THE RESET

Also by Elizabeth Uviebinené

co-authored
Slay In Your Lane: The Black Girl Bible

co-edited
Loud Black Girls

THE RESET

*Ideas to Change How
We Work and Live*

———

ELIZABETH UVIEBINENÉ

HODDER*studio*

First published in Great Britain in 2021 by Hodder Studio
An Hachette UK company

1

Copyright © Elizabeth Uviebinené 2021

A CIP catalogue record for this title is available from the British Library

Hardback ISBN 9781529347432
Trade Paperback ISBN 9781529347487
eBook ISBN 9781529347470

Typeset in Celeste by Palimpsest Book Production Limited, Falkirk, Stirlingshire

Printed and bound in Great Britain by Clays Ltd, Elcograf S.p.A.

Hodder & Stoughton policy is to use papers that are natural,
renewable and recyclable products and made from wood grown in
sustainable forests. The logging and manufacturing processes are expected
to conform to the environmental regulations of the country of origin.

Hodder & Stoughton Ltd
Carmelite House
50 Victoria Embankment
London EC4Y 0DZ

www.hodder-studio.com

CONTENTS

For my fellow Thinkers and Doers

INTRODUCTION

—————

'The activity of work reminds us that we – as individuals, as communities and as a society – can build our own future.'
— Institute for the Future of Work

BURNOUT. INFLEXIBILITY. PRESENTEEISM.

Three words that reflect the plight of the modern workplace.

Loneliness. Anxiety. Depression.

Three words that characterise the strains of modern life.

Believe it or not, these two sets of struggles and strains are *inextricably linked*. But that realisation didn't come to me overnight.

When I first pitched the idea for this book, it was with the mindset that what was needed was a reappraisal of work and the way we think about it. I wanted to take time to dive into the way we work, to try and explore solutions to an environment that wasn't working for so many of us, that had been so entrenched for so long that its problems felt almost insurmountable.

Then Covid-19 hit.

What I thought I knew about the world of work was upended. And much to my surprise it was still very much up for grabs.

It's maddening that it took a global health emergency of world-changing proportions to force a proper conversation about how we work. Suddenly that need for change had become incontrovertible and understanding how we work and live was no longer on the fringes. It had become a fixed theme in our lives.

The pandemic revealed a capacity for change that individuals and businesses had massively underestimated. It accelerated changes that were already underway, embedded in transformation programmes that corporations had claimed would take years to be brought to reality and while businesses had to rapidly adapt, so did we. For white-collar workers, the sudden shutdown of the physical workplace overnight was difficult yet manageable, people adapting mentally and physically to working from home. And one of the things that has surprised me most about the workforce's response to the pandemic is how much more resilient we are than we give ourselves credit for. It also turned out the technology we needed to make such a change possible was already there: it was just the incentive for businesses that had been missing all along.

In the wake of the pandemic, there was an influx of comments about this 'new way of working': *'we can do our jobs from anywhere now'*, *'oh, we've mastered the art of remote working'*, *'it's the end of the office'*, *'the end of the 9 to 5'*. Everywhere you looked there were discussions and articles about the future of work. The great migration to the countryside as people could work 'anywhere'. The complete home working space makeover.

The British Council for Offices ran a survey and found Covid-19 had changed the working patterns of white-collar workers for good. Few staff said they intended to return to their offices five days a week, with most saying they were going to combine remote working with a few days a week in the office.[1] Looking at this it sounds like good progress, but when you dig into it, it feels like *how* we're working hasn't changed at all. People are still sitting in front of their laptops all day, eating desk lunches, sitting in Zoom meetings they can't be bothered to be in and with the barrier between home and work now removed, they are also extending the work day well into the evening. And amid all of this, many still aren't finding satisfaction in their work.

The problem was this 'new way of working' was riddled with the same problems and mindsets as before.

I watched all of this happening and wondered how we'd come full circle – with a few 'experts' telling us the new rules for working. Even though the workforce is multi-generational, multi-geographical, multi-cultural and technology-enabled, we were verging yet again on the one-size-fits-all solution. That made me wonder if anything could or would actually change.

Essentially rebooting the same machine in a slightly different way – 'working from home' or 'tech-enabled businesses' but having the same fundamental approach of staring at a screen, obsessing over productivity and working in isolation – will produce the same results. We're just switching back on the status quo and replicating some of the unhealthy behaviours that got us here in the first place.

So while there was a new fixation on how and where we were working, my optimism for a genuine overhaul of our relationship with work dwindled. I also noticed another conversation happening, one about what work means to us.

In our pre-Covid world, it was easy to get wrapped up in the busyness of the office environment and avoid the fundamental question of whether we found our work fulfilling. The pandemic exposed the very bones of our work lives. We could see it for what it really was, without the distractions of our zombie-like commutes and HR teams selling perks as culture.

We couldn't go to work, and we couldn't do much else. In lockdown there were no restaurants, cinema, friends, exercise classes. There was very little of anything except work. Just us, our laptops and our jobs. I'd been thinking about how I worked anyway, but 2020 got me thinking about *why*. I started by finding a definition from the Institute for the Future of Work that put work 'at the centre of people's lives and families'. More than just a source of income, it's part of our individual and group identities 'offering a sense of fulfilment and purpose' and tying us to each other.

I am not a believer in the idea that work has to be where you get meaning and fulfilment out of your life. Sure, we spend a substantial amount of our lives at work rather than with family or friends, so it's understandable how we got here. But work is enmeshed in our identities, and this is a much larger conversation than the one about what tech allows us to do in terms of remote working. In a society where our personal identities and careers are so closely aligned, imagining a truly new way of working can feel frightening. It can even feel like a barrier to that change.

Have we reduced the conversation to this home vs office debate because it's an easier question that the one we actually need to tackle: why are our personal identities so tied-in with our jobs? I don't want to talk about the communication platforms Zoom and Slack. I want to talk about 'autonomy' and 'empathy'. I want to find a way to integrate greater choice and trust into how we work and live. I want a new social contract.

Never has the interdependent nature of us as individuals, our work, and our communities been clearer than now, and we've reached the point where we are finally starting to think strategically about the role of the office and the role of work in our lives. We're thinking about the dynamic that sits at the heart of it too; not just *where* we work but *how* and *why*. Technology might be the enabler of how we can work in the future but it's not the sole answer.

My investigation into how an individual works suddenly seemed quite big. When you write books, you're positioned as an expert on said topic. I'm not an expert on work, I'm just curious. And my curiosity made me want to talk to the real experts, and to bring those experts to the heart of the book. I didn't set out with some preconceived notion on what I'd say. I wanted to speak to the people who'd tried things already, who knew about the history of work on a global scale, who'd tested and considered and had something important to say.

I set out on this journey with one question: As individuals, how can we change our relationship to work? I didn't expect it to open up a whole Pandora's Box. Because the thing is, once you change one thing, everything changes. One conversation led to another, which led to another. I didn't set out on this project expecting to speak to politicians or an architect. I didn't think I'd be considering the infrastructure of our cities and the demographic of our country.

This book started with a simple desire to explore our relationship with work, and how it was impacting our lives. But one thing became clear very quickly – if we want to reset how we work as individuals, we're going to need to reset a lot of things. The more I explored the subject of work the more I realised it was the crucial link between each part of society and changing one thing would change everything.

Over the last few months I've realised that if we reset how we understand work as individuals, we demand our businesses change. Once our businesses change, our communities change and our cities change. And if we have new communities, spread throughout the country, then everything changes. And through all those conversations and all the research I've conducted, it became clear that the areas for change fall into six distinct categories. That's six fundamental *resets* to change how we work and live.

It starts with us as **individuals**. Because if we're going to really benefit from the radical shift of the pandemic, we have to rethink how we fit into an ecosystem. If we rethink how we fit in, everything resets around us – the work **culture** we exist in, the **business** we work for, the **community** we're a part of, the **cities** we live in and the **society** we shape. The reset starts with you, but it doesn't end there.

I'm not an expert on business, and I'm certainly not an expert on politics and the environment, but I've spoken to a lot of people who are. They've all realised it's time for a fundamental change in what 'work' means. Everyone is demanding change of one sort or another, and each change is closely tied in to the next. We can't just rethink one strand of society; we need to rethink everything together. We need a fundamental reset.

You might be thinking this book feels a little light to

change every element of how we work. And you're right, we've got a long way to go. I'm writing seven months into this paradigm shift, and everything is up in the air. My hope is that *The Reset* starts as a conversation on how we could reimagine our work environment as we move towards a future that is less about what is best for big business and more about what is in the best interests of the worker. The old system is simply not fit for that purpose.

This book is intended to be optimistic, positive, provocative and open. It's not definitive, exhaustive and restrictive. We're all pieces in this puzzle and we have the responsibility to understand what we can change about ourselves and where we can step aside and let someone else create a change. *The Reset* asks us to engage in work and life at the same time. In each of the six chapters, I've explored a major theme we need to change. Some of these are on you the individual, some are on all of us collectively.

This is not a book of predictions of what the global workforce will look like in a post-Covid world, a self-help book on how to work better post-pandemic, on how to work better at home or on how to increase your productivity.

Researching this book has meant exploring vital questions about work and life in a society that's changing rapidly, but it all comes back to one core question: *what's possible now that would have seemed impossible before?*

Many businesses and individuals have conceded that things need to change. We've all sensed this is a very unique opportunity to redesign and reimagine our work lives. People are using this time as an opportunity to reflect. I'm a firm believer that there is no work life vs life. There's one life. And this is our big chance to reset.

Elizabeth Uviebinené

Chapter One

YOU

———

YOU

YOU

'Best career advice that I can give: don't ever attach yourself
to a person, a place, a company, an organisation or a project.
Attach yourself to a mission, a calling, a purpose only. That's
how you keep our power and your peace'

– Erica Williams Simon[1]

AS BUZZES GO, it was pretty potent. That sleek little black
rectangle in the palm of my hand, vibrating with potential
connection and glamour: my first Blackberry; a signifier
that I was busy, important, needed and connected. It was
the same day I had my first glass of Prosecco, part of the
fancy welcome-to-the-team lunch that the company would
roll out to new graduates. All creating the ultimate welcome
to the world of work – a prized package. My new device
promised an urgent, staccato pace to my life. It was 2013

and I was very much in *like* with this piece of tech. I was happy to be always on and available, naively without any real idea how draining and destructive this relationship would one day become.

At the start, the endless buzzes would see me checking my inbox in the evening just for the sheer novelty of it. By the end, I'd be on holiday checking in because I'd become well and truly trapped. Today the sheen has worn off and, boxed in by the expectation that I will always be on the other end of a text, I go through days where I've turned off the pinging notifications to just get on with life. But as tech utopias go, it's a hollow victory.

We were duped by this Brave New World and all it promised. My work phone moved quickly from being a demonstration of value to a tool of control, and everyone, at every level, was swept up in the wave. The backlash against tech and devices has grown since my first day, and for the most part we know we shouldn't be shackled to our work. Yet somehow we still are, all the while railing against our addiction to our phones, as our fingers tap the table, desperate to unlock screens. Like the proverbial tree in the forest, if your WhatsApp doesn't ping, do you *really* exist? Certainly not in any meaningful sense, when plans are made, projects organised, work conducted and socialising happens all on our phones, 24–7. Plus who knows? Someone *really* important might have just messaged you. The question is though, is it ever actually *that* urgent?

As I recall my first day in that office, I had no idea of the effect the 'always-on' culture was going to have on me. When I joined that company, I had a clear mission; I knew what I wanted to achieve there, how I wanted to grow and evolve. Within a short space of time, I'd lost that sense of purpose in the blinding light of my various screens. I didn't realise how difficult it was going to be to switch off from devices and platforms designed to keep us plugged into networks and 'gaming us' into hanging on the screen for the next dopamine hit of content, whether an Instagram post or an email from our line managers.

As my life became faster and work became more integral to my identity there seemed to be no way to get off the merry-go-round, but the challenges and enforced go-slow of Covid-dominated 2020 has resulted in a fundamental shift in the world and our priorities. And as we were forced to stare at a screen for every second of work, we realised we wanted to look away more when we weren't working. It made us rethink how we work, but also, it's fair to say, *why* we work.

Much has been said about 'productivity' and how it's fueling my generation's obsession with robot-like efficiency. This conversation has obscured an important one about what it is to have a purpose and mission in our working lives. Not everybody needs to have a purpose with their work, in fact I'm of the opposite opinion – that not everything has to be seen through the prism of work in order to live a life that is fulfilling. But it's a discussion worth having.

Interestingly, an American study conducted by BetterUp in 2017 revealed that 9 out of 10 employees would be prepared to earn less in exchange for meaningful work.[2]

We all need to have an awareness of where we sit on this scale. Some people want to seek purpose in work. They want what they do to be enmeshed with their identities outside of work. Other people see work as a tool to live with a purpose outside of work. Where do you sit on this scale? Working out *how* you work is one thing, but understanding *why* you work is probably at the heart of the matter.

During the first lockdown, we experienced a unique opportunity to see how we as individuals could, in our own way, rethink how we work. Working at home on a day-to-day basis made us confront some of the values and toxic attitudes we had towards our work. Hopefully, being confronted by these attitudes head-on may be enough incentive to change them. Because the truth is, change starts with deciding what you want.

Know when you're losing yourself

stop letting work be your identity, and stop feeling trapped by that identity

In 2019, I wrote an article for the *Financial Times* called 'How to Avoid Burnout and Thrive at Work'.[3] Burnout is a state of emotional, physical and mental exhaustion caused by excessive and prolonged stress. The headline hinted at a quick fix, but the piece itself argues otherwise. I knew the key to tackling chronic burnout wasn't a 45-minute yoga class and a juice cleanse. How could it be? The symptoms are bleak. It's an overwhelming exhaustion, feelings of cynicism and detachment leading to a sense of ineffectiveness. An occasional moment of 'self-care' just won't do.

Burnout has particularly gained momentum in today's discourse and, in 2019, the World Health Organization (WHO) declared burnout an 'occupational phenomenon'. However, the term was first used in the 1970s by the American psychologist Herbert Freudenberger in research for his book *Burn-Out: The High Cost of High Achievement*, where he defined it as the 'extinction of motivation or incentive'. In truth, the concept of burnout has been around as long as people have been working, but the workplace now looks completely different to how it did in the 70s, and I'm not just talking about the aesthetics. Modern work culture prioritises a constant state of connectedness, availability and quick responses – whatever the hour. And that's a major catalyst for burnout. How we do our work has increasingly become unhealthy.

We're told if we pick a job we love, we'll never work a day in our lives. But that simply isn't true. Just because you enjoy something, it doesn't mean it isn't stressful, challenging and often demotivating. Besides, picking a job we love runs the risk of ruining our positive relationship with that thing if we don't address these issues. Satisfaction often isn't a result of *what* job you do, but instead *how* you do that job. When I revisited my article and started reading about burnout, I found a poll by Gallup that identified five factors which lead to burnout: unfair treatment, an unmanageable workload, lack of role clarity, lack of communication or support from a manager and unreasonable time pressure. These concepts aren't unique to one industry or role.[4] They're challenges faced by lawyers, retail assistants, consultants, dentists – and probably you, too. The fact that it's a theme across all ways of work should tell us that this is more than a set of specific issues. This is about how we allow work to define every part of our life, and the fallout from that.

So, if we start from a place of understanding that *anyone* can suffer from burnout, what steps can we take to understand our limitations and cultivate a healthy attitude towards work? The first, I believe, is identifying the parts we get wrong.

There are very real reasons that we, as a generation, all feel so deeply fixated on work. We've come into a working world recovering from recessions, trying to make enough to survive amid rising living costs and greater competition for roles as certain industries become more automated. It's made us desperate to hustle hard. In that environment, we simply don't know how to take proper breaks, and we're applauded for coming into the office when we're ill and soldiering on. We've rebranded second jobs as 'side hustles' in our attempt to catch up economically. We frame it as: who wants to be one thing these days? But more often than not the reality is: who can afford to just do one thing these days? No wonder 32 is now the average age of reaching burnout and 37% of Millennials don't feel empowered enough to take a lunch break. That lack of empowerment is a very real issue that needs to be addressed.

When I was told that my burnout piece was one of the most read that month, I wasn't surprised. For me, it was emblematic of a larger problem, one that I could see and feel every day as I started my commute. The last two decades have seen burnout become an epidemic in offices throughout the UK and half a million people in the UK suffer from work-related stress to the point of being unable to continue. Some comments on my article said I should 'stop being a Millennial snowflake', but they missed the point entirely. Burnout isn't a Millennial affliction. It's a twenty-first century one.

Burnout goes deeper than the economic reality of living in the early twenty-first century too. It's psychological. It's tied up in how we view work, and what we think it says about us. For a long time, I let work define my identity and I became trapped by this identity that was supposed to give me freedom. Many of us think being successful at work is essential to who we are. Success at work means being the most productive, most dedicated, most machine-like version of yourself. And whether you're working in an office, or you're working at home, self-employed or not – if you feel that way then nothing's going to change.

It's an intergenerational truth that we see work as a status symbol. In particular, it's how hard we work that's considered the status symbol. We're clocking more hours than ever, and research shows that employees with higher social status have more job satisfaction and increased perceived performance.[5]

However, what makes Millennials different is that we increasingly see burnout as a mark of that status. We seek to wear this burnout as a badge of honour, like a work of art we've spent months painting, admiring it whenever we have a spare moment. We relish 'the cult of being busy'. In the past, wearing a fancy piece of jewellery was how you let friends and rivals know you'd made it; these days, the currency of social position is time. Busyness is the new status symbol and we wear it with pride. And we all do it to various degrees. The more I've read about burnout, the more it feels like something we're not only expected to feel, but *encouraged* to.

We say we wish we had more time to ourselves, but I've come to realise it's not what we actually want. A study by Silvia Bellezza, from Columbia Business School, looking into how we signal status through our use of time, showed that we aspire to have a busy schedule over having more leisure time.[6] When we look busy, we get our ego stroked. Even while we're feeling totally burned out, and it's impacting our lives negatively, we're still getting something from the fact that we're 'busy'. We're romanticising the very parts of our work that are giving us burnout – looking busy, clocking long hours, checking our emails over dinner. In fact, we're so busy being busy, we're not taking the time to re-evaluate what actually makes us happy and fulfilled. In the same way we get an ego kick from being 'busy', we also feel shame when we're taking a break. According to a YouGov poll,[7] carried out in 2018, the majority of Brits check their emails while they're on holiday. Before this generation of connectedness, the always-on generation, this wasn't even possible of course. But it's worth saying that we're not just looking at social media on holiday and messaging friends at home – we're *working*.

We begrudgingly admire our friends who don't have a second to spare, who relentlessly pursue new revenue streams and side hustles. When the choice is between thinking or doing, we want to be doing. My generation's obsession with productivity and self-improvement has seen us devour articles and books about the *6 Habits of Highly Successful People*, and worship the CEOs that wake up at 5 a.m. And I get it.

We're encouraged to overwork, but subtly, by comparing ourselves to each other and through the cultural obsession with success. We're made to feel guilty if we aren't busy. I realised this when I started to almost like feeling burned out. I'd start every conversation with, 'I'm so busy . . .' and I'd cancel dinners with friends because . . . you guessed it I was so busy. If I didn't feel burned out then I wasn't doing enough. If you've ever sat at work staring blankly at a monitor, only to snap back to reality with an overwhelming sense of guilt for daydreaming, you'll know what I mean.

But science says these moments of absent-mindedness can be extremely powerful. There is significant evidence to suggest that individuals must be free to daydream[8], seek solitude and engage with new experiences if they're to continue developing their creativity. Something as simple as leaving the office for a quick walk can help us be more creative and solve problems. A working culture which encourages employees to take walks, move around and do what we need to do to help us recalibrate would ultimately benefit the bottom line. Put simply, when we can't fully switch off, we can't fully switch back on. Our ability to relax, to be bored and to stop, enables us to be productive, creative and turn all the way up. We need to stop being chained to our desks – both physically and psychologically – whether that desk is in an office or our homes.

For me personally, two symptoms of burnout stand out as particularly bad. The first is that it drains motivation, which hinders creativity. We need to be encouraged to think freely, take risks and explore. The World Economic Forum ranked creativity as one of the most vital skills for employees in 2020, and while this attribute is heralded by employers, the activities that help us be creative are stigmatised in the workplace because they don't appear productive. I don't mean easels in the corner of the office, I mean the sort of opportunities that allow our minds to wander and creative ideas to emerge. Our infatuation with appearing busy prevents us from daydreaming and certainly from absent-mindedly staring out of the window for any length of time. It prevents us from thinking and reflecting. And that means it stops us understanding what we can really offer. It detaches us from that sense of purpose we bring to our first jobs.

The other symptoms of burnout really got to me too – being cynical in work started to transfer into my life. The lack of hope and faith I had towards everything around me was suffocating at best and depressing at worst – and I wasn't producing my best work. I was on auto-pilot and if you've ever sat next to a cynical colleague at work, you'll know that it is highly contagious. It undermines your work, your health and your relationships. It is self-defeating on many levels.

We're already waking up to the negative impact of burnout and I see a shift happening as more of us are aware of the importance of good mental well-being and health. A 2020 VICE study[9] found that 88% of respondents said overall health and wellness is important to living their best life. Yet only 8% actually rated their health as good. That's a stark gap, and a clear indication that something has to give.

The conversation is changing, and in the last few years we've focused more of our discussion of mental health on the impact of burnout. I'm listening too – these days I'm trying to be conscious about the language I'm using that glamourises overworking and working against all odds. I'm muting people on social media who are glorifying their 'hustle'.

Beyond this, we need to educate ourselves on the long-term implications of chronic burnout. Research shows that burnout is a predictor of Type 2 diabetes, coronary heart disease and prolonged fatigue.[10] What might feel like short-term inconvenience – being burned out – can lead to life-altering health conditions. It's also time to switch out those conversations around 'productivity' to ones that emphasise meaningful work instead, otherwise we run the risk of continuing to glamourise false productivity – the appearance of being busy. With rapid technological developments and digital infrastructure, we shouldn't need to work 60+ hours a week anymore. Both Unilever and Microsoft in Japan have trialed a four-day week for employees[11] and true productivity was actually increased in this latter example. We've all woken up to a valuable lesson – prioritise personal time the same way you would prioritise an important meeting.

In today's world, we have no choice but to create new behaviours and boundaries to prioritise personal time. Our routines make us overstressed and dangerously under-rested. There are many different 'solutions' and 'quick fixes' that are touted as solving these problems, but one thing I know for sure is that we need to stop being so proud of working too hard. We need to stop celebrating the very things that are driving us to burnout. And we need to stop admiring other people for perpetuating a belief that systematically destroys our motivation, creativity and ultimately, capacity for work and life satisfaction.

More than that though, we need to rediscover that sense of purpose we brought to our first jobs. Before we got distracted by constant emails and messages, we thought about what we wanted to create and do. Before we told people how hard we were working, we were telling them how interested we were in certain things. I don't think we should just learn to value productivity less; I think we should try and remember what makes us feel valuable.

Know yourself

work out what makes you feel fulfilled, and who you want to be at work

Redesigning our routines and finding space in the day has been one of the unexpected positives to come out of the first lockdown. Work no longer feels separate from our personal lives, and while this has had its drawbacks, it has also encouraged us to think more clearly about how our career fits in with our lives. For some of us, it has been a pivotal moment to question how we could ever have accepted hours-long commutes and lunches chained to desks. For many, there has been a recognition of the impact on us of making time for our hobbies, families and domestic lives.

Without our bosses hovering by our shoulders, there is freedom to engage with work on our own terms. We can put a load of laundry on at lunch time or go for a walk around our local community. Around 32% of us have taken up reading during lockdown[12] and as the evenings and weekends became expansive and open to opportunity, finding a new hobby didn't seem like an obligation to help spice up your CV, but a chance to rediscover creativity. The figures speak for themselves: according to a YouGov Poll, UK consumers spent an additional 24% on hobby supplies and 21% on books in 2020.[13] For some, there was the rare opportunity to create something, purely for pleasure. It was less about the end result and all about the process.

This freedom has opened people's eyes to their individual experience of work; whether through bypassing the office politics for a solitary tea break or taking a little more time for breakfast in place of a commute. It has allowed us to consider the different elements of our character outside of work too. Previously we've been rushing between office and social life, fitting things in on an ad hoc basis. The lockdowns have been an opportunity to pause and consider who we are as individuals and, beyond the obvious, the role work plays into our lives.

As I've learned more about myself, I've found myself

wanting to understand if people I was inspired by had shifted too. I got in touch with Ete Davies, CEO at Engine, an advertising agency, I've admired for a long time. He's been called Engine's 'disruptor in chief' and he has a reputation for innovation and energy. I wondered if he hated the slow pace of lockdown. We quickly got on to how he had replaced his morning commute with activities that were emotionally fulfilling and which helped him to set up for the day.

'When I'm working on ideas I quite like collaborating and working through things with people. But to get to the point where I can do that, I need time to think in silence, and think deeply and reflect on things. The mornings without the commute – and I generally get up quite early anyway – have given me a lot more time in my day just to find clarity before the day starts. I listened to this podcast about the Miracle Morning, and things that you do within it. So I adopted that and spent a small amount of time meditating, which personally I'm not great at because I have an overactive imagination, but I do try to use that time to focus and centre myself. And then I spend a bit of time just reading, typically one subject or article relevant to work, and then I do something that's of personal interest. I found that it really helped reframe the morning and the start of the day. It's one of the things when we start to go back –

and I'll have to go back into the office a couple of days a week – the commute will take that time away from me, but I've enjoyed that.'

The Miracle Morning Ete was talking about was introduced by Hal Elrod, who, without any doubt, could not have had a pandemic in mind as a testing ground. And yet, how we construct our morning routines has found its way under the microscope on a global scale. For many, our commutes transformed into exercise routines, family breakfasts and mindfulness practice. Not everybody wants to meditate, but it works for Ete. As for me, I learned I like to work first thing, especially if it's anything that requires me to use the creative part of my brain. It's in the afternoon that I want to take a break and do something social or admin-oriented.

Mornings are just one moment to recalibrate, and there are many other moments throughout the day that let us carve space out where we needed it for us to use on the things that helped us feel like ourselves. The more I spoke to different people the clearer it became that many of us made meaningful progress in developing a sense of identity, through building gratifying morning routines and making time for passions outside of the workplace. We have learned more about who we are.

While most of us ditched banana bread baking as soon as we escaped lockdown, those moments of creativity or meditation may have had a considerable beneficial impact on our working lives. I'm not saying everyone has to find their inner artist or yogi, but I am suggesting you find space to better understand what brings you fulfilment. I came across a study that said people who engage in creative activities outside of the workplace perform better on creative tasks inside the workplace.[14] That really stuck with me, that investing time in something else could improve what I'm working on. What's more, these hobbies help us to recover from periods of stress, and reduce our risk of burning out.

I was really interested in this phenomenon of greater creativity, and how bringing hobbies into our routines would fulfill a side of our identities we've been ignoring and with that actually improve our work. Or even help us find entirely new work. In the month of April 2020, Etsy saw twice as many new shops open on its platform compared to April a year before[15] which speaks to the yearn for creating.

Understanding what brings us fulfilment is beneficial: for our souls and ourselves, but also for the creative parts of us that work often demands. By looking inwards in this way, everybody wins. We're happier, and we bring our best ideas to work.

Know your value

work out what your strengths are, find time to build on them, bring them to the team

I've been asked a few times how my life has changed since the first book came out. When I was in my corporate 9–5, as much as I enjoyed it, I was never bringing my full self to work. It's structuring my own work over the last years that has meant fully embracing all parts of my personality and individuality. Now, within a work day, I can do a corporate speaking gig, head over to a school, speak to students, and finish the day off at a meeting with my editor without ever having to worry about changing some aspect of my appearance. I've found this particularly empowering in navigating the world of work as a young black woman.

This is something that resonated with Ete, who is particularly interested in how a system of conformity can prohibit good work. He said:

> 'The need to try and force people to conform and to fit into a stereotype, or to fit into a solution by which the system can dictate to an individual how to behave, how to think, how to exist, is fundamentally flawed. Because it's not liberating for the individual, so you wouldn't get the best out of anybody in that sort of situation and it leads to deep frustration within the person because they're not living their life to fulfilment.'

Individuality isn't something that's celebrated in the corporate world. Most of us admit to hiding elements of our personality at work, despite the fact that studies have shown that encouraging individuality in the workplace improves employee well-being. If we know finding fulfilment in ourselves makes us happier and helps us work better, why don't we bring those things to work with us and make them part of our day?

We don't usually prioritise bringing our whole self in our working lives, but I know from my experience that being able to move between different contexts and present one consistent persona can have a positive impact on well-being. To me, this still seems rare. But thinking about it now, it's how nearly everyone has responded to Zoom meetings, which have become key to working and communicating. I wonder if one of the most important things about the lockdowns isn't just seeing how we work, it's also about seeing other people in a new light, too, and letting them see us.

When the boardroom was replaced by the Zoom waiting room things happened – kids wandered into the frame or we darted off camera to grab our Amazon delivery – and no one found a flattering camera angle. A whole new content pillar was born on the internet: Zoom etiquette. What to wear, which background to use and how to position your webcam for an effective meeting. Like a socially distanced Big Brother parody, we got a rare, intimate glimpse into our co-workers' lives on every conference call.

Seeing our team outside of the workplace context, with their favourite mug in hand and a family photo in the background is a gentle reminder that they're human too. And while we know how to act in a meeting at work – be on time, look engaged, don't fall asleep – the rules haven't been quite the same in the lockdown. As we have adapted, we have adopted new ways of interacting and we have showed more of ourselves in the process.

I'm a big admirer of Rachel Botsman, who's written several books on trust, power and influence. I thought she'd have something interesting to say about this idea of our private and public selves. Unsurprisingly, she's found the impact of lockdown working fascinating:

'People feel this sense of relief and they're seeing a different dynamic because so much of work is about appearance. How am I judged for the way I behaved in that meeting or what I was wearing? Or all these things, even how you work, how you write. I think a lot of it is that people's energy is not going into appearance, however you interpret that. It's actually being channelled more into the work.'

Think about your last Zoom meeting. Did you even have your camera on? If you did, were you dressed up like you would be for the office? Were you pretending to write exhaustive notes like you might have done in a conference room? Or were you listening to the person who was speaking, and offering responses when you knew they'd be valuable?

Everyone wants to live their life to fulfilment, right? And what's more fulfilling than knowing who we are, and then being that person in every place we inhabit. We need to follow our instincts more and allow the person we present at work to align more closely with who we really are. It's clear that we perform best and enjoy our work most when we can be ourselves and where our work fulfils who we are. The first can be answered by encouraging a lack of restrictions in work, in supporting each other's choices and breaking down barriers of formality. The second is a little harder. It's working out what makes us feel like we have purpose. Remembering what our purpose was before we entered the working world, and doing what we can to fulfil that, even in a small way. This doesn't have to relate specifically to the job that you do, and those tasks; it can be as simple as the *way* you approach those tasks.

This used to be called finding our vocations, but I like to think of it as owning our true selves.

I spoke to Ete about the idea of uniting who we are with what we do, and the fact we've moved so far away from doing something that's right for our character, or identity. He had this to say on those jobs that are tied to a craft, in other words jobs that are really closely aligned with who we are.

'The reason that's more fulfilling is because there is no split of the individual. Everything that they're doing is joined in one, psychologically and emotionally. That must

be a relief, for those of us that are sort of living duality or multiplicity between working life, personal life, social life. That's got to take a toll on you, I think, even if it's not a visible one. It's got to have a lasting effect on you, having to switch between all of those different environments. You have to let the individual celebrate themselves as they are and in that freedom typically we've always got better creative work. I found that it's actually harder work when you're trying to force people to fit into these boxes.'

If you've chosen a job you wanted to do, there are probably lots of moments that you feel that connection between your work and your identity. I love so much of what I do in branding, and when I'm putting together a creative pitch, getting my ideas onto a page and presenting it in a way that's going to connect, I feel fulfilled. Obviously, we can't all just be doing the bits we enjoy all the time, but I found what Ete said about fitting into boxes interesting. So many roles are the same across different teams and companies, but perhaps if we brought a fresh approach or angle to an individual job, we might reshape how it fits into a company. We might fit the job to the individual, rather than the other way around. We're all conforming to a set way of doing things, and perhaps if we had freedom over how we approached even the challenging or tedious aspects of our job, we'd feel better connected with ourselves. If we can find meaning in the different parts of our work, we might feel better prepared to engage in them positively.

Ete mentioned a Japanese concept, Ikigai, meaning 'a reason for being', which I found particularly interesting in the context of work and fulfilment. The Ikigai model helps us assess what the world needs, what our own emotional needs are and what skills we have to offer. The key to fulfilment is to align each of these in one 'life mission' – all elements fit together so that all aspects of your life align with one another. Individuals following Ikigai aren't trying to build a portfolio career; they're trying to align their internal needs with the needs of the external world. It's a holistic approach which is a far cry from the constant personal development inflicted on so many workers of today. It's finding your niche and refining your skillset.

In preparation for the post-pandemic world, we'll need to do plenty of soul-searching to figure out how we rebuild. The Ikigai framework provides a great structure for us to determine the work that has value for the external world, and for our internal world too.

We were facing a drought of good jobs before the pandemic hit, with think pieces and studies exploring the erosion of middle-income jobs as automation displaced workers across a number of industries. Both the creation of good jobs and adequate retraining are crucial for rebuilding the economy and maximising workers' skill sets. We need to find a way to align our economic needs with the wealth of different talent and experience across our communities. If we can work out where our value lies, and bring it to work, we're making huge steps towards finding fulfilment.

Ask your boss if you can get involved with a project outside your usual scope of work; moving laterally through a company enables us to explore hidden talents and understand our own limitations. Other times, we face the type of creative drought that requires a more complex intervention. Sabbaticals can provide a unique opportunity to gain inspiration and also find separation from the day job. Sometimes it's the distance that helps us to see things clearer.

Sooner or later, we all get stuck in a rut at work. Spending 40+ hours a week working, it's easy to get lost in the cycle of it. When Google[16] explored what makes a good team, in 2016, the researchers discovered that psychological safety was a top priority for staff. Employees needed to feel secure and confident enough to take risks in the workplace. A culture that supports an employees' individuality, values their opinion and trusts them to get stuff done stimulates higher productivity and job satisfaction. When we create spaces where workers feel supported, they're more likely to test new ideas and challenge outdated work models. The key to cultivating better teams is enabling and supporting people to be individuals too. If we think about how we fit into our teams at work, are our individualities – our quirks – allowed, encouraged and valued?

The last few years of burnout have made it clear we need something better. Not just for ourselves, but for our colleagues, too. We want to create strong teams where everyone feels fulfilled and if we're trusted to create those, then we'll see better work, too.

Chapter Two

CULTURE

———

CULTURE

———

'Culture is the new business currency'

– Cassandra Stavrou

I REMEMBER THE first time I stepped into a tech office. I was part of a mentoring programme and jumped at the opportunity for a day out of the bubble of campus life at university. It was like corporate Disneyland. I'd spent various internships in rooms set out like a grid, with flimsy dividers and off-white walls. Suddenly it felt like they'd finally figured out what a workplace should be. There were plush furnishings, a gym looking over central London, unlimited free food, a rooftop garden, padded boardrooms in chintzy patterns and vibrant colours. And they threw in a puppy too! Finally, a workplace fit for a new generation of workers, which would of course incentivise a new breed of uber-productive workers.

My friends started going for interviews at tech places and start-ups, and in each one they'd be told proudly about the 'annual birthday leave policy', free lunch on Fridays and company away days in Ibiza. And all these companies would talk about all of these things in the same breath: 'office culture'. In fact this idea of 'good' culture became synonymous with these fancy tech-driven companies. Google 'wasn't evil' and Apple 'thought differently', and most of them built these glossy campus-style offices full of Googlers and Amazonians. These businesses were leading the charge, proudly telling us that they were done with traditional offices, that they were a community or a 'family' and if we wanted to be part of the gang, our reward was free food and beers on Friday afternoon. They didn't talk much about the emotional well-being of existing employees, but I'm not sure that many of us noticed or asked.

It definitely looked and sounded great. I don't think any of us realised those gyms, sofas and well-stocked fridges would form a straitjacket. We had everything we needed, so why would we ever want to leave?

I think we've all started to realise those perks are a quick fix to a big issue. And at the same time that burnout took hold, there were even darker stories emerging. Sexual harassment and racism at the heart of our favourite apps, misogyny in tech-bro culture, goal-oriented growth at the expense of both employees and users. To clarify, these issues have always existed; they're not the creation of these types of companies

– the problem was we were happy for these companies to take the lead for a new blueprint of what good culture should look like. By doing so, we enabled the really bad things that can rear their head in any business to be glossed over.

The problem of culture ran much deeper than the question of where to position the ping-pong table. Culture had become everything and anything and now meant nothing, just empty gestures without much follow through.

Culture isn't a free haircut
Culture isn't a nap room
Culture isn't an all-inclusive holiday

Culture isn't just about the exciting perks, but that's what it's come to represent for many of us. What's really damaging about that thinking is that it makes culture about what a company 'gives' us, when it should be about people. Focusing on perks on the side rather than how we treat each other creates an environment where things like racism, misogyny and mental health crises can flourish. I'm not saying those problems haven't always been there in offices to some degree, but if we're constantly being burned out, do we really need a free breakfast? Wouldn't a consolidated reconfiguration of our workloads and how we work be more preferable?

A free lunch might give employees an endorphin kick of nutritious value, but if they're returning to the same office tension and unmanageable workload, these short-term perks aren't going to have any lasting impact. Holidays, free food, fancy office design – those things may attract talent at first but does it truly create culture at a deeper level? According to CIPD, in 2017 only 5% of companies offer onsite child-care[1] – compared to 32% offering free food. That's not investing in employees' futures, that's focusing on attracting a 23-year-old with a good degree and a big appetite. After all, what sounds sexier – a ping-pong table and free cocktails on Fridays or childcare provisions?

After talking about an individual's place at work, I started to realise that nothing can change for the individual if the business doesn't respond and adapt to their needs. If this continues to happen then nothing is going to change. If we want to reset how an individual relates to work, we need to reset what happens when we're there.

Cassandra Stavrou is co-founder of popular healthier snack company Proper. Cassandra is an incredible voice on a new type of business, one that's conscientious, innovative and focused on what's good for the team. I loved talking to her because it felt like she was at the helm of the future of leadership. And she definitely had something to say about the perk culture of so many offices.

'. . . [It] is very hard to retrospectively bolt on that sort of stuff like, "Oh, we're gonna try and build culture by having gin tasting every month." That won't cut it. You *have to do the groundwork and you have to build it from the bottom up. It has to be right through the business.'*

Now, I'm not averse to a gin tasting, but Cassandra's on the money. Culture has to permeate every thread of the business: it can't be just added on top like sprinkles on an ice cream. It's got to be about what each of us is bringing to the company, and what we're getting back in return.

Culture is a commitment to each other. It's a statement that each of us is going to invest time and energy in each other, and a demand that our business leaders do the same back. We have to change the way we work with each other, and that goes both ways. For me, culture has always been the invisible glue that holds a company together. It's the shared values, attitudes, standards and beliefs that make up an organisation. It doesn't require you to see your colleagues every day; it requires things you can't actually always touch, and for some people it simply comes down to, 'It's the way we do things around here.'

I think there are three areas we've been getting wrong in how we treat each other. Three areas that we can reset to make culture meaningful. Communication, trust, investment. And none of them involve a free ping-pong table.

COMMUNICATE PROPERLY

Picture the scene. A global pandemic has meant the entire country is on lockdown. You're stuck in your home for all but an hour a day. The news is terrifying, with reports from overcrowded hospitals and predictions of an unprecedented economic catastrophe. You're still trying to get your work done, because you can't just down tools – it's Friday afternoon and you're facing a weekend of bread-making and television. First though, you've got the office Zoom quiz.

Catapulted away from casual Fridays and free pizza, and hunkered down behind our kitchen table-cum-desk, we needed answers and we needed support. Did we need 40-person quizzes on a screen? Probably not. But the truth is that it was an attempt at keeping us connected, and some people needed that. Businesses moved quickly to answer our needs – from the logistics of meetings on tech, to replicating the social and informal interactions that make up so much of our day.

The most obvious signs of a toxic workplace all come down to how we're communicating with each other. It's an environment where information isn't shared widely or where it's unclear what needs to be done. It's feeling undervalued and where your work isn't recognised. It's a situation where there's an 'in' group, who support each other and look out for each other, at the expense of those on the outside. It's over-communication and too many pointless meetings.

What we need is communication that feels practical, conscious and connected to the bigger picture. At the start of lockdown, Cassandra made practical steps to helping her team feel connected. She told them:

'Let's just try and get through the next hundred days together. And this is how we're going to do it. And this is how we're going to support each other. And these are the practical steps we're going to take as a team, be it, you know, little weekly coffee calls across the team, or the least remote, remote worker rewards or access to breath workshops and yoga and lots and lots and lots of practical measures were taken to make sure that they felt supported.'

Cassandra focused on the entire team, and spoke to everyone about how they were going to stay connected with each other. She didn't tell the senior management team and ask them to pass the message on 'as they saw fit'. She created communication policies that applied to everyone, and she included everyone in them.

I'm really fascinated by the idea of democratisation of information, especially in the context of trust. Research from Professor Veronica Hope Hailey identified that maintaining trust between teams in times of disruption requires active maintenance of this relationship.[2] It's easy for this trust to break down when employees work remotely, and businesses don't have a clear strategy for enriching their relationships. But the flipside is that many remote teams find they can coordinate access to information, simply by not being in the office where informal conversation was happening. Without the easy transmission of whispered office rumours, the spread of information can feel more democratic.

Workplace culture is an amalgamation of the formal and subtle behaviours in a workplace; and while many of us have missed those water cooler chats during the lockdowns, it has also removed the trickle-down nature of internal business updates. Access to information goes a long way in helping employees feel like they're in the loop.[3]

Sure, it's great that technology allows us to keep in touch, maintain contacts and meetings and have quizzes. But a very simple all-company email, a shared file that's updated or a team instant messenger for updates – those things are vital in making us feel on an equal footing with our colleagues. The best companies use the immediacy of tech to share information quickly, clearly and to everyone.

So what can we all do to shift the narrative around office politics? Democratise our communications. If we're able to transform how we interact with each other so it's democratic and equally shared, we should also be able to expect that sort of openness and conscientiousness from our business leaders. When we're communicating and sharing our needs, we should receive that sort of honesty back. We need our leaders to **communicate openly.**

To state the obvious, we live in an age of communication, and there's a sense that the more a person communicates the more they care. But somewhere along the way we've confused what genuine communication means with just being told things.

The best leaders set the parameters of how and when

they'll be communicating with their team, and then invest in the quality of that communication, like Cassandra seems to have done. I came across a study which said the quality of communication in the workplace directly influences how much an individual trusts their boss.[4] I know that's probably not surprising, but it's amazing how often business leaders don't help their team feel included.

Once again, Covid forced business leaders to reconsider their communication approach outside business as usual. In the scramble to sort out tech and protect the underlying economics of the business, I'm sure communication slipped down the priority list for a lot of leaders. And who can blame them?

But some people took the opportunity to centre communication, and Cassandra is one of them. When Covid hit and our offices were emptied, Cassandra wrote a Medium blog about the first 100 days and shared it.[5] Instead of saying 'This is how we're going to do things,' or even, 'I want to hear from you about how to do things,' she put her hands up and said, 'You know what, I don't know, this is scary and I need your help'. She expressed a vulnerability that stretches way beyond deliberate communication.

She told me why she made the decision to publish so openly:

'I felt pretty anxious when Covid-19 hit. No one could have predicted the enormity of the impact, the tragedy,

the loss of freedom. And it's stuff that none of us have ever experienced before. And that the team will have been feeling incredibly anxious – "Am I going to have a job?". "What does this mean?" Very quickly I felt that communication and really, really careful choice of language and support was so important, especially when everyone was distressed. I really believe in quality, regular communication. I think that's so important.'

We're all just people at work, often confused and anxious and struggling. That applies to the most junior team members and the CEO. But how those at the top act sets the tone all the way down. If we can all be a bit more open about how we're feeling, we'll go some way to dismantling the idea that we should struggle on in silence.

And remember, this is a two-way contract. So as well as sharing, our leaders should be listening. They should **communicate responsively.**

Are you wondering whether anyone is listening? Or if anyone cares? The most important thing to ensure is that there are also channels that enable employees to respond to what's being said. Otherwise, there is a complete disconnect; the contract is only one way. Cassandra talks about an 'ongoing dialogue' with her team:

'It's all about regularly communicating with the team. Last week I said, "I know there's loads of conversation

around, is there going to be an office in the future? I'm really open to your suggestions. If you've got any ideas, send me an email." You know, book in some time . . . I'm playing around with some ideas in my mind. Include the business and the team in that journey. Sometimes businesses feel the pressure to have everything figured out day one. And that's when you start to become a bit too rigid. It can be an ongoing dialogue with the team.'

The honesty of saying to your team, 'You know what, I don't have all the answers, and that's OK,' is refreshing and incredibly effective. Cassandra told me she brought this dialogue right to the heart of her Covid response, so it didn't just shape the conversation, it actually shaped how the company worked.

'We're working out the right balance for the kind of new office environment. Is it three days a week? Is it whatever you want? Is it that we all try and pick a couple of days where we all try and be together? And we're just trying out different things this month. We might then flex it the month after. And I think that builds trust with the team because the communication is in both directions. It's not just mandates from the top.'

She told me they'd also created an engagement survey so there were established opportunities for the team to give ideas and feedback. They're starting with a dialogue, they're showing that conversation will have an impact, and they're giving people the chance to respond so it stays fluid.

For Cassandra this wasn't a sudden culture change, it was always at the core of her business. When Covid hit and everyone's offices were emptied, we were fully reliant on the relationships we had cultivated up until that point. In her business, Cassandra had fostered openness and trust, so when she built a blog about the first 100 days and shared it, she knew she could trust her team to respond well. It was a two-way contract of trust. It depended on her having built a team who trusted her and listened to her, and her doing the same back. This is a lesson for future leaders; we are still dealing with the pandemic and its fallout and may be for quite some time, and it won't be the last challenge we face, so building trust into the foundation of our businesses is always a good investment.

The pandemic resulted in a rapid escalation of shared technology resources, and the introduction of a huge range of HR resources. And the best were in response to feedback and engagement from employees. Some companies had a working from home allowance to pay for resources and equipment, which helped address some inequalities. Others, knowing that their employees were feeling anxious, offered free membership of headspace for their teams. They were asking and they were responding to needs.

Flexibility is at the heart of the conversation in this book.

What's essential to making it work is communication running both ways. Employers won't be able to rely on their in-house policies and perks to cultivate that: it has to be deeply embedded.

A new culture will have to place an emphasis on the emotional bonds between employees, their jobs and colleagues. It's paramount to building a positive, borderless culture. Casual Fridays don't matter so much when you can work from your bed, in your pajamas. What matters is feeling like part of a team. Because if we're resetting our culture to allow hybrid working, we have to reset what that means practically and socially. We have to think carefully about how to communicate and how to stay connected so everyone still feels part of something.

TRUST PROPERLY

When we first all switched to working from home, I thought that it could be a real step forward – essentially, a move that forced employers to trust their workers. They could no longer see them hard at work at their desk or taking notes in meetings and during presentations, so instead they would simply have to trust that workers were engaged and produc- tive. But some bosses had other plans. Shortly after we went into the first full lockdown, I came across some news articles that astounded me. A software called Sneek was letting employers see their team on their laptops. All. Day.

Although the company says the app was never designed

to spy on anyone, Sneek takes a photo every few minutes and uses them to create a wall of faces. And they can take those photos without the person knowing. I dug a bit deeper. According to the research company Gartner 16% of employers were monitoring their employees through such methods as 'virtual clocking in and out, tracking work computer usage, and monitoring employee emails or internal communications.'[6]

Sixteen per cent . . . In the middle of a world-changing pandemic that's destroying lives, sixteen per cent of employers are concerned that their teams are slacking.

Like some kind of twisted virtual take on presenteeism, some employers decided to spy on their staff through their webcams. And with every keystroke and open tab being monitored, it's no wonder some employees could never fully relax working from home. Instead they were kept on high alert; knowing they weren't trusted, they focused on being seen rather than truly engaging in work. Hello burnout and anxiety.

For a hybrid model to work, and for an individual to feel empowered and supported with a more flexible work style, there needs to be trust between them and their employer. That should be obvious. But this lack of trust runs deeper than a response to a pandemic.

The truth is that when I read about the companies who had been caught spying on their employees during the Covid lockdowns, I was shocked, but I wasn't altogether surprised.

Barclays got caught in the act using employee monitoring software a few years prior to the pandemic,[7] and it's become a common feature in the finance industry. What was particularly disappointing was the fact that employees never consented to this. Who would?

We're all familiar with the idea of the surveillance state. So while the spying crossed a privacy boundary, the deception from business leaders was equally as immoral. Leaders claim transparency as a value that benefits their team, but ultimately it reflects their desire for control. This becomes obvious when you realise that the transparency they espouse only runs one way. So often we hear HR teams and business leaders talking about 'trust' as an essential value of their businesses. But I don't think they're living up to it that often.

Perhaps, like 'culture', 'trust' has become a word that's meaningless in a corporate world. I loved talking to Rachel Botsman about trust. Rachel is an author and world-renowned expert on trust and what it means for life, work and how we do business. She explained to me the ambiguity about what trust means.

> *'People use the word "trust" a lot, but when you ask them to define what it means, very few people could actually define not just what it is, but how it worked. Boards started saying "should it become a value?" and "should we have a trust strategy?", but no one really knew what it was.'*

It's like some strange version of *1984*, where all the things corporations talk about as important to them are exactly the things they don't actually demonstrate. For me, it's simple: having trust means letting people choose how they work, and accepting that they know what works for them better than any HR member or manager possibly could.

This is the start, middle and end of a strong work culture, it often comes from the top, but it has to exist at every level. I've isolated three core facets of a company built on trust, each of which is essential to a strong culture.

1. INTENTION – START FROM A PLACE OF TRUST

When you start a business, day one, you make a decision about how that business will be run. You might adapt and change along the way, but you start with an intention. You employ people and you start a relationship. How you start that relationship is up to you. And trust is a big one, because how can you expect someone to trust you to lead them if you don't trust them in response?

Sereena Abbassi, the former global head of culture and inclusion at creative agency M&C Saatchi, had an interesting perspective on this.

'The old system tells us you have to earn trust, but wouldn't it be incredible if we approached running our companies in a way where you're trusted until proven otherwise. People need to feel empowered. People need to feel like they have

autonomy; the majority of people want to feel like they've got a level of agency. Traditionally we spend more time with our work colleagues than we do with our nearest and dearest. I find it fascinating how you can work alongside someone every day and not trust them to deliver. This idea of presenteeism, it just blows my mind. Like if I can't see you, you're not doing work. It's absolutely ludicrous.'

We have to start from a place where 'you're trusted until proven otherwise'. Nothing grows if you don't have trust. But what does that look like in practice? It's saying to someone when they join your company 'work how you want, but deliver'. Look at results. Look at communication. But don't build a relationship by constant surveillance. That shows a fundamental lack of trust.

There are more and more companies that are built on a principle of trust. It's at the core of their business structures. Matt Mullenweg set up WordPress, and he's often at the forefront of innovations in tech and business. I heard him on Sam Harris's podcast, Making Sense,[8] talking about how his business was responding to Covid, and what they were doing already to shape culture. I was blown away when he said his company only gets together in person for 26 days a year. Outside of those creative conferences they're free to work exactly how and where they want.

Can you imagine starting at a company and not meeting your colleagues for months? I'm sure that's not how it feels in practice, but for me it makes more sense to strike a balance between remote working and office working, to enable employees to make decisions on their work patterns that are fulfilling and emotionally supportive. Google's chief executive Sundar Pichai settled on a hybrid model, identifying the value of shared community spaces for creativity and collaboration, while acknowledging how home working enabled more flexibility for its employees too. I like that approach. Allowing employees to choose, to be part of a physical space and part of a digital one. After all, for every person who has found that home working has benefitted their productivity, there are others who find that they rely on time in an office environment to get certain tasks done.

This is the vital component of flexible working – starting from a position of choice, building systems that rely on trust. If you're putting flexibility and freedom to choose at the core of your business structure, you've got to follow through on that.

We need to understand leadership as a device to create structures with trust at their core. It's having the power to change the environment your team is working in – whether that's physical or metaphorical. In our conversation, Engine CEO Ete Davies said he thought leadership was ultimately about 'bringing people together and creating an environment where they can work successfully together. If I can create that environment, then everything else takes care of itself.'

That speaks to me. And I didn't just hear that idea from Ete, it came up again in a conversation with Joanna Lyall, who after 20 years rising through the ranks to become UK managing director of Mindshare, and who is now the UK CEO of Brainlabs. Joanna talked about a type of leadership that didn't breathe down people's necks, but stayed close enough to offer emotional and practical support. A sort of boss that creates boundaries and gives freedom within that space. She said, 'My role is not to be an expert. I'm not there to tell them what to create, what to publish, what to do. I'm there to create a framework that allows them to be brilliant.' She's basing this on the expectation that if you've hired someone, you can rely on them. You don't need to watch them; you need to free them. Sounds good.

2. CREATING POSITIVE, MEANINGFUL FRAMEWORKS

How do we make sure we keep trusting each other? Well, let's start by implementing policies that mean something. Let's put positive frameworks for choice in place and make sure people use them.

This comes back to the tech perks, and all those things that look amazing on the outside but are meaningless if they aren't underpinned by trust. I remember everyone chatting about Netflix's unlimited holiday policy. But then we started hearing that every single thing employees did at Netflix was appraised and if they weren't performing they could be fired at any one of their reviews. And there were reviews every two weeks. In this context, taking as much holiday as one wants suddenly doesn't look so appealing, right?

Unlimited holiday has become the poster child for tech companies that want to talk the talk, but don't walk the walk. Reed saw a 20% increase in jobs offering unlimited holiday between 2017 and 2018. But that increase is more common in modern companies that are built on goals and metrics – and if you're constantly being evaluated on what you're delivering, are you going to take that two-week trip to Spain? Is anyone shocked that in fact people take less holidays when it's unlimited?[9]

As Proper co-founder Cassandra Stavrou says, 'There is a massive gap between living and breathing the themes and the policies that you want the business to stand for and ticking boxes.' It doesn't mean anything if businesses say their employees have choices, but make them feel psychologically that they don't.

One area Cassandra raised with me feels like one of the most important battlegrounds of this conversation: equal maternity and paternity leave. There's been a huge cultural shift towards equal and shared paternity leave, and it's considered the essential step to closing the gender pay gap. But the reality is that men often don't feel free to actually take it. Without companies actively encouraging men to take the time off, it's a meaningless perk.

Serena William's husband, Alexis Ohanian, wrote an incredible article in the *New York Times* about this issue.[10]

The co-founder of Reddit, Ohanian took up his own company's policy of 16-weeks' paid paternity leave and it was a revelation to him. But when he looked into it, he found that fewer than half of fathers took up a paternity leave policy. Why? Because they don't feel supported by their companies, believing they'll miss out on promotions, become obsolete or might even be fired. Welcome to life as a woman!

This is an example of a fundamental shift that business leaders need to make. It's OK to be proud of positive or progressive company policies, but they have to really encourage employees to utilise them – otherwise, what's the point? These policies aren't just pulled out of the ether: they are created with the intention of real change, solving an existing issue and may have real economic value too. Take equal paternity leave. That's not some nice gift to men to allow them more time with their babies – although that should be a given. It allows women to go back to work too; it brings mothers back into business at a time when so many have to choose to stay at home because of how unaffordable childcare is.

I spoke to Anna Whitehouse, who's an influential voice on parenting. She immediately made the connection between the impact of becoming a mother on a business:

'Focus on the bottom line, focus on actually, what's good for business here because ultimately treating people like humans in a humane way is good for business. It's good

for the community. It unites people. And the tech is absolutely there. And I am an exhausted mother who piped up. It's no more complicated. I was hacked off with the system that was going to effectively – if it continued as it was – stunt my girls' careers. They were going to start their jobs perhaps at 21, like I did, looking around the room and wondering where the women are beyond 30, beyond childbearing age. Why aren't the men at home with their children? And I cannot raise my girls, you cannot raise your nieces, sons, the kid on the bus opposite you; we're not talking about your own families, we're talking about the next generation. We cannot raise them to . . . we can't raise them for a fall.'

When men don't feel encouraged to take advantage of paternity leave, it affects women too. And it massively affects the business. That's just one example. But everywhere you look at these policies they're created for a reason. Having holidays is good for your mental health, and you return better able to work, free food supports those who can't afford overpriced sandwiches.

Is there a role for perks at work? Of course there is. But the option to work from home shouldn't be a perk. We need to get better at distinguishing between the two. Perks can boost employee morale but they aren't the heartbeat of why you choose to work for a company – or they shouldn't be! I was most definitely reeled in to join companies in the past based on such things but I have realised the more sexy the perk appears, the more frustrated the employees. Perks can be part of employee culture but shouldn't be used as a substitute.

It's not enough to create policies though; we have to embed them in our culture, and simultaneously nurture a culture where employees value the policies and feel there is mutual benefit in applying them. Businesses have to encourage employees to take advantage of these policies, and make them feel trusted to have the freedom to do so.

3. TRUST IS A TWO-WAY CONTRACT

It's not just about trusting employees to do their work and not monitoring them, it's about trusting them to understand their work and decide for themselves how to manage it. And crucially, how to work with each other. Because usually you're part of a team, and you need to trust everyone else just as much as you need to feel trusted from the top. We all need to create clear parameters for our work, so we can support greater agency in each other.

Trust needs to be built on relinquishing control. Whether you're a business leader or a junior employee, you have to let others have agency and input. It's Rachel Botsman who drew the link between trust and control, explaining that 'it's genuinely hard for people because they like control . . . If we really want things to change, we need to transform our relationship with the things we can't control.'

This is where we've gone wrong previously. It's differentiating between real trust in the workplace and an environment that's all about control. What kept coming up in the conversations I was having was that management styles never really kept up with culture messaging, and what we considered to be trust was often the opposite. Rachel researched this and found that companies that describe their culture as high trust use 'power, reporting, and accountability measures which are actually the opposite of trust'. She said, 'There's a legacy of a generation of management and leaders who never really learned how to trust people. They grew up in an era of oversight and micromanagement. So when the technology and expectations and people's cultural values shifted, that was still at the heart of many organisational cultures.'

This gets to the heart of the problem with culture: the world has changed and everyone knows trust is a value to be celebrated in the workplace, but our structures and styles of working are so built on monitoring and oversight that none of us actually knows how to relinquish control.

One part of that two-way contract is a business that creates a framework that asks for a reasonable contribution and states clearly what the employee has to do. And that applies to all of our interactions at work – setting boundaries in the expectations means we don't deal with as many surprises. Put it this way, if I've been asked to write something to a brief, I need to be able to ask all the questions before I start, and get clear responses. If I get a two-line response, I might not deliver what's required, and that doesn't help anyone.

I think it's about being honest, about acknowledging what element of control you need to retain on a task, and what elements you can leave to someone else. Rachel also touched on this idea.

> 'People are not very good at being open and honest around where they need to be controlling. And what I found is, I tell people who I work with, "Look, I am finickity about design." So if you put something out there and it has 22-font type on one side and 26, I will notice it. I am not an anal person, but I was trained as a designer. So this is what my eye is going to see.'

This is the difference between giving someone a task, then when it doesn't meet expectations making that person feel like a failure, and giving someone clear instructions on the parameters for success. If you can take clear instructions and then follow them with your own approach, you'll feel empowered and supported at the same time.

I'm going to come back to autonomy later in the chapter, but the thing I really take away from what Rachel says is this idea of a 'high-trust relationship'. That we should be building a foundation of trust in all members of a business from the top to the bottom, but that we should also be maintaining that trust in the workplace. And this is *high* trust – it's meaningful, and it's deep.

We don't just need to reset our idea of trust so we start from a basis of believing people are working rather than checking they're working. We also need to reset our idea of trust so we respect our colleagues and assume they know how to do their work without our control at each stage of the business, wherever you work, you need to trust that the people you work with will deliver what they need to. Give up control.

BE INVESTED

The last, and most important, thing we need to reset is being invested in each other. That means leaders putting energy into the growth of their teams, and employees believing they have a stake in the business. That's the heart of a two-way contract. Both of you put something in – both of you get something out.

Starting from the top, if we want to create a communicative and trusting culture, then we should be on the lookout for businesses that **nurture development**.

Ultimately, businesses need to fulfil their purpose. On a structural level, employees contribute their human capital or skill toward the end goal – providing a service, or delivering a product. The corporate machine is dependent on each individual doing their bit. So every worker must in some sense, be aware of and aligned with the company mission. Anyone who's worked in a company will have seen some version of an employee handbook, mission statement or even just the unwritten office protocol that they're expected to pick up over the course of their employment. They are designed by managers and HR teams to make it clear to the employee what's expected of them.

Now I'm not saying we shouldn't expect businesses to ask something from their employees. That as well as the clear tasks of the job, they're also being asked to participate in the company, to align with its identity and be part of something bigger than that list of tasks. But the question we should all be asking is: what does the employee get back? Where is the employer's handbook about what their employees can expect of them? If the only thing business leaders can offer their employees is a wage slip, attracting and retaining talent becomes a whole lot more challenging. In 2018, a study found that the average Briton would spend over 3,500 days of their lives working.[11] We need to enjoy the journey and make sure that there's some reward, and that only partially relates to the zeros in our bank account.

Cassandra Stavrou has talked about what she owes her team quite bluntly: 'It's not just, "Oh, we'll pay you every month and that's kind of our bit done." It has to go further.'

She says: 'I'm so grateful that they've chosen Proper to spend three, five, seven years of their career with. I feel a real responsibility to make that time fun, enriching. Develop them. That's my bit of the bargain . . . It's a two-way contract and more business leaders are starting to understand that.'

It has to go further. Fulfilment comes from growth, and growth comes from space and resources. Studies have shown that people are 12 times more likely to leave a business if they don't feel like they are developing.[12] If a business nurtures its employees, they're not only developing an invested and engaged worker, they're also investing in their own future. In the context of these smaller companies that are growing quickly, leaders, like Cassandra, who have emotional intelligence can inspire their employees in a way that's harder in a more established framework.

That's also Ete Davies' brand of leadership. 'It's always about enablement . . . but the central job and the central role for the leader is to enable the people that you have to achieve their full potential, to do great things and to feel like they are contributing.'

This isn't thinking about leadership as the management of a system, financials or growth. It's not a top-down approach where you're getting people to do something for you. This is leaders having the humility to know that their team has the ability to do something and recognising that it's their job to give them everything they need to do it. Strategy and vision are good in a leader, in fact, let's be honest, they're essential. But if there is just a P&L and a business plan, this won't breed success.

What we're saying is that a good organisational culture

supports employee's needs and makes them the focus of growth. The best bosses will be the ones who release control, and take a more flexible approach to structure, offering more of a skeleton, a loose framework which empowers employees to make their own choices. And through all this, a really great leader will provide empathetic support.

This is a huge deal. It transforms the role of a business leader, to the extent where current bosses may no longer fit the needs of what's required from them. It will change how leaders are recruited in the future; we already know that emotional intelligence is an important trait for individuals in these roles, but could it become the basis of what makes a good boss? That picture in your head of a business leader – is it a white man in a suit, standing up in front of everyone? Me too. But maybe now's the chance to do something different. Maybe it's time to **nurture autonomy**.

As you develop a better understanding of what you're really offering at work, you need a business culture that gives you space and support to bring it and thrive. A leader's job should be to make employees feel valued and developed. And the employee's side of the bargain is taking ownership.

Cassandra's 'The Next 100 Days' blog started by speaking directly to her employees – 'Continue to be a builder. That means we need you to make decisions. Think things through. Trust your gut. We will back you. There will be no blame if it doesn't turn out quite right.' Just like the rest of us, she had no idea how this was going to go, but she wanted her whole team to help her work it out.

By approaching management in this way, Cassandra was asking her employees to be stakeholders, not just participants. Feedback channels become feedback loops, where employees feel empowered to share their ideas too. It's about sharing what you want as a leader, but leaving some elements on the table.

And as we begin to navigate new ways of working post-pandemic, there's an opportunity to bring everyone, at all levels of a company, into discussions like never before. I've read some fascinating think-pieces and studies on this idea of active involvement in decision-making. It's about empowering employees to be part of the development of the company, engaged in its growth and responsible for its foundations. Cassandra calls this 'builder mentality', which she thinks is vital because

> 'Exposing your fallibility and empowering the team to be part of figuring it out is so motivating versus saying, you do this, you do that . . . We want people to join who are excited at the prospect of not having all the answers, but being part of finding the solutions.'

That idea of making everyone shareholders and creating an environment that encourages people to feel invested resonated so much with me. I know that things like 'owner mentality' sounds like every other corporate motto, but if we want to think about culture differently, then that concept has to be built into the bones of businesses. Let people in. Hell, put them on the board. So long as it breaks down the 'us vs them' mentality.

So we've come to the real heart of culture here. The conflict at the core of good culture, which so many businesses have fallen down on. Good culture means a two-way contract where we're all equals. But is this the central fear of business owners? That they are, by necessity, relinquishing power if they change culture? Is it business leaders holding back any meaningful change in culture? Is that hierarchy where all our problems come from? That's certainly what architect and co-founder of Dark Matter Labs, Indy Johar, thinks:

'I would be provocative enough to say that our thesis of management and organisation is really still coming back from a world of slavery and a world of Kings and Queens, and it comes from a thesis that one person can tell the other person what to do. That the efficiency of command and control is something valuable. And we have lived in this model of what I'd call kingships and serfs, and management theory is the last vestibule of holding onto that.'

This idea of feudal hierarchy feeding into capitalist hierarchy is fascinating, and worthy of an entirely different book. But it's worth thinking about – this idea that hierarchy creates an environment of control. As I hope I've shown in this chapter, control is the enemy of culture. We may not be able to totally flatten the structure, but can we try and keep the spirit of equality in mind as we grow? Sereena Abbassi said:

> 'I think a lot of businesses start out on this so well-meaning, and they're like Yes to flexibility. Yes to honouring the fact that we are individuals and there shouldn't just be this one size that fits all . . . And then they grow, they scale up and then they sometimes get bought or sold and they just become inherently conservative with this very, very rigid mindset, which doesn't actually honour all the wonderful individual people and stories that the organisation has. It just becomes very standardised.'

I agree. Think how any business starts. It's just one person, with an idea they believe in. They start building a team, then they get investment and they have other people to answer to, and the business grows and is successful, and suddenly they're more distant from the team, and there's more pressure to just succeed and grow. So is resetting culture about making sure that sort of huge growth doesn't happen? Or is it about ensuring all the small details of a corporate structure are carefully thought about?

Indy calls this the 'boring revolution'. It is 'the stuff we don't discuss', property rights, employment rights, employment contracts, title deeds, warranties. He says, 'Your employment contract is a thesis of control. What would it mean if you were invited to care? What would an invitation to care really look like? We've constructed a whole legal domain infrastructure which is actually an extension of control, which I think has reached the end of its limits.'

What this means is asking employees to be equal partners at the beginning. This isn't just asking them to be part of how the creative and the output works, it's asking them to be in control of the very core of a business. This is really revolutionary, and I'll be honest, it might just not be possible in most businesses, and it's also not an overnight thing. But surely this is the way we should be thinking at the moment; and surely we can at least start looking for it in the businesses we apply to work for, and demanding it of the businesses we do work for?

Covid stress-tested the idea of a business culture removed from the physical space of the offices. And distributed teams have already proven that culture can transcend the workplace, with huge progress in both the tools and processes to help remote teams to communicate, collaborate and consolidate their relationships.

With trust, and communication, businesses can encourage a way of working where we truly feel that we can be flexible. In that world, hierarchy will be less relevant because those managerial status symbols won't be as visible. And crucially each person will have autonomy. They'll be trusted to manage the work they're doing, and invested in creating something substantial with that work. If we're communicating freely and we feel trusted to make our own decisions, surely that business structure is going to become a web instead of a pyramid?

Culture isn't about perks; it's a commitment. It's a two-way contract where both parties – the business and the employee – are putting value in and getting value out. It's communication, trust, and investment. All the perks in the world won't make up for having a manager who treats you badly.

Chapter Three

BUSINESS

———

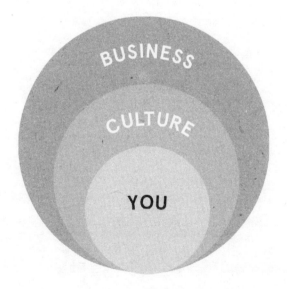

BUSINESS

———

'Didn't think Channel 4 knew there was life outside the M25'
– banner across the new Channel 4 HQ in Leeds, 2019

THE WORD 'PURPOSE' has permeated through the business world in recent years like a lightning bolt through company mission statements. From Patagonia's dedication to Ethical Consumption to Ben & Jerry's activist history. You can't move these days without a brand declaring that they're ethical, sustainable, diverse – basically they're good for you.

And who can blame them, the power of purpose is a great motivator. Consumers expect it; 94% of us believe the brands we love should have a strong purpose, and 83% agree that businesses need to deliver a positive impact if they're to earn a profit.[1] It motivates employees – according to the

Edelman Trust Barometer[2], and three quarters of employees believe their employer should make necessary changes when they see them, and not just when they're demanded by the government.[3] Employees no longer want to be left in the dark by their superiors either, stating that they expect bosses to speak out on issues such as racism, diversity and climate change. People want to work for employers who align with their values and practice transparency in the workplace. And even investors look for it – in the UK alone, in 2020, 78% of them stated that ethical investment (investing in companies that are green or socially conscious) was more important to them compared to five years ago.[4] and two thirds of them had increased investments in sustainable funds over this period too. But those considerations haven't always been at the top of investors' minds.

The free-market economist Milton Friedman and his philosophies of maximising profits as an overriding and self-evident goal have long defined business. That's how capitalist societies think about business. And this way of thinking has shaped our entire lives.

It's hard to imagine a society or even a business that doesn't put profit ahead of everything else. I was looking into how business is taught and in one textbook, *Foundations of Business*, it was described as 'the organised effort of individuals to produce and sell, for a profit, the goods and services that satisfy society's needs.' That doesn't sound too far from the Friedman model. Until we look at those last two words, *'society's needs'*. For far too long we've seen this as consumption, convenience and competition. But with 2,825 global billionaires holding more wealth than the 4.6 billion people who make up 60% of the world's population, something's not adding up.

Sure, businesses are creating plenty of profit, but who does that benefit? According to the UN, the world population is on course to grow from seven billion in 2020 to more than nine billion by 2050. With today's consumption of resources already equivalent to 1.5 Earths, it's clear that the way ahead is unsustainable without serious intervention. According to the WHO and WWF respectively, seven million people die every year due to the effects of polluted air[5] and, by 2050, without action, the amount of plastic in our oceans will outweigh the number of fish.[6] Friedman's argument that for a company to pursue anything other than (legal) profit would be 'pure and unadulterated socialism' is starting to feel outdated. And it's particularly alarming when we look at how this growth-obsessed doctrine is destroying the planet.

We need a society in which the services and goods we need don't come at a terrible social or environmental cost. What's clear is that the clock is ticking, and future demographic and environmental trends will only magnify the challenges of a world that's been asset-stripped in the name of profits over everything.

Businesses shouldn't continue to add to this destruction;

they should help prevent it. And people are starting to realise that. I'm not an economist, nor have I started a business, but my work as a brand strategist has opened my eyes to a shift in public perception – that profits should be a by-product of serving a purpose.

This isn't about businesses simply stating that they have a purpose, it's about putting in place some key things that mean they act with purpose. Slapping the 'sustainability' banner on a website isn't going to cut it anymore – they need to practice what they preach right the way through the entire business.

A piece in the *Financial Times* sheds some light: businesses will define their purpose in different ways, 'but the model that replaces Friedman's framework must recognise that all companies "are embedded in a political and socioeconomic system whose health is vital to their sustainability"'.[7]

How your business operates might feel like it's outside of your control; you're just one person, but I believe it's important that we all think about these areas independently and reconsider our own values. That's really thinking about the right place for us to work or shop. And I hope that businesses will take note too – because increasingly, the things they took for granted that would attract talent, guarantee profit and make a business 'successful' just aren't enough.

Ultimately, we should be asking: 'How is the world a better place by this company being here?' And if the answer is that it's not . . . well, then we should see it as an opportunity to take our money – and talent – somewhere else.

Rethink growth

There's increasing recognition that it's time for business to play a bigger and far bolder role in tackling society's most challenging problems. Businesses just don't stand outside of the collective. In fact, without the vast human and financial capital and global reach of multinational corporations on board, our ability to solve the world's most pressing problems is *unimaginable*.

But there's a dark side to this too. Pre-1800, corporations were public service organisations which had to act in the best interests of the people. After the Civil War, corporations in the new United States were given the same rights as individuals under the 14th Amendment. This means that today corporations still have the same rights as people, and they can become worryingly entrenched in politics.

What makes corporations so powerful in terms of global impact, is that they can create political action committees and spend lots of money lobbying governments. The bigger their profits, the greater their impact on society as a whole. And it's highly unlikely we'll see Exxon Mobil lobbying for carbon negativity any time soon.

Businesses may not be able to solve all the world's problems, but they have power to be at the forefront addressing many of them. Things are changing, and as the world looks just a little bit like it's falling apart, the currency people are looking for is changing too.

No one is recognising this shift, and the need for it, more than Labour MP for Nottingham, England, Nadia Whittome. She was elected aged 23 and refused the standard parliament salary, keeping only the 'average worker's wage' and donating the rest to charity. Nadia is part of a new wave of people demanding more. When we spoke in summer 2020, she was angry with so much of Boris Johnson's government's response to the pandemic, and more generally about the implications of a society that puts profit over people.

Nadia has spent her life in Nottingham, a city that often tops lists of the UK's poorest cities. That's in large part because of the very low employment rates: only 57% of 18–64-year-olds were in work in 2017.[8] That's the lowest in the country, and it's a great burden on and pain to the communities that live there. It's not surprising Nadia feels so passionately about how jobs and businesses act in her home city.

She told me that the 3.7 million in 'insecure work' – one in nine of the workforce – was the main reason why inequality is so widespread in Nottingham. 'We've had 10 years of austerity. The Marmot Review [into health inequality in England] showed how life expectancy has stalled. And then we've seen that Covid has widened the gap between the rich and the poor.'

It's a statistic I hadn't quite grasped before speaking to Nadia: *one in nine people are in insecure work.* It suddenly makes the conversation around the middle classes working from home feel really irrelevant, and it points to the urgent need for businesses to step up. Nadia thinks we're facing a 'jobs' massacre like nothing we've seen before'. She made a direct link between government, business and poverty over Covid, commenting that 'what's happened during this crisis is the government has bailed out capitalism, but it hasn't given people power'.

Nadia is looking around her and seeing her generation forced to spend a third of their income on rent, not being able to get on the housing ladder, while record lows of council housing are being built and existing council housing is being sold off at low prices. 'None of that is necessary,' she says. 'In fact, the opposite is necessary. Like we need secure jobs. We need secure housing.' The problem is so clear. And the link between businesses, the economy, government and resources are even clearer.

Yet, despite her obvious frustration, Nadia sounded a note of hope at groups asking for change. She talked about collective action, mentioning Extinction Rebellion, Black Lives Matter, climate strikers and outsourced cleaners fighting for their rights with the IWGB, the Independent Workers of Great Britain union. That's coupled with community movements like mutual aid, trans people fighting for their rights, sex workers etc. 'I think for me, that's probably the greatest source of hope . . . community learning and those community movements,' she says.

I talk more about community in Chapter 4, but what's important is how many of these groups are emerging and demanding more from businesses. Demanding they respond to climate change, that they pay their workers fairly, that they ensure rights for everyone in their business.

Society is waking up, and in particular the younger generation. Nadia is an inspiring person to talk to, because of her passion and her hope. 'I firmly believe in the power of our generation and I'm looking forward to the next generation of politicians, lawmakers, teachers, teaching assistants, people working all jobs across society, because I think all jobs are very important. Society wouldn't function without any one of us. I think we really will start to see real change then.'

As more and more people enter the world of work, have money of their own to spend and a choice in how to spend it, and where they work, we just might see a shift in what businesses prioritise. It's time to reset our expectations for what business goals should look like and, hint, exponential growth is no longer as desirable – or sustainable – as it once appeared to be.

Economist Kate Raworth created a new economic model called 'Doughnut Economics', which lays out an economic system and structures based on sustainability. The twenty-first century goal, she asserts, is to meet the needs of all people within the means of the living planet. This doughnut is a ring of societal benefit between the social foundation of what society needs and an ecological ceiling for what the planet needs. This, she shows, is where the world's economies can operate in a 'safe and just space for humanity'.

For Raworth, as for most visionary thinkers, 'the economy is embedded within, and dependent upon, society and the living world.' It's sort of mind blowing that a lot of economic thinkers put society and the living world aside in the quest for a 'value' on the stock market. Doughnut Economics starts with the rejection of endless GDP growth and the acceptance of an immutable truth – that nothing grows forever. Healthy systems in nature develop until they are grown, and then they concentrate on thriving. We need to do the same.

The implications of a perspective shift that focuses on thriving rather than growing or winning are profound. And businesses reflecting that perspective shift would be transformative. Of the UN's 17 Sustainability Development Goals (SDG) for 2030, outlined in 2015, at least eight are directly and powerfully impacted or even determined by the actions of business; such as decent work and economic growth, industry, innovation and infrastructure, responsible consumption and production, and partnerships to achieve the goal. The remaining nine are indirectly so, in an interconnected, globalised world. What's amazing is that this is already happening. A 2017 report by KPMG showed that

43% of the world's largest 250 companies now link their sustainability reporting to the SDGs, including Samsung, General Electric (GE) and Ford – and at the 2020 Davos conference, US billionaire Marc Benioff proclaimed: 'Capitalism as we have known it is dead.' He summed up the zeitgeist, by saying, 'This obsession we have with maximising profits for shareholders has led to incredible inequality and a planetary emergency'.[9]

Of course, Benioff, with his billions already safely in the bank, might not be the best person to pronounce the death knell of classic capitalism, drawing up the ladder after himself. But such high-profile statements do underline the message filtering though. As a global community we've recognised that we will all have to play a much longer game to deal with the damage done to our psychology, societies and global systems by the rapacious 'value acquisition' of the past century.

But how do we actively effect that change in a meaningful way? One answer can be found in B Corporations.

Certified B Corporations (B Corps for short) are businesses that meet the highest standards of verified social and environmental performance and public transparency. Making themselves visible and accountable, they're taking the lead in yoking profit and purpose together to build a more sustainable economy. And most importantly, they're drawing a line in the sand that may ultimately encourage everyone to be bolder. The more I read about them the more I feel they might be our chance at a wider culture shift. Simply, it's business as a force for good and in the last financial crisis of 2008, certified B Corps were 63% more likely to survive than any other businesses of similar size.[10]

It's a movement that is gathering momentum, not least because it's what the consumer wants. A new generation of customers are demanding more transparency and ethical engagement than ever before, so that B Corp status is becoming increasingly prized. And these days, it's something people notice.

Cassandra Stavrou, founder of B Corp status Proper, compared it to what a Fair Trade stamp means to profits. It's 'that marker around your governance, the way that you treat the world, the way that you treat your team.' As Cassandra says, it doesn't mean 'our work here is done, we've got the stamp; it's saying we recognise we're trying to do the right thing, and we're going to continually try and get better and better.' It means a business is evolving and adapting. It's still changing to meet goals. It's just that those goals aren't *just purely* economic growth.

This matters: change demands innovation and if there's one thing capitalism loves, it's innovation. It's about putting positive social growth in the same frame as economic growth and seeing them as intrinsically entwined. Cassandra gets this: 'Innovation plus competition is a really, really powerful relationship. With customers more demanding and more discerning than ever before, it requires a situation where businesses have to get better, have to be more representative, have to care about the climate, if they want commercial success.'

It's not just about getting a certificate – job done – move on. It's about seeing that certificate as a marker of what you want to do, and what you care about. Cassandra asked me to imagine a world where all companies will compete not only to be the best *in* the world, but to be the best *for* the world.

Spanning 60 countries and 150 industries, the movement is gathering pace. It makes good economic sense too: B Corp-certified brands in the UK grew 28 times faster than the national economic growth rate of 0.5% in 2018, according to the Office for National Statistics.

I'm not going to say we should only work for and use companies with B Corp status. But I'm saying it's something simple to look out for, a clear indication that the company has the intention to do something good. So look out for it. It might be surprising that companies explicitly focused on something other than economic growth are growing the most economically. But think about everything we've covered so far, and it seems to make sense. Businesses supply the consumer, and as I've said already, the consumer is changing. They want something worth buying and businesses that answer that need are doing something right. And that means right across the business.

Rethink product

The fashion industry is one of the biggest global polluters, and fast fashion in particular is an example of the social and environmental damage companies can do. If we look at the supply chain of a T-shirt for example, growing cotton requires an enormous amount of pesticides which threaten biodiversity, spinning cotton generates 394 million tonnes of CO_2, dying cotton requires fresh water and the transportation and continued washing and drying of a garment saps resources further. For all of this effort, £40 billion worth of clothing hides in the back of our wardrobes, and we continue to demand new styles every season.

When it comes to questioning a brand's integrity, often we need to look deeper than the top-level PR and marketing. It's no surprise that the world's top polluters in the oil and gas industry are key funders of climate denial groups,[11] but it's an insult to consumers when these companies try to mask this with soulless green PR.[12]

An increased awareness of the role mass productions have on the planet is having a big impact on the spending habits of Gen Y and Gen Z. I know I've changed, and so have my friends and the people I speak to. It's taken a while, but acquisition as a goal for life is starting to look flawed and unsustainable.

Research shows that consumers make buying decisions based on the value they attribute to items – whether that is their ability to impress others, fill up a psychological hole, distract or something else entirely. Now more than ever, when people consider a purchase they are thinking about its origins, use of fair and sustainable production methods or longevity and recycling potential. With consumer spending driving approximately 60% of global GDP, according to the World Economic Forum, the choices we make matter, and the power of consumption drives change.

There is a central tension at the heart of this. Ultimately without a consumer there is no business; so consumer spending drives natural extraction and production output, with a massive impact on water, land and energy use. And we all know what that impact is doing to our future.

The act of buying something has become much more of a political act now. It is as much about acknowledging and consenting to the product's behind-the-scenes practices and its ethos as it is about the function of the thing itself. While the end product may have been presented to the unthinking consumer at the point of sale in previous decades, today's consumers are waking up to the wider implications.

All this might seem so far from where we started – being conscientious about how we prioritise and value our own time, for example, but if you think about it, consumerism is simply an extension of that. Choosing where we put our time, energy and money can have a huge and direct impact on our quality of life. And more than that, it has an impact on the communities we are part of and the planet we live on. What we consume not only sustains us, but it differentiates us – and in late capitalist industrialised nations, it also defines us. Consumption and identity are intertwined in a free market where choice becomes a synonym for hierarchy and ethics.

But as the world's issues become more and more pressing, choice is also becoming interchangeable with values. The demands of consumers are changing – where once price, quality and availability were the main drivers for consumption, provenance and authenticity are now climbing up the list of factors that consumers cite as important for their economic exchanges.

So what can businesses do to meet new demands for integrity? They can be transparent about their supply chains and then ensure those chains meet expectations. Ultimately, if transparency of the supply chain becomes a – or even *the* – choice point, then it demands a complete rethink of what a business is. And also what a business says. I've spoken a lot in writing and on stage about the importance of storytelling to connect with customers. In a competitive online market, gaining brand trust and loyalty has never been so crucial. We're now in a world where multiple communication channels refract your 'company soul' in all directions, putting brand at the very heart of business.

In this new world of visibility, and accountability, there is no point talking about how good you are as a company and then paying your cleaners below living wage or sourcing products from sweatshops. If you build a business with this sort of cognitive dissonances, and you're found to be unethical, well you might not recover.

Cassandra Stavrou agrees. 'The internal and the external of businesses and brands is merging and business integrity is more important than ever. Long gone are the days where you can have this shiny, exciting external brand that's being communicated to consumers, while internally you might not be treating your team well or upholding the values that you talk about. You're very quickly found out. The internal and the external are becoming symbiotic. And it starts with your consumers needing to be able to pull back the layers and find your values run through to your core. Consumers are more discerning than ever before and if you're found not to have that level of integrity, they rightly will just go somewhere else.'

In the same way that building a company culture with policies and mottoes that don't mean anything substantial for employee's lives doesn't work anymore, building a business with a shiny brand that hides bad practice won't wash either. As consumers, if we want brands to act right it's time to do so with our money and spend it in better, more ethical ways. This does require more research on our part and more conscious spending choices.

We need to make sure our businesses are living up to their brands. The idea that we can dictate consumer choices by voting with our wallet is fundamental to free market capitalism. It ensures the businesses that survive are the ones we value most. And if we're to go along with the concept that companies are driven by their consumers, then consumers need to be savvy too. It's easy to say we support climate activism and fair pay, but then continue to buy sweatshop clothing. As consumers, if we want to see changes to the way companies are run, we have to stop buying into them. I would like to stress that the onus is not solely on you. As Maxine Bédat of the New Standard Institute told the *Financial Times*: 'We need brands to speak about what they're doing to reduce impact and be honest and transparent.'[13]

However, access to transparent information is a key barrier to consumers being informed. How can you exercise your purchasing powers to choose ethical products when 'the clear lack and untrustworthy information makes it challenging to navigate multiple packaging messaging and prevents consumers from buying ethically. The abundance of labels – ranging from voluntary certifications like Ecolabels or multi-stakeholder initiatives such as Fairtrade International – make it incredibly difficult for consumers to understand who and what to trust' says Nesta.[14]

Though it seems like a lot for you as an individual to take on, it is becoming easier. For example: ethical rating apps, such as CoGo, are also becoming integral in the fight for greater transparency to answer the needs of more conscious consumers. And not surprisingly, according to a Behavioural

Insights Team study, rating systems can in fact be much more effective at nudging consumers than product-based labels as they capture the overall company's performance.[15]

These are indisputable active steps to ensure our businesses are performing at a higher level. Rating systems aren't everything, but similarly to B Corp status they are a badge of intent, and a sign that a business is doing more than just profiting. It's not your responsibility to force businesses to care, but as I've said before, you can show what you value with how you spend. Businesses are waking up to a change in consumer needs, and they are proving that they *can* adapt if they *want to.*

Rethink talent

I grew up in a London that felt like a truly multicultural city. Shops, restaurants and most importantly people from all over the world. So stepping into my first corporate office for the first time, I was pretty surprised. This didn't look like London. Everyone who worked there looked the same, with similar perspectives and ideas. Except me. And if I didn't feel like I fit into the business, how could that business possibly make things for people like me. Logically, if a company's corporate social responsibility pamphlet stressed a commitment to diversity, while not embodying that in the workers it hired, does that company really value diversity at all? They have to embody their values, inside and out, if they want us to believe it.

I wonder what it would have felt like to go to an interview at a business and see a team of people who looked like me, or at least didn't all look like each other and not me. Businesses need to attract talent that comes in many forms, reflecting the larger society.

Talking to Ete Davies about talent made me imagine an office made up of people who felt supported. He talked about a business built solely on the 'talent of individuals, their knowledge, their experience, their skills, their passions'. And that's a business that could respond to crises and build growth because it had the right people in place. Ete focuses his energy on hiring the right people and creating a frame-work in which they can succeed. He recognises that valuing people, first and foremost, is the key to making a business thrive in a sustainable, lasting way. And part of valuing workers – and making them feel valued – includes how, and most importantly, where the business works.

Flexibility isn't just about allowing people to work from home and the implications of the room in your house you're working from, it's about where that house is. It's about allowing people to choose how and where they live so long as they are contributing to the business. And it's also about trusting them to know and choose for themselves the best and most effective way for them to contribute. What's really exciting is the change that will have on what the business creates.

How many times in the last few months have you heard people on the radio or TV talking about the 'move to the country'. All middle-class voices talking about keeping a flat in London and otherwise moving to Sussex and growing vegetables while keeping their city job. I mean, that sounds great. But I don't think that's the most important part of this picture. We're not thinking on a big enough scale of how shifting to flexibility could have a serious impact on businesses themselves.

Instead of thinking through this one-size lens of 'what happens if we let our employees live anywhere', why don't we think about 'who could our employees be if they can be anywhere'. It's not about putting a new layer on an existing structure. We're talking about genuine, impactful flexibility at the heart of a business that allows for a whole multitude of approaches.

Businesses are damaged by the elitism of a London-centric, white, middle-class demographic. Letting those people work from the green belt isn't going to make a difference to the business. It's not just Covid that's made people think about this, and some businesses have already been making bold steps to diversify. The BBC moved to Salford, and my own publisher, Hachette UK, have announced plans to open offices in cities throughout the UK. This spread throughout the country is going to be one of the most important and impactful ways we're going to change the idea of work. But at the most basic level, taking away how it will change infrastructure, lives and politics, that idea of decentralised business is going to transform the output of the business itself.

Alex Mahon, CEO of Channel 4, made one of the biggest shifts at Channel 4 by opening an office in Leeds. This is one of the most important media companies in the UK, and not so long ago it was based in its entirety in London, which meant all of its employees lived in London, and so needed to be able to afford to live in London. That means a pretty narrow pool of potential employees to create content for the whole country. That's certainly what Alex realised.

'Can you really represent the UK? Can you really represent all the opinions, all the points of view, the perspectives, who people are, what their views are, where they come from, if you make all those decisions from London? The people you've got in London all have similar sensibilities because that's where they live day to day. If you want to represent what the UK is, you have to think about people both coming from and being based in different places because points of view in the UK are pretty widespread now. And the biggest thing that the Brexit referendum has taught us is that there is a very wide range of opinions and we thought really there's demand for people to be represented.'

I'm sorry to put Brexit in this book. But it matters. We all know the mainstream media completely missed the fact that outside of London people just weren't happy and wanted something different. Whatever the right thing is, it's a huge problem that the media didn't pick up on that. Our viewpoint was so narrowly focused on London, and that's because so many of our businesses, where the money is, are based in London. People didn't feel represented, because they weren't being adequately represented. The Brexit vote took place in June 2016, and Alex started at Channel 4 in October 2017: her first priority was representation.

'Whether you see that in terms of political opinion or ethnicity or gender or class or wealth, or where you come from originally, there is a demand from audiences to see authenticity represented with equitable power on screen . . . our thinking was how do we represent the country better? Because we are meant to represent Britain, but it was what we do on screen. So the biggest thing is 50% of our money is going to be spent out of London. But to do that, we wanted a set of people who lived in different places and came from different places. So opening offices in Bristol and Glasgow and Leeds was a way to represent that. And the way we went about finding those places was to let all cities pitch openly so that we wouldn't make the decision based on our own preconception of what other places might be.'

It is a major, substantial business decision to be adaptable and flexible. Outside of the new HQ in Leeds, there was a banner billboard that read: 'Didn't think Channel 4 knew there was life outside the M25'. I couldn't love that more. It's an acknowledgement of where we've been going wrong, and a clear statement of intent. Let's not just get out of the bubble, let's get rid of the bubble.

That bubble damages communities, but it also damages culture. Our most exciting culture doesn't come out of bland corporate spaces, it comes out of interaction, community and the messiness of life. One thing that came across so clearly in my conversation with MP Nadia Whittome is how much she really loves Nottingham and how proud she is of its culture: 'We've got the Television Workshop; Shane Meadows who directed *This Is England* is still based in Nottingham. We've got amazing emerging talent, like, well, Young T & Bugsey aren't just emerging talent anymore, they're massive, but they're from Nottingham. And you know, we've got a great art scene as well. We've got the community recording studios in my constituency where a lot of artists start out. These things have grown organically, from an area that is really connected. Nothing really goes on inside [London's] Zone 1, where there are lots of Starbucks and Pizza Expresses.' But where Nadia lives Nottingham's 'got just the most buzzing, vibrant cultural scene'.

This is at the heart of how a business needs to fundamentally reset. It's about being flexible, yes, but making sure that flexibility is there for everyone, and that it allows the business to help everyone, and in turn be shaped by places. Nadia said that when big businesses move to cities or towns 'that doesn't necessarily mean that workers are going to benefit or that the local area is going to benefit. So I think they also need to seriously reassess their structures. I mean things like paying all workers the real living wage, so that the jobs that are created as a result of that are good jobs'. Because if a business really puts time and care into the places they are investing in, they can really change that community and get the best from it.

Alex Mahon of Channel 4 gave me a list of the things she thought about for a new HQ, and it reads like a manifesto for a new type of business.

'How the place could change us and what impact we could make on the place. We thought about that alongside the normal measures like, what was the availability of staff? What was the demographic mix? What people in digital were there in the cities, but it was also about what's that partner-ship, and did we feel we could embed fast, and did we feel that we would also help make the right kind of changes in the city? So it was that kind of combination of things. So some places we thought, we'll make no difference here what-soever. You know, we're too small. But some places we thought, well, if we worked with the city, actually they're going to help us hugely, but maybe we can make a little bit of a difference *too. And it was that combination that helped us think about things as well. And we didn't make all the obvious choices, right?'*

It's bold and innovative and you know what, it's going to be good for the business. It's going to mean the culture Channel 4 puts out is more reflective of the people watching it, and it's built on a wider range of opinions and ideas. And by bringing business to a new location, it's helping the people who live there already massively. That's a positive value.

Anna Whitehouse speaks passionately about this and I couldn't agree more:

'The irony is the companies that were saying no to perhaps mothers, women, people living with disabilities, humans, for business reasons – flexible working requests were rejected daily for business reasons – suddenly had to implement some form of flexibility for business reasons within 24 hours when Coronavirus hit. And I think that is . . . the really frustrating thing is companies had to Zoom in, they had to log on, otherwise they would have had to shut down. When cold, hard cash is on the table and is at risk of being taken off the table, it is very funny to see – it's not even funny, it's frustrating to see – how quickly companies can adapt. And I think, you were talking earlier about those living with disabilities, I think that – moving this away from women, away from mothers

– those living with disability, seeing companies open their doors to working from home within a 24 hour period. How galling is that? You know, how frustrating and painful is it to see companies making it possible when they said it was always impossible? Because ultimately what it says is they didn't want those individuals working for them, and that is painful discrimination. And I think I cannot hear from another inclusivity and diversity officer wanting me to talk on another panel. I like to just employ people and allow them to work in a way that works for them. You know, this is about every-body. It's about men committing suicide on construction sites, it's about a woman in a wheelchair who can't get on the tube, it is about a mother, it is about people. And I think people are talking about being family-first, people-centred: stop talking, start doing.'

Talking to Anna made me think of the way Cassandra Stavrou described the intentions of Proper, that people, community and world make up the three pillars by which they divide up their business. She said, 'The way that we divide the business is under three pillars. So [number one is] people, how we treat our team. Number two is commu-nity. So how do we support the wider community and use our platform to have a positive impact? And the third is world. Ensuring that we've got the lightest footprint possible. And under each pillar, there is a really comprehensive plan, action-based targets, accountability across the team for all of those targets. It's only when you get to that level that it starts to really happen and make a difference.'

It's not as simple as letting people work from home, talking about your 'don't be evil' brand. It's about putting those things at the heart of what you're doing. It's ensuring that everyone in the team is a shareholder, invested in and empowered by the business. It's ensuring that the business is doing something beyond making money, it's bringing value to the staff, the consumer and ideally the world. It's ensuring that you are attracting the talent that are achieving those aims, whoever they are and wherever they live.

The best way to figure out whether the companies you work for – or are spending money at – are the right ones is to do your research. Figure out what your moral code is around money. If you want to support ethnic minorities or local community brands keep an eye out for Black Pound retailers and Buy Local schemes. Understand the changes you want to see in the world and use your purchasing power to move them forward.

Chapter Four

COMMUNITY

———

COMMUNITY

'I long, as does every human being, to be at home wherever
I find myself'

— Maya Angelou

WE'RE LIVING THROUGH a loneliness epidemic. I know
that's a very dramatic start to this chapter but it's the ines-
capable reality. Hear me out: you may not see it but you've
felt it. When social commentators look back at this time,
what will they see? The busy, connected flow of modern
societies? Or a cloud of loneliness that hangs over us like
the fractured memory of a nightmare you just can't shake
off? This will come as no surprise to anyone swiping right
for the umpteenth time or finding themselves alone on a
weekend with the days spooling out in empty hours.

Loneliness by definition is a solitary pursuit, hidden from

a wider view. But a 2018 survey from the *Economist* and the Kaiser Family Foundation showed that more than two in ten adults in the United Kingdom (23%) say they always or often feel lonely, lack companionship or feel left out or isolated.[1] And more worryingly, if you look carefully, you can see the shadows of it in statistics of poor health, depression, financial inequalities and even suicide rates.[2] This is the hidden cost of a world too busy to be a society. It's safe to say that loneliness is bad for our health.

We haven't always been conscious of this deep societal loneliness, so what went wrong? Why now? First, the way we live has changed dramatically. As the late twentieth century rolled around and our networks expanded, we became truly globalised. Family members were settling further afield from each other, sometimes even in other countries, and ambitious young people were going where jobs and opportunities took them, pulling up any fledgling roots as they went. By the twenty-first century, to live near your family, or to stay in one place for an extended period of time, seemed a bit defeatist to many young people. After all, where's your ambition? The world is your oyster, right?

And it wasn't just a physical phenomenon. Once upon a pre-internet time, society – perhaps even 'reality' itself – was a solid ground and a shared experience. Now it's a hall of mirrors thanks to social media and online forums, and we find ourselves lost and gazing at others, untethered by the bindings of true connection. Longevity, blood, everyday interaction, conviviality, help: words of a physical universe that we barely inhabit these days.

Now let's add the generational differences. Studies have called Millennials the loneliest generation, which is kind of ironic seeing as we became the most connected generation because of technology. We see the world without borders, we logged in one day and have never needed to log out. Alarmingly, 42% of Millennial women are more afraid of loneliness than a cancer diagnosis, by far the highest share of any generation.[3] One YouGov Poll found that nearly a quarter of all Millennials could not name a single friend.[4] And each generation gets lonelier, a 2018 Cigna Health study found Gen Z reports the highest levels of loneliness of any age group.[5] And none of this data even reflects the impact of lockdown on mental health.

We're the generation that only knew the curated feed, curated people and curated life, which often makes it difficult to create real meaningful connections with others. We've swapped conversations for likes and building relationships for shrewd networking. Forced to adapt and hustle wherever we found ourselves – home, work, satellite experiences – the idea of community slipped off our to-do list. Almost old-fashioned in its requirements of contribution, continuity and responsibility, it appealed less and less, while the empty space around the individual grew. It's too easy these days to fool ourselves that connection through a screen can bridge the gap between the individual and something bigger than ourselves. Or that work hours and structures can fill the emotional needs of a life that ultimately demands more than the ego to function. With a culture so focused on the hustle and performative workaholism, how does one spend time making and maintaining meaningful friendship. This requires time and if, as a generation, we feel like every waking moment must be filled, that can be a challenge.

Although the connection between loneliness and social media is well established,[6] it can't solely be blamed for our increased sense of isolation. A study by social psychologist Daniel Perlman in 1990 found that before the existence of smartphones, social media, and even before internet use was widespread, young adults were the most likely to be lonely. This decreased throughout people's lives until they reached old age, when it began to increase again moderately.[7]

I'm of the school of thought that community is in our nature and at heart, we are collaborative and social beings. We are naturally inclined to cooperate in order to not only survive, but thrive. This is something I connected on with Indy Johar, who suggested our inclination to collaborate has sustained us as a species.

'What's interesting about humans is that they are one of the most collaborative, complex, rich civilisation species and their capability has come entirely through their collaborative capability. And we are able to create instruments and mechanisms to advance our collaboration, and to go

from what would be a threat of war to a thesis of collaboration has been a choice. We've been able to transcend our thesis of competition and to create frameworks of more and more radical collaboration in order to actually be able to be the civilisation that we've been able to be.'

The idea that humanity is community and that the best things we have ever done come from collaboration doesn't feel revolutionary. And yet for some reason we aren't investing in communities like we so clearly should. Connection has been replaced by independence, and we're constantly being told to focus on the 'self' and look inwards – 'you do you'. This idea implies that looking outside ourselves is somehow selling ourselves short.

Is 'living your best life' at all costs making you happy? Or is it that the more time you spend pounding the treadmill, reading self-help manuals and comparing what you have to what other people have, the more time you spend feeling alone.

We've never been so alone together. And if loneliness is the enemy, then it is a stealthy one with no one cause and no clear answers in the current model of 'modern life'. Living close to people is no guarantee of connection with them, natural meeting points – from churches to community centres – are under threat, in decline or increasingly commercialised, and it takes many hellos and small conversations to create the net of everyday community.

What's clear is that we need to unlearn some habits, starting with the assumption that we are all individual islands and therefore function in a vacuum and in isolation – and then to rediscover that connection largely comes from contribution, not consumption.

Grow your local community

look around you, invest time and energy in the people you live among

I often wonder what 'community' actually means today and the role it plays in our daily lives. Is it a group of people with the same interests, or the same purpose or the same identity? Is it an easy term for a collection of people in a shared space? Or is it a demand for unity and investment in other people's lives? Is it simply the idea that we are not alone?

When I used to live and work in Canary Wharf, in east London, I struggled with the fact I couldn't feel settled, but looking back it's not surprising. Canary Wharf becomes a ghost town on the weekends, the fancy stores and restaurants hold shape, but the people disperse. It's all glass walls and empty places. And most importantly, there was no real sense of community. Perhaps that's partly because I didn't have the time to invest in new relationships; I lacked incentive or simply – didn't want to. But if that was true of me, then it was definitely true of everyone else who lived around me. We might nod in a corridor or when we passed on the pavement, but I don't think I knew a single person's name. But hey, I told myself, that's London for you. I realised I never felt settled because deep down I craved a sense of community, that feeling was something I missed deeply. A strange loneliness niggled at me in the quieter moments, so I moved back south of the river and I now live in Croydon. Depending on who you ask, that's either London or not. If you're asking me, and despite the CR0 postcode, I'd say look at a map and tell me if it's inside the M25. So it's London and that's settled!

I was surrounded by people I knew in a place that I loved, but somehow the community I sought didn't really materialise because I still spent the majority of time commuting into Canary Wharf every day. I was forever running for a train to make an 8.30 a.m. start, running for the last train home post-'after work drinks'. So I only really saw the community I lived in while I was rushing past, throwing a wave over my shoulder as I headed into the station. Exhausted by a week of work, I'd perhaps get more of a sense of place on a late Saturday morning, but not much. I only got a snippet of what my local area had to offer and the relationships I developed were fleeting and restricted.

When my job became flexible and I didn't spend swathes of time in the city it opened up a new lens through which

I saw my community. I was having lunch in the local restaurant instead of Pret a Manger, going to the nearby community meetings and I was more invested in what was happening around me. I wanted to understand the people I lived around and to have a voice in the community we were a part of. I developed relationships that started with pleasantries and grew into something more meaningful. We even started a WhatsApp group.

If I'm painting some idealised vision then let me be real: I still took lots of things for granted, spent more time online than outside. But just these glimpses of my local environment got me thinking about how different our communities would look if everyone could work more fluidly on a permanent basis. What would we spend more time doing, and more importantly, who would we be spending more time with? As we swap time commuting with time in our community, could we invest more in local relationships?

One thing strikes me as clear, investing energy in community is the most important way we can have an impact beyond ourselves. We just have to start by paying attention to what is around us.

The pandemic changed the world. What happened in 2020 was a catalyst for testing our networks and our relationships. Everyone faced the same situation – albeit at different levels – and this enabled us to form and strengthen our relationships to support each other. The relationships either sank or swam. On one level our physical world felt smaller but we felt more connected on both a global and a hyperlocal level. Stuck inside during the lockdowns or restricted by the tiers we were allocated, the opportunities for real-life conversations diminished and we moved to online communication as the primary form. Some of our networks expanded, and people were looking to engage in them more thoughtfully. And then as we left our warm houses on a Thursday evening to clap for the NHS and our carers, we'd check in with neighbours and throw a wave to residents further up the street. None of these relationships were ones which many of us valued and invested in before the pandemic, but they were the ones we have grown to rely on.

In times of hardship, uncertainty and fear, community is more important than ever. We rely on those around us for solidarity, support, guidance, information and empathy. Covid paradoxically reduced the radius of our lives and expanded the circles we were interacting with. What makes the lockdown periods so interesting is that despite being isolated, our communities have been determined to pull together.

As different demographics faced different challenges, what we sought out of our communities was changing. Strangers offered extra toilet roll to their neighbours on Facebook groups, Londoners walked the dogs of people they'd never even met. Communities filled the gaps left by limited state support. By week three of the first lockdown, individuals reported feeling that the community had 'come together'.[8] When we consider the number of grassroots groups that sprung up to deliver care packages to the vulnerable, and online residents' groups who offered necessities for those unable to purchase them during the panic-buying stint, our new hyperlocal version of community pulled together at an impressive pace.

This desire to support people around us and connect on a hyperlocal level didn't go unnoticed. I spoke to London Mayor Sadiq Khan about the wave of community care that came out of lockdown, focusing on faith communities. He said:

'One of the things we saw during the pandemic was remarkable, remarkable examples of people demonstrating civic duty. And by that, the faith communities in particular making sure people have food, making sure people were being looked after, speaking to your neighbour, you know, heaven forbid in London, getting to know your neighbours, getting to know people on your street, the Thursday evening clap for carers. That shows there is an appetite, a hunger for social bridges across communities and neighbour to neighbour, community to community. And we want to take advantage of that going forward. And actually, yeah, technology is great, but you can't beat human contact, human interaction.'

You can't beat human contact.

We learned a lot of things in 2020 but valuing our local community has got to be the most important. How do we try to keep the sense of comradery we gained? Can we reset our relationship with the community so we're putting it first? How can we foster community? A community is an evolving and adapting thing. It requires input on so many fronts. In some cases that means the extraordinary demonstrations of care we saw during the lockdowns. In others it just means spending time. And, crucially, spending money.

When I spoke with Ete Davies about a more flexible approach to work, he identified the positive impact a shift to localism could have on neighbourhood small businesses. He talked about the inherent value of spending time – and money – in our communities, 'when people are more rooted in their local community, they're redistributing focus and in a lot of cases, wealth back into their local community.' He gave the example of buying a coffee and that if you're staying local and buying it from your neighbourhood café, that money is staying in the local community rather than going to a chain in central London. He said that 'can only really be a good thing for the redistribution of wealth, around the country'.

Community feels like something that can be intangible, but it sits at the meeting point of economics and society. It's where people can support each other and grow together. And investing in that growth is your choice. Walk past Starbucks, go to your local café; when you hear about a restaurant opening nearby, go to it. See a sign for a small yoga studio, give it a go.

We don't need to start big to create a sense of community. We can take steps to bring our money to our local places of business. We can strike up a conversation or invite our neighbours for a drink, or we can, if we want, participate in what's going on in our neighbourhood.

Civic duty covers so many things. If we spend more time in our local communities, we care more about it – that means taking an interest in local politics, signing petitions, showing up to protests or demonstrations. What happens in our communities becomes more interesting and affects us more personally when we're spending most of our time there.

This can be anything from tending to a community garden or protesting with a local activist group. There are amazing groups that use community projects to battle loneliness, and they're often targeted at older people. Groups like Garden Buddies invite elderly people to get together to tend a shared garden and also May Project Garden is a good example of grassroots community.

MP Nadia Whittome was involved in Story Parks, involving putting books in parks so children could pick them up and read them. She said, 'When that was first piloted, people said that that would never work, that in Nottingham people would nick the books; that hasn't happened. And that's no surprise to me.'

Trend forecaster Karen Rosenkranz told me about a group

of birdwatchers in London called Flock Together, started by two black men. 'So it's also about bringing people of colour together and feeling that [they] have a space in nature, as a group who's often under-represented in that space . . . they meet every two weeks and go bird watching.' She said, 'I think that's so amazing to see these initiatives where people, really young people go, "Oh look, there's all these things at our doorstep." It's not like you need to travel.' She mentioned Hackney Marshes, in east London, and the various woods around south London, vast open spaces within a city, right on our doorsteps. Karen is dreaming of a 'shift in society, away from the urban', commenting that we've been 'city-centric for the past two centuries, now it's good to shift the perspective a bit'. It's as simple as looking around and seeing what's out there. Going for a walk, taking in nature, looking beyond the concrete jungle.

The more time we spend in our communities, the better we understand the people around us. When you volunteer at a soup kitchen, or attend your council meeting, you can see the direct impact of your contribution. Nadia believes in giving power back to communities:

'So we don't need top-down decision-making. We should be using this as an opportunity to decentralise power, to give people power in our communities. I think one of the things that we spoke about in another one of our conversations was about powerlessness. How for years,

decades, even, forever really, working-class people and
minoritised, marginalised people have felt and have been
disempowered.'

Your participation makes a difference for the people nearest to you. When local councils make unjust decisions, residents can exercise this civic duty by coming together and standing by one another.

These small acts – building well-being and strengthening social ties within the community, which in turn encourages more participation[9] – add up and make an impact. Studies have shown that volunteering has a clear and beneficial impact on low self-esteem. Giving back is good for our psychological well-being and life satisfaction. It's win–win.

Start with looking around you, foster relationships and put your own energy and time in. You don't know what you might get out of it, but you don't know how it might shape who you are, and through that, how you work.

Grow your work community

understand the people you work with, in and out of the
office, help them, get to know them

So much of the conversation around flexible working centres on technology, when successful flexible working should also be judged by our attitudes to community. While empathy can't quite be automated yet, our ability to connect and collaborate with others is vital to the business ecosystem.[10]

I've spoken about changing culture and rethinking the structure of our businesses so we have more autonomy and are doing something more worthwhile. The missing piece? Making sure we're coming together meaningfully and still feel part of a bigger mission.

When I first became freelance, I gained more freedom in how I worked, but I also lost a central hub of the office network and colleagues. Bursts of inspiration are so often sparked by the people around us, and I missed that. I also lost that sense of shared purpose which can be a motivator, that feeling of being part of something far bigger than ourselves. While it's possible to get used to the solitude after a while, and it can actually be conducive to more focused work, I still found myself looking for a sense of community. I became more interested in workspaces and communities that were cultivated for women with similar job experiences to mine. It's probably one of the most consistent pieces of advice I give people going freelance or looking to change their approach to work: find your tribe, find your vibe.

Meeting new people is how we discover opportunities, both professionally and personally. This is the power of 'weak ties' or casual acquaintances. Close family and friends tend to circulate in the same social pools as we do. It's much harder to gain new perspectives or fresh ideas from people we are already very close to. Our casual acquaintances have a level of distance from our own lives that can be beneficial in introducing us to new opportunities. Research has also shown that building new networks can boost happiness, knowledge and a sense of belonging.[11]

The world is a crowded place; as businesses grow, what begins as a community of 10 employees may become a legion of 200 or 20,000. The building I was working in had around 20,000 people coming in and out every day. That's thousands of employees, many of whom will never even meet each other. How can we maintain a sense of community in a workforce that multiplies exponentially? How can we carry this through to a flexible working model?

This is a consistent challenge that many business leaders face as we shift to greater flexible working. And no wonder – being part of a strong community makes us happier and keeps us healthy, both physically and mentally. According to the Fair Society, Healthy Lives review, a landmark study looking into the health inequalities in England, individuals who participate in their communities feel like they have more control over their lives, and tend to benefit from this psychologically.[12] Happy and healthy employees are more productive, more emotionally fulfilled and less likely to leave a company.

So how do we ensure we're connected with our colleagues and feel part of a strong work community? Well, one idea is to make it someone's job – there have been calls for companies to start hiring community managers, and some are listening. To think, we appoint a head of product, finance and marketing quite freely, but don't extend that same effort to a role which cares for the people doing those jobs. It seems archaic. The Mom Project, a platform which links mothers looking to get back into work with job opportunities, hired a community manager responsible for growing the talent pool and boosting engagement. So far, it looks like it's been beneficial to the business and employee well-being. Similarly, in an effort to create spaces that support people while breaking down barriers and humanising work, Fidelity has also invested in creating that position – in particular to help organise what it's calling 'work neighbourhoods', to foster connection.

So there are things a business can do to create community, but all good communities are authentic, and often that means starting from the bottom. In Ete Davies' mind it all comes back to the idea of empowerment and autonomy. That builder mentality I spoke about in Chapter 2, Culture. As Ete said, communities in the workplace 'are collections of individuals finding their ways to work together'. He added that when we give more decision-making control, empowerment and freedom to the individual to decide how they engage with an organisation or their local community, then we will see 'human evolution in terms of our working culture and our working practices'.

It's going to be up to us to use that framework to build

strong communities that help us flourish. From my experience the most successful in-work communities have been created by the employees, but crucially supported by the business. Examples are charity committees and learning groups – these are communities created by employees that enrich the company and benefit the individuals who work in it. So, perhaps now is the time to set up a formal group dedicated to shared interests or to discover which skills people in your team want to develop and set up a group for doing so.

And it's not just formal networks and events. Maybe you were chatting with an ensemble of colleagues in the kitchen at your office and spontaneously organised Friday drinks. Or a random conversation with your manager revealed a hidden skill utilised in a new project. Or perhaps you overheard a team member discussing a challenge you've also been facing, so you decide to work on it together. These chance meetings may seem trivial at the time, but they're fundamental to our relationships, and to our careers. In a collaborative world, community is a crucial piece of the puzzle in the future of work. It uncovers hidden talents, empowers colleagues on a shared mission, fosters innovation and makes the general experience of working more enjoyable.

From funded and purposeful office networks, to informal company sports teams, to even more informal social activities, it's the employees who create the tapestry of engagement that is office culture. When we're working flexibly, or remotely, we need to be particularly conscious of keeping those communities together. While many of us flourish at home, others relish the chance to be in the engaged communal space of an office. We can have the best of both worlds, but we need to make sure our communities work for everyone.

Sadiq Khan picked up on this complex environment of mixed desire for in-office working, and illustrated how different demographics needed different things from their working environment, the Millennials, for example, whose bedrooms might also be their offices or who craved social-isation. He was speaking specifically about Covid lockdown, but a lot of the ideas stretch beyond that. He said, 'When it comes to people working from home, actually it's those who are sharing homes – that's the Millennials, if you like, or those with young children – who are really struggling . . . and are desperate to come back to work. We in City Hall, for example, made our office Covid secure, and can bring back about a quarter of our staff and those who are the keenest to come back were the youngest staff.'

Young people are less likely – or able – to have created home environments that suit work, and simultaneously have a desire for socialising that perhaps wanes over time. Older employees are more likely to have comfortable homes, to be further out from the centre and to have families and lives that make socialising less integral to their work lives.

And that's not even taking into account the range of factors that have an impact on how and where we work, from disabilities to finances. When we are creating communities, we need to be thinking about everyone.

This idea of prioritising the community we work with doesn't just have to be about the 50 people, or even the 20,000 people in a company. It's about learning and evolving in our work, and that sort of development can be helped by all sorts of people. For all we know it's our fiercest rival who can best help our development. If we focus less on being so competitive, and start being collaborative, we might create some of our best work. We need to develop communities that are vehicles for the sort of creative thinking we're pursuing as individuals.

I think co-working spaces are a really good example of the difference between productivity and creativity. These have been big news in the last few years, and often not for the right reasons – shady founders, elitist set-ups, meaningless culture. The thing I hear, time and time again, is that for all their talk about free yoga, lectures and coffee shops, most people come in, sit at their desks head down and then get out as soon as they can. But perhaps we can create spaces for work that *are* meaningful – and that's about putting community at their centre.

I wonder if it's also about changing the demographic. Instead of convenient spots for the exact same groups of people who are in a traditional office, albeit ones with the nerve to set up on their own, what about places that integrate with the community and other businesses. Sadiq stressed the fact that he wants 'high streets to be a place for socialization as well.'

If you're working from home, sat at the same desk, could you create a local spot for working that feels part of the community? 'Is it possible to have shared workspaces in high streets? So if you want a break from working in your bedroom or your office, go to that shared workspace on the high street.' And he tied this expressly to wider culture, to socialising outside work. It's not about doing the same work outside our homes, it's about bringing the community into work, so if we're going to a co-working space it's genuinely to be part of that community. Our already struggling high streets have been hit hard by the pandemic[13] but we have a chance to rebuild them with hubs, bespoke office models and casual community spaces that encourage human connection and collaboration, something I'll explore in the next chapter on The City.

If we make community the core of our work and our life, and make a greater effort to participate meaningfully, then we won't miss the connection of the traditional office five days a week, especially if we have multiple, overlapping communities to tap into. Our networks are essential to our success, but they're also vital to our happiness.[14] We need emotional connection to survive as individuals, and thrive as professionals. Once we've discovered the power of genuine connection, can't we bring it back to the digital space that was often making us feel so lonely?

Grow your digital community

look beyond the people right in front of you, make connec-
tions and bring people together

Virtual space counts for something. As I've mentioned earlier, often it counts for something negative – an endless stream of alienating information and images that make us feel like we're not enough. Breaking down our obsession with scrolling through aspirational content is key to feeling connected. But that doesn't mean turning away from social media in its entirety; it means redefining how we use it. Online communities aren't perfect, but they allow us freedom and a space to connect and offer a sense of belonging. Once we have that technological freedom, how can virtual space encourage our growth and sense of community?

This is particularly important when you look at groups who are often ignored by traditional power structures. When we spoke, Anna Whitehouse commented on the value of online communities. Anna became a parent and felt discon-nected – she set up Mother Pukka to connect with others, and through that created a resource for mothers. I was particu-larly fascinated by how she highlighted the importance of the online community for women. She asked who was looking after pandemic patients, when they came out of hospital? 'Women. Who sets up WhatsApp groups within their communities to make sure everybody has everything they need? It's women. Who is taking on the burden of homeschooling and childcare? It's women . . . The playing ground is not level to start with going into this pandemic.'

As flexible working grows, we need to ensure that all groups feel supported. As I mentioned in the introduction, self-employment is at its highest, according to the 2018 ONS report – growing from 12% of the British population in 2001 to 15.1% in 2017.[15] What's particularly interesting is that this is being driven by women. You can chart this increase in the rise of female-only networking groups and business communities, designed to support women moving away from the traditional office-based 9–5. They're an example of how we can form supportive, interesting work communities off the back of greater flexible working. Over the last 10 years, we've seen groups like For Working Ladies, HerHustle network and She Can She Did create communities for female professionals, who haven't been fully supported in the conventional workplace business. This is women collaborating and communicating for clear purpose. It's active growth and engagement.

If you're a creative professional, you've probably already heard of The Dots. Pip Jamieson spotted a niche for a creative professional platform when she was looking to build her network, but LinkedIn felt cold and uninspiring for creatives looking to connect. Pip noticed how white-collar work was becoming more fluid while she was working for MTV. The Dots is an example of a business community that links people in a way that isn't dictated so much by job title, but more by people's preferred work style. Historically, we were born into communities; now we get to pick them.[16] Which means, we also get to find places online and in real life that fully support us, and where we can add value.

Pip explained the genesis for her business to me, and it's a classic story of having a need for oneself and meeting it in a way that works for lots of people. She said, 'I just wanted to build a professional network, which was geared for a modern generation.'

'I was surrounded by friends that were just working in a really different way, people adopting more fluid-based careers . . . We just were working very differently than that "I'm going to spend 10, 15 years of my life in the same corporation" . . . people were just wanting different things from their careers. So they were wanting more flexible work, they were exploring working remotely, all that was opposite to that corporate world. But yeah, I think on a deeper level, the people I was surrounded with – while money is so fundamentally important, we all need it to keep food on the table, so were other things,

like actually valuing the people you work with, actually learning and growing, actually enjoying your job and actually working on things that have purpose and meaning, not just going to work on something that you didn't really care about.'

She encompasses so much of what I've spoken about in this book – that urge to work differently, to work in a way that suits more parts of your life. But she also spotted the need for a tool to support that way of working. That's innovation. What's really brilliant is that from the beginning she was thinking about *everyone.* She explained, 'I'm very dyslexic, for example, and I felt [work] wasn't a space where I could be open about my dyslexia because I'd be judged for it. And the whole reason I started The Dots was to really democratise opportunities and open up those to everyone and celebrate our differences and create a safe, inclusive, network that allowed everyone to be themselves.'

So often social media can feel exclusive – who's in, who's out, who looks the part. Valuable online communities like The Dots put all that aside and focus on space for anyone. We need to build democratic spaces into our online systems. In the same way that the Facebook algorithm is designed to get us addicted and then keep us hooked, or Instagram raises the most aspirational posts to the top, we can, if we choose, build positivity into our technology. That's what makes The Dots so valuable. It's not just a mission statement, it's built into the technology. Pip explained how their algorithm works:

> '. . . *Everything we've tried to build at The Dots is around a positive community. I deeply dislike Twitter, for example, I just find the way it's built just perpetuates negativity and abuse. And for me, community-building is about support and helping each other . . . So everything we've tried to build is around that. So for example, with our algorithm, people actually come higher in a search on The Dots if they are kind and helpful to other people. So if they ask questions on The Dots that other people like, they come higher in search results, and if they answer questions that other people like, they come higher in search results. So we've tried to build a way, which reinforces positivity and kindness.'*

The catalyst for changing our approach to community is recognising that communities are no longer things we're just born into. We now have access to global networks at the swipe of a screen, which means we can join communities and connect with people from *anywhere in the world*. If we put aside all the negatives of screen time and social media – and there are many serious negatives – we can consider the value it holds if we use it in the right way. Because it allows us to break down barriers, and find our tribe. You don't have to be the only woman in an office of men, the only person of colour in a totally white office, the only person with access needs in an office. You can find a community to help you grow, even if the one immediately around you doesn't understand. You can build a community structure that brings value to you, and one where you're adding value too.

And that's a message that stretches beyond work, and is a sign of significant change in how we live. During the lockdowns everyone started sharing posts from Nextdoor, the localised social media platform, to check in with residents and provide a sense of community. And while a community may look different online, its essence is the same. It's about bringing people closer. This is the opposite of most social media, which is just about amplifying yourself. We need digital communities to be about the collective, not the individual. For example; one of the things I enjoyed the most about the first lockdown was an app called Clubhouse. It allows users to connect and talk to anybody around the world and operates via rooms: each one has a set topic attached to it and is moderated. What I found so interesting about the app in the early days was people's desire to connect to other people via just voice and exchanging ideas and opinions. The immediacy in which the app grew among people really spoke to what I feel was a longing for connection.

I was listening to a podcast by author Bruce Daisly called Eat Sleep Work Repeat. He was interviewing Jillian

Richardson, who wrote *Unlonely Planet,* and she spoke about the loneliness of when she moved to New York for the first time. The paradox of big cities is that we can be alone while still being surrounded by others, something Covid has brought sharply into focus. She told Bruce, 'I had no consistent community – people who would wonder where I was if I didn't show up. I was disconnected. At the time, I thought that I was the only one who felt this way . . . but I was VERY wrong.'

Bruce observed: 'Jillian found that one of the most relatable things that any of us can do is confess to others that we're lonely as she realised most people were not satisfied with their friendships.' [17] Her response was to create the Joy List – a list that originally was made to connect people across New York with other like-minded individuals and now sets about connecting anyone virtually.

Interestingly, a 2020 study by the Global Web Index, has shown that what we share online, and why we share it is changing.[18] We're moving away from social media as a method of broadcasting ourselves, and instead using it as a tool for interaction with community at its heart. So as well as changing how and what we're sharing, more of us are sharing with our online communities than ever before.

We need to reset how we think about 'community', so it's not just a word for the people you happen to live or work with and instead is a way to describe connection. Covid opened us up to the idea of community in a new way, and it's up to us to carry that on. If we can do that, we might just help people feel a little less lonely.

I want to leave this chapter on something Sereena Abbassi said to me about culture. It's not really about work and resetting society, it's about the very meaning of connection:

'Me and my brother formed a relationship with our Iranian family in Iran. Most of my mum's family are in London . . . You can forge really strong, powerful connections with people and not be in the same physical space because actually physical distance doesn't mean that there can't be emotional closeness. And, for me, culture really is just about values. It's not culture that binds us really it's values that binds us. Because if you think about the UK, the UK is made up of lots of different cultures. So if it's not culture, it's values. And I think those values, they're not bound by place, they're not bound by time. It's about what you're wanting to work towards. It's who you want be in this present moment and how you want to be moving forward. What sort of world do you want to create? What sort of business do you want to create? What kind of business do you want to be in the world? And I don't think you need to be in a physical space in order to have that, to do that.'

If we reset our idea of community, we transform what our professional networks look like but also what our social ones are, too. Communities will continue to be built around choice and shared interests, as opposed to just lineage and proximity. People can choose their tribe. And it doesn't have to be just one. It's giving us the power to connect with the people we want – online or next door. It's about resetting our idea of people, because anything is possible when a community comes together, and that starts with feeling less alone.

Chapter Five

CITY

———

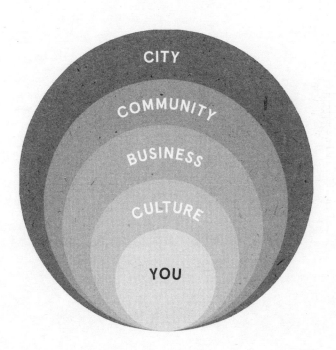

CITY

———

'Cities are places of opportunity, and their success is the result of centuries of re-use and re-appropriation. Change is the one constant in cites, change is exciting and change is the engine of progress.'

— Amanda Levete[1]

CITIES ARE BUZZING, energetic and noisy and when we're young we are meant to be 'plugged in' to where the action is, right? Cities have always been a rite of passage for the hungry and aspirational. They're fun, exciting and youthful – who didn't want a job in the city when they were 21? My friends and I all did. It was the top of our to-do list as the clocks started ticking and our time at university came to a close. For us, it was all about stress-testing how ambitious we truly were. If we couldn't make it in a big city, like London, we couldn't make it anywhere else, right?

Similarly, cities have also always been about money and creating economies of scale. But archaeological excavations also show that early cities were variously religious hubs, political bases and cultural centres. How the civic space was used reflected the social body, in all its complexity. Cities are still all those things, but they've also grown and expanded with civilisation. So, what will archaeologists discover when they dig up our post-industrialist cities? In centuries to come how will our obsession with money leave its mark? And how closely entwined are our relationships with money and the city anyway?

Let's go back to the real boom of the relationship between the metropolis and the economy. The idea of the city as primarily a centre of commerce was set in the seeds of modern industrialisation and dense urbanisation around key ports, railways and highway hubs in the 19th century. London quickly grew to become the global financial and trade centre, with the world's largest port fueling this growth. It's no wonder the population expanded from around one million at the start of the century, to six million by the end. It was a bustling, purposeful industry and goods flowed in and out.

After World War Two however, manufacturing contracted significantly. As workers traded the factory floor for the cubicle office, between 1960 and 2015, manufacturing in the UK faced the biggest decline in Europe. As this rush of import and export moved out from urban centres, it was white collar work and head offices that became the central preoccupation of city dwellers. This was a trend that accelerated in the 1980s when property and financial booms meant the city came to embody prosperity, excitement and opportunity.

Prime Minister at the time, Margaret Thatcher, deregulated financial services and made enormous investments in the London docklands, places like Canary Wharf as new business hubs, fueling growth in service-based industries, and in doing so, hammered one more nail in the manufacturing coffin. These policies came with a cost of greater unemployment and inequality as many northern cities saw a big drop in their employment rates.

However, life for some was spontaneous and glamorous and the highs outweighed the lows or pushed them to one side anyway. And that's how it remained. Until now.

In reality, as the years rolled on, those famous London streets paved with gold became increasingly tarnished. These days, money tends to be the deciding factor in whether we're having a great time or hanging on by our fingertips, particularly in the capital. And even if we happen to be somewhere in the middle, it's just a grind. Trying to buy property at a hugely inflated price or paying rent increasingly out of line with wages, winding through packed or gridlocked commutes, paying through the nose for meals and drinks out 'in town' just to make the city visibly, viscerally 'worth it'. Look at what's on our doorstep, we said, waving our hands toward a centre of theatre, museums, dining and shopping from the window of an isolated shoebox in Zone 3 – and yes, it was a bounty within a 40-minute tube ride.

A 'man who is tired of London is tired of life', so the saying goes, but most of us are just plain tired of trying to survive the concrete jungle. While other cities in the UK are marginally less expensive and challenging to live in, the fact remains that all large post-industrial cities represent a way of living and working that's far removed from the ideal. They're still a tractor beam for the young and people seeking their fortunes. Come to us they beckoned as businesses threw up gleaming HQs, seducing the young and starry eyed and taking advantage of the workforce concentration. But they've lost their shine.

Then came the huge dystopian experiment in home working for white-collar workers. In the UK the proportion of those working from home rose to half in April 2020, from a previously paltry 5%, and, according to a report by Cardiff and Southampton universities, some 90% of workers *do not want* to return to full-time commuting to and working in an office.[2] With a tantalising vision of a more equitable future, who can blame them? In life sometimes we have to be pushed or we'll never be ready.

From remote working to de-densification (the process of making an area less populous), increased surveillance and community activism, Covid-19 chipped away at the marble of urban life like a craftsman determined to reveal a new shape of things. At some point though, and more likely sooner than not, the chisel may finally slip . . . and when that happens, what elements of city life will be splintered from the monoliths we have been so used to? Time will tell.

One prediction is that there'll be a mass exodus. We'll all pack up and move to the country for the rural dream, or just to smaller cities and towns. It's an option, and one I'll discuss in other chapters, but is the answer to just leave cities? Occasionally the thought of leaving the city has crossed my mind. Cheaper houses, cleaner air, more work-life balance. But then . . . but then . . . the career ladder and dreaded FOMO meant I was unwilling to relinquish my place. For the truth is that for all our longing for balance, the off-kilter, dirty, sexy city, with its concentration of businesses, opportunities, transient people and networking, is presented as the only real choice for the ambitious. However tired we are, it's seen as the only option for those with a lust for life.

And more importantly than what a city offers is the fact that leaving just isn't an option for many. There are those who can never imagine living elsewhere, and there are those who don't have the option to imagine living elsewhere. Instead of, 'Are we going to abandon cities?' I find myself asking, 'Who is this city for in the first place?' Is it only for the uber-rich and big business? Or is it for everyone who lives in it? In fact, I am not an advocate for an abandonment of big cities: I want there to be a shift in priorities.

Instead of heeding the cries of the middle classes and moving to the countryside, we should focus on making our cities work for everyone and not just the privileged few. Every time we switch on the radio, someone seems to be calling for a mass migration from the centres to the outskirts, but unless you have a flexible job and the capital to do so, this so-called solution is impossible for most people. And this just moves the problems of the cities to the countryside, without resolving the core issues of equality and opportunity.

For me, the opportunity to reset how we inhabit cities is one of the most exciting elements of this book. Did I think I'd be talking about cities when I started having conversations about our relationship to work? No. But it makes sense. Because cities are a vehicle for our ambition, a representation of the things we value most. And if we are resetting our own desires around work, how our businesses provide the things we really need and what communities are worth investing in and cherishing, well inevitably we're going to have to reset the places where we do all those things. Cities reflect us, they provide a mirror to our lives and the things we say are important. If we're re-thinking what's important, the city is going to change whether we want it to or not.

So how will the places we live in change if homeworking becomes more of the norm? What new communities will grow in lieu of centralised commercial centres? And what will be the principles at their core? I've taken a few journeys into central London as I write this book and I've been thinking about the relationship between space, community and value. How do we inhabit space in a way that's intuitive? How can we shape a city for the community? How do we create value for all in a place where we've always sought to create wealth? Ultimately, how do we reset our relationship with cities to make space for everyone?

Live locally

'Build back better' and 'the new normal' are two phrases that worked hard for their money when the pandemic hit. But what exactly does that mean for the social and physical fabric of our cities? Changing the flow of movement through urban spaces has had a profound impact on everything from public transport, air quality and housing to retail and roads. When the dust settles – and it's going to be a long time before we see the true impact of the pandemic on our cities – we might just see a substantial change in the very bones of our big cities. And that doesn't just mean the infrastructure at the centre, it means those things right outside our front doors. One of the most vital considerations in any city is how we're using the space around us, the very buildings, parks and roads that make up our local areas.

If we bring greater flexibility into our lives, and people are not travelling into metropolitan hubs for work every day, demand changes and with that so does the planning developments and business practice. For many, the expectation of a permanent move to working from home more often is already affecting their decision-making. In the UK, the price of one-bedroom flats fell in August 2020 and prices for larger flats and houses rose, while research by the Nationwide bank found that over 40% of Londoners are moving out of the city, or have considered doing so, as a result of the pandemic, predominantly for quality of life reasons, if they can afford it.

People are starting to realise that if they can work more flexibly, it's going to be more important where and how they live. Our homes aren't somewhere to commute from, they are somewhere to live. With the transition to remote working, they've become the places in which we spend much more of our time. Living in a studio flat didn't feel like such a big deal when all we did was sleep there. The combination of workplace and living space naturally requires more room for us to be able to switch off from the day job. With this in mind, it's no surprise that commuter towns saw an increasing amount of interest from city dwellers. The town of Chessington, for example, which lies 16 miles south-west of London, saw lettings searches increase by 99% during the summer of 2020. Without the cosy comforts of the office, or the worry about a lengthy daily commute, workers are prioritising spacious homes over 'prime location'. And if they can afford it, they are seeking both.

When we're making big decisions about where and how

to live, what do we look for? Schools are a big factor, as is green space, and what about proximity to family and friends? All these things are about community, but if we're constantly travelling into the city for work and culture, how much are we really getting out of that community space? I've talked about community already in Chapter 4, but it's with greater flexibility and engagement with our cities that we could really embrace what that idea of a local community means.

One way to broaden this new sense of flexibility and to effectively change the way we live is through the concept of the '15-minute city'. It's an idea developed by Sorbonne professor Carlos Moreno, advocating for localisation as an answer to the environmental damage of cities. Essentially, these cities are built in such a way that residents are able to meet most of their needs within a 15-minute journey by foot, bike or public transport which increases the quality of life of the residents and is beneficial to the environment.

Traditionally, cities were designed so that residential areas were separated from business districts. This makes sense, when one considers the pollution and disruption caused by factory work. No one wants smoking chimneys or delivery trucks passing in and out of their road. The problem is, these outdated city structures mean we often have long commutes to work, travel across cities to meet our friends and the nearest restaurant is two separate tube lines away.

These days, our move to a more service-based economy means work and residential spaces can integrate quite neatly.

The 15-minute city is guided by four key principles:

- every neighbourhood should have access to services, particularly food and healthcare
- housing options are diverse to cater for a variety of needs
- the air is unpolluted and there are plenty of green spaces nearby
- more people can work closer to home or remotely

With a 15-minute city, the hour-long commute is a thing of the past; local office blocks in every neighbourhood would enable employees to work closer to home. Meeting friends for dinner wouldn't necessitate a city-center venue, localities would have leisure and hospitality options much closer to home. Without frequent unnecessary journeys, air pollution would decrease too. In Professor Moreno's model, employees would work and socialise close to their homes, with a 'village' feel to each area that is a result of the redistribution of infrastructure usually concentrated in a city centre. From a business perspective this might mean headquarters redistributed to nodes throughout a city or geographic region, or co-working hubs to allow others to collaborate close to home. It might include cultural, educational and social resources all on your doorstep. It could be parks, gardens and galleries. It's the idea that everything you need to live is only 15 minutes' walk away.

For London Mayor Sadiq Khan, the seeds of this are

already in place. His take on the 15-minute city is focused on the idea of healthy high streets – beleaguered in an age of online shopping. We spoke about it in the midst of the pandemic, when social distancing had also reduced footfall. Under his vision, this traditional spine of local infrastructure gets a fresh new investment and becomes home to a wealth of options for the local community:

'More than 99% of businesses in London are small or medium-sized,' he explains. 'We're working with them as well as the leisure sector, entertainment and councils around ways that we can improve high streets. We've got to think about the diversity of our high street.

'What is entertainment? What is the culture there? How can we improve the experience? The "new normal" will have to involve improving our high streets. Some cities use the phrase "a 15-minute city", where everything you need is within 15 minutes. We're doing the same thing but calling it "high streets for all", and the idea is what's on your doorstep will be the thing that you need.'

Look out of your window. Imagine a street that has working hubs, community gardens, art and learning centres, cafés and communal open-air spaces. Imagine if that road, congested with traffic heading into the centre, was reduced in size and replaced with benches and squares for human interaction. In essence, the new communities could, to use a popular business phrase, be more about bringing your 'whole self'.

And it's already happening. In Germany, the community of downtown Hamburg is networked together by pedestrian paths, bike lanes and public transport.[3] In Barcelona, Spain, Mayor Ada Colau created 'superblocks' to direct traffic to the perimeter of blocks focused on pedestrians and public spaces. London is making these steps too, with Low Traffic Neighbourhoods (LTN) rolled out across the city, clearing cars and vehicles from local areas. LTN zones aren't universally supported, and there's no doubt they inconvenience some people, but they are an interesting step in putting the environment and local public spaces first. Pedestrian-only shopping areas demand residents explore on foot and ditching the car for a scenic view dotted with green spaces has been proved to support good mental health and physical fitness. This human-centric infrastructure encourages individuals in the community to connect with one another; multi-use spaces enable them to spend time in the community without the pressure to spend money.

As we reset (or start) our relationships with the people we live near, we will need to reset the functions of these spaces. The places outside our doorstep should be opportunities for us to connect, support and innovate. For example, in late 2020, plans to rewild Nottingham city centre were published. It's a bold vision for a post-retail landscape – an urban oasis that could help link the city with Sherwood Forest. The trust's CEO Paul Wilkinson said, 'Transforming the Broadmarsh [Shopping Centre] into a natural greenspace would bring people together and start putting the city's nature into recovery at a time when natural greenspace has never been more valued or needed.' As the city looks to the future post-pandemic, the Nottinghamshire Wildlife Trust believes that everyone should have the opportunity to live in 'a healthy, wildlife-rich natural world, and that we all depend on contact with nature for our well-being'. They're calling it a once-in-a-generation opportunity to transform Broadmarsh into a space for nature, and people, signaling a new greener future for the city. Such a bold, green vision could set the city on a course to a greener economic recovery, boost tourism and stimulate inward investment.[4]

This idea of us all living locally, having office hubs and all our amenities within 15 minutes has got me wondering about the wider effect. If we have the opportunity to live locally, how will that impact demographics? Will there be less gentrification, or more? Will places develop an even stronger cultural feel? How will gatherings such as sport events be impacted? And the biggest question of all: if we are investing in our local area, what happens to areas that don't have money to spend on them? How do we spread the wealth if we're focusing it locally? If it seems like I'm asking a lot of open-ended questions in this chapter, it's because I am. This truly is our opportunity to come up with the best way forward, to design spaces that work for everybody.

Live fairly

When I asked you to look out your window and imagine a community space did you think 'Huh. I can see that already?' Well, then perhaps you already live in one of the informal 'villages' that already exist within many large cities. In London, for example, the residents of Dulwich, Crouch End, Clapham or Highgate would argue that they already live in vibrant, green and valued city spaces, with distinct local character and fulsome amenities on the doorstep.

Interestingly, though not perhaps surprising, the proportion of freelance workers in these affluent areas is also relatively high, fostering an environment in which people are already working and living simultaneously. House prices are high and white-collar work dominates, making them exceptional cases rather than blueprints for the future. What we're looking at is the exceptionalism of wealth, and what I'm talking about is making that accessible to everyone. For the true 15-minute city *everyone* must have the opportunity to work where they live, and live where they work. And I'm just not sure that's realistic.

As we are all celebrating the uptake and potential of remote working, isn't it vital that we don't overlook the structural inequalities inherent in basing a new work order on white collar possibilities alone? I posed this question to Sadiq Khan when we spoke.

'For Londoners this pandemic hasn't just reflected the

inequalities, it's amplified them,' he agreed. 'The problem is, if we're honest, only those in managerial positions or with office jobs will have the luxury or choice to work from home. If you're a manual worker, drive a bus, work in a factory, clean the stations or do social care then you don't have the choice . . . And what we've got to be careful about is that we don't inadvertently increase the choices and life chances of those who are already doing pretty well, and not improve those of the people who are perhaps not doing so well. So, it's a real challenge.'

The opportunity to work from home certainly isn't an equal one in the US. Approximately 37% of jobs can be carried out from home – education, professional services, and managerial positions leading the way – jobs which are held predominantly by white, middle-class people.[5] For those lacking a university education too, teleworking opportunities are greatly reduced. For anyone outside of the white middle-class category, the remote jobs available are low-skilled and low paid. This split exists outside the US of course, and any changes we make to a city need to account for the different work opportunities available to people. We need to adapt, and adapt quickly.

Let's start with working where we live – it's not enough to just encourage flexibility so white-collar workers can sit in their nice houses and get deliveries. And it's not about creating co-working spaces that only go halfway to a solution, focused on capacity, rather than radical new alternatives to an unyielding system. We don't want privileged employees to act as dislocated satellites, physically present in a community but with their heads in the city centre. We can't just have rich areas with people at home investing in them, while poor areas remain the same. I think the challenge is allowing for flexibility but encouraging integration.

I've spoken about the ways in which individuals can reset their relationship to a community, but there are huge opportunities for businesses to foster that shift. We can demand more from our businesses to support the communities in our cities. We've talked about businesses moving from rigid workplaces to flexible ones, and encouraging a team composition that reflects a range of different work styles. But to really democratise space and work, businesses could aim to create fulfilling roles for all the people in a community. I'm talking about equitability between the higher-paid and lower-paid staff, and I'm talking about job opportunities outside the established demographic. There's two clear ways they might do this – creating working hubs within communities and making a progressive choice about which communities these hubs are in.

First, what are these hubs? And how can they make a business work better for the community?

There's an architecture firm in New York called HLW, and they're at the forefront of a movement to decentralise businesses. They've advocated for 'distributed nodes throughout multiple locations', meaning mini office hubs that could, in their view 'result in more mixed-use office buildings that serve a more diverse cross-section of workers'. This comes back to the co-working set-ups I spoke about in the previous chapter. It's human nature to seek connection and physical interactions, and while it may not be imperative to every task during the working day, having the option to use spaces for creative work or thinking could stimulate new ideas and enhance a sense of community. Mixed-use office buildings could also make an office space work for a different type of employee with different needs.

The Ascent building in Singapore is a multipurpose space designed to stimulate chance meetings between individuals in social and professional settings. It's home to Merck group, Prestige Biopharma and Olympus technologies just to name a few. Developers embraced synchronicity in its restoration of the building in Science Park 1, designing a space that seamlessly integrated green spaces, coworking spaces, restaurants and exhibition space. They understood that the companies they wanted to attract – ones which value innovation and rely on knowledge workers – would need a collection of spaces to stimulate creativity and problem-solving.

Beyond making hubs enticing for different workers, businesses can also make sure they are available for everyone. When selecting the locations for mini offices outside the centre, perhaps they could choose some in affluent areas, but also some in areas with less wealth. They can encourage workers to step just outside their 15-minute area and bring some of that creativity and money to a new space.

In the UK, outside of London, MediaCityUK is the only creative and media hub in this country. With a mission to regenerate the Manchester docklands and attract talent, MediaCityUK has become a significant contributor to the local and national economy, in an area that's long been ignored by cultural and financial power. With 250 businesses calling this location home, and the introduction of a technical college to train the next generation for media and creative roles, this development is an example of how locations can attract, develop, and retain local talent with meaningful work.

Ultimately, businesses have a huge amount of power to make cities more fair by how and where they focus their resources. They can make sure these nodes are built to support a different range of employees, instigating training opportunities and looking specifically to the community for hiring. Instead of just a demarcation for resources, that 15-minute space could be a framework for hiring. Build a space for one's workers and then look to hire workers from within that community, too, looking beyond the sort of people always hired. If we radically rethink how businesses work within a city, we can start to build an economy that everyone feels a part of.

And then there's the space around us.

Anyone who's tried to live in a city knows space is at a premium on some fronts (ahem, home ownership) and ignored on others. Think of all those spaces, especially around poor communities and housing estates, that feel like wastelands. It's one thing for businesses to build exciting mini hubs, but imagine if we could step out the door of that space into an environment that's been designed for a present and actively engaged community, rather than one that's created to push people into the city centre. This is about reconstituting the space around us to suit the broad communities who live there.

Anna Whitehouse sees this as part of a 'flexible working utopia'. She says, 'My sort of flexible working utopia would be a world where we ebb and flow between the office and home. You know, I think there's been a lot of kickback on how we're losing community by working from home. And I've had people saying, look, you know, people don't like it. Yeah. I'm like, can we please just park flexible working in one corner. That is the umbrella. That is the utopia. Working from home is one tiny fragment of that.'

I read a Deloitte blog which said the age of urbanisation isn't over. 'Cities are indispensable to human progress,' it says. 'The so-called agglomeration benefits of cities and the way in which, as scale and density increase, output and productivity rise are well understood. These gains arise because cities foster specialisation, learning, relationships, competition and the exchange of ideas.'[6]

It's this second bit I'm interested in. It's a given that an increase in density means an increase in productivity and output. Hooray, more money! But what else can density of people bring? It can allow learning, relationships and the exchange of ideas. Cities are already incredible places of learning and culture, with universities and museums acting as entire worlds of knowledge. But I don't think that knowledge feels like it's for everyone most of the time. If we live miles out of the centre and take 40 minutes to commute into work every day, are we really going to come back on the weekend for an exhibition?

Don't get me wrong, there are already incredible examples of local culture and learning – from small theatres above pubs to council-run courses. But as more and more libraries close, and funding for the arts is cut, how do we preserve and prioritise those spaces throughout cities?

The big sites of ideas and learning in the centre of a city like London are incredible. But what I want to focus on is how the *whole* city can be shaped for intellectual and social growth. The architectural firm HLW talks about the importance of cities for helping people thrive, which they define as 'the joint experience of vitality and learning'. It's about redistributing the resources and wealth around a city so everyone can have this opportunity to thrive. A world where only a portion of the city has the resources to live happily, in a space that's been designed for growth and learning, is not the world I want to be part of. We need to actively invest in each part of a city. We need to invest time, and we need to invest money.

According to the British Arts Council, access to the arts can increase community cohesion, make residents feel safer, and have a positive impact on neurological conditions such as Alzheimer's and Parkinson's.[7] Stour Space in Hackney is an example of a multi-functional space which offers opportunities for individuals who wouldn't typically have access to arts education and resources, from a weekly 'pay what you can' night at the café, to affordable art classes and cheaper living space. As an employer, Stour Space provides local jobs, as well as the training to support local talent in securing work.

Unfortunately, the artists who created this community are slowly being forced out by rent increases. The irony being that this community's creators are being pushed out by those hoping to buy into it.

Stour Space was created by activated community members, without the protections of government. But these sort of projects can be developed by councils too, and at scale. The Idea Store is a great example of how local government can invest in networked services that empower communities. These education-focused community centres provide adult learning and library services across London, reaching individuals with little access to these kinds of resources. Following the first location in Bow in east London, in 2002, sites on Chrisp Street, Whitechapel, Canary Wharf and Watney Market have sprung up too. The courses range from upholstery to dance, and they are available to everyone in the community – whatever their finances. It's funded, promoted and supported, and it has the ability to be a life-line for growth.

Let's imagine government support was focused on providing a network of the resources formerly concentrated into city centres. Imagine the sort of urban design and care that's taken over the inner ring of London being replicated throughout the city. Instead of rushing past run down shop fronts or bleak playgrounds to get to the tube, those spaces could really come alive. They could be redesigned for a community that's actively engaged in their worth. It could be possible to reshape the city so each part of it flourishes. Every area of a city could be designed so it's inhabitants can create, grow and learn. At that point, a city can be unleashed from its central economic preoccupation, it can be reset for the demands of the world now. It can be remade for everyone.

Live collectively

I've been reading a lot about futurists, who are dedicated to exploring the potential for human society to adapt to a changing planet. For futurists, resetting the city is not just about creating new spaces that optimise our work but new spaces that optimise us instead. It's a pretty fundamental shift and one that might be hard to fully grasp until the impact of the pandemic has unfolded. Our society has had hundreds of years of prioritising work and maximising productivity, networking and raw ambition. It's going to take a bit of time to realise what's possible if we're focusing on personal and collective growth.

If we change our relationship with cities, then what and who are they for? Could we be making the city, as a concept, redundant? Or can we preserve the wonderful things about a city, while making them greener, fairer and more valuable places?

Modern cities developed as economic hubs, growing out of the need for a meeting place to exchange goods, eventually consolidating economic power there as a result. As the cities became the focus for wealth they also developed as a crucible, a melting pot for social, intellectual and cultural capital. We have historically thrived in cities, and they've been magnets for the nomads too, who bring diversity, innovation, ideas. They've been energetic places, buzzy and brilliant. For all the inequality and fixation on wealth that have crippled many of the lives attached to cities, the flipside of that is the opportunity that happens in pockets or for people in the right place at the right time.

Can we preserve that value even as we reconsider the need for economic growth concentrated in a single place? And could the concentrated diversity and energy within a city, which so fosters an outlook on the world that's tolerant, global and outward-looking, be adequately replicated by local, smaller-scale living? It could be argued that if we move to just living in a small area, our villages, our view on the world will become smaller, our simulations less, our echo chamber brought into real life. So much of the last decade has taught us the perils of isolated perspectives, so how do we make sure we're still thinking global, even while we're encouraging personal growth and freedom locally?

I think the age of urbanisation is far from over. We need cities, we love them and human progress still depends on the existence of cities – indeed, research shows that as scale and density increase, output and productivity rise. Look at London. It's got huge flaws, as I hope I've expressed above. But 8.9 million people, all up close in one city, trading experience, time, energy, collaboration, money and talent, will always produce more innovation than 80,000 or 8,000 people in another spot. It's a numbers game. Digital communities and increased connectedness might mitigate this slightly, but they can't replace the immediacy of physical population density.

But how do we change that game for the better, harvesting all the gains of the traditional city in a new model that links vibrant neighbourhoods into something bigger than the sum of its parts? How can cities truly respond to environmental and social needs as well as economic ones.

No one is thinking about this more than Sadiq Kahn, who is banking a lot on the 'green recovery' of the capital. He's seen the pandemic as an amazing moment for communities to come together, exactly in the ways we covered in the previous chapter. He also sees revitalising 'the local' as a way to knit the shattered capital back together, possibly in a new and environmentally friendly way. Crucially, he sees this investment in local areas as part of a bigger picture, a story of the whole city. He said, 'What I don't want is what I call a bagel-type recovery where the centre gets hollowed out. We have lots of really good activity in the suburbs, but we don't want to lose the joy of central London in London'.

There are huge steps to be made in making sure people across the city can benefit from the possibilities of a city. A major part of that is investing in local areas fairly. Another part is making sure the city centre remains vibrant, vital, and a focal point for positive growth. Ian Mulcahey, urban planner at design and architecture firm Gensler, believes many of the ideas behind the concept are emerging organically, as urban planning discussions continue. He explains: 'There's currently a weird analogue debate going on that people will either work from home or in the office, but we see more of a blended environment, where they'll work in both, but also in transit and in places like co-working hubs and the foyers of art galleries. Things are already gravitating that way, but ultimately it's about moving from rigid workplaces to a range of different work styles based on what people need to do.'[8]

The fact is that professional spaces help us express our professional identities, and they give us energy and interaction that needs to be replicated in some form. With this in mind companies themselves might want to rethink the synergy between home and office and repurpose their city centre buildings to be somewhere that employees come to do some parts of their work, but not all of it. Could we have a central office with a predominant function like all-company meetings and then nodes throughout the city for other ones that reflect that area. The knock-on impact of getting rid of banks of desks for the battery hens of the 9–5 and replacing our 'offices' with a set of centres for different purposes could be huge. And without the need for desks for *everyone* at the same time, we could redesign an office into mixes of meeting rooms, social areas and spaces that encourage collaboration, learning and connection instead.

In addition, mixing business offices with amenities such as event spaces, restaurants, and gyms would allow these sectors to complement rather than compete with one another. And I'm not talking about those in-office gyms that talk us into staying at work, or identikit restaurant chains. I mean a creative energy that evolves naturally and shapes an area. In this model, we have that shift of infrastructure and energy in our local areas, but also allow central hubs to continue to thrive. If businesses are using their central space in an interesting way, then commercial hubs could develop the sort of 'local' feel of the places we live in. The current model of large employment centres surrounded by dispersed residential communities then becomes redundant as the city is knitted together in a more sustainable, healthy way, combining all the elements in the right places needed to collapse the divide between work and life.

Sadiq Khan gave me this food for thought: 'Question: in the future, will people want to travel an hour and a half for their studies or for work or for leisure, entertainment? Probably not. We've got to make sure town centres or high streets cater for people's needs and pay more attention to what I call "the experience". Shop retailers will now have to think about how they can entice you away from shopping from home to, for example, Oxford Street. That same applies to work. How do we entice you to want to come into Canary Wharf or the West End, if it's the case that we need footfall going in there?'

Cities must be able to identify what makes them unique, the talents, skills, and resources they already have, and how these can be presented on a global scale. Norwich – one of the smaller cities in the east of England – recently established itself as a Sharing City.[9] This global accolade is awarded to cities which embrace sharing platforms such as Airbnb, Uber and Deliveroo, while maintaining a collaborative and community-focused approach. Supported by two leading UK universities, a world-class research centre, and a diverse young talent pool, Norwich has been a leader in innovation and creativity for years. By establishing itself on a global stage, the city has been able to develop sharing platforms of its own, too, that focus on local priorities, such as social inclusion and climate change.

If we have *choice,* we're asking businesses, companies and cultural centres to step up so we *choose* to use them. Rather than big offices forcing us to compete and exhaust ourselves to suit their success, we're encouraging competition and growth, so it suits us. Instead of giving power to property companies to build empty flats for investors, can we now shape a city around those already here instead, and use its spaces and people to develop interesting environmental responses and bottom-up culture. Can we transform cities to hubs for positive progress, rather than just sinks for talent and wealth for capitalist growth, resetting our businesses so they are attracting different talent and reflecting different communities? Cities have always been diverse, but can they be equal and decentralised? In a world upended, it's worth placing our bets.

Chapter Six

SOCIETY

———

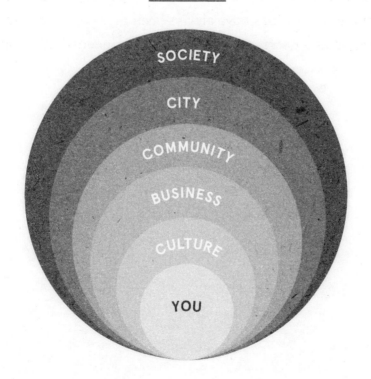

SOCIETY

CITY

COMMUNITY

BUSINESS

CULTURE

YOU

SOCIETY

———

'The visionary starts with a clean sheet of paper, and re-imagines the world'

– Malcolm Gladwell

'WHAT IS YOUR idea of a good day?' Over the years, I've asked my friends this question many times. The first time I asked it most of them were frankly a bit stumped. They just didn't know how to answer this bold invitation to be happy. What was a 'good' day? Where to place the emphasis, what to do with the expansive freedom to choose? For many it felt as if I was asking them what they would do if they had won a million dollars.

I'd unpacked it for them a bit more, bypassing their puzzled, panicked expressions with a second question. 'I mean, if everything you're working towards now went your way, would that ladder up to what you constitute as a good life?' From the macro: where would you live? To the micro: what time would you wake up? And to the mundane: how would you split your day? The answers that came back were compelling and persuasive. But interestingly, what they said was a 'good life' was rarely what they are aiming for with everything they do in their life currently.

Life in a modern world gallops along at a pace, bolstered by a series of unquestioned 'norms': work is good, busy is best, cities are exciting, money is scarce, time is scarcer still. Who has time to challenge 'truths', who has the energy to campaign when the bills need paying and rents keep going up and the job market keeps shrinking and we're all just so . . . goddamn . . . tired. Asking what a good day was then, perhaps, in retrospect, a bit of a trick question when the options seemed so limited.

And then 2020 arrived.

Our worlds shrank in some ways: physical space, travel, opportunities; and grew in others: time, tech and existential angst. And in a world where solid realities melted away amid the hallucinogenic trip of a shifting social paradigm, we were given an unexpected opportunity to reconsider what indeed constitutes a good day . . . and a good life. I suspect if I asked my friends this question now, they would still be equally at odds as to how to answer, but for very different reasons. We lived in the throes of the biggest collective shake-up in living memory and few if any of us have fully decided what exactly it means for the future yet. But at least we're all fully considering the question now.

'Some things will snap back into the way they were,' Ete Davies says. 'But the box has been opened on others now, and I don't think people will go back to the way things were before, because they've seen something different. This is a step forward for humanity. This was a global reminder of mortality, and people are starting to re-evaluate things. I think it's going to hopefully push us forward in positive ways.'

A large proportion of people don't want things to return to 'how they were'; a world based around rigid office-based (over) work where we are expected to fit our 'lives' into small boxes and live as lonely satellites, divorced from natural community to make enough money to enable us to carry on doing more of the same. It was never that good a deal, was it?

Priorities are the new pathways. And working out what is important to us has become imperative. In part this is because it's easier to work it out in the negative space of lockdown (there is nothing like being told you can't get on a plane to convince you that all you want to do is spend your life travelling. . .) or it's just the thrilling fact that everything seems up for grabs now. What seemed implausible, nay impossible last year, now seems entirely possible.

Are you ambitious and looking for the opportunities of a big city but want to live outside the metropolis? Feel compelled to downscale your job for more balance or jettison the commute to spend time in your community. No one is laughing and anyone that says that that's 'not how things are done' clearly hasn't been paying attention.

Stepping out of the work-driven mentality into a wider version of ourselves could be 2020's most lasting legacy. The idea that stress, depression, pollution, loneliness and over-work are not necessarily natural byproducts of modern life is one for me.

In my opinion, 'a good life' depends on who you are. As individuals we decide certain things early on that we consider to be essentials of 'a good life' and we're constantly trying to move toward this state below the surface of our everyday lives. But sometimes we don't know what it is we are working towards; the problem being that a good life is neither a fixed state nor something free of contradictions. Is a good life sitting in an orchard writing a novel, or working yourself hard in the City in a high-powered role? One could argue it could be both, even to a single individual. Human beings are rarely one-note tunes.

Plus, I've always had a suspicion that life is actually just a tapestry of experiences. And that rather than seeing our life as composed of separate things, the coagulation of some of which constitute a good life; work, home, family, sleep – we might be better served by seeing it as a whole, living on a spectrum governed by principles rather than goals. In that way too, we can tap into parts that make us whole that we have neglected in the tension of trying to keep up.

Exploring what gives us joy and satisfaction and finding purpose and meaning in our lives seem to be more useful lubricants through life than chasing a vision of success anchored in consumables, status and locations. In that way too, we could dispense with that most modern of maladies, the feeling that we are somehow 'not enough' whether that's rich, successful, good looking or just hitting the 'right' things at the 'right' life stages.

Karen Rosenkranz pretty much summed it up when she said, 'I think we've done too much work, too much travel, consumed too much, the calendar is full, this feeling of being on a treadmill and always wanting more and more and it's never enough.'

The big question is what does a good life really mean to us? Does everything we are working on right now ladder up to that? And if not, then what are we choosing to reset to achieve it?

So, now I'm asking you directly: if everything went your way, what would a good day look like? When would you like to wake up in the morning, where would you like to be, what feeling would you like to have and why would you feel excited about your day? You don't have to have all the answers yet, I certainly don't. But one thing's clear, this is the time to reset and flex out these choices.

Choose how you work

People my age write books about how to squeeze the most productivity out of our lives – hell, I've talked about it, thought about it, even written about it too. But my heart is genuinely torn between knowing that the obsession with productivity is a slippery slope and recognising that being able to have a vibrant career does demand you do things that you may not want to do, and in ways you might not necessarily want to do them.

The first thing to understand is where we have choice in work, and where we don't. Where we're being pushed into a corner, where something is being presented as a choice when it's not, where we're free, and also the things we just can't change. As I discussed in Chapter 1, so much of our attention is focused on the outward appearance we're presenting, we're giving less thought to recognising the choices in front of us.

Anna Whitehouse talks about the frustration of things that are presented as choices, that are really just the reality of circumstance. She said when 'you look at the States, I think recently there was a stat, 40% of new businesses are female-led and they were almost celebrating that fact and I don't think there's much to celebrate in that, because you have to ask, was it a choice for all the women forced into being self-employed to support their families? Heralded as "mompreneurs" when actually you're talking about some of the 54,000 women made redundant on maternity leave, or who've had their flexible working requests denied. That's not choosing the entrepreneurial dream, that's a restricted choice because of discrimination.'

Gender pay-gap, invisible labour, misogyny and racism in the workplace are all huge problems in society that are having an impact on how we all work and the choices we make about our lives. And we can see these restrictions everywhere, from lack of diversity in media jobs, to lack of access to so many physical spaces.

Not giving people choice and freedom clearly and directly impacts minority groups, but the truth is, that sort of society negatively affects everyone. Anna set up Flex Appeal, which campaigns for flexible working. After arriving late to collect her daughter from nursery one afternoon, Anna was reprimanded by a staff member and decided she needed to change her working hours. Her employer rejected her request, and ever since, Anna has been hosting nationwide events to put pressure on employers to provide remote working options.

One of Anna's sponsors for Flex Appeal is Sir Robert McAlpine, a construction firm who implemented flexible working in response to the number of male suicides. As Anna said earlier, this is everybody's issue.

So the most important thing is that we all work towards a society where everyone is free to make choices about how they work based on things like their skills, ambitions, circumstances and lifestyles. Anna put it simply, 'I think all we want – you, me, anyone else fighting for a different working world – is choice . . . is to give people the choice of where they work, how they work and to do it in a human/ humane way.'

It's about elevating a humane approach to work, opening up choice to everyone and making sure it's not just the loudest or most powerful voice in the room that is deciding what choice looks like. The pandemic rewrote our imaginations and with so much in flux, it made us all feel that if we can work out what we want and ask for it then we might truly be able to change the way we live.

Anna Stansbury, Inequality and Social Policy Scholar, Harvard University, said in an interview for the BBC, 'For the world of work, one of the biggest effects of the pandemic has been to illuminate the utter lack of voice and influence most people have in their workplace . . . Employees in retail, in office jobs, in hospitality have hesitated to return to long days of working in enclosed spaces with poor air circulation – but have often had no real choice in the matter.'[1]

This is the reality for most people. Most people can't just buy a second home in the countryside, or work exactly how they want, because of economic systems. Anna Stansbury predicts this having a huge impact on younger generations, that 'it will manifest itself over the longer term, in a generation which has viscerally experienced the risks of not having a meaningful voice in their workplace – and who will put substantial emphasis on organising for, advocating for, and voting for measures to strengthen employee representation and workplace democracy in the future?'

And what if that future is now?

As Gen Z begins to enter the workplace, demands are changing on employers themselves. Millennials had already set the groundwork by daring to imagine life was as important as work and then recognising that running around trying to keep up was not a worthy goal. But it is the cohorts to come that will really push for change in the workplace, and they're doing it already. In our conversation Sereena Abbassi spoke about the new wave of individuals coming into the workplace and shaking things up.

'I was at a protest a couple of weeks ago, and by and large, the people there were under the age of 25. And it's because that generation has realised that this archaic idea of work and the system actually doesn't serve them. So much is inaccessible to that particular demographic, such as home ownership and so much is unstable too they've probably seen many redundancies within their family. They've also seen tuition fees skyrocket. I speak to youngsters all the time who say, "I can't deal with the mental stress that going to university and graduating with that much debt will leave me with, so I'm just not going to do it. It's not an option for me."'

Raging revolutionary thoughts aside, we have to work within the matrix of this life, and that means (for the moment anyway) capitalism and paying the bills, and dealing with the tension that comes between wanting to lead a life of purpose within a transactional system marbled with inequality. But these Gen Z protestors are showing us the way. They are opening us up to a conversation where we don't just accept the status quo, instead we ask what our choices really are.

Abraham Maslow's hierarchy of needs has always fascinated me. This psychological theory presents a pyramid that should – theoretically – lead to a fulfilling life. It's structured by how vital those needs are to human life, the base layer being the most, the top the more aspirational. And while the lower layers are made up of factors such as food, water, shelter, health, friendship and self-esteem, you need to make it all the way to the top for self-actualisation. All of which suggests, if we want to feel fulfilled and find work that is purposeful, we need to meet our own mental, physical and emotional health needs – indeed, prioritise them – before we can truly live with purpose.

But what happens if we stop looking at the choices presented to us, and instead consider the choices available to everyone? This is what Karen Rosenkranz views as the essential shift, taking back true choice. She says, 'People need to ask for [change], and I think a lot of people will make that shift now. It's about daring to ask for more flexibility. The idea of hustle culture is very unfair, because it puts all the responsibility on the individual . . . I think we have to push back now as employers or freelancers or people working in the system and say, "I'm not going to continue to work that way."'

Not everyone can demand change at work, but we can only create a cultural shift if we ask for choice and freedom where we can. If we assess our lives, work out the choices we need and ask for them. If it's not possible, at least you asked, and at least you are part of the conversation. While it might not be vital to you, the changes you embrace might make a difference to someone else. This is everybody's society and so it's also everybody's problem.

This is what Anna Whitehouse understands as the core choice we have to make about work – it's choosing to challenge norms and ask for more for everybody. She says, 'The first thing is to know that you have a voice, that it's not for activists or the government, or, flexible working experts to fix it's for everybody to fix.' She also told me about James Clarry at Coutts Bank, who implemented flexible working – something incredibly rare in banks. He went against the grain and when he was asked why said, 'Well, you know, productivity has gone up 30% and my staff are happier. Why wouldn't I do it?' He stepped outside his immediate needs and choices to think about choice for everyone. As Anna says, 'What we need to do is stop asking permission to change the system. Each and every one of us can do it.'

Is it fanciful to assume that all workers can have a voice?

Perhaps, but our attitudes to work cannot be policed so easily – en masse, attitudes change structures, and as individuals, the more we speak up the more we empower others to do the same. Asking for change, asserting our needs, resetting our professional lives so that they suit us and work for us, rather than moulding ourselves and our lives to those of an employer.

And within those needs, the aim to stop annexing our personal lives in our working ones. In dissolving the rigidity of the late-capitalist fervour for work, the personal and the professional can finally cease to be warring factions. Forget corporate blurb. Bringing your whole self to work takes a revolution not an HR pamphlet.

Sereena Abbassi told me that she, like many, sees capitalism evolving into a more conscious phase. 'I don't think we'll ever get rid of capitalism entirely – but I think it is going through an evolution and I think it makes sense that alongside that evolution, the place of work also evolves.'

We're not going to totally break the system of work. But by making conscious choices, and asking for what we want, we might just shift the landscape. Change happens incrementally as well as through an upheaval. This was the core of Indy Johar's theory of change, and he talked in our conversation about the power of small movement. He said, 'Most people look to move the 50% in the middle. I'm not interested in the middle, the middle doesn't move like that. I'm interested in moving 3.5%, because actually that's all you need to do to be able to shift the trajectory of where the future is going to be made, and how it'll be made. So the question for me is always how and where do we influence the 3.5%? In order to shift the trajectory where value and new forms of value are being uncovered.'

It's up to all of us to try and be the 3.5%. We're being called upon to work out what is important to us – and then live it. I'd say that despite the navel gazing of the self-help industry we haven't really had to confront this in such an in your face way before.

So much of life in the twenty-first century, has sustainability at its core. Yes, we could keep grinding on in the shadow of a previous paradigm that denies us the right to change it up with any real traction, but is that really going to power us through our lives? And is it going to provide Millennials and the generations that follow with the impetus and drive to evolve and solve the world's biggest problems? Or create a more holistic system in which unchecked growth is finally debunked as an economic and social strategy, and the metric of well-being becomes the only sensible option?

Well-being is at the heart of our new world of work. Businesses might not frame it quite like that, but that's what it is – the curtain has been pulled back on the myth of work as life's prime meridian.

Let's hope that forward motion is slower, more considered, sustainable and inclusive. And once you've worked out how to bring choice into your work, you just need to bring it into your life.

Choose how you live

The baseline is that the choices we make will continue to shape our world. As work evolves, so too does the way we live and principally where we live. As you know, I'm not an advocate for the privileged to just upsticks and move to the countryside or coast, and I believe we need to make places work for people – *all* people. But I want to take this time to reconsider the idea that the city is where life is.

Everything I said in the previous chapter about The City stands true – it's a melting pot, an energy-rich meeting of minds, perspectives and ideas. But there is another choice. We need to know we can choose the city and it will give us meaning. But we also need to know we have a choice to live outside of it. For so long, the city has drawn talent to it to feed the machines of big business and big opportunities in everything from media and creative arts to law, medicine and banking. To live outside was to have a high tolerance for commuting or else to mark yourself out in some way as too relaxed to hit the big time. Only those in senior stages of their careers could make the satellite life a success, blessed with the ability to work from home or grace the office once a week.

Working from home has revealed the agility of many types of work, this is no longer an unvarnished truth. People of all ages have begun to think about 'moving to the country', or elsewhere, and trying out a different pace and style of life, something borne out by rising prices in rural areas in the UK.

Friends of mine are really thinking about where they want to live now, rather than taking it as a given that they will remain in London because 'this is where life is'. One, a perennial renter, told me last week that she is now moving to Margate. For her, as for many, it is not for a 'quiet life' but to increase the ability to be creative and connected. And to be a little bit more still, as Sereena Abbassi also attests. She has just moved from London to Bristol. 'I just feel like for the past two-and-a-half years I've been on a hamster's wheel. It is nice just to stop and to be in one place.' For others though, the idea of the hectic city experience is still a powerful bias to get past.

When I talked to trend forecaster and ethnographer, Karen Rosenkranz about it, she brought up the mental barrier that has held us in thrall to staying in cities, even when the experience has been tough. Karen has written a book called *City Quitters*. She helps clients identify and prepare for socio-cultural changes and specialises in spotting these nuanced shifts for a range of different businesses. 'There's a pressure that in order to be cool and produce really forward-looking stuff you've got be in [the city]. It does make sense to some extent,' she says. 'London is one of the most vibrant cities in the world, for example, but I also think there is a lot of interesting output happening outside major cities.'

The ways in which this shapes how we live can be subtle

but profound. The reality is that our environment shapes our disciplines and our boundaries. If I know there's a Tesco down the road or Deliveroo then that convenience means I'll work later and get dinner later, for example. I succumb to the fact that I can always be 'always on' because everything around me in a major city is always on.

Of course, no one has ever said (explicitly) that everyone with ambition or a desire for a vibrant life should move to the city but the unspoken implication is pernicious. Hey – you can see it in my own perspective on cities in the last chapter. And because of that mental barrier here we stay, held in the grasp of metropolitan mythology, seduction of scale and the idea that this is where we belong. And more importantly, that we wouldn't belong anywhere else.

'People fear that they will be isolated and lonely and won't find like-minded people or a community outside the city,' says Karen. 'We always think of a city as such a diverse environment with so many different cultures and people, but then when we live there we often just hang out in very small circles of people that are just like us. When people move out, suddenly they interact with people of different ages and who do different work and maybe have different political views. And that can be challenging but it's also refreshing.'

This idea of difference is really key, especially at a time of echo chambers and polarisation. Can we choose a path that brings us into contact with other people? Might doing so bring us a new perspective? We're focused on concerns that if we leave, me might fade from sight, or won't make friends. And if you weren't born in a city, that leaving might be a backward step to our early life before we moved to the big city to find the streets paved with gold. But can't we focus on the positive potential of choosing something else?

We need to understand where we'll feel most able to live with purpose, and freedom, wherever that is, without being restricted by ideas we've been fed. We need to be making choices for the right reason. Karen said she noticed that many people were moving out of the city not just to have a quiet life, but 'to be able to work better to protect their creativity, their artistic freedom and those things'.

There's this idea that people who choose not to be in the productivity of city life are doing so because they've given up on their career and want to settle down and have a quiet family life. But can't the opposite be true? Karen certainly thinks the tide is changing, and people are making active choices about where they will be able to grow. She works to create places for people to work and live differently, because in her view 'a rural context influences creativity'.

This idea of returning to nature to foster growth and creativity is an interesting one. These days, attention is pulled in so many directions, and at a rapid pace. Switching from sending a text, to typing up a Google doc, to watching Netflix in quick succession is leaving us with something scientists call attention fatigue. Separating from the screen and taking a walk in the park is one way in which we can actively reset our brains and, by extension, our creativity.[2] As important as it is to find activities which inspire us and encourage us to think in new ways – like playing an instrument for example – it's also vital that we have moments of silence, without expectation, where we can simply enjoy the state of being. It's no coincidence that most people have their best ideas in the shower.

Choosing to live closer to nature is just one positive choice. It's as positive a choice as choosing to live in a city because of its multiculturalism. Or abroad because of the country's culture. It doesn't matter what we choose – it's about making that choice for the right reasons. We should be working in a place where the things we choose are purposeful and enriching.

Along with how and where you live, we are reconsidering everything; from how we travel, to what is sustainable and how truly our lives align with our values. We've woken up and found it's hard work, because the truth is choices *are* hard work. No matter how much we might rail against a status quo, it is most often the easiest route to 'let it slide'. We shrug and say, 'this is how it is' and put up with less than optimum conditions because we feel powerless and daunted by facing down what appears to be a monolith but is, in truth, a social system composed of our daily decisions. But if we truly want a life well lived, where we are alive to our own possibilities, and feel that we are not an arbitrary system set up to profit and benefit the few and not the many are in control of our destinies, then we have to be willing to put in the work. And that means making mindful choices, based on real and authentic motivations that come from the bits of us we spend a lifetime being too busy to look at.

We need to be constantly asking ourselves valuable questions to steer our decisions. Karen Rosenkranz lives by this policy, and thinks it's about asking: 'Why are you doing this? And who are you doing this for? Are you really happy with the work you're producing? Are you just doing what you think you're supposed to do?' These sorts of questions illuminate a path and a purpose. And they ask us to re-evaluate success. I talked about social media with Karen and the idea that we're so focused on showing what we've done we've forgotten to ask if that's what we really want. Her response: we need to 'find your own rhythm or your own measures for success'.

Making one big decision about our lives will result in the other parts demanding our attention. Rather like dominoes, changes tend to fall, one by one. Where we work may determine where and how we live and vice-versa in myriad ways but that also impacts who and how we interact with, where we shop, what contribution we can make to a community and a whole host of other daily decisions. And it's hard to make these decisions on autopilot.

In the end it comes down to one belief: that life can be different. One question: what are we choosing now? My friends may still look at me bizarrely when I ask them what a good day looks like for them, but my enquiry no longer provokes anxiety or confusion. There is a feeling that this is now a pertinent question to ask of all of us.

The gift that 2020 gave us was space and a chance to work out what is good and bad in our lives and reimagine it to be more sustainable and more fulfilled. There is new potential to create a 'good life', however that looks to us, with new choices on the table that were unimaginable even a year ago. Careers, community, relationships, how we work as individuals, how businesses operate, how we communicate, how we can be better citizens, where we live and how they are all linked – everything has been affected and is now up for grabs. And while there are certain things we cannot control externally, we are always, ultimately, the point of power in our decisions of how to respond.

What are we choosing to reset? We want to create a broader vision for the future and a path for a new life based on the things and people we value. It's all possible.

I hope this book has helped steer you to make new choices for your own life.

NOTES

INTRODUCTION

1 BCO. Majority of workers plan a return to office, but home working here to stay. https://www.bco.org.uk/News/News46982. aspx

CHAPTER 1

1 Williams Simon, Erica (@missewill), Twitter post June 6, 2018, 10.33 p.m.

2 Achor, S., Reece, A., Rosen Kellerman, G. & Robichaux, A. (2018, November 6). '9 Out of 10 People Are Willing to Earn Less Money to Do More-Meaningful Work'. *Harvard Business Review*. See: https://hbr.org/2018/11/9-out-of-10-people-are-willing-to-earn-less-money-to-do-more-meaningful-work

3 Uviebinené, E. (2019, April 26). 'How to avoid burnout and thrive at work'. *Financial Times*. See: https://www.ft.com/content/e99f97a8-4650-11e9-b83b-0c525dad548f

4 Wigert, B. & Agrawal, S. (2018, July 12). 'Employee Burnout, Part 1: The 5 Main Causes'. *Gallup*. See: https://www.gallup.com/workplace/237059/employee-burnout-part-main-causes.aspx

NOTES

5   Kim, E. S. & Jung, C. S. (2015). The Effects of Status Symbols in the Office on Employee Attitudes in a Human Service Agency. *Human Service Organizations: Management, Leadership & Governance*, 39(4). https://doi.org/10.1080/23303131.2015.1046008

6   Bellezza, S., Paharia, N. & Keinan, A. (2017). Conspicuous Consumption of Time: When Busyness and Lack of Leisure Time Become a Status Symbol. *Journal of Consumer Research*, 44(1):118–38. https://doi.org/10.1093/jcr/ucw076

7   YouGov. (2018, August 15). 'The majority of employees check work emails while on holiday'. See: https://yougov.co.uk/topics/economy/articles-reports/2018/08/15/majority-employees-check-work-emails-while-holiday

8   Godwin, C., Hunter, M., Bezdek, M., Lieberman, G., Elkin-Frankston, S., Romero, V., Witkiewitz, K., Clark, V. & Schumacher, E. (2017). Functional connectivity within and between intrinsic brain networks correlates with trait mind wandering. *Neuropsychologia*, 103:140–53. https://doi.org/10.1016/j.neuropsychologia.2017.07.006

9   Arbit, J. (2020) 'The Pandemic Has Heightened Young People's Dedication to Their Health'. *VICE*.

10 Salvagioni, D. A. J., Melanda, F. N., Mesas, A. E., González, A. D., Gabani, F. L. & de Andrade, S. M. (2017). Physical, psychological and occupational consequences of job burnout: A systematic review of prospective studies. *PloS One*, doi:10.1371/journal.pone.0185781

11 Kelly, J. (2020, December 1). 'Now that working from home has proven successful, Unilever is trying out a four-day workweek'. *Forbes*. See: https://www.forbes.com/sites/jackkelly/2020/12/01/now-that-working-from-home-has-proven-successful-unilever-is-trying-out-a-four-day-workweek/?sh=6514a0a41ab0

12 Enever, W. (2020, May 7). 'Will COVID-19 change how we spend our time post-lockdown?'. *Savanta*. See: https://savanta.com/view/will-covid-19-change-how-we-spend-our-time-post-lockdown/

13 YouGov. (2020, June 4). 'How are Brits spending money during COVID-19?'. See: https://yougov.co.uk/topics/consumer/articles-reports/2020/06/04/how-are-brits-spending-money-during-covid-19

14 San Francisco State University. (2014, April 16). 'Creative activities outside work can improve job performance,' *ScienceDaily.* See: www.sciencedaily.com/releases/2014/04/140416225322.htm

15 Marketplace Tech. (2020, May 8). 'Etsy is doing very well during the pandemic.' See: https://www.marketplace.org/shows/marketplace-tech/etsy-face-maks-covid-19-pandemic/

16 re:Work. 'What Makes a Team'. See: https://rework.withgoogle.com/print/guides/5721312655835136/

CHAPTER 2

1 CIPD. (2016). 'Labour Market Outlook: Focus on working parents'. See: https://www.cipd.co.uk/Images/labour-market-outlook-focus-on-working-parents_tcm18-17048.pdf

2 Gustafsson, S., Gillespie, N., Searle, R., Hailey, V. H. & Dietz, G. (2020). Preserving Organizational Trust During Disruption. https://doi.org/10.1177/0170840620912705

3 Larson, B. Z., Vroman, S. R. & Makarius, E. E. (2020, March 18). 'A Guide to Managing Your (Newly) Remote Workers'. *Harvard Business Review.* See: https://hbr.org/2020/03/a-guide-to-managing-your-newly-remote-workers

4 Thomas, G. F., Zolin, R. & Hartman, J. L. (2009). The central role of communication in developing trust and its effect on employee involvement. *Journal of Business Communication* 46(3):297–310. https://doi.org/10.1177/0021943609333522

5 Stavrou, C. (2020, March 16). 'The Next 100 Days'. See: https://medium.com/@cassandra_stavrou/the-next-100-days-b189e360c7b

6 Gartner. (2020, May 6). 'Gartner identifies nine trends for HR leaders that will impact the future of work after the coronavirus pandemic'.

See: https://www.gartner.com/en/newsroom/press-releases/ 2020-05-06-gartner-identifies-nine-trends-for-hr-leaders-that-wi

7   Christian, A. (2020, August 10). 'Bosses Started Spying on Remote Workers. Now They're Fighting Back'. *Wired*. See: https://www. wired.co.uk/article/work-from-home-surveillance-software

8   Sam Harris. (2020, March 24). *#194 – The New Future of Work: A Conversation with Matt Mullenweg*. [Making Sense]. See: https:// samharris.org/podcast/

9   Hannah, F. (2019, February 22). 'Unlimited holiday: a perk that comes with pitfalls'. *BBC*. See: https://www.bbc.co.uk/news/business-47338096

10   Ohanian, A. (2020, April 15). 'Paternity leave was crucial after the birth of my child, and every father deserves it'. *New York Times*. See: https://www.nytimes.com/2020/04/15/parenting/ alexis-ohanian-paternity-leave.html

11   Skoulding, L. (2018, October 2). 'How long does the average UK employee spend at work?'. *AccountancyAge*. See: https://www. accountancyage.com/2018/10/02/how-long-does-the-average-uk-employee-spend-at-work/

12   IBM. (2014). The Value of Training. See: https://www.ibm.com/ training/pdfs/IBMTraining-TheValueofTraining.pdf

CHAPTER 3

1   Zeno. (2020). The 2020 Zeno Strength of Purpose Study. See: https://www.zenogroup.com/insights/2020-zeno-strength-purpose

2   Edelman. (2020, January 19). '2020 Edelman trust barometer reveals growing sense of inequality is undermining trust in institutions.' See: https://www.edelman.com/news-awards/2020-edelman-trust-barometer

3   Ibid.

4   RecruitUK. (2020, April 6). 'Looking beyond returns: the rise of

ethical investing'. See: https://recruitukltd.co.uk/looking-beyond-returns-the-rise-of-ethical-investing/

5   WHO. Air Pollution. See: https://www.who.int/health-topics/air-pollution#tab=tab_1

6   WWF. (2018, June 6). 'The holiday plastic choking our oceans'. See: https://www.wwf.org.uk/updates/holiday-plastic-choking-our-oceans

7   Edgecliffe-Johnson, A. (2019, January 4). 'Beyond the Bottom Line'. *Financial Times.* See: https://www.ft.com/content/a84647f8-0d0b-11e9-a3aa-118c761d2745

8   NTU. (2019, March). 'Laying the foundations of a good work city: mapping Nottingham's employment'. See: https://www.ntu.ac.uk/about-us/news/news-articles/2019/03/nottingham-missing-out-on-employment-growth

9   WEF, Davos. Benioff, M. (2020, January). See: https://www.cnbc.com/2020/01/21/stakeholder-capitalism-has-reached-a-tipping-point-says-salesforce-ceo-benioff.html

10 Peters, A. (2020, March 31). 'How businesses could emerge better after COVID-19, according to B Lab'. *Fast Company.* See: https://www.fastcompany.com/90483730/how-businesses-could-emerge-better-after-covid-19-according-to-b-lab

11 Greenpeace. 'Exxon's Climate Denial History: A Timeline'. See: https://www.greenpeace.org/usa/global-warming/exxon-and-the-oil-industry-knew-about-climate-change/exxons-climate-denial-history-a-timeline/

12 Monbiot, G. (2019, June 26). 'Shell is not a green saviour. It's a planetary death machine.' *Guardian.* See: https://www.theguardian.com/commentisfree/2019/jun/26/shell-not-green-saviour-death-machine-greenwash-oil-gas

13 Chapman, O. & Bekar, B. (2020, November 11). 'Purpose over profit: how the COVID-19 pandemic is urging us to work and

buy ethically'. *Nesta.* See: https://www.nesta.org.uk/blog/purpose-over-profit/

14 Behavioural Insights Team. (2020, January 29). 'A Menu for Change'. See: https://www.bi.team/publications/a-menu-for-change/

15 Indvik, L. (2020, November 3). 'Sustainable fashion? There's no such thing'. *Financial Times.* See: https://www.ft.com/content/d174e7d7-97c4-43fc-8765-95075e5fcce7

CHAPTER 4

1 Economist International. (2018, September 1). 'Loneliness Is a Serious Public-Health Problem'. *Economist.* See: https://www.economist.com/international/2018/09/01/loneliness-is-a-serious-public-health-problem

2 Michaelson, J., Jeffrey, K. & Abdallah, S. (2017, February 20). 'The Cost of Loneliness to UK Employers'. *New Economics Forum.* See: https://neweconomics.org/2017/02/cost-loneliness-uk-employers#:~:text=The%20research%20finds%20that,on%20productivity%20and%20staff%20turnover.

3 Everyday Health. (2017). 'State of Women's Wellness'. p.31. See: https://images.agoramedia.com/everydayhealth/gcms/Everyday-Health-State-of-Womens-Wellness-Survey-PDF.pdf

4 YouGov. (2019, July 30). 'Millennials Are the Loneliest Generation'. See: https://today.yougov.com/topics/lifestyle/articles-reports/2019/07/30/loneliness-friendship-new-friends-poll-survey

5 Cigna. (2018, May 1). 'Cigna's U.S. Loneliness Index'. See: https://www.multivu.com/players/English/8294451-cigna-us-loneliness-survey/

6 Amatenstein, S. 2019. 'Not so social media: how social media increases loneliness'. *Psycom.* See: https://www.psycom.net/how-social-media-increases-loneliness/

7 Perlman, D. (1990). Age differences in loneliness: a meta-analysis.

See: https://www.researchgate.net/publication/234637847_Age_Differences_in_Loneliness_A_Meta-Analysis

8   The Young Foundation. (2020, July). 'How Covid-19 changed community life in the UK'. See: https://www.youngfoundation.org/wp-content/uploads/2020/07/The-Young-Foundation_Corona Report-Final.pdf

9   Russell, A. R., Nyame-Mensah, A., de Wit, A. & Handy, F. (2019). Volunteering and Wellbeing Among Ageing Adults: A Longitudinal Analysis. *Voluntas* 30:115–28. https://doi.org/10.1007/s11266-018-0041-8

10 Gleeson, B. (2015).'5 aspects of emotional intelligence required for effective leadership'. *Inc.com.* See: https://www.inc.com/brent-gleeson/5-aspects-of-emotional-intelligence-required-for-effective-leadership.html

11 Leslie, I. (2020, July 3). 'Why your "weak-tie" friendships may mean more than you think'. The Life Project, BBC. See: https://www.bbc.com/worklife/article/20200701-why-your-weak-tie-friendships-may-mean-more-than-you-think

12 The Marmot Review. (2010). 'Fair Society, Healthy Lives.' See: https://www.parliament.uk/globalassets/documents/fair-society-healthy-lives-full-report.pdf

13 Robinson, R. & Humphreys, A. (2020, September 22). 'Debate: Has pandemic-induced online shopping killed the high street for good?'. *City A.M.* See: https://www.cityam.com/debate-has-pandemic-induced-online-shopping-killed-the-high-street-for-good/

14 Pak, M. (2018, October 25). 'Networking is key to success in life, NOT (just) business'. See: https://medium.com/@mariyapak/networking-is-key-to-success-in-life-not-just-business-a54ef68ceb9d

15 ONS. (2018). 'Trends in self-employment in the UK'. See: https://www.ons.gov.uk/employmentandlabourmarket/

peopleinwork/employmentandemployeetypes/articles/trendsin-
selfemployment-intheuk/2018-02-07

16 Garber, M. (2017, July 3). 'What does "community" mean?'. *The Atlantic.* See: https://amp.theatlantic.com/amp/article/532518/

17 Bruce Daisley. (2020, October 19). *Community 4: a champion community builder shares her advice.* [Eat Sleep Work Repeat]. See: https://www.globalplayer.com/podcasts/episodes/7Drbzns/

18 Beer, C. (2020, January 7). 'The Rise of Online Communities.' *GWI.* See: https://blog.globalwebindex.com/chart-of-the-week/online-communities/

CHAPTER 5

1 Levete, A. (2020, November 9). 'Coronavirus: Will our day-to-day ever be the same?: Can our community relations become more meaningful?'. Worklife, BBC. See: https://www.bbc.com/worklife/article/20201109-coronavirus-how-cities-travel-and-family-life-will-change

2 Felstead, A. & Reuschke, D. (2020). Homeworking in the UK: before and during the 2020 lockdown. *Wiserd Report,* Cardiff: Wales Institute of Social and Economic Research. Available for download from: https://wiserd.ac.uk/publications/homeworking-uk-and-during-2020-lockdown

3 Rodriguez, L. 'Making our communities more liveable: examples from Germany and Scandinavia'. *SmartCitiesDive.* See: https://www.smartcitiesdive.com/ex/sustainablecitiescollective/road-map-making-our-communities-more-liveable-examples-germany-and-scandinavia/131416/

4 Dingel, J. I. & Neiman, B. (2020). How many jobs can be done at home? NBER Working Paper No. w26948. Available at SSRN: https://ssrn.com/abstract=3569412

5 Deloitte. (2020, October 5). 'Home working and the future of

cities'. See: https://blogs.deloitte.co.uk/mondaybriefing/2020/10/home-working-and-the-future-of-cities.html

6   Arts Council England. (2015). The Value of Arts and Culture to People and Society: an evidence review. See: https://www.artscouncil.org.uk/sites/default/files/download-file/Value_arts_culture_evidence_review.pdf

7   Everett, C. (2020, September 29). 'How the "15-minute city" will transform work'. *Raconteur*. See: https://www.raconteur.net/workplace/15-minute-city/

8   Norwich Sharing City. (2017). 'The UK's first sharing city'. See: https://norwichsharingcity.co.uk/

9   Norwich Sharing City. (2017). 'The UK's first sharing city'. See: https://norwichsharingcity.co.uk/

CHAPTER 6

1   Stansbury, A. (2020, November 9). 'Coronavirus: How the world of work may change forever: Will all workers now have a voice?'. Worklife, BBC. See: https://www.bbc.com/worklife/article/20201023-coronavirus-how-will-the-pandemic-change-the-way-we-work

2   Suttie, J. (2016, March 2). 'How Nature Can Make You Kinder, Happier, More Creative'. *Greater Good Magazine.* See: https://greatergood.berkeley.edu/article/item/how_nature_makes_you_kinder_happier_more_creative

ACKNOWLEDGEMENTS

First of all, a special thank you to my editor Harriet Poland for her encouragement, patience and confidence in me from the very first time I told her about this idea on a rainy and cold day in a coffee shop in London. Most importantly her friendship; I couldn't have done it without her.

I'd like to thank the Hodder Studio team for all their hard work and efforts in putting this book together during a very unprecedented time! Izzy Everington, Dom Gribben, Dan Jones, Vero Norton, Callie Robertson.

Thank you to all my contributors: Ete Davies, Alex Mahon, Pip Jamieson, Anna Whitehouse, Indy Johar, Sereena Abbassi, Karen Rosenkranz, Nadia Whittome, Cassandra Stavrou, Joanna Lyall and Sadiq Khan. Your insights and expertise were invaluable in making this book what it is.

And last but not least, a huge thank you to all my friends and family who put up with my countless WhatsApp messages while trying to bring this book to life during a very crazy time in history. Love and appreciate you all.

THE ZERO CONUNDRUM

A Serial Murder Mystery

JOHN DUBY J.D.

Commonwealth Books Inc.

THE ZERO CONUNDRUM
This edition published 2021 by
Commonwealth Books Inc.,
All rights reserved

Library of Congress Control Number:
2021946052

ISBN: 978-1-892986-33-7 (Trade)
ISBN: 978-1-892986-28-3 (e-pub)

First Commonwealth Books Trade Edition: September 2021

PUBLISHED BY COMMONWEALTH BOOKS, INC.,
www.commonwealthbooks@aol.com
www.commonwealthbooksinc.com

Manufactured in the United States of America

To my daughter, Reagan Duby, whom I love
most in this world, and my beloved
stepdaughters: Luvi, Eris, Abby, and Carolina.
To my twin sister, Jennifer, and her
husband, David Tippet, for their love and
support in my life.

ACKNOWLEDGEMENTS

To my author friend, Betty Henderson, whose dedication to helping me and whose editing skills made it possible for me to write this book, I am forever grateful.

To Richard Lawrence of the Eaton Literary Agency for his guidance and concerted efforts with *The Zero Conundrum*.

PROLOGUE

Jack Garvey, a Supervising Special Agent with the Behavioral Analysis Unit (BAU) of the FBI, was confronted with a case that stumped the FBI for nearly a decade. The challenge it presented seemed more indecipherable than merely daunting, which was why it was given to Jack.

His mission was simple in its objective—confirm the existence of and then find one of the most-prolific serial murderers in American history. Jack's starting point was far more problematic. Where did he begin when he had a list of *don't knows* as long as a world-record anaconda? No one knew who was killed, where, why, and there were no eyewitnesses. The perpetrator so far left absolutely no forensic evidence. Without those elements, how could he demonstrate the commonalities between methods of killing or the *modus operandi,* the MO, and the killer?

MOs were commonly used to group murders of a specific serial killer as a starting point in looking for evidence that could lead to his apprehension. Working with local law enforcement as the bodies piled up, Jack found no consistency of methodology in the monster's numbers.

Jack Garvey's challenge was to find the serial murderer, or murderers, before there were more innocent victims. The only thing he knew was the cryptic notifications the FBI received came from many large cities in the U.S.—that and the fact that results were expected, despite that many other good agents tried but failed to find their man.

Jack, a good chess player, enjoyed the game's tactics and strategy. The creativity of chess taught him to see, in his cases as well as in his games, solutions others didn't see on the board. That and his driving intellectual curiosity and determination helped him checkmate his quarry.

Not limited to chess, however, he enjoyed any puzzle to the point of near obsession. That was evident in the way he approached his cases. He was driven by an insatiable need to know, solve the puzzle, and understand how his prey thought. Those attributes explained his success in the FBI.

CHAPTER ONE

The two-person tent was lightweight, designed for hiking. It could be popped open in a moment for immediate shelter. He liked it, because it came with a convenient large carrying case with shoulder straps for easy transport. It looked out of place pitched in the living room of a circa 1910-style red-brick four-flat in Chicago's New Town.

For nearly half a century, the flat was right around the corner from John Barleycorn, a unique, high-ceilinged pub that showed Laurel and Hardy and Charlie Chaplin silent films. The dimly lit establishment's walls were adorned by models of historic sailing ships, like *Old Ironsides,* or doomed ships like the *Titanic, Lusitania,* or the ironclads from the Civil War to World War Two's *Bismarck.* The models were crafted with amazingly accurate detail and perhaps eerily foretold the tragic events to come.

He enjoyed the pub's ambiance, though he could almost see, like a phantasm, how it was tainted by the ritual seduction of men by manipulative women. He saw the creatures wherever he looked at Barleycorn's. The tent was in that particular four-flat because of one of those women.

The flat had an array of furniture, each chosen for its impulsive appeal in the moment, with no thought devoted to creating a room that was either thematic or coordinated. Each piece was clearly procured where budgetary constraints and functionality predominated the tenant's thinking. The furniture was haphazardly strewn about the room to make space for the tent, a camouflaged shelter completing an image of unabridged disarray. Inside the tent was a living, writhing creature.

1

CHAPTER TWO

He wasn't the kind of person to drift. Concerted planning and attention to detail were his dominant traits. Still, he tried to figure out how he came to be who he was. His ambition was two-fold: to be the most-prolific serial killer of all time, and *never* get caught. Being caught would end the immense pleasure he anticipated deriving from his predominant pastime of punishing women for their inherent nature.

His history didn't have the usual indicia. He was never physically abused like Jeffrey Dahmer and many others. He never tortured small animals or committed arson. It was almost universal for serial killers to have done both. For him, inflicting pain on animals would be demeaning. What satisfaction could be derived from harming a less-sentient being? No, he would inflict excruciating pain on humans, specifically women.

Why do women invest their every waking moment to domineering and manipulating men, even an inoffensive, retiring man like my father? he wondered.

He came from an upper middle-class family. His father, a college professor, praised his son's genius IQ, which he said eclipsed his own. He could've been a high-school valedictorian, his mother constantly reminded him.

He did well enough to get by, but most subjects bored him. He dropped out of college after one year. Still, he could be a prolific reader if a subject interested him, like forensics.

Unlike his retiring, bookish father, he had a gift of gab. His father taught law, something he *was* passionate about. Talking about the law, he waxed poetic. Maybe that's where his son became persuasive, evolving to become manipulative himself. What he disdained in women he could not see in himself.

When his father wasn't talking about the law, he barely spoke. He claimed he saved his passion for the law. His son believed he refrained out of fear of confrontation with his wife. Their conversations always ended with an acerbic tone of voice from her, if not vicious and denigrating toward his father and extending to their son.

Seeing sadness and resignation in his father's eyes, he wondered how his mother ever respected the man enough to marry him. Had she gradually worn him down to such a pitiable state? Had she simply figured that as a Doctor of Law and soon to be a professor, he had enough status to justify some of her ego, while she simultaneously saw enough weakness in him to nourish the dark side of it?

Unlike the fervent dedication his father brought to the law, no visible passion was exhibited between his parents, which wouldn't surprise anyone who knew them. Beside his retiring ways, Drake, his father, was rather bookish-looking as well. His five-foot-eight height, male patterned-baldness, and a beard that looked like a fallow farmer's field, contributed to the image of a defeated man. His intelligence and well-mannered ways appeared to be his only redeeming attributes. His son felt his father's constant, enduring love, no matter the man's weaknesses.

His mother, Phoebe, was all about appearances and how she looked to others. She was five-foot-six and fairly attractive, although not nearly to the extent she imagined. When the couple went out in public, she religiously mentioned she should have worn shorter heels, but she never did. The physical stature it gave her affirmed the dominance she displayed to others. Those displays weren't just for her personal edification in public. They were a fact of family life.

She had a reasonably nice figure, although Jenny Craig for a few weeks wouldn't have hurt. Phoebe's amazing blue eyes could warm someone or cut him in half. For himself and his father, it was most often the latter.

She asserted they weren't touchy-feely people. Hugs for their only son didn't exist. When Drake hugged him, she claimed he was jockeying for advantage, so he stopped. Their son minimized this as a mere twinge of pain that was in reality a sharp, penetrating wound. His mother's rejection extended differently to each of them. She rejected her spouse, because he was unworthy of her, while she treated their son with contempt, because her husband was his progenitor. Phoebe was openly contemptuous of the idea she could have had any part in birthing such a pathetic child, so akin to her husband.

That persisted, because Drake was too timid and afraid of rejection to protect his son. Rather than viewing this as a weakness in his father, he saw Drake, whose love was all he had to cling to, as a victim of Phoebe's devious designs.

Still, whatever the metamorphosis of his hatred for women, it wasn't ambivalence toward sex. For him, he knew, he couldn't enjoy a woman or accept what could be surrendered or worse, given. There had to be a nexus with the rage he felt. He was ready to experience the orgasmic confluence of the sex act, a homogenous exorcism of his desire, but it had to be combined with the imposition of pain and, ultimately, death in a manner worthy of his genius.

CHAPTER THREE

Zero was his covert, internalized name for himself. It had its origin in a job he had the summer before he started his first and only year at the local junior college. His attending a junior college was a great disappointment for both his parents. He went there while camping out at his family home, having already decided his college experience would be short-lived.

The summer job was bathing twist drills in acid. He donned thick plastic gloves and took cubic metallic bins of twist drills to drop into large, concrete sinks filled with acid. After initial de-burring of the drills, the acid removed any remaining imperfections. He was indoctrinated into a program broadly followed by many manufacturers across the country -- Zero Defects.

Formerly QC, or quality control, was thought of as a concerted effort to minimize the inevitable errors employees made. Zero defects proposed that the acceptance of this inevitability proliferated the mistakes QC sought to minimize. The idea was to start with the proposition that mistakes were avoidable.

The job was endurable, but the men at the factory constantly taunted him.

"Have you ever eaten pussy?" they asked.

At eighteen, with the naïveté born of isolation from his classmates, he had no idea what the question meant. He was probably the only person in his high-school class who didn't. Having his naïveté exposed felt like being stripped naked. Every day, Zero wanted to run away, but he had to wait for the buzzer signaling the end of shift.

The constant taunting enraged him. Zero blamed it on the women who closed doors in his face throughout his high-school years. "You're such a spaz! Come back, when you know what to do." Sometimes, the comments were more direct and brutal. "I'll bet you've got an Oscar Mayer wiener under there. I'm looking for Moby Dick."

Drake and Zero became accustomed to knuckling under to Phoebe. More than that, they learned to ignore their own inclinations. Drake's bottom-dwelling self-esteem paralyzed him. Zero alone couldn't stand against his mother—at least, not yet. Girls sensed his lack of confidence. The pretty ones treated Zero with indifference or what seemed to him contempt. The shame showed in his bowed head, his inability to look people in eye. For Zero, it fed a blazing hatred that coaxed, then demanded, he erupt. Although he didn't then, he was ready later.

His ambition was to be the most-prolific, undiscovered serial murderer in history. He would never be identified, because he would carry out his acts with intense, detailed, precision planning and would generate zero defects in their actualization. He would live a life of self-delivered exhilaration beyond anything anyone else ever experienced.

He was left with only his searing ambition. The truth he would admit or recognize was that he preferred the fullness of embers that burned but never extinguished to an empty shell. He told himself his father was gentle and muted, rather than express the actual cowardice and weakness Drake lived.

Zero's maternal grandfather's black-and-white photograph hung prominently in their living room. He was Phoebe's role model for Drake and Zero. His picture revealed a tall, strikingly handsome man, certainly the reason why Zero stood six-foot-two. His maternal grandfather had the posture of a banker, not a lumberjack, and showed it in stark contrast to his sheepish father. When the three of them went out together, with Phoebe in heels, Drake appeared like a dwarf behind them.

In black-and-white, his grandfather's photograph didn't reveal Phoebe's penetrating blue eyes, but she assured Zero they were as blue as the Italian grotto in Sorrento. She recalled in detail her trip there with her father when she was a teenager, claiming he would've made an excellent lead for a James Bond movie. "The name's Bond, James Bond."

Zero never met the man, because he died fairly young, but Zero hated him, too, for giving his mother those eyes and the arrogance revealed in his photo.

He extrapolated his own introduction with a different bent. "The name's Zero, and I have a license to kill you."

CHAPTER FOUR

Before Zero pitched his tent, he'd been looking for Number 1 for a long time. He couldn't help ruminating about the metamorphosis that brought him to that point. He knew proximity to any woman he desired not only aroused him but filled him with a fervor to inflict punishment on her.

He wanted to hurt his mother, too, but he avoided her whenever he could. When his father died of cancer, he blamed her for having made his life miserable. He considered inflicting punishment on her then, but he held off in a way he couldn't explain. He rationalized that a single act would be too transitory and wouldn't satisfy his smoldering rage. Were there cultural mores that stood between him and such an act? Was killing the woman who carried him for nine months a bridge too far?

Zero was certain that inflicting pain and death on many women was the only way to assuage the burning, acidic hate he carried. He felt a compulsion to discover what brought him here. His mother was controlling. She was a Christian woman who used her religion like a battering ram to silence dissent at home, but all Zero saw was her hypocrisy.

He and his dad enjoyed fishing. For a time, after church on Sunday, they grabbed the small military-green skiff with its 15-horsepower outboard and went fishing for bluegills, bass, crappie, and catfish. They always went to the same cove, a quiet calm place hidden from speedboats and water skiers. The secret was to entice the bass from the reeds with one's favorite lure vibrating slowly past without tangling it in the same reeds. The island of tranquility was the only peace in Zero's young life.

It was short-lived. Phoebe decided Sunday must be exclusively for adoring God. She couldn't stand seeing Drake and her son sharing something that didn't include her. Zero felt his mother couldn't tolerate seeing them happy, even for a brief interlude. Certainly his father, a devout Christian, felt worship was important, but he disagreed with Phoebe's rigidity.

Phoebe prevailed. Zero had his own thoughts. Did God think that robbing him and his father of their special time together somehow made the day holier? Sunday services were followed by a church-sponsored group Bible study for youth. Phoebe conducted her self-aggrandizing version of further Bible study and contemplation at home. Zero felt she was the epitome of a self-important Pharisee. The Apostles were fishermen. How big a catch might Zero be missing? Was this augmentation of their daily prayers necessary to love God? Zero wanted to love God as his father did, but over time, Phoebe drove her son further away.

Drake, too, acutely felt the loss of their special time.

"Take him fishing on Saturday," Phoebe said.

"You know my professorship depends on being published. With my classes and class preparation during the week, I have to dedicate Saturday to writing. Full professors are expected to publish," he whined.

"It's not as if you're a *Harvard* professor, you know. No one ever reads *your* books. Who cares about a book from a professor at a Podunk university?"

Either Drake's writing or his shared pastime with his son had to go, which meant no more fishing.

Zero tried to capture the moment when his animosity toward his mother took hold as a permanent facet of his thinking. He would never forget winning first prize in a science competition in sixth grade. He worked very hard on it. His project consisted of building a little car that contained dry ice that emitted gas through a hole at the bottom, which floated the car. There were different surfaces to demonstrate the impact of friction and gravity on inertia. He used sandpaper for one because of its rough surface. Control was perfectly smooth. He had two uphill ramps and one that declined. The impact of each variable on the speed of the car was graphed to illustrate how it affected inertia and how that comported with the laws governing inertia. His graphs and other visuals were done very colorfully, and the entire project had an appealing presentation. He felt very proud of it.

The first thing Phoebe told him was it was a very good effort. "I think, however, that the exploding volcano I saw is more impressive and should have won instead."

He was crushed.

After the science project, Zero was imbued with the determination to continue to disappoint his mother, to create a polarity between them that would express his developing aversion for her and a growing understanding of how his father suffered at her hands.

Drake was considered very bright by his colleagues, but he and Phoebe insisted that Zero was even brighter, and that was probably accurate. Phoebe and Drake heard it from the boy's teachers. Before the scient project, Zero's math teacher recounted how the boy could make mental calculations that would have made Einstein envious. No one who met Zero missed his quick intelligence, but all he heard from his mother were his shortcomings. With his new resolve, that gradually became satisfying.

After the science fair, he allowed his grades to slip.

"You should be valedictorian of your high-school class," Phoebe repeated.

When she spoke to him in that tone, he always focused on the four or five furrowed wrinkles on her brow.

"Instead, you're wasting your talent."

There was never any discussion over what happened or why he had such an abrupt turnabout. There was only perpetual denigration.

One day in open congregation, Zero's pastor asked him a question about Christian doctrine. Zero's answer was wrong and prompted a few chuckles from the congregation. Zero wanted to hide. He felt like crying, but he was too proud. He wanted to run, but Phoebe held his wrist so tightly when he struggled that he felt prickly needles presaging numbness in his fingers. She kept him at her side while she apologized for her son's error, as each parishioner exited service that day. Each apology cut him like a scalpel, a death of a thousand cuts.

When he entered public high school, Phoebe ridiculed Drake for not earning enough to send him to a private Christian school with a $13,000 annual tuition.

Ultimately, he met a girl he liked and asked her to the homecoming dance.

"You didn't ask me before inviting her?" Phoebe demanded. "She's *not* of our religion!"

She forced him, with tears running down his face and his voice breaking with embarrassment, to call the girl and withdraw the invitation.

Phoebe immediately picked up the phone and called a close friend in the congregation.

"Debbie, your daughter is a freshman at North High, isn't she?" Phoebe asked.

"Why, yes."

"Does she have a date for the homecoming dance? My boy would love to take her, if she isn't committed already."

The skinny girl named Pamela wasn't someone Zero would ever have been interested in. That marked the beginning of his withdrawal from encounters with the opposite sex. This evolved into a philosophy of taking control of the relationships his mother denied him. He wasn't sure how yet, but that would evolve, too.

A sense of futility led to withdrawal from everyone but his father. Zero's withdrawal became antipathy, which led to disdain for all things Phoebe. Finally, disdain became hatred.

As he matured, Zero realized he was physically attractive, as women approached him. His social awkwardness, however, almost immediately drove them away. His intellectual superiority was obvious, and he made no effort to conceal it, which also had a chilling effect.

Continuing to mature, Zero learned to be charming, but in his adolescence, girls felt an undefined discomfort with him. Rejection followed rejection, each time building on the hostility he felt toward women, a feeling previously limited to his mother. All women were like Phoebe, incapable of empathy, compassion, or understanding. The women to whom he was most attracted withheld the affection he desperately craved. Later in life, he developed the social skills to be successful in his work. He would never allow a woman to consider him a failure, as Phoebe systematically did to his father.

Phoebe constantly reminded Drake of his homeliness. He was fortunate to have her, given his diminutive stature, baldness, scruffy beard, and lack of professional progress. Phoebe related to herself as someone men desired. She went so far as to believe that extended to the pastor of their church.

Drake was five-foot-eight and hunched over, his self-esteem barely an inch off the floor, which Phoebe constantly reinforced. His social ineptness made him incapable of the political maneuvering that could lead to a department chairmanship.

Phoebe was in the habit of apologizing to Drake for wearing high heels that made him look shorter than he was, but she still wore them.

Without heels, Phoebe was five-foot-six, had an attractive figure, was well-endowed, and had a pleasant face. An objective view would have added she wasn't aging well.

When logic failed her, Phoebe reminded Drake that he better appreciate what he had, as no other woman would want him. Her conviction that this was true provided her with the leverage to impose her will on him. When they argued, she often threatened him with separation or divorce. Drake, certain she was right about his lack of attractiveness, felt trapped. More than anything, he feared separation from his son, since most women were given custody of minor children, and isolation from what he perceived as his family. The thought was devastating.

Zero's parents never tried to shield him from their arguments. It was as if he were a piece of furniture. He heard his mother diminish

Drake. His father always resisted for a time, then he crawled back into his shell.

Zero, feeling his father's anguish, saw his tortured soul. Zero's hatred for his mother took concrete form, and he began viewing all women through that lens.

When Drake became ill with cancer, he was in incomprehensible pain. His colon cancer metastasized throughout his body and even into his bones. Phoebe refused nursing assistance, not just to impose her controlling ways but out of sheer meanness and spite. She got a hospital bed for him through hospice. When the pain became unbearable, he held the bed's side rails until his knuckle were white. Soon, he begged for a shot of morphine.

Zero couldn't believe his father could sweat so profusely. When the pain was at its worst, perspiration rained from his outstretched palm.

Phoebe became his caretaker to save money, rather than using affordable hospice care. Every aspect of Drake's remaining existence fell under her purview. Why not? It was *her* family. Often, she withheld his pain medication, telling him it was too expensive, and he needed to show strength as an example for his son.

At twenty years of age, Zero decided to give his father an injection that Phoebe withheld. As the morphine coursed through Drake's body, Zero felt he finally became a man, because he defied his mother and helped his father. The unintended consequence was that Phoebe withheld medication more frequently, causing Drake to suffer unimaginably.

When Zero couldn't stand watching it anymore, he accepted a job in retail sales and moved out. Just before Drake's death, he helped his son get a better job through a friend who pitied them. Shortly afterward, Drake passed away. Zero saw in his father a man who loved his son, was at al times gentle and well-meaning, and, most of all, long-suffering at his wife's hands.

Phoebe used Drake's wake as another opportunity to put him and her son on display, pointing out their inadequacies at every opportunity.

"Drake was so brilliant. It's too bad he was so socially inept that it never led him anywhere," she told anyone who would listen at the wake. "He never did make department chair," she added with an exaggerated sigh.

"You know our son," she said. "I'm afraid the apple hasn't fallen far from the tree."

Zero, thinking back to that moment, decided to strike back at his mother by proxy with every arrogant, attractive woman who denigrated or rejected him.

CHAPTER FIVE

Jack Garvey thought he wanted to be a lawyer. He had a Bachelor's from Northern Illinois University, but he didn't want to pursue advanced degrees in psychology. He couldn't see himself listening to poorly adjusted, chronically depressed people sobbing on a couch. That would be too depressing.

Instead, he imagined himself conducting withering cross-examinations and delivering brilliantly conceived final arguments that would win the day for his clients. While attending law school at the University of San Francisco, he landed a plum job working as a law clerk for a renowned criminal defense appellate attorney. Jack quickly learned that criminal defense buried attorneys in an infinite amount of computer research. They had to find applicable precedents, attend forensics seminars, fashion motions alleging error by a judge admitting evidence that should have been excluded at trial, and pointing out evidence that wasn't admitted that should have been. Criminal defense attorneys looked for tactics like ineffective assistance of counsel where it was alleged the defendant hadn't received adequate representation or pointed out errors in jury instructions that were given or excluded. The research was endless.

There were two distinct parts to the appellate process. The appeal tried to identify errors within the transcript of the trial. The other part was the *habeas corpus*, which translated as "to have the body." The penal system had no right to continue to incarcerate someone if an error occurred outside the conduct of the trial.

That meant the defendant would either be released, or, more commonly held but granted a new trial. If it was a death-penalty case, the error could be at the "guilt phase," determining the defendant's guilt, or at the "penalty phase," if he or she was sentenced to death. In a *habeas corpus,* that could mean there was juror misconduct, such as discussing the trial before it was given to the jury, or introducing evidence from an extraneous source not presented at trial.

Bill Oppenheimer, the attorney Jack worked for, was in a bind. His normal PI, in the hospital undergoing an appendectomy, couldn't take care of a crucial, time-sensitive witness interview for the *habeas* as it was referred to. Recognizing Jack's agile mind, Bill approached him.

"Would you be interested in conducting the interview in San Quentin?"

"Sure."

Oppenheimer spent significant time preparing Jack, filling him in on the case and the relevance of that particular witness.

Jack fell back on what he gleaned from his psychology background—how to put people at ease, how to focus on the interviewee and not the interview, how to draw the person out. The result surprised Bill with its comprehensiveness, and, most importantly, the relevant information it developed. It was beyond anything Bill expected from an untested clerk.

Oppenheimer continued using Jack for investigative work, and Jack loved it. He found his niche.

CHAPTER SIX

Zero was what many women called a "hunk." At six-foot-two, he had an admirable physique he assiduously maintained without the body-builder overkill. His dark-brown hair was neat and businesslike. His carefully trimmed mustache, reminding some of Clark Gable, gave him an air of intrigue. He had an enviably attractive square jaw and an inviting smile, making him approachable. He had no trouble encountering interested women. His countenance and suave mannerisms, cultivated since high school, gave him the ability to attract women with a skill most men would envy.

He viewed it differently. Each woman was a predator. They all perused a room, classifying all available males, dismissing most and casually moseying toward their first victim. Since most men made consummate asses of themselves fawning over a beautiful woman, it sometimes took awhile to find the one she would invite to her bed for the night.

His first foray in the glorious and much-anticipated ceremony had to be not only perfect in execution but also symbolically unassailable. She had to be *the* most-beautiful, most-desirable woman, the one every man in the room wanted to seduce, so her destruction would engender sympathetic commentary.

"She was so young and had so much to live for!"

It would be ceremonial in the sense of a religious rite. While he never bought into religion, he wanted to inject a sense of solemnity into it, making it a momentous occasion.

He met Number 1 at John Barleycorn's, a restaurant and pub near her place. She was tall and slender, with lustrous black hair and a pronounced arrogance that communicated superiority.

John Barleycorn's, an informal place on the near north side of Chicago known as "North Town," was frequented by college students and young professionals. That was where he got his first glimpse of Number 1. She wore skin-tight jeans with the compulsory threaded holes, accenting every curve and line on legs that never seemed to end.

After taking in her legs, he raised his gaze to take in her entire torso. Her pert, moderately sized, braless breasts, enticed with pronounced nipples through a white, silky, alluring blouse. She returned his gaze in a way that said, *Here I am. Come and take me, if you're worthy.*

Zero let her cover the distance between them. He and Karen exchanged pleasantries. Zero scrupulously sidestepped the innocuous BS beautiful women were accustomed to hearing. Using creative lingo and practiced humor, with calculated aloofness that tempted Karen, he chatted with her. She eventually invited him to her flat just around the corner. Zero begged off, referencing a report due the next day at work.

"I just stopped in here briefly for a couple drinks," he explained. "After I unwind, I need to delve back into my portfolio."

He understood what he withheld at first would make her more determined in her conquest.

Such women were accustomed to winning. With her appetite whetted, Zero wangled an invitation to dinner a week later with one stipulation. He insisted it be an uninterrupted evening—no phone calls, friends, or business -- just them. He tactfully suggested it would be to honor their privacy on their special night.

Just what made it special, he didn't say. That week gave him time to prepare.

CHAPTER SEVEN

Along with numerous law firms interviewing the best and brightest of the USF law school class who passed the bar was the FBI. With his interest in investigation, it was the only interview he wanted. The FBI conducted exhaustive background checks before giving applicants the opportunity to test their mettle and become a Special Agent.

There was an interminable series of interviews, not just with Jack but with his classmates at Northern, USF, and even high school, plus a criminal background check, polygraphs, tests, and more. The most-competitive candidates had an advanced degree like Jack's Juris Doctor and perhaps some social science discipline like his psychology degree. The FBI merely preferred three years of related experience. That's where Jack's *habeas corpus* background with Oppenheimer came to his rescue.

As Churchill said, that wasn't even, "The beginning of the end, but the end of the beginning."

Initial training lasted forty weeks, the first twenty of which were in dorms at Quantico, Virginia, where the FBI had numerous and diverse facilities for training. The different functions and specialties ranged from foreign intelligence and terrorism to their largest forensic laboratory.

With a background similar to Jack's, the ultimate hires would most certainly be successful. Only five percent of those who began training at Quantico were accepted as Special Agents. Jack Garvey was among those.

The training was more rigorous than he ever imagined, even realizing it would be comprehensive. He thought law school was tough, and it was particularly difficult to stay focused and finished when he realized lawyering wasn't for him. The same stubborn determination to complete what he started carried him through. Going from law school to Quantico was like piling exhaustion upon exhaustion, but the prize was better than a Superbowl ring. He wanted to get into the Behavioral Analysis Unit as a profiler. That was the stuff of movies, functionally existing within the Bureau, as the FBI was called by its agents.

The BAU, highly sought after, generally took eight to ten years. Jack's extraordinary perception, hard work, and occasional lucky break accomplished it in three, the earliest a Special Agent could achieve such an assignment. The progression within the Bureau was from Special Agent to Supervising Special Agent to Managing Special Agent to Executive Special Agent, ultimately reaching Assistant Deputy or Deputy Director, highly politicized positions. Jack didn't want that. He had to keep his hand in the field in some capacity. Jack's rank was Supervising Special Agent, and he enjoyed that just fine.

The concept of profiling was spearheaded by the famous John Douglas, the seminal advocate for profiling as a tool, particularly for identifying behavioral consistencies among serial murderers and terrorists. Jack read several of Douglas' books after he retired from the Bureau. One in particular, *The Killer Across the Table*, focused on psychological and pathological information developed from interviews with famous murderers that aided in future profiling. Jack was certain that was his direction. Attaining it at the age of twenty-nine was a miracle.

That was seven years earlier, and Jack became highly regarded in the BAU. His work in the unit was well thought of. He participated in gathering evidence and developing a profile that led to the identification of Leonard Albright, an abhorrent kidnapper/serial rapist and murderer of young boys. Jack reveled in the thought that, if he never made another contribution as an agent, the part he played, along with many other agents and local law enforcement officers in the Albright case, justified his career choice and the commitment that came with it.

When Albright was captured, Jack saw a scrawny, bearded, disheveled street dweller similar to those found in the country's crumbling metropolises—a regular Charles Manson. He also saw evil. Did he see evil in the man because he knew of his heinous acts or because Jack had a mystical ability to sense the devil?

Jack's sense of satisfaction with his contribution to the case didn't mean his dedication waned. As he learned more through ongoing training, especially in experience and judgment, Jack realized his abilities and potential impact were incrementally broadened, and he had definite plans to put those assets to work.

CHAPTER EIGHT

Zero knew to commit a series of murders without being caught, every detail had to be anticipated and viewed under a proverbial microscope.

The first thing he studied was why most serial murderers were caught, and he compiled a list.

1. They had a prior criminal history, so he (virtually all serial killers were men) would be looked at earlier and with greater suspicion. Zero had no such encumbrance.
2. The *modus operandi*, or MO. Ted Bundy, for instance, frequently feigned an injury to gain the sympathy of his prospective victims. Albert DeSalvo, the Boston Strangler, wore work coveralls and pretended to be a plumber or from the gas company to gain entrance, then he strangled his female victims, afterward mimicking the painful physical therapy he did daily on his handicapped son. Zero would plan each murder with a different MO, so they would be impossible to connect.
3. The killer lived in or operated in a specific geographical area where law enforcement could focus its efforts and utilize the press to disseminate information to the public when appropriate. The Green River Killer, Gary Ridgway, who was suspected of killing a total of seventy-one victims, was one of those. Not only did it protect the public when information could be released, but it could also invoke a response that could potentially identify him.

Zero would commit each murder with its unique MO in a different locality.

4. The predator often chose a specific kind of victim. Ted Bundy was attracted to college co-eds. Ridgway chose prostitutes. Once police realized the Green River Killer was selecting only prostitutes, their efforts could be concentrated on venues where they recruited their johns. That wouldn't be the case with Zero.

5. Forensic evidence could be connected to the killer. The principle method involved DNA, but hair, fibers, shoeprints, fingerprints, tire tracks, and many other items were routinely left behind by even careful perpetrators due to a lack of knowledge of forensics on a practical level, by carelessness, or often panic. Zero wasn't one to panic, and he studied forensics thoroughly.

6. Many times, after successfully evading authorities, a sense of invincibility overtook the killer, generating error. In others, there was complacency or a desire to be caught or stopped. Zero felt contempt for his contemplated victims. There was no possibility he would allow complacency or narcissism to be his downfall.

As he planned for Number 1, he reviewed his preparations. He sufficiently emphasized his absolute need for privacy, ostensibly to deliver the perfect love-making experience. It would be a perfect scenario. He bought a two-person tent, connected by a two-foot tunnel. That was ideal for keeping his victim in one room, and the tools of his trade and items he wished to use in the other, thus isolating forensic evidence. Shoe size could be conveyed by carpet impressions, but he had a solution for that.

The floor of his ceremonial room of the tent was sprayed with liquid rubber, sealing it and preventing any seepage of evidence that might be found in carpet fibers underneath.

He was ready to lose his virginity in an unequaled eruption of sensations. True, it would include sexual climax, but it would be the uninitiated celebration of the taking of the most-precious thing his targeted female had—not her life, although he would take that, too, but her dignity.

CHAPTER NINE

The day of Zero's coronation arrived. *Coronation* was the only word that worked for him. Many entertainers were coronated by public acclaim: Elvis Presley, the king of Rock and Roll; Patsy Kline, the queen of Country; James Brown and Aretha Franklin, the king and queen of Soul.

Zero, however, would be self-acclaimed. He had a plan to celebrate his accomplishments publicly yet anonymously. He would be the emperor of serial murder.

Number 1's alias was Karen, who would instantly be the most intriguing, most-sought-after, most-desired woman in any room she entered. Her lustrous hair fell sleekly down her back, four inches past her erect shoulders. It was as black as a moonless, starless sky. Her face had the oft-idealized high cheekbones synonymous with glamour.

At five-ten, taller when augmented by spiked heels, Karen had the longest, most-voluptuous legs Zero ever saw. Contemplating her braless breasts that she shamelessly displayed to the lascivious men at John Barleycorn's, including those not-so-furtively elbowed by their spouses, immediately aroused him. That was how he encountered her the week before.

Karen sized him up, too. She imagined him as a Chippendale, one of the legendary male strippers that past-prime, middle-aged women went to see and drool over, usually after a divorce or an active sex life had passed from their marriage. Young women could still marvel at the sex appeal of handsome men who could have inspired Michelangelo's David, although with a much-larger penis.

Zero was a devotee of motion pictures, especially older films. Karen reminded him of Hedy Lamar, the Delilah to Victor Mature's Sampson, voluptuously directed by Cecil B DeMille as the biblical temptress in 1949. The unfortunate cinema ignoramuses among modern society would have to Google her to encounter Lamar's incomparable beauty. Karen was the Number 1 he was looking for and would be his twenty-first birthday present to himself.

When he met her at John Barleycorn, there was an instant connection. Not only was he physically attractive, but he used his simmering hatred for women like her to imbue himself with a disingenuous charm that he cultivated to hide his natural inclinations. Somehow, offering to slice her to pieces seemed like a tactic with little prospect of success.

For instance, he hated his mother, but he could manipulate her to do what he wanted despite the many disappointments she expressed about him. Recognizing his seemingly dormant intelligence, she had high expectations for Zero. His academic accomplishments were lacking, his job more suited to someone of a lesser station in life. Still, he could get her to cosign for a car he wanted.

After working on it, he found he could easily manipulate others, too. He could get better grades than he deserved, especially with female instructors. He was able to obtain employment even when his qualifications were sketchy or nonexistent. Always, there was an underlying motivation. When there was nothing he desired from a person, he found it difficult or impossible to extend himself or even be cordial. Then he appeared detached, ambivalent, or even hostile.

He wanted something from Karen, his Number 1. He adopted an easygoing, receptive personality, focused on listening, flattering, and availability. Karen invited him to spend the night of their first encounter after only two drinks' worth of conversation and one dance. He cultivated her interest. Most people wanted what it seemed they couldn't have. If one had curly hair, one wanted it straight or vice versa. If one were short, he wanted to be tall.

Zero used that in two ways. His inaccessibility on the first night made her want him all the more. To implement his plan, he needed time to prepare.

He also had to itemize all the paraphernalia he would need for his scheme. He explained he was leaving on a camping trip with friends the morning after their rapturous night together and consequently would have a lot of gear with him when he arrived. He explained that returning to his loft to get the gear would delay his departure for the trip.

Karen readily agreed.

CHAPTER TEN

"Wow," Karen exclaimed. "You weren't kidding about bringing a lot of gear with you. Well, come in. I'll find someplace to stow your stuff," she said after a brief, inviting kiss.

Zero set his things in a niche in the hallway of her comfortable-looking condo. It was furnished with trendy, modernistic, mismatched furniture that communicated that she was successful, if esthetically challenged, a professional who had arrived.

Zero glanced at the apartment. Like many of the currently in-vogue condos, it had a fashionable great room. The spacious room contained a bar that separated a modern appliance kitchen from comfortable furniture, strategically placed to avoid creating habit trails. What segregation existed came from a demarcation between hardwood floors near the kitchen and bar and the larger area of plush carpeting flanked by a fireplace complete with a large, protective, dingy bronze-colored screen. That was where he would plant their little honeymoon suite.

"How about a cocktail to get things started?" Zero mused.

"What suits your fancy?" she asked, turning toward the bar and displaying her back to him.

Grabbing her in a choke hold, he quickly rendered her unconscious. He learned it while obtaining his varsity letter in high-school wrestling, although it was illegal to use in competition.

Karen would recover quickly, so he moved expeditiously. It took just a moment to observe every magnificent curve of her limp body. She was a work of art, a masterpiece.

He wrapped her hands behind her back with duct tape, placing a Ping Pong ball in her mouth and taping it closed. She would be incapable of anything more than a muffled scream, inaudible to neighbors, although Zero would hear and enjoy it.

Quickly opening his large duffle bag, he removed the two-room popup tent. After donning latex gloves, he moved furniture away from the center of the room. The tent popped into position in seconds, by which time Number 1 was regaining consciousness. The enclosure he prepared with sprayable rubber was on the left. Before she was fully awake, he stuffed her into that end of the tent.

Once she was fully aware of her circumstances, he cut into her clothing with scissors, so he could roughly rip the clothes off, leaving only remnants behind and a halo of fabric around her. Naturally, the slut wore no bra, just like at Barleycorn's.

Zero sought to reassure her, although he was confident of the outcome. "Don't worry, Karen. After I rape you, I won't kill you, not unless you ask me to."

He already taped her legs spread-eagled to the rubberized tent floor with several pieces of Gorilla tape that was amazingly adhesive. He applied multiple pieces of tape across her shoulders. She couldn't roll or writhe in a way that would create a disturbance for nearby tenants or in the condo below. With her wrists taped under her body, Karen couldn't resist.

Donning two additional pairs of latex gloves over the pair he already wore, took one of several plastic bowls from the duffel bag, and filled it with bleach. Concerned that fibers might have attached themselves to Karen's neck while he choked her, he entered the space where he lay and looked for evidence, washing any away with bleach. Karen reacted with muted protests. Zero smiled like an attending angel, enjoying her obvious terror.

Next, he entered the second room of the tent and removed his clothing until he was completely naked. He placed his clothes neatly into a sealable plastic bag, so no trace evidence could attach itself to his clothing. He would dispose of the clothes later.

He reentered Karen's space. He wouldn't diminish the sexual experience by wearing a condom, but he also didn't want to leave any DNA behind. He was prepared for that.

Anticipation made him erect. He entered her and came almost instantly, over her nearly inaudible protests.

"How was that?" he asked, taunting her. "I'll do better the next time."

After he satiated himself two more times, it was time to eliminate his DNA.

He previously dragged his duffel bag into the second compartment, so he could easily access the articles he had so painstakingly prepared via the two-foot tunnel. Reaching through the tunnel, he grabbed an electric drill with a one-and-a-half-inch-diameter wire-bristled router.

"I'm sure you understand that I can't leave my semen behind in any detectable form." He imagined her impending death was akin to cleansing the world of a parasite, similar to Phoebe. The rape was merely a bonus, like the gold Nazis took from Jewish teeth. Death was the goal.

He inserted the battery-powered electric drill with its metallic bristle-equipped attachment into her vagina and began routing it out, spraying blood over her creamy white, supple thighs and the rubberized tent floor. Her predictable reaction was very satisfying. Her intense screams, faintly heard only by him, elicited a smile from Zero that, in detached isolation, could have been perceived as benevolent, like a photograph devoid of any background.

When he finished with the drill, he returned to the bowl of bleach, suctioned the bleach into a one-inch-diameter, eight-inch syringe, and injected the bleach rhythmically into her vagina, mixing the bleach with her blood and his semen. He stroked the syringe into her almost as if making love, leaving toxic bleach in place of semen, then he suctioned the remaining gelatinous liquid back into the horse-sized syringe. He deposited the love juice into another of his plastic bowls.

The absolute exhilaration he felt exceeded his expectations. He anticipated he wouldn't indulge in sodomy, but he changed his mind.

"I promised you I wouldn't kill you unless you asked me to," he said. "Do you want me to kill you?"

She shook her head.

"Well, let me recover for a bit, then. When I have, I'll sodomize you. I had no idea I had such endurance. You were hoping for that, weren't you? I hate to state the obvious, but that'll necessitate another cleaning operation. Can you imagine what that high-speed drill will feel like in your butthole, your anus, your ass, Bitch?"

His repeated nouns made her contemplate the next experience.

"I'll expect you'll say no again, proving you're just a stupid cunt, or will you?"

Her eyes went wide in all-encompassing panic. Still, she clung to the hope of some miraculous rescue. Tears streamed down her face. She recognized on some level the futility of further resistance. Still, she clung to the hope that somehow, some way, she could avoid what Zero was intent on doing.

After a brief interlude, Zero sodomized her as promised and returned to his drill, bleach, and syringe.

"Did you know I was a virgin?" he asked. "I never raped or sodomized anyone before," he added in obvious pride. "I'm quite sure you imagined yourself very good at lovemaking. I'm certain you're correct. It was a nice birthday present for me."

Tears streamed down her face. Her eyes pleaded with him. Realizing he would continue to inflict unbearable pain until she capitulated, she began nodding vigorously when he asked if she wanted him to end her life.

"Are you asking me to end your suffering?" he asked, feigning incredulity.

Karen confirmed it.

"Well, all right, then. Of course, I still need to complete my cleaning operation." The drill began to whir, and she fainted, only to be revived by Zero.

Strangulation was the death he decided to impose on Karen. The police would be able to determine the cause of death, but they wouldn't find any fingerprints or palm prints even if they used super-glue, a trick occasionally used when other techniques failed. Three layers of latex gloves would foil the advanced forensic method known as DNA touch technology. Strangulation would also help establish a misleading MO for the killer.

Placing his hands around her neck, he squeezed, gradually increasing pressure until she lost consciousness. Sometime later, she woke, surprised to be alive and still in pain from her horrible ordeal.

He smiled widely, as she returned slowly to complete awareness. He repeated the technique several times until he became bored with her renewed terror and finally increased pressure until he finished her.

CHAPTER ELEVEN

Karen's apartment was built during a construction boom in Chicago in 1910 in a popular red brick until it was renovated as part of an urban-renewal initiative. Formerly, it held four apartments, one on each floor, but it had been renovated once previously. Originally at street level, which rose over time, the first-floor apartment became a garden apartment with steps leading down a half-story. Part of the lower floor encompassed the HVAC systems and janitorial storage. The other three levels had huge apartments with multiple bedrooms and bathrooms but were remodeled and contained two reasonably spacious apartments on the second and third floors. The fourth floor accommodated a single apartment suited to someone with bohemian proclivities due to the constraints from the gabled roof.

Part of the renovation included new security systems. It was moderately priced for the New Town area, which meant it was expensive. The New Town lifestyle appealed to youth and the artistically inclined, as well as hangers-on from earlier times. It was akin to New York's Greenwich Village, for Chicagoans with a bohemian bent.

Karen's apartment was on the third floor. The security system's modernization meant the cameras on the second and third floors had wiring that hung loose, unconnected. Zero had already cased the building and was delighted at the electrical contractor's procrastination. Absent that, he would have chosen a different target, not his perfect Karen.

His objective was to do the cleanup that would ensure no forensic or other evidence was left behind that could potentially implicate him. Several bowls of various sizes nested together. He filled each with water from bottles he carried in his tent pack for cleanup. That would avoid his having to use tap water, which offered several hazards for retaining forensic evidence, such as spills from repeated trips to the source. Zero placed the largest bowl in the right-side compartment, which he retrieved to bathe himself thoroughly, leaving every potential trace of blood and forensic evidence in the rubberized left side. He searched for any sign of blood or other indicia inadvertently carried outside the tent.

While there was blood from his routing operation with the electric drill, most came from using a machete honed to razor sharpness. He cut through blood and bone like butter, minimizing blood splatter. Chopping her body into manageable pieces allowed him to roll up the tent, retaining all the tools he used in his ceremony. The blood soup that remained was returned to small, manageable bottles through a funnel, saving time and preventing the police from recouping it from a toilet or bathtub or drain, as a less-intelligent perpetrator would certainly have done.

The only two problems he foresaw were the extensive quantity of liquids, primarily bleach, blood, and water. He couldn't roll them up in the tent when he was ready to depart. Second was the potential to leave impressions on the carpet that might identify his shoe or foot size, but he was prepared for that, too.

He had two large, foot-square tiles with straps attached, which he tied to his shoes that would leave diamond-shaped impressions behind. He took the bottles of water and bleach, which would have been too heavy to carry upon his exit, and poured them into the dirt in the several planters just outside the windows of Karen's apartment. He knew about them from his earlier surveys of the building. Even sharp forensics specialists wouldn't start digging in the dirt. If they did, it would be impossible to recover anything. If the liquid killed the plants, the evidence would be so degraded it would never be of use to the police.

He disassembled the two-compartment tent, rolling it up with his tools and Karen's body parts enclosed, protected from seepage and the potential deposit of forensic evidence by the rubber coating. He stuffed it back into his oversized duffel bag, which had originally been designed to contain an artificial Christmas tree, which he tossed out.

Zero placed the bag near the apartment entrance. He used Karen's vacuum to remove any potential remaining evidence and shoe impressions from when he initially entered the apartment, then he emptied the contents into his duffel bag, assuring nothing was spilled.

After washing the plastic container that contained all the vacuumed particles and once again emptying the contents into his bag, he walked toward the door. Looking through the convex peephole, he saw no one on that early weekend morning, so he set the duffel bag in the hallway before stepping out and removing the tiles from his shoes. He dropped those into the bag and zipped it shut. When crime-scene detectives began scurrying up and down the stairs to the third floor, his own imprints would be erased.

Zero went directly to a prearranged dumping site, removing only the body parts with his latex-covered hands. He carefully raked his tracks with branches from the scene as he left, knowing that the body parts would eventually be found by hikers. It was important to his plans that they be found.

Going to a lake some distance away, he tied the duffle bag and its evidence to the vacant rowboat he placed there. He rowed to the deepest part of the lake, used a battery-powered drill to puncture the hull, and then swam back to the shore in the dark to make his triumphant exodus to his vehicle. Tracks recovered from that area would have no connection to Karen's remains miles away.

Zero's career had begun.

CHAPTER TWELVE

Several days after his exhilarating ritual, from a large city far removed from the site of his triumph, Zero posted an envelope addressed to the FBI in Quantico. When opened it would reveal a very common generic decal in red to signify the blood of his victim still attached to its original backing. On it was the number 1 and nothing more—not yet.

CHAPTER THIRTEEN

Mike Hennessey, Jack Garvey's Managing Special Agent, was "aces" in Jack's book. He couldn't have asked for a better or more-knowledgeable mentor. Jack was assigned to him when he reported to the BAU seven years earlier. After ten years with the Bureau, Jack distinguished himself as an agent with out-of-the-ordinary skill sets, and his promotion to Supervisory Special Agent was accomplished in the minimum allowed time, an auspiciously rare occurrence.

Jack came to know Mike very well. Mike was a man who was truly dedicated to serving his country in a way that could save lives or at the least deter additional loss of life if there was no other alternative. The FBI was committed to the concepts of obedience to orders and abiding by procedure. Jack was taught that the rules agents lived by were developed through experience and validated repeatedly in practice.

Few agents, if any, were as rigidly determined to adhere to the book as Mike. Once he became a Managing Special Agent, he doubled down. Mike felt the Bureau's policies protected his men and women and conformed the agents' behavior to bring about more-predictable outcomes.

While his approach to his job was inflexible, Mike was much more pliable. People were very important to him. If an agent was going through a divorce, experiencing serious illness with a close family member, or involved in a shooting or in other ways off balance in his work or personal life, Mike was there for him.

He could have a drink with someone off duty and discuss things in a sincere, empathetic way. He could wait with one of his agents at a hospital, when work allowed, when the man's wife was in labor or during a loved one's terminal illness. In short, Mike was there for all his people all the time when circumstances permitted. To a person, especially to Jack Garvey, Mike was loved and his agents respected his other love affair, the one with the book and the Bureau.

Mike's only other love was for his wife, Deidre, and their two children, a boy and a girl. The boy was away at college, and his daughter, Grace, was a leading high-school cross-country star in Virginia. He made every meet he could, but only Deidre could attend every competition. He accepted that it came with his job, but he hated the trade-off even though he loved the job.

One day, Mike suddenly appeared in the door to Jack's office, and Jack knew something was up. Mike filled the door like few people. Jack's five-foot-ten stature was dwarfed by the six-foot-four, 250-pound former linebacker. His thinning, reddish-blond hair made him look like a younger, larger Jack Nicklaus. When his patience was tested, the first indication was the large jaw muscles inflating like balloons filled with helium. When he looked like that, everyone knew they didn't want to meet Mike Hennessey in a dark alley.

"Jack, I know you're working on some things," Mike said, "but I'm reassigning those projects to other agents. I have something out of the ordinary, and I think you're the best person to figure this one out."

He closed the door and sat opposite Jack. "I've left instructions to hold all calls. This will take awhile."

The two men regarded each other intently, Mike taking one of the only two visitor chairs in the room. Jack always felt his office was depressing, covered by slate-gray paint and mitigated only by a print of Renoir's *Luncheon of the Boating People,* Jack's favorite Impressionist painting. It did little to improve the space, but he enjoyed it, however out of place it seemed in his cubbyhole.

Jack didn't like leaving tasks unfinished and was tempted to object to the change, but Mike had already taken action, so it was a moot point. He knew Mike well enough to know that was unusual, so Jack was interested.

Because it was so out of the ordinary to have Supervisory Special Agents' work interrupted so abruptly, Jack simply said, "Shoot."

"For some time now, we've been receiving mail from a variety of locations throughout the eastern U.S. The first few didn't get much attention, because the envelopes included no notes or anything that could be linked to a specific crime. The envelopes are printed with our Quantico address, but each one in common, although diverse, stationery envelopes. They're widely distributed by a variety of vendors and are virtually untraceable to the point of origin.

"Each envelope's address was printed on a different computer each time. One was a laser jet. Another was an ink jet. The others came from different printers, all with similar fonts but definitely different machines. The various mailings had as little in common as possible to make them impossible to trace, although we might have expected that."

"You know, sometimes I can be impatient, Mike. What the hell was in the envelopes?"

"A number, from one through sixty-six, *in order.* Each was a decal, a very common type you can find in any Wal-Mart, Target, or craft store. They're impossible to track without a location of origin, probably impossible even if we knew it.

"Of course, we tried to correlate the dates the envelopes arrived with, particularly, murders, since the inference is that there's a possible serial out there. No correlation was found. Similarly, an attempt to correlate the locations from which the numbers were mailed also failed.

"The only thing we have going for us is that virtually all were mailed from the eastern part of the country."

"There must be something more," Jack said, his face showing his confusion, which changed to astonishment.

"No, Jack."

"So what you're saying, Mike, and let me thank you for this in advance, is that you have a non-case. You have no crimes, no location for a crime other than the postmark on the envelope, which appears to be intended to mislead, and no date for a crime. There's no hard evidence except that something may have happened to someone, somewhere, and it was probably in the east, right?"

"Yes. Don't feign indignation. This is exactly your kind of puzzle." Mike grinned.

Jack wouldn't have admitted it at the time, but he was intrigued.

CHAPTER FOURTEEN

"Well, that's intriguing, all right," Jack said with a trace of sarcasm. "It should be a proverbial needle in a haystack. The problem here is, we don't even know where the damn haystacks are! How long have you been getting these numbers? If we're dealing with a repeating offender, sixty-six is a big number. Also, what's the history of our efforts so far? What kind of support can I look forward to?"

Although Jack loved a challenge, he was already asking himself if they needed an investigator or a clairvoyant.

"You're just full of questions," Mike said. "Rightly so. We've been getting these envelopes every couple of months for about ten years."

"Ten years? Are you fucking kidding me? That's as long as I've been with the Bureau!"

"There goes that goddamn self-righteous bent of yours. It's the one thing about you that pisses me off. The envelopes, because we really didn't have anything substantive to go on, were initially treated as a training challenge for new recruits. You know the kind of thing—we test their creativity to see if anyone comes up with an idea that might lead somewhere. When the number hit ten, though, it started getting increasingly serious attention.

"The project was assigned to a couple of special agents, who began by looking at some of the correlations you and I discussed. The agents' names are in the file on your desk. With those kinds of numbers, if indeed there is a serial criminal—we can't assume they would be homicides—maybe someone was counting bank robberies."

41

"Come on, Mike. You know this doesn't smell like anything other than serial murder or an unusually dedicated hoaxster. I don't think either of us believes that. The pathology is all wrong for any other kind of crime."

"Of course, I agree, but that ground had to be covered. Usually, we study the concentration of murders in a geo area, but we can't find a pattern. The same thing for a particular MO. That's perhaps the most-puzzling thing. These guys almost always have a consistent routine, a way of going about their business. Most often, it revolves around a specific way of getting their rocks off. We couldn't identify multiple murders that could be characterized that way for grouping.

"No matter which way we looked at it, we came up empty. That's why you're on it."

"Give me a break, will ya? You know as well as I do that every Special Agent is good at what he or she does. You're counting on my being luckier than they were."

"If I didn't know you better, I'd say you were fishing for compliments," Hennessey chided. "There are a couple of differences, Jack. We all go about investigation in a very methodical and planned way that reflects the experience of the Bureau. Like most things, you take methodology to an extreme. That can be good or bad. It can pay off, or it can get in the way. You can get bogged down chasing loose ends that lead nowhere. You've been exceptionally productive, but you know you've chased down bad leads into some rabbit holes."

"Yeah, OK. And?" Jack felt impatient again.

"You have one other attribute that makes you the right man to chase this one down. You're the most-tenacious agent I ever saw. You take it as a personal affront if things don't go your way. You refuse to let go. That's what this one is all about. The other guys who tackled this said they reached a dead end. When you do, you just tunnel under it."

"And the support, Mike?"

"Yeah, well, we've had to reassign your other cases and the agents attached to them. That limits our resources. All we can offer you are a couple rookies, brand-new agents. Their names are Cheryl Hancock and Roy, believe it or not, Rogers."

"*Roy Rogers?* You're friggin' kidding me!"

They shared a belly laugh. When Mike laughed, the pictures on the wall vibrated.

"You think the kid even knows his namesake? It's probably a childhood fantasy for the guy's dad," Jack said. "I hope he doesn't turn out to be a hockey puck."

"Actually, I'm doing the best I can for you. They each completed their first forty weeks of training at the top of their class. They're the two best from the latest crop. Their personnel files are included in the material I gave you. That's what you have to work with. They're about as different as Mutt and Jeff. Their backgrounds, approaches to problems, and ways of thinking couldn't be more different, so I think the combination will work out well for you.

"I've taken the liberty of scheduling a meeting for you tomorrow morning at eight AM. You can review their files tonight and get acquainted with them then. Once you get started on this, you're not going to get much rest. The Bureau always says you're on call 24/7. Figure working Monday through Saturday until we get a handle on this. This might be a long haul, so you'll want one day to rest. I don't want you thinking I'm getting soft, though.

"My guess is, if we're really after a serial, he's shooting to eclipse Ridgway's seventy-one believed victims, or maybe Sam Little's claimed ninety-three. We can't ignore that the perp is sending us numbers. Those numbers are leading up to something, and since we both know this is most consistent with a serial, I can't think it's going anywhere else.

"Anyone who kills that many enjoys it," Mike said. "I don't want him to make either one of those numbers, Jack."

Mike thought for a moment. "I also want to take a little time to fill you in on the two agents I selected for you. Since they're both right out of training, they don't even come close to having the three-year minimum to be an official BAU Special Agent. This will be unofficial support and should be kept under wraps to avoid embarrassment. You know my Executive Special Agent, George Walker. He understands we have to do something, as the qualified agents you've been working with have to stay with those cases.

"However, you also know that George tends to be a bit stubborn. He thinks these numbers may be just an elaborate hoax. He's a Trump guy, and you know how they're into hoaxes. It took a lot of persuasion on my part to get this far. If your instincts and mine are correct, he can't afford to ignore those numbers, either. Until we can bump him off the fence, we'll have to work with what we've got.

"You'll learn about the newbies on your own, but a head start on what makes them tick won't hurt. Ms. Hancock's dad is Al Hancock, one of our own, retired. I know you won't treat her any differently, but Al and I are still close friends, and I've known Cheri, the name she goes by, all her life.

"She has a Master's in psychology obtained to take her in the direction of the BAU. I think she has the goods to get there someday. In the meantime, she's pretty excited just to be involved. She lost her mother when she was young and idolizes Al. Since she was a little girl she wanted to follow in his footsteps and is unusually dedicated.

"Cheri is an outstanding athlete, a cross-country runner, and she maintains her conditioning. I'm pretty sure she could leave you in the dust, Jack. My Grace is trying to beat Cheri's still-existing state record in cross-country.

"Her commitment goes deeper than just wanting to be like her dad. She has a good grasp of academic psychology, but it doesn't end there. I don't believe in ESP any more than you do. I'm sure she doesn't, either. We have relied on your instincts to the benefit of the Bureau more than once. She has the uncanny ability to look into people and understand the unspoken, even the deliberately concealed. She has the highest scores in cognitive perceptual psychology ever recorded in the Bureau. Sorry, Jack, but someone has finally eclipsed you.

"Understand, though, she's no egghead. She has practical skills. Cheri is head-turner gorgeous. I mention that, because, in exercises, she used that to draw in other agents and then lower the boom on them in sanctioned tests. Finally, she's tough as nails. Her desire is always to ingratiate herself to others unless her mission dictates otherwise, and then she's dangerous.

"Being athletic, her self-defense skills, including martial arts from an early age, plus our own training, make her formidable. Cheri is a team player and very trustworthy. That should give you some good insight into her.

"Let's turn to Roy Rogers." Mike couldn't help smirking. "He takes a lot of ribbing about his name. Few of our recruits these days remember Roy Rogers and Dale Evans of movie, and mostly TV, fame. *Die Hard* makes more of a connection, and that's enough for his fellow recruits to give him a constant ribbing. He takes it well, though.

"He isn't your typical agent, and the Roy Rogers moniker of a dashing hero doesn't fit very well. He's on the short side for an agent, retiring in manner, and not likely to come to the forefront unless he has something relevant to say. If he has something to say, it's worth hearing. As good as Cheri is with perception and observation, Roy is with statistics, odds, and determining which fork in the road to take. That allows him to avoid going down some of those unlikely rabbit holes you occasionally take, Jack. We believe he has a genius IQ and would be best used working on probabilities. His forte is cross-referencing all these numbers, where they were mailed from, and potential nexuses with obscure bits and pieces where others might see no correlation.

"You'll have to hold your sometimes autocratic style in abeyance. Don't say, 'Do this because I told you to.' That'll drive him away. Instead, watch him for signs of impulses and draw him out. Once you make him feel a full member of your small team, he could take you places you'd never find otherwise."

"Sounds like something to work with in terms of potential," Jack said. "If we do have a serial out there who has murdered dozens, more practical experience would be better. Why isn't that the case?"

"You must have missed the part where I said I was bucking George on this case. He feels this is too bizarre to be anything other than an elaborate prank that draws resources away from other, more-vital, projects. Counterterrorism has always been a priority, especially in recent times with the Boston Marathon bombings, insurgent murders on our military bases, or pedestrians being hacked with machetes or run down by trucks.

"Go home and get some rest tonight. Give a little thought to how you want to lay out a plan of action on a case where all the normal approaches haven't worked. While you're resting, review the files I gave you."

"Gee, thanks," was all Jack could muster.

CHAPTER FIFTEEN

The following morning, his two inexperienced agents sat in Jack's office, making their introductions. He reviewed their files carefully the previous night. Each was top-of-the-line, but he needed to know more. Were they narcissistic, ego-driven, aggressive, team players, or ambitious self-promoters? What were their individual strengths and weaknesses beyond Mike's evaluation? Mike was a good judge of character, but Jack liked forming his own opinions.

Roy was clearly analytical. He placed highest in his class in deciphering code or problems that required drawing inferences from statistical data. That could be useful in the present case, because of the overwhelming amount of data that needed to be sifted through. Was there a relationship between when the mailings were made and where they were sent from that connected to a known homicide?

Mike's assessment that Roy wasn't anything like the dashing cowboy of his namesake was true. Roy was the quintessential nerd, not someone who usually came to the Bureau. He could do almost any kind of mathematical calculation, multiplying into the trillions or dividing to four or more decimal places in his head with no effort. His file delineated that with certainty. Testing his mettle beyond being a human calculator was something Jack would have to assess over time.

Notes made by his teachers at the academy highlighted another aspect of Roy that Jack could relate to—his indomitable determination. Because of his diminutive stature and the kind of martial arts training some recruits had before joining the Bureau, Roy was an easy target for others when it came to self-defense and the physical capabilities needed to meet the Bureau's standards. He was in danger of being washed, his other attributes notwithstanding.

Rogers worked tirelessly, putting in extra hours even after the exhausting pace of routine training. What he lacked in size and strength, he made up for in technique. He learned to use leverage rather than brute strength, intelligence and quick thinking to his best advantage, and he was soon throwing the other recruits around the room with aplomb. Jack didn't like the kid for his self-defense skills. He liked him, because he refused to let obstacles stop him long before they were apparent to others.

Cheryl Hancock's intuition couldn't be calculated. Her ability to spot theoretical perps in training exercises was also the highest in her class. Her own built-in polygraph gathered signals about people long before they were apparent to others.

Following in her father's footsteps was far from an advantage, despite the added motivation it brought. Al Hancock had a distinguished career with the Bureau, which always prompted people to make comparisons, a heavy burden when added to the inherent stress a recruit normally faced. At some point in the future, when Cheryl Hancock had a track record of her own, it would be different. In the meantime, she faced constant pressure, much of it self-inflicted, to prove she was as good as her old man. That could help motivate her or become destructive. Time would tell.

The two new agents complimented each other very well.

Cheryl was all business, something she had in common with Jack. That was probably a good thing for the team. There was no hanky-panky, as the old song from Paul Revere and the Raiders went in the '60s. Jack's dad played those old songs constantly, and they stuck in Jack's head and were there to stay. No hanky-panky was a good thing, because Agent Hancock was stunningly beautiful. She stood almost five-foot-six, had a slender build, and very attractive features.

Her shoulder-length blonde hair curled underneath. Occasionally, she tucked the right side of her hair behind her ear. Jack quickly saw that happened whenever she was puzzled about something or en-

THE ZERO CONUNDRUM - 49

grossed in thought. Her well-shaped ears were relatively small and cute. Her waist was small, and her curves came from a *Playboy* sketch, all of which Jack ignored, like deleted files from his computer—or so he told himself.

To use a vulgar expression, Jack would never "shit where he eats." His job dominated his life. He often thought that the old adage about no one dying wishing he spent more time at the office didn't apply to him. He would fill his time with an occasional dalliance with an attractive woman, but never someone from the Bureau. No woman had ever turned his head enough to achieve a lasting relationship. Playing chess on the internet or going to a movie filled his limited free time, but most often, his thoughts drifted back to his job. He could check his more-prurient interests other than what was necessary to fill his physical needs, then move on.

One reason Jack was still single was that he avoided intra-agency entanglements. Most agents were ambitious and looked for relationships outside the Bureau. He knew of instances where people sabotaged their careers. The infamous example of Lisa Page and Peter Strzok came to mind. Ms. Hancock may have gotten him onto that train of thought, but Jack was deliberately derailing it.

Jack was more concerned about Mr. Rogers, given Ms. Hancock's obvious attributes. They finished the standard forty weeks of training together, and Mike was perceptive enough, and nosy enough, to have made inquiries. He would never have placed them in the same assignment if there was something between them. Still, Jack planned to keep a wary eye.

"It's nice meeting each of you," Jack began. "I know you have questions, and I'll answer them to the best of my ability. There's just one thing I want to say: I know you're each committed to a career with the Bureau, but if you can't bring it to this project, I can't use you. I don't mean commitment in the usual sense but my own brand of commitment, the kind that meets my own definition."

He paused. "Commitment: the thing is already done. Only the doing remains." He let that sink in. "I'm serious. Write it down." He repeated it.

"That means we're going to complete this assignment and do it successfully, no matter the obstacles. We're going to do it in spite of limited resources, in spite of a team that, while we respect your innate skills, doesn't have the breadth of experience as a team we normally would. No excuses."

He paused again.

"You've both been briefed, so let's get to your questions."

Just as Jack had lots of questions, so did his two new agents. He drew inferences from the questions they asked.

Roy was focused on the numbers. How many crimes would they have to sort through to find a pattern? What kinds of patterns should they look for?

Cheryl, who had already expressed her wish to be called Cheri, wanted to know the psychological profile of someone who would concertedly send out such cryptic numbers over such a long period of time. Were there any parallels in case studies Jack was aware of?

After feeling each other out over morning coffee, they began to relax, dissipating the initial discomfort they felt with the situation. There was no way of beginning the job that was not, in some way or another, abrupt.

"OK," Jack said. "Normally, we go about trying to solve a crime in much the way you'd complete a jigsaw puzzle. You use the road map given on the box cover. You put known pieces together and gradually add others until you have the full picture. We can't do that here.

"We need to be more creative, the old cliché of thinking outside the box. First, let's get one thing clear. I have ten years' experience, and you don't. I couldn't give a damn! We need to do a lot of brainstorming. There are no stupid questions or stupid ideas. No one should dismiss another person's thoughts. Sometimes, it's the most off-the-wall concept from the least-experienced person that pays off. Please remember that.

"Let's look at what we know. If this is an undiscovered serial killer, he's a damn successful one. He's unconventional, and that means our approach must be the same. We've been getting these numbers for ten years. We know from consistencies we can identify that these mailings and these decal numbers are almost certainly coming from the same individual. While the paper stock and a variety of printers have been used, the numbers are in numerical order. They come from common stock that is easy to trace to the manufacturer, but it's impossible to isolate the points of origin.

"Next, we know all the numbers are mailed in the eastern U.S. Why? What are the implications? Roy, I want you to tackle that as your initial assignment. Look at the dates and locations the numbers were sent from and see if you can recognize a pattern. This has all been done before, but we need to go over it as though it's new ground.

"We know this person by nature must be methodical as hell, even in variances we can't see yet. What does that say about him? It could be a woman, but we know how rare that would be for a serial. Let's play the odds for now and assume our target is male. Assuming, from the very limited facts we have, we're dealing with such a person, can we deduce anything about him and his personality? Working, as you are now, in a support role for the BAU, you have resources that can help you develop a profile, however sparse our limited knowledge may be. Cheri, I want you to work on developing such a profile because of your psychology education. It'll be more complete and progressively more distinct as we develop information.

"If anyone doesn't give you the support you need, or is dragging his feet, let me know. For right now, plan on meeting in my office every other morning at 8:00 AM for a powwow. I won't insult either of you by telling you to keep a low profile on this. Maybe I just did. Any questions?"

There were none. Jack knew they were still rookies, and that mattered. There was excitement being involved in a presumed serial murder case of such proportions. It could make them jump too fast and waste time with dead-ends. Recognizing their temporary status could also cause reluctance to jump in when they should, passing up an opportunity.

"Oh, one other thing," he said. "I'll get a copy of the current file delivered to each of you immediately. Read it cover to cover and let me know if you see anything. It could be potentially useful or a miscalculation that could prejudice our thinking. I'll consider it and most likely shit-can it. The people who worked on this didn't produce a result. They're good people, but we can't build on a nonproductive foundation. To be successful, our thinking has to be original and lead us in new directions."

CHAPTER SIXTEEN

Jack's team gathered for their first meeting over morning coffee. Jack had what he called "unadulterated" coffee, black, strong, without cream or sugar.

"Let's start with your reviews of the current file," Jack began. "Roy, why don't you lead off?"

"I didn't see any glaring errors in the actions the prior agents took or any defects in their reasoning. I would make just one observation. First, the mailings were looked at from every conceivable perspective. The facts we could ascertain were scrutinized for each factor involved.

"The common stock of the envelopes showed that each envelope not only used different but also all-but-untraceable stock. Such stocks are very common and widely distributed from a variety of retailers. It would take an exemplar from a particular manufacturing run, of which there are literally tens of thousands, to pinpoint when that run was made. With that exemplar, other threads and factors could be compared. At this point, we have none.

"The typefaces were a consistent san-serif but were printed with different *name-brand* printers. This is significant, because my research shows that sometimes a perp would use different machines to throw us off, but they all came from the same office. Generally, such machines tend to be the same name brand.

"DNA was considered. The envelopes were sponged, not licked closed. Finally, how many mailings were there from what cities? There was some duplication, or repeated mailings from some of the same cities. There was no pattern, such as the same cities in the same order or at consistent intervals. While the origin cities had homicides at or near the dates of those mailings, they didn't fit a serial murder scenario."

"Clarify that," Jack said.

"In the vast majority of cases, the homicides that occurred could be eliminated, either because a perp was apprehended, such as a husband who dispatched his wife after a domestic dispute or for a different motivation. Examples of that would be looking for the perpetrator who killed in the commission of an armed robbery or where a victim was killed gang style, or there was evidence of a drug connection. Once no connection could be made among homicides in a proximate city or a potential serial homicide within a relatively finite period of time, the agents moved on and tried to find a connection to the next mailing. I'm not assailing the agents...."

"Quit trying to cover the butt of someone you don't know. If you find something that could've been done better, that's what we're looking for. Get to the point, Roy. I'm not trying to be a hard ass. You're here, because Mike Hennessey thinks you can contribute. His track record for identifying talent is pretty good."

"Well, what I noticed was that a next step of trying to draw inferences from the fact *there were no obvious connections to be made* was never taken." He carefully emphasized his words. "What I mean by that...."

"I know what you mean by that, and it's a good observation. Was there no nexus by design? Were the mailings in both location and timing meant to mislead? Can we extend our analysis to finding that nexus with a different location or different time or both?"

"Yes," Roy said.

"May I add something?" Cheri asked.

"You don't have to ask permission, Cheri. If you have a thought, jump in," he said somewhat benignly for him.

"I think we should emphasize location, or other locations in this instance, more than time. I think we'll find the period between the act and the mail is shorter, not longer. This person is sending these mailings not so much because he wants to be caught but because he wants to be recognized, even anonymously. He's been too careful about concealing information that could connect him to a murder while also being too methodical about sending these mailings after committing his handiwork to want it to be hidden altogether. He's playing a game, saying, 'I'll let you know *approximately* when, maybe within preordained parameters. See what you can do with that.'"

The room was silent for a few seconds, while the others assimilated this information and formed their thoughts.

"That's a good hypothesis," Jack said. "It could be wrong. It sounds logically based, and it also has the advantage of narrowing our focus a bit, something we can certainly use. Let's proceed on that basis for a moment, if only because it *does* narrow the focus. Let's also remember that we're doing it. We may need to adjust our thinking down the road. Roy, what else?"

"One of the things we have to accept is the sheer weight of the numbers and their relationship to what we're trying to do. Making assumptions is a dichotomy, because it's both dangerous and necessary. Is there an assumption we can make from the fact that virtually all these mailings came from major cities in the east? I believe there must be. Even so, it's not much help. We've been receiving these for ten years. In that time, there have been a known reported number of homicides in the U.S. of 200,136 through the last fiscal year. Of those, about 60% or 121,326 in states east of the Mississippi River. Established Bureau analysis suggests that between 1%-2% of these would be perpetrated by serial killers.

"That means that roughly 1,200-2,400 murders may have been committed by serials, and we're trying to pinpoint a perp who committed sixty-six. It's an immense task to limit those sixty-six to one person or possibly two, as in the instance of the Hillside Stranglers, out of that total range of murders. I don't know of any instance where three perps conspired to commit serial murder.

"Only one mailing came from the western U.S., specifically Honolulu. I think we must concentrate on the significance of that one.

Why the departure from the norm? There could be any number of reasons—vacation, visiting family, a seminar. It's a very popular location for vacations. For the other cities, it could be next to impossible to connect to the perp, but I'll see what I can come up with. I'm afraid that's all I've been able to glean so far."

"That's very well-done," Jack said. "Cheri, fill us in on your work."

"In trying to develop a profile, however vague, I had to looking at what we have and how it might apply to the general profile of a serial killer. I'm also trying to look at the converse, or what we might learn from any *departures* from that norm suggested by what we know, as thin as it might be.

"Most often, serial murderers aren't the isolated loners they are depicted to be. Albert DeSalvo was married, had a son, and was devoted to both. He committed bizarre post-mortem reenactments of the painful physical therapy he performed for his severely handicapped son. Ted Bundy had a girlfriend. At one time, she was even his fiancée, even while he continued his heinous murders. Far from a loner with poor social skills, he could be very engaging and was a popular law student. His ability to gain others' confidence was a big factor in his successful abductions.

"Look at what we know, which is very little right now, I think we can conclude this person is very intelligent. That's not always the case. Here we have a person who, by mailing these from the very first murder, had a definite plan, one designed for long-term implementation with an expectation of success. By inference, he had to believe that despite sophisticated forensics and modern technology, he could evade detection. For this man, the murders, whatever else motivated them, were a compulsion to demonstrate a high level of intelligence, probably one superior to others who perceive themselves as intelligent. I consider that central to his motivation.

"In addition, I believe he's single. The amount of travel he obviously does, combined with the frequency of commission of these crimes and their planning, leaves little time for any kind of viable relationship.

"Finally, there's little we can conclude about his level of education. He could have a PhD like the fictitious Hannibal Lector or be a high-school or college dropout. I think the latter. This would explain, at least in part, his compulsion to demonstrate his intelligence. There's something more that figures into his motivation, but we don't have enough to go on in that respect. I'm afraid that's all I have so far," she said almost apologetically.

Again, silence pervaded the room. Finally, Jack said, "This is good work. I can see why Mike selected you two. I've been interviewing the agents who worked on the case previously and talking with very senior agents and managing agents, including Mike Hennessey.

"No one came up with anything more that what you two have produced. In fact, less. Sometimes, fresh eyes and fledgling enthusiasm can be an asset. Roy, I want you to look at Honolulu. What caused our serial to change his habit? What was unique about the locations at the time the mailing was made?

"Cheri, I believe the reason for the extensive travel involved with our guy is probably work-related. Nothing else I can think of could account for it. Even a trust-fund baby with unlimited financial resources wouldn't be likely to travel this extensively or be limited to such a defined area. Major cities like New York, Chicago, Philly, and Boston might have some appeal, but comparatively mundane engagements like Columbus, Ohio, on a repetitive basis would not. Consulting would be less consistent. I'm sure it's work-related. Focus on the kind of work the perp might be doing. With so little yet developed, that's a big task, so do what you can.

"I'll talk to law enforcement in a few of the major cities from which we have received more than one mailing and see if I turn up anything. See you both in a couple days. Call me if you have questions. Thanks."

CHAPTER SEVENTEEN

Number 67 was important to Zero for several reasons. It would mean he had successfully killed two-thirds of 100 fucking bitches and evaded detection. After Number 1, he made it a tradition to kill one on or as close to his birthday as possible. He would vary it from year to year to avoid establishing a pattern.

Close but no cigar doesn't blunt my ecstasy much, he thought.

Even Zero admitted he had a dark sense of humor. If it wasn't somehow perverse, it didn't amuse him. He learned to feign laughter convincingly for his clients, but what amused him would have been repulsive to them.

Number 67 would take place on his thirty-first birthday on July 10, marking the tenth anniversary of his glorious career. He chose another exquisite torture for his victim. Finally, he was within "shooting distance" of passing Gary Ridgway's seventy-one confessed killings. He would accomplish that in the current year, as a New Year's gift to himself.

Shooting was a vulgar way of dispatching a victim. Some might beg to die just to avoid a shot in the kneecap. He thought of Carl Malden shouting at Steve McQueen in *Nevada Smith,* after he was shot in both kneecaps.

"Finish me! Finish me! You haven't got the guts! You haven't got the guts!"

He loved that movie, including the part where Suzanne Pleshette died of a rattlesnake bite while cursing McQueen. It was satisfying to see women dying while feeling betrayed and desperate, as desperate as his father had been for his shot of morphine.

The punishment inflicted on the two characters in the movie fell short of the ongoing, unendurable pain that filled him with euphoria. Each failed to demonstrate the creativity worthy of his genius. He would finally satisfy his mother's fondest desire. He would be the valedictorian of serial murder.

His conquests anticipated death several times before succumbing. Ultimately, they surrendered to it gladly. He kept his promises. He never inflicted a lethal act on anyone who didn't ask for it. They rarely obliged the first time he asked. He had to give each a chance to change her mind. Otherwise, how could he be sure?

Zero realized that was an obvious rationalization, so he could be entertained a little longer. As George Hamilton hissed in a vampire farce, "Never a quickie, only a longie." Zero's stream of consciousness was fixated on finding some nexus with old movies that day for a reason he couldn't quite grasp. Usually, he enjoyed watching movies that involved murder or infliction of pain. His favorite was a scene in *Schindler's List,* where an officer's gun, pointed at a kneeling Jew, continued to misfire. Each time it misfired, the intended victim flinched until the officer borrowed another's sidearm. That became his inspiration for reviving his victims so he could prolong their agony.

He first saw Barbara, his "intended," clad in a bikini at a public beach in Wisconsin Dells. She had brilliant red hair, probably Clairol 67, he assumed. She had a beautiful body. Her calves were well-shaped but looked disproportionately thin when viewed with her athletic, firm thighs. He judged she spent a lot of time in the sun, as her copper body testified. Her face belonged in a Michelangelo bust of a noblewoman.

Zero took a break from his job and liked to swim. He never chose a number in a public setting. Like with Number 1, he always found the next one in a crowded, dimly lit bar, and he never targeted a woman in the company of anyone else, because that was an unnecessary risk for attention-grabbing conflict. That would be a defect, which didn't fit with his Zero Defects agenda. If he considered that a bad idea, a public beach with possibly hundreds of witnesses was absurd.

At the beach, he took a quick swim and found the farthest reach of sand, where he tossed down a large beach towel as far from the others as possible. Barbara swished across the hot sand in her tong, giving him every opportunity to view her attributes.

"Hiiiiii," she said in as alluring a drawl as she could muster.

It reminded him of Hillary Clinton speaking with an African American affectation.

"No one told me it would be easy. No one told me I come too far."

Barbara's attempt rang equally hollow. She had no genuine drawl. "You're delicious!" she observed.

She would have made an excellent barker at a slave auction.

"Thanks. You're pretty delicious yourself, but I'm taken," he said matter-of-factly, trying to discourage her. She was the embodiment of all three things he hated—an alluring woman who knew it, a flirt, and simultaneously disingenuous. She wasn't out to make friends. She wanted to get fucked. He would love to accommodate her, but he met her in an all-to-public setting.

"A *female* significant other?" she asked. "It would be a shame if you were gay."

At that moment, he began considering her for Number 67. The very idea she thought he might be gay made him want to vomit. However, as he committed to himself at the commencement of his glorious pursuit, he wasn't about to get sloppy or overconfident.

"No, worse than that," he replied. "I'm married."

"Funny. I don't see a ring," she said in her noxious purr.

"It's a little loose, and I didn't want to lose it swimming. I'm just as married, though. Got my tenth anniversary coming up."

"Well, I'm a bit married, myself. Can't show you a ring, either, but I have a ring finger with a tan line where the ring usually is. I don't see a tan line on your finger. My name's Barbara."

"OK, Barbara. Nice to meet you," he lied. "We just met, and you're being pretty provocative. Where's this going?"

"To bed, I hope. As I said, I'm married, too, but it took me half as long as you to get bored."

"Tempting, but I'm ready to towel off in a second, then I have to hit the road."

"Too bad," she drawled again.

Then he *really* hated her. She wasn't willing to take no for an answer.

His decision was made.

"I admit, I've wondered what a little charge-up might be like. You know, from the same old thing. I'll be back in a few days. Maybe we could get together then."

"I'd have to be sure I can get away. We both need to be very discreet, no?"

"Tell you what. There are plenty of cabins for rent around here. When I return in the next few days, I'll rent one and give you a call. Don't worry. I'll be discreet."

"What's your name?"

"Zach Smith," he lied.

Barbara wanted to exchange cell numbers, which made him imagine Number 67 on his speed dial. He claimed to have no cell coverage where he was going and would have to call her.

Having come prepared, she took a permanent marker from her hand and wrote her number on the palm of his hand, sealing her fate.

"Don't you worry. I'll get away." She grinned with bright white teeth that flashed against her copper color.

He decided that Number 67 would take place on the tenth anniversary of Number 1.

CHAPTER EIGHTEEN

Zero, searching for cabins in the area, needed one with a generator. He couldn't canvas them in person, which was too risky, so he called until he found one that met his requirements, including relative isolation and available on the tenth of the month. He explained he needed the generator for some vital work on his computer, and he couldn't risk being without electricity.

"Heard you have a lot of thunderstorms hereabouts in the summer," he said over the phone.

The proprietor wanted a credit card, a deal-breaker for Zero.

"I'm driving right now," he said quickly. "Also, I won't get in until late. Do you have a drop box? If you'll trust me, I'll put in an extra 50% in cash."

The man considered for a few seconds. Zero almost heard wheels turning.

"OK, but don't tell my wife. She's not a very trusting person. She says I'm too trusting. That's half the reason I'll do it."

Zero liked the guy for that.

He planned to put 150% of the money into the drop box, protected by his latex gloves. That would buy him more time before the body was discovered. He would exchange the cash he had for other bills to avoid the chance of fingerprints. As always, he practiced Zero Defects.

He called Barbara from a disposable cell phone he bought with cash.

"Yes, I can talk," she said.

"Can you get away?"

"Yes. The fact that it's a bit later is made to order."

Number 67 was imminent.

CHAPTER NINETEEN

The log cabin Zero chose sight-unseen was made of light-colored logs. He didn't know anything about wood, but he supposed some would view the cabin with its sturdy, prominent beams in the ceiling, a romantic setting. Such thinking was antithetical to his purposes and foreign to his personality, but he judged it would make a very short, good, first impression on Number 67, at least for a few brief moments. Then she would wake up helpless, terrified, and desperate for hope in a hopeless situation.

"And the greatest of these is hope," his mother preached.

He figured out how to connect extended jumper cables to the generator and had them ready. The cabin had a living area, bedroom, and a bathroom off the bedroom. He deposited the cash in the nighttime drop box, got the key from under the mat, and parked behind the cabin, backing up to a moderately dense forest. As he looked deeper and deeper into it, the focus transformed into impenetrable black.

He stole license plates for his arrival and departure and would discard them soon after he finished in a prepared location. The body would be left along an obscure but lightly and regularly trodden trail in the woods a short distance away. He determined that after a brief scouting expedition with the use of a small LED flashlight as his only source of light.

The path was used infrequently but often enough for the body to be discovered in a day or two, if not within hours, once it was daylight. By that time, he would be well away, as he planned to leave before dawn.

All Barbara could have told anyone about him, if she had a close confidant as most women do, was his alias of Zach Smith. The cops could obtain a phone number from her phone, but it would show only a cheap disposable untraceable number.

Barbara arrived at their prearranged time of ten o'clock.

"Hey, Barbara, welcome to Shangri-La!" he said cheerily.

She entered, admiring his choice of cabin. She wore a sexy black wraparound dress with plunging neckline. It could be worn to a cocktail party or a sexy rendezvous, where a flick of the sash would reveal almost every aspect of her torso. Zero imagined she was being deliberately provocative. She whirled around, enjoying the pleasant trappings of the cabin.

The next thing she knew, she woke up with her hands secured by duct tape behind her back, her mouth filled with a Ping Pong ball, and taped shut. Zero always marveled at the invariable widening of the eyes when his victim understood her precarious position, even though the danger wasn't yet fully comprehended.

He assured her he wouldn't kill her unless she specifically asked him to. The mere mention of the word "kill" presented a terrifying possibility. That terror fed his fantasy, giving him an immediate erection. Over time, he learned to build his endurance and resist the temptation to come too soon. Zero raped for dominance and tortured for exhilaration. He teased himself, deliberately procrastinating his fondest activity.

For Zero, sex was merely foreplay. Moving slowly, he would graduate to the ultimate gratification, the infliction of unimaginable pain on a beautiful young parasitic woman. Naturally, he could not only imagine it but recall it. Every one of the sixty-six prior numbers was imprinted on his memory. He frequently relived them, although the real thing was always best. Mere recall wasn't enough to satisfy him. There always had to be another.

Because he had never been so brazenly propositioned before, he would make Number 67 pay for her arrogance. He made women pay for their despicable existence. They had to pay for their desirability, rejection, and domination, reminding him of his mother's domination of his father. No woman could covet his physicality as Barbara did and be allowed to live.

He laid her in the bathroom, removed as much clothing as he could without disturbing the restraints , then taped one leg to the pedestal that supported the sink and the other to the toilet seat beside the washstand, where he raped her repeatedly. He never sodomized women for the pleasure of it, only to demean them. For the time he had them, he didn't own just their bodies, he *owned them.*

When he sated his sexual cravings, he left the bathroom briefly, tripping the power off, expunging the lights in the cabin to create the impression of a power outage, and started the generator. He snaked the jumper cables through the open bathroom window.

He turned on the lights again. When Barbara saw the cables, her eyes widened. He repeated that he wouldn't kill her unless she asked. He often wondered if that gave his victims hope, or if they realized the end was inevitable.

The generator was set to low rpms, so he could repeatedly shock her without accidentally killing her. Her death had to be a deliberate act.

He attached the cables randomly for a few seconds and watched her jump and vibrate, making inaudible screams, before he removed them and let her settle, observing the burns marks where the cables were attached.

"You don't want to die, do you?"

Predictably, she shook her head.

After numerous electric shocks, she reached the limits of her tolerance and began nodding. Saying he wasn't convinced, he shocked her again. He thanked her for introducing herself, adding she was correct in thinking herself very desirable and sexy. Her husband would miss her. Finally, he filled the bathtub with water and saw her eyes widen again.

He returned to the generator, not wishing to endure any greater shock than he had when he attached the cables the first time, and switched the generator to the *Off* position.

Returning to the cabin, he reattached the cables to Barbara, one to each prominent breast. She lay in the water, which covered her from midthigh to near her armpits, her pronounced breasts just clearing the water like newly formed islands.

Going back outside, he stood on a stepladder to observe her final agony, peering through the window in a "Here's Johnny!" imitation of Jack Nicholson in *The Shining*, pulled the cord, and restarted the generator. The lights at first went brighter, then they dimmed, as he watched her body convulse rhythmically through the bathroom window.

What a tenth anniversary celebration it was.

CHAPTER TWENTY

Jack's office was neither cramped nor spacious. Roy and Cheri sat across from him in semi-comfortable but moderately priced Steel Case chairs common to many offices. Cheri noticed something was bothering Jack, and Roy soon did, too.

"We received Number 67 in yesterday's mail."

Their mouths opened with questions immediately, but he waved them off.

"I kept it under wraps until today's meeting for a couple of reasons. First, we always check for prints. Our guy never leaves any, but this is the second time we found a print with a history. Both were for misdemeanors that allowed us to make an ID. Both belong to postal employees who encountered the envelopes in the process of forwarding them.

"I want you to understand something about me, and more importantly, about what I expect from anyone who works with me in an investigative team. *This happened on our watch!*" He raised his voice without yelling, and his tone wasn't accusatory.

Jack waived off their protestations. "I said it happened on *our* watch. You need to understand that. There is no recrimination attached to my statement. You two have been on the case for little more than a week. There is nothing any of us could have done to prevent there being a Number 67, but we're working this case, no matter how long, and someone's dead. It happened on our watch.

"Accept that. When we stop accepting this accountability, we open the door to excuses every time we fall short. I know you've been working hard. I want you to return to what you're doing with increased urgency and intensity, and we'll meet tomorrow to review our progress."

CHAPTER TWENTY-ONE

The following morning, Jack said they had a new agenda.

"Number 67 was mailed from Chicago," he began. "As you know, I've been talking to local law enforcement at every location from which a mailing was made. I haven't gotten to all of them yet. I'm only talking to the head guys, chief of police, county sheriff—the head guy or gal." He gave Cheri a brief smile.

"One of the earlier mailings came from Madison, Wisconsin, and it was one of the places I called. I got a call back from the Chief of Police there, Bob Johnson. He knows most of the law enforcement in and around Madison.

"One of the nearby counties is Adams County, and Chief Johnson heard from Sheriff Al Kuhl. By the way, his given name is Aloysius. I was told he doesn't respond well to his formal name, even in jest, so don't. If we knew him, and he had a sense of humor, we might needle him. From what I understand, though, he doesn't have much of a sense of humor where his name is concerned, so it's Al.

"Sheriff Kuhl had a homicide in his county. The victim was a woman, and there's ample evidence of torture. I won't go into much detail before we get a close, firsthand look at the situation. It's a long shot that this is related to our case, but we need to take a look.

"Adams County is in the part of Wisconsin called the Wisconsin Dells. I don't know if you've heard of the area, but it's important to set the scene. It's beautiful, with rivers, dunes, and high, colorful rock formations along the riverbanks. There are good restaurants in the towns and many quaint, unique shops and stores. The Dells encompasses four counties and attracts hundreds of thousands of tourists every summer and fall.

"Three reasons this is important. First, tourists in an area for a short period of time rarely develop a motive for murder. Second, the year-round residents, since the Dells is an affluent, expensive place to live, are less likely to commit homicide versus a more economically or depressed urban area. Third, this is the only homicide in Adams County in two years. The county had only eighty-four crimes last year, and sixty-nine of those were petty theft. It's not exactly fertile territory for a grisly murder. Our perp had to rent a cabin, remotely located, for the scene. Locals don't often rent cabins.

"We have tickets for a flight in two-and-a-half hours."

"Who's we?" Roy asked. "Are all of us going?"

"No, Roy. I need you here. Your work is our best hope of finding a common link between the number we have and a specific crime or crimes. You have training in statistics and an incredible facility with numbers. Your role on this team is the most critical of all. I need to keep you here, endeavoring to discover that link. I know you're anxious for field experience, but I—we—need you here."

"Yeah, I understand." Roy, slightly deflated, acknowledged Jack was right.

"Am I going?" Cheri asked.

"Yes. Viewing remains isn't just about the objective forensics we can garner. There's also perceiving what kind of person would function as the perp did here. That's where we can use you. Before my JD, I had an undergraduate degree in psychology. You have a Master's in Psychology, combined with innate insight into others. That's what your file says, and we need that.

"If we're going to make that flight, we'd better hustle, Cheri. Get your essentials together. Prepare for two or three days.

"We'll meet together to discuss things once we're back."

CHAPTER TWENTY-TWO

When Jack and Cheri flew into Madison airport, they were greeted by Chief Bob Johnson at the gate. Cops with credentials could do that, and he left his marked car at the curb outside.

Jack wondered how Cheri felt sitting in the back behind the screen, not usual for Special Agents, even new ones. Bob drove them to headquarters, where he had an unmarked car waiting to drive to Brighton, the Adams County seat.

Jack did the introductions, having already spoken with Bob on the phone. "We want to get up there ASAP, so this will save us time. If you hadn't alerted us, we'd be getting a rental right now."

Jack was five-ten but wished he were taller. He sometimes wondered why all the cops he met were six-foot-four. Bob was tall and very skinny. When he sauntered toward them, he resembled a walking stick figure.

"Can you fill us in on who we'll meet in Brighton?" Jack asked.

"There'll be Sheriff Al Kuhl. You'll find him a cool character. Maybe he's trying to live up to his name. He's committed to his job but protective of territorial jurisdiction. That'll give way to wanting to solve the crime, but he'll want a solid basis for anything you do. He isn't comfortable with any suggestion of lack of capability on the part of his people. Doesn't matter to him how infrequently they deal with a homicide. You'll warm up to him though, I think.

"The most-helpful person will be the Chief Medical Examiner. You wouldn't think a small county like Adams would have an exceptionally competent ME. Dr. Joseph Carr, former head of forensic pathology at the University of Ottawa, is renowned in his field. He was widely consulted, even internationally, and occasionally by the FBI. Some of your compatriots in Quantico are familiar with him. That might help you get additional cooperation if you need it. Don't think you will. Carr is in his 80s but hasn't lost a step, I hear. Came here to slow down, but I don't think he'll ever stop. Loves it too much. Came here, because he always liked the Dells."

"Detail rundown, Bob. I'm appreciative. Knowing the lay of the land is very helpful," Jack said.

As if thinking out loud, Cheri said, "Jack may've told you I'm a new agent. I expect to see a certain number of cadavers before I'm through. I just can't understand how someone could look forward to seeing them every day. I expect an undertaker gets paid better, to boot?"

"We have more homicides in Madison, but most often, the ME sees deaths from car crashes, heart attacks, or a disease that needs a name put to it," Bob replied. "I see cadavers, because I have to. Never could figure out why someone would choose to do it. Must be a little perverse in some way. Thank God some people do it for whatever reason. You'll like Dr. Carr. Everybody does."

They thanked him and picked up the black, full-sized sedan and were on their way to Brighton.

Before checking into their hotel in Brighton, Jack drove directly to city hall and asked for Al Kuhl. The officer at the front desk looked hesitant until Jack flashed his credentials.

"We heard you guys were comin'," he said. "Sorry, Ma'am," to Cheri.

The sheriff came out immediately. "Hello. I'm Al Kuhl. Bob told me you'd be visiting."

"I'm Jack Garvey." He turned toward Cheri. "This is Special Agent Hancock." He used her formal title to increase her stature in her own eyes and make her feel more integral to the investigation.

"Nice to meet you. This is a very old building, and the halls are a bit meandering, so I thought I'd better escort you personally." He seemed more cheerful than Bob led them to expect.

"Very hospitable of you," Cheri said, wishing she hadn't spoken and blushing slightly.

Kuhl had a more-expansive office than Jack expected. Thinking of his own cramped office, he felt a bit envious. Glancing up, Clark noticed an elaborately detailed chamfer that traced the perimeter of the ceiling. He lamented the loss of craftsmanship in the name of "modernism."

As if reading Jack's mind, Al said, "Chalk it up to early twentieth century architecture. Unfortunately, they still have the furniture to match. These hard oak chairs play hell with my hemorrhoids. Sorry, Agent Hancock. We're hicks around here."

They sat down. "You're interested in the cabin murder, as we're calling it, right? You'll want to talk to the ME, of course. Normally, I'm somewhat protective of my jurisdictional prerogatives. You may have heard."

They didn't give Johnson away.

"We've got a great group of professionals here, but the circumstances of this case.... Let's just say I wouldn't mind some help on this one. Murders aren't that common here, but this is far from ordinary.

"Let me give you what we've got so far without treading on Dr. Carr's territory. I think we're dealing with a slick operative. First, no one saw the person who did this except the victim. A male, we're certain, because it was a man who reserved the cabin. The perp had to be strong, too. No semen is evident, but that's not surprising based on the condition of the corpse. Still, I think it's likely rape, but Dr. Carr will fill you in on that better."

"Why do you say that?"

"It appears the perp went to great lengths to avoid using a condom or leaving semen. There was probably rape involved, based on that. As I said, you'd best get that from Dr. Carr.

"This guy convinced Beau Williams—you'll want to interview him; he and his wife own the crime scene cabin and a few others up northwest of town—to put a cabin key under the mat. He told Beau he couldn't reserve the cabin, because he was driving and couldn't get to his wallet and couldn't remember the card number. He promised an additional fifty percent of the room rate. Said he'd leave the cash in the night drop box."

"Did he?" Cheri asked, summoning the courage to speak again, knowing the answer would tell her something about the man. Was he able to distinguish between right and wrong, which could be used to counter an insanity defense? More significantly, it could be a view into his thinking and what other motivation he might have had related to making payment. If he paid with cash, could they lift any prints that might be the perp's?

"Yes," Al said. "We instantly recognized the value of that as evidence. Emily, Beau's wife, had already taken the money and deposited it in the bank, as she does each morning. It was before the body was discovered. Knowing Emily, Beau probably caught hell for accepting cash. By now, the bills have been handled by several people and mixed up with thousands of other bills.

"The guy who rented the cabin insisted it have a generator. I think it would be better to get this from Dr. Carr. He's learning more about this as we speak."

Jack immediately saw the possible connection with the autopsy, although he couldn't define it completely.

"The body was found by hikers just off an infrequently used path," Al continued. "It was in an awful state."

"Let me guess," Jack interjected. "Dr. Carr's bailiwick. Can you at least tell me if you have an estimated date and time of death?"

"As near as we can tell, it was the early morning hours of July 11. She was found by the hikers the early afternoon of July 12. We've got the hikers' names, but we've interviewed them thoroughly. All they know is seeing her body off the trail and being smart enough not to disturb anything. There were two couples. One with a strong stomach stayed while the other three couldn't wait to meet us. One of those led us back to the body where the first one waited."

"I understand from Bob Johnson the victim was married," Jack said. "Did the husband report her missing?"

"Yeah, but not until the early afternoon of the eleventh. Apparently, she had a habit of staying out most or all night, but she usually came home by early morning. Husband's wealthy, a bit older, but a nice guy according to most people hereabouts. Rumor has it his money didn't stop her from being something of a tramp."

Jack and Cheri exchanged glances. Could the victim's casual morality help them profile the killer?

"Dr. Carr has the photos that were taken when we arrived on the scene," Al said, giving Jack a knowing shake of the head. "One thing I can tell you, and it's one of the things that make me say this guy is a slick operator, is that it looks like the dirt driveway, including behind the cabin, was raked and displaced to remove tire tracks or footprints. The asphalt road in front of the cabin was hosed down for some distance. The guy must've come prepared with a spade and garden hose. Beau keeps a hose at each cabin. He doesn't keep them attached to the spout, because they can rust into the spout in this climate. Beau said the hose didn't appear to have been disturbed. He recognized the ways he always coils them. The man must've brought his own. We'll be sending Beau's down to you at Quantico just in case. This guy was a very smart cookie."

"I can see why you're protective of your turf. Sounds like you did a good job of preserving the evidence."

"I think you'll feel the same after you see Dr. Carr."

CHAPTER TWENTY-THREE

"Joe," Kuhl said in a friendly way, although a bit overboard, "these are our compatriots from the FBI. This is Jack Garvey, Supervising Special Agent and Special Agent Cheri Hancock. Not too much around here would warrant this kind of privilege," he added, tongue in cheek. "Give 'em everything you've got, and tell me everything they come up with. See you folks later."

Dr. Carr, in his eighties, wasn't quite what they expected from his description. He had severe curvature of the spine, that made him resemble a 100-year-old Hunchback of Notre Dame, only skinnier. He was balding on top and had long, white hair, like Benjamin Franklin. His spinal curvature was so bad, he mostly faced the floor. That meant his hair hung down beside his face instead of on his shoulders. Jack wondered if that worked better for looking through a microscope.

"Feel free to interrupt with questions," Dr. Carr said in a deep, gravelly voice with a hint of mischief. "It's better than missing something, because you couldn't remember it later. I tend to move at the speed of light, I'm told, despite my years. I'll try to cover things in a methodical way where things hang together for the most part. We identified the body. Her husband confirmed it a few days ago. Her name is Barbara Cox. Her husband is an important real-estate developer around here.

"Clinically, she is five-foot-eight and twenty-eight years old. The cause of death was electrocution, suggested from pairs of burn marks on various locations all over her body. There were marks from jumper cable clamps spread wide on her flesh on her arms, legs, neck, and her minimal love handles. The clamps were deliberately spread wide to grab a large amount of flesh. My vision is that, while the cables were connected to her flesh, it would look similar to a flexed biceps. The spread of the clamps would exert more pressure, too, making them less likely to slip off. These caused burn marks where she was shocked.

"The burn marks are particularly pronounced on her breasts. I believe that's where the cables were attached when she was immersed in water, which was merciful. She endured a lot of torture before the *coup de grace.*"

"Often we see such torment imposed by someone with a simmering hatred of the other person," Jack said. "It's very often the result of a close relationship, such as a spouse.

"Her husband, I understand from Al, has an iron-clad alibi at some party or something for his associates. Barbara was supposed to attend but begged off at the last minute. Al didn't tell you?" he asked, surprised.

"He just said the husband reported her missing. I was already sure he wasn't the culprit."

"Al does that. He eliminated the possibility himself, and that was good enough. The cause of death was electrocution. We could tell that the lividity, the pooling of blood in the lowest extremity after death.... Sorry. Forgot who I was talking to. That with the relaxed rigor mortis suggested she was dead for about a day.

"I found further evidence to suggest that was an accurate estimate. The perp was gone before daylight on the eleventh, and she wasn't found until the twelfth. I'm no entomologist, but I've worked with them in a number of cases. There was an unusually large number of parasites in this specific situation, and an unusual variety, for reasons I'll explain.

"It all points to her death occurring in the early morning hours of July eleventh, based on discovery of the body in the afternoon of the following day, the twelfth. I believe she was raped as well."

"Yes," Jack said. "The sheriff suggested you would explain."

"Do you two have strong stomachs?"

"Usually," Jack said.

The ME turned to Cheri.

"I'm new with the Bureau," she admitted. "You might say I'm untested in that area. All I've seen are photos."

"I'll get you two a couple of barf bags just in case. With my stature, I'm not very good at cleaning up puke."

He left the room and returned with a pair of the typical semi-transparent cylindrical blue bags and gave one each to Jack and Cheri. They followed him into the morgue, where he unceremoniously slid out a glossy silver slab covered in a white sheet. The ME turned it back, and Cheri made immediate use of her bag.

Jack viewed many dead bodies before, but that one turned his stomach more than any he could remember. He barely stifled the urge to copy Cheri.

Jack gave Cheri a break and didn't resume until she recovered. He wanted her input, which was why he brought her along.

"Ready to resume?" the doctor asked without much empathy. When they nodded, he continued, although he showed a little more sympathy and some barely muted amusement.

"As you can see, much, most of the tissue and much of the bone in the pelvic area is missing. Specifically, starting from the bottom of the pelvis structure at the ischium on both sides, which come together at the pubic symphysis." Looking down, he didn't see their puzzled expressions, continuing as if teaching a class on human anatomy to a group of would-be doctors.

"Those are completely gone. The pubic bones, which support what you would call the hips, were shattered and missing in part. In the process of removing most of the pubic area, the coccyx was broken and removed in part as well. The coccyx is what is commonly called the tail-bone. It isn't easy to remove it."

The two agents had numb, semi-informed stares. The Bureau trained them in anatomy, but it wasn't delivered at Dr. Carr's lightning speed or in such overwhelming detail and technical jargon. Still, they understood that any resemblance to a normal pelvic region was missing.

"I can see only one reason for this," Dr. Carr said. "The entire vagina and any semen contained therein was removed. Thankfully, this was done postmortem. If not, it would have killed her, anyway."

Cheri and Jack were thankful for that.

"There are no wolves in this part of Wisconsin. A bear would've been strong enough to do that, but it wouldn't have been done this way. This was done by a strong man. The most minute shavings of metal were found on the surface of some of the bone striations. We'll send those fragments to Quantico's lab, too. My guess is some type of spade was used, probably one that came to a point, as opposed to a flat edge.

"If she was raped, and the tape residue on her wrists, ankles, and face suggest it, Mrs. Cox's killer was removing his semen and any potential forensic evidence, or trying to."

CHAPTER TWENTY-FOUR

Jack and Cheri interviewed the Williamses, who owned the cabin where Zero stayed. Neither saw nor heard anything on the evening of July 10 or the morning of the 11th. Beau said the man's voice was "average" with no discernible accent. Throughout the interview, Beau was constantly castigated by his shrewish wife. Jack and Cheri learned nothing worthwhile.

They saw the photos of where the body was recovered, and they learned nothing new when visiting the site, even though they tried. They agreed to return to the hotel, revitalize, and meet for dinner at a restaurant in the hotel at eight o'clock.

They wore business casual to be comfortable, which was suitable for an agent. They were still FBI, even if no one else in the restaurant knew it.

Jack couldn't help musing that Cheri looked good in anything. He ordered trout almandine, and Cheri had the filet mignon, medium rare. Both were bourbon people, and the first sips helped take the edge off their mood.

"How's the stomach?" Jack asked mischievously.

"That's the last time that'll happen," she replied sternly. "I'm starved. You trying to ruin my appetite?"

"Not at all." They agreed to avoid shop talk.

They finished their meals and refused dessert, opting for the *digestif* of Irish coffee. Jack's had Jameson's whiskey and Kahlua with whipped cream, while Cheri had Jameson's and Bailey's and no whipped cream.

"Did we learn anything today that is relevant to our search?" Cheri asked.

"Yes, we did. We learned that Barbara Cox was Number 67."

CHAPTER TWENTY-FIVE

Jack's team assembled in his office at their usual 8:00 AM the morning after he and Cheri returned. Jack briefed Roy on what took place and used the time to check Cheri's recall. He wanted her impressions. He was especially interested in her take on whether Barbara Cox was Number 67. He deliberately avoided any discussion on that point on their trip back.

Cheri felt she was on the hot seat. She knew Jack wanted support for his conclusions, although it seemed a quantum leap to her, and she wanted to do her best.

"If we start from the assumption Mrs. Cox was Number 67, I would look at this through the lens of the sparse conclusions I made developing a speculative profile. Based on the amount of travel our serial does, I already concluded he's most likely not married or in an ongoing relationship.

"The condition of her body when it was discovered, as Jack described, portrayed a level of savagery and brutality on a scale that, even in his experience, is almost without parallel. It's hard to imagine how someone with that kind of rage, if it's directed toward women in general, could maintain any kind of relationship for anything more than a transitory period.

"The Number 67 envelope was mailed from Chicago rather than nearby Madison, Wisconsin, which is consistent with Roy's hypothesis. It was sent about five days after the murder, also consistent with trying to obscure any connection to Mrs. Cox.

"The forensic evidence that one would normally find—semen, fingerprints, fibers, or any source of DNA that is usually left in some degree—was completely absent. The pain inflicted on the victim was almost unimaginable and is consistent with a sociopath who has no sympathy and is unable to extrapolate a sense of humanity. These indicia reflect a sociopathic individual with the intellectual capacity to repeat these horrific acts on an ongoing basis. That he could do so while denying law enforcement discernible forensic evidence on a long-term basis is stupefying given the sophistication of modern forensics. Our tests are sensitive to obtain identifiable DNA even from a mere touch, so their lack is amazing. Our guy left none.

"This profile could fit any number of the 3,000-4,000 serials the Bureau estimates may be at large at any time in this country. I defer, of course, to Jack's superior experience, but I can't say I understand the confidence with which he puts his theory forward, that Mrs. Cox is Number 67."

"I want to direct this to both of you," Jack said. "If you're going to defer to my opinions instead of putting forward your own ideas, your participation in this investigation has no value. I'll admit that Cheri had the fortitude to at least call my opinion into question. That, for a new agent, is rare. Once again, if your analysis reflects only my thoughts, that renders your own opinions impotent. Express your opinions without referencing mine, please.

"Don't misunderstand me, either. Your analysis and perceptions were excellent." Although it wasn't his intent, he saw he made Cheri uncomfortable. "I'll get back to you on my conclusions, but first, I'd like to hear about Roy's progress."

"The first step I took was to look at the locations where the mailings were made," Roy began. "Of the sixty-seven, several were repeats from certain cities. Looking at the frequency of the mailings might give us a lead concerning the perp's home base. Number 67 was the third we received from Chicago. There were four from New York, and we have multiples from Miami, Tampa, Detroit, Cleveland, Philadelphia, and Boston. There are a few other locations with only two mailings. Single mailings came from cities like Memphis, Nashville, and several more. There's a discernibly higher number of mailings from larger cities. One can say without being challenged that the number of mailings from each city is proportional to the city's population. If we're looking at business travel, which seems likely, larger cities would logically be visited more frequently.

"Previous agents tried to correlate the dates of the mailings with nearby homicides without success. I couldn't do any better developing a pattern. If Jack's right, and the Dells murder note was mailed five days later from Chicago, it could be an indication that the mailings have consistently been made from a city where the murder didn't take place. If that was by design, it explains the inability of prior agents to develop any kind of identifiable pattern that would help further the investigation.

"There was, however, one aberration—the mailing from Honolulu, which is west of the Mississippi. I googled the month of October for activities in Honolulu and found a staggering half a million tourists, with 464 conferences and attendees from business, medical, education, and fraternal organizations.

"If we could identify a murder that took place at the time of that particular mailing, connecting it to one of those half-million people would be all but impossible unless a relationship existed between the victim and the perp, and that doesn't fit with our serial."

"Sounds like you hit a dead end," Jack surmised, breaking one of his cardinal rules to jump ahead.

"Respectfully, Supervising Agent Garvey, you're selling me short," Roy said with unexpected fortitude. "If I can't immediately ferret out the murderer from half a million people, that doesn't mean I'll quit. If I can't find him, maybe I can find the murder itself.

"And I did. It's reminiscent of a mob hit, with the feet set in concrete and the body tossed over the side. Except it was a she, and the feet set in concrete were near the water's edge in shallow water—the depth varied with the tide," he said almost gleefully.

"How'd you learn that?" Cheri asked, amazed.

"I contacted the Honolulu police for the specifics."

Jack was impressed with the young agent, although he was also hopping mad. "You did that without my authorization? Who the hell do you think you are? I made it clear that contact with local authorities was a function I would fulfill in this investigation. You're a damn rookie! We gave you an opportunity that someone fresh out of the academy never gets, and you forgot Rule One: Follow directions. Evidently, I need to find someone who can."

CHAPTER TWENTY-SIX

"Jesus, Jack!" Roy said, completely cowed. "I was excited. I reacted impulsively!"

"Don't do it," Cheri implored. "You said he's a rookie, and he made a rookie's mistake. Roy and I work well together, and he may have come up with the first lead of value in this case!"

Jack seething, tried to compose himself, knowing he didn't make good decisions when he was angry, no matter the justification. "There are good reasons for my filling that role, including avoiding backlash from locals for treading on their jurisdictions and giving up information we don't want to divulge, or even knowing when to mislead them and why we do that." His anger faded slightly. "You get one second chance Roy, and this is it. Tell us what you learned."

"A pediatrician from Philadelphia, Dr. Sylvia Bacardi, attended a conference in Honolulu. She originally arranged for just the conference, but she called her office and arranged to stay an extra week, continuing her room at the Honolulu Marriott. The police eventually heard from associates and family that she never checked out of her hotel and never returned home. Eventually some snorkelers in a secluded area of the Oahu shoreline found a cement block with what looked like human tissue in two holes in the block with a driftwood pole in a third. They notified the police.

"Very little tissue remained in the block, mostly bone and nail, badly degraded. It was about one week since Dr. Bacardi was reported missing. Police interviewed professionals who attended her conference, *Diagnosing Rare Conditions in Adolescents,* as well as staff at the hotel after the other attending doctors had returned home, but they got nowhere. Since she was from Philadelphia, I thought there could be an eastern connection," he concluded sheepishly.

Jack didn't want to destroy a promising new agent, but neither could he tolerate a maverick who didn't follow directions. "Roy, I meant what I said. I don't usually give second chances, and I never give a third. Straighten up and fly right. You did develop potentially significant information, so you deserve credit for that."

He paused, studying his off-balance agents. "Cheri, you did nice work, too. In a minute, we'll discuss where to go from here.

"The gorilla in the room is how I concluded that Ms. Cox is Number 67. There are two reasons, one compelling, one not so much. Forensic science has accelerated in terms of capability at a geometrically increasing rate. To avoid identification long enough to become one of the most-prolific serials ever would require someone from within the forensics community, or someone who has read extensively in the field. I think the latter.

"The second part of my two-legged tripod is instinct. My instincts tell me Barbara Cox is Number 67. My instincts are far from infallible, but they worked well for me in the past. One, the timing was right, just a few days before the mailing. Two, while Madison was the closest city of any size, Chicago isn't that far from the Dells. Three, the savagery with which this murder was committed reflects the kind of rage that would sustain a massive number of crimes over so long a period.

"The murder in Honolulu in close proximity to the mailing of Number 60, if I have that right, may lead somewhere, or it may not. There are several reasons I tend to think it won't.

"First, the reason our Numbers haven't correlated with any known serial is because our perp consistently mails them from another location. That militates against Dr. Bacardi's murder fitting our conclusion.

"Second, the killing of Cox shows an active involvement in the torture and death of the victim. Freezing someone's feet in concrete is more of a passive act, however horrific the death might ultimately have been.

"Finally, and this takes us back to Cox again, our perp engaged in repeated tortures extending his exhilaration in his victim's death."

"May I take a shot at poking holes in your theory?" Cheri asked.

"You know you can," Jack replied.

"I'll take them in order. Dr. Bacardi was from Philadelphia and extended her time to take a vacation. Perhaps our eastern U.S. traveler made contact with her in Philadelphia, and their meeting was pre-arranged. The nexus between the perp and the victim would indeed have been from a different city and consistent with the pattern.

"As for the passive nature of the killing, that's an assumption. We don't know how she died or how long it took. If our guy created the conditions that resulted in her death and stayed to observe the consequences, he may well have felt an active participation in her death. Lastly, depending on the actual cause of death, repetition of pain may well have been part of the scenario."

A hush fell over the office. Jack mulled over Cheri's comments, trying to look at them objectively and not let his ego reinforce incorrect conclusions. He paced as much as the small office allowed.

"We'll meet here tomorrow morning at eight again," he said, walking out.

CHAPTER TWENTY-SEVEN

Cheri and Roy were apprehensive the following morning. Jack greeted them and rocked in his high-backed chair before speaking.

"You may remember my saying that sometimes, it's the least-experienced individual, with the least-cluttered mind, who breaks a case open. Roy, you didn't follow directions, but you turned up some salient information. Cheri, your reasoning may have put us, *may*, I say, on the right track.

"My plan is for Roy and me to head to Honolulu." Roy's face broke into an expansive grin. "I'm still the person best suited to speaking with the locals, but your being there to introduce me will provide some continuity. Also, something you've already heard could spark additional inquiry.

"Cheri, you're going to Philadelphia to interview Dr. Bacardi's family, friends, and professional associates." He wished dividing the work that way didn't make so much sense, and Cheri was the one accompanying him to Hawaii. "Frankly, we sorely need more manpower to pursue this line of investigation.

"Before we can request that, we have to prove these Numbers we're receiving are connected to actual crimes. We don't have anything concrete—pun intended—to connect either Cox or Bacardi to this investigation or even our theories. It's getting the attention solely because of the length of time and the consistency with which the Numbers have been sent, as well as the concerted effort not to leave fingerprints, to use common stationery incapable of being traced, and, most importantly, the body count.

"There's some sentiment from higher-ups that we're like a dog chasing its tail. Only Mike Hennessey's dogged insistence in support of this investigation is keeping us afloat. Before we got it, the Bureau had already invested significant resources without result, which doesn't sit well." Jack became more enthusiastic.

"Cheri's observations are cogent but not enough to satisfy the skeptics. Cheri has, as she should, questioned my conclusions about Ms. Cox. In my opinion, her analysis of what we know is right on. However, profiles have been proven wrong, especially when predicated on paper-thin facts and extrapolations from those facts. Still, her profile resonates with what I see, too, but it's not enough to get us more resources.

"One other thing. The guy we're looking for was able to attract a beautiful woman married to a very successful man who had a whole bunch of money. My impression is that she wasn't randomly picking up some run-of-the-mill guy. Ask about Dr. Reynolds' physical attractiveness. I have a feeling it may be relevant, and get pictures if you can, Cheri. Use your skills to get her friends and colleagues to feel comfortable with you, then draw them out. It'll be difficult, because you're dealing with the death of someone important to them, but they'll probably want to help bring closure to a painful experience.

"Also, we won't put all our eggs into this one basket. I'll continue talking with other law enforcement in other jurisdictions to see if we can scare up any more leads. From now on, I'll focus on crimes, regardless of the MO, that involved torture. If I find anything, I'll check with you, Roy, for any proximate connection with the mailings. We need to allow for a week's variance. Number 67 was mailed 200 miles away and five days after Cox's death.

"We should prepare for our trips. Roy, you'll contact Chief Sandy Tuttle who you talked to and arrange an appointment ASAP. We'll need to talk to the ME, too.

"I just got word Mike Hennessey wants to meet tomorrow morning at our usual time in my office. Any questions?"

There were none.

CHAPTER TWENTY-EIGHT

Mike, having called the meeting, began. "Jack filled me in on your activities and the Wisconsin trip. No question that you're performing to my expectations. Knowing Jack, he hasn't gotten into the political aspect of this case. I learned a long time ago to trust Jack's instincts. The brass, however, finds actual evidence more compelling.

"What gave this investigation impetus was the fear that, if these numbers *are* a serial and not an elaborate prank, then two things should be true—first, a lot of people are already dead, and second, there is an infinite number of potential new victims.

"The Bureau has been looking at this seriously. There's pressure to find something substantive. No one has yet threatened to shut down this case, but the limited resources we're permitted are a concern.

"When I talk about resources, I mean the number of staff and the budgetary allocation. Right now, that's nowhere close to Gary Ridgway in the Green River case, for example, the comparable number of potential victims notwithstanding. In his case, numerous bodies were recovered, all prostitutes, from the Green River. We have nothing like that here.

"The concern is that the Bureau would be embarrassed if we were drawn into a sustained but elaborate hoax. The other side of the ledger is that we could be caught flat-footed if there really is a serial. Why didn't we get him sooner? Believe me, the Executive Special Agent and the Bureau would rather get him late than never. That will still save lives. That thought is what keeps us going.

"Let me be crystal clear," he said. "I want all of you to focus on what you're doing. Let me handle the behind-the-scenes stuff. Jack tells me we have identified Number 67. I believe him. It is, however, to others in the Bureau, a quantum leap. If you let it, urgency will destroy an investigation. It makes you jump too far ahead of where you ought to be, but that urgency exists, and it's up to you to handle it. Jack?"

"Thanks, Mike," Jack said. "I won't add to what he just said. I don't need to."

Roy and Cheri noticed Jack was unusually tense, with his shoulders higher than before.

"I've become a telemarketer," Jack said, "selling chiefs and sheriffs in the East on a far-fetched theory. Local officials told me anecdotes from their recollection of cases that could fit the description of torturing the victim and repeatedly inflicting non-lethal wounds before the *coup de grace.* Usually, they involved animosity with roots in domestic violence or long-standing conflicts. There have been rapes, too. Most deaths related to those involved strangulation, not horrific acts like the Cox murder.

"In one case, hatred between two business rivals led to a gruesome outcome. Convincing any of these people to initiate a time-consuming look over a ten-year period for cases that involved torture without a real definition of what that might mean or a definite MO, well.... They didn't buy it. There were a few though, despite the sheer number of cases to be reviewed, who said they'd look into it.

"We have to be multitaskers, continuing to look on multiple fronts. We're looking at Honolulu now, but I still have doubts that it fits.

"Roy, get contact information from Tuttle for Bacardi and pass it on to Cheri. You'll need to build on it, Cheri, identifying additional persons who might know something about her Honolulu plans. Each of you should firm up your appointments. Before I head out with Roy, I'll keep calling other locals. Eventually, we'll find another murder that looks like Cox."

CHAPTER TWENTY-NINE

Zero met Dr. Sylvia Bacardi in what would have been his usual grazing ground, a bar. She left a boring party with a group of doctors telling lies about their most-recent surgeries or near-impossible diagnoses that might never have occurred.

Sylvia was a small woman, five-foot-two and slender. Her blonde hair was pulled back in a bun to fit the image of most of her colleagues at the conference. She draped the jacket from her light-gray suit worn with conservative white blouse, across the back of her barstool. When Zero came into the bar, his eyes were immediately drawn to her.

A brief introduction gradually turned into genuine conversation. Each was stimulated by the other's intelligence. He was the first man she met that satisfied two of her criteria—clearly intelligent and strikingly handsome. The rest, she figured, would be learned.

Her companion's thoughts were more of a dichotomy. She was the rare woman who could challenge him intellectually, possibly the first in his experience. He was startled to have such an engrossing exchange with a woman, something he thought was impossible. He felt himself enjoying their banter.

Zero found himself thinking, *This doctor is a good doctor*, although he was still her superior, because he would eventually become the best serial murderer in history. He felt the itch, too, because it was nearly three months since Number 59.

It was a moot point, however, from several perspectives. He hadn't had the time to prepare. He came to Honolulu a week early to make the necessary preparations for the upcoming AAUS trade show.

Normally, the Western Regional Manager would have done that, but he was ill. Even with COVID-19 two years in the rearview mirror, every illness the guy got had to be a major deal. Zero also had to remain after the conference to handle meeting with their Hawaiian broker.

Sylvia was flying out on Friday when her pediatrician's conference ended. Since it was already Wednesday, the whole thing was impossible.

Then he had an epiphany. Normally, he wouldn't have been so bold, but he could tell her that he wasn't just making a pass but wanted to get to know her better.

Was there a way she could extend her stay for a week? Sunday was all he needed.

CHAPTER THIRTY

Dr. Bacardi was shocked and flattered by Zero's proposal. "That's a bit more than a pass, Zach. I'd say that's taking a swing at a grand slam."

"I was afraid you'd misunderstand me. When I said get to know each other, I meant exactly that, to hang out together and have some fun. No agenda or expectations." He tried to sound humble.

"Look, you're a nice guy. I haven't talked to someone as well-read and intelligent as you in a long time. I'm split between wondering if you're for real or just another guy with more patience than normal trying to get to the same place. I have a medical practice. Shall I call my PA and ask her to reschedule any appointments she can't handle? It's absurd," she said gently.

"Yes. I look at you and see a dedicated physician, someone who's still young and who doesn't manage her practice. It manages her. Maybe I'm wrong. Maybe take two weeks off every three months. My guess is it's three days every two years." He used his instinct, every tool he learned in a successful sales career. The fact that he might like her made her destruction a necessity.

"Not that bad, but you're closer to the truth than you know.." Biting her lip, she sounded a little sad.

"I'm afraid I've embarrassed myself," Zero lamented, taking the first step in his *lost sale close* technique he learned in a seminar. He was quite good at it.

"Zach, I shouldn't admit this, but I'm intrigued. You cut right to the quick with me, but you aren't as transparent."

Or as easy to manipulate, he thought. "Well, I'm kind of self-quarantined, you might say. I lost my wife three years ago to breast cancer. Her name was Magalina. He met her in Puerto Rico. She was just 27 when she found a lump in her breast. By then it was too late. The hospital told her to watch it and see them again in six weeks. The cancer was a rare type, the fast-moving kind. She fought it for over a year, but we knew all along what she was up against."

Sylvia was very sympathetic. As a physician and a woman, Zach knew exactly how to approach her.

CHAPTER THIRTY-ONE

Dr. Bacardi called her office and took a week's vacation to be with Zach Jones. Whether he was Smith or Jones, Zero was a sincere, convincing manipulator. He was Captain Ahab, intent on ridding the world of the evil White Whale. Antithetical to Herman Melville's novel, though, was the idea that women truly encompassed evil in the world. Melville's Ahab had but one target on which to visit his hatred.

Zach explained he needed to work during the day to prepare for a convention in the upcoming week and carefully deflected questions about which convention, what he sold, or anything else about his deceased wife.

Sylvia loved people and rarely saw their bad side. She loved her patients and was loving to everyone else. Zach had only to tell her he'd rather focus on their exploration of each other, which he did while being completely disarming.

He related to her intellectually. He actually felt himself starting to like a woman. Her artistry in almost making him succumb was maddening. He took comfort in knowing hers would be one of the most-horrifying, and therefore the most-gratifying, adventures of his career.

Zach and Sylvia spent Thursday and Friday night dining together. Thursday, he enticed her to have elaborate room service on the balcony of her hotel room. He needed a bathroom break when room service arrived, apologizing to Sylvia and leaving cash and a generous tip on the table.

Friday, he chose a Hawaiian luau and paid in cash, unbeknownst to the doctor. He later explained he'd been detained for the luau and asked if she could take his receipts and put together two plates of food and a bottle of champagne he reserved and find a spot as far as possible from the hot fire on a hot night. She interpreted that as romantic. Her resistance was weakening.

Finally, Zach gave her the bad news she'd be on her own Saturday, but he had something extra special planned for a private outing on Sunday together. He rebuffed her growing interest and attempts at physical interaction, deigning to kiss her, faking passion, and promising he would unleash his true feelings for her on Sunday.

Saturday was work-related, although not for his employer. Zero worked on his preparations for a triumphant experience, a new zenith of rapture. Sunday promised to be a pinnacle of creativity and a self-ordained tribute to his genius.

CHAPTER THIRTY-TWO

Sunday, Zero picked up Sylvia at her hotel. He maneuvered his company's hardtop rented vehicle, equipped with stolen plates, away from cameras that would otherwise have obtained identifying photos of his face.

Sylvia was enthusiastic about getting out of the city and curious about his surprise. He explained they were on their way to a secluded place where they'd be totally alone and would have an elaborate picnic, complete with good wine, food, and his special surprise.

After an hour's drive, he took a side road leading to a beach shielded from the road above by a cliff that hid a large entrance to a volcanic cave.

"You've outdone yourself with the setting," Sylvia said.

Zach carried what appeared to be a very heavy picnic basket, while she carried a lightweight plastic tarp for the picnic spread.

Zero knew he would have to drug her to accomplish his scenario. He was amazed at how easy it was to obtain date-rape drugs like Rohypnol or Ketamine on the street. He chose Ketamine, because it was an anesthetic, acted immediately, and, depending on dosage, rendered a person unconscious for a significant period. His street vendor called it Special K.

As Sylvia bent over to spread the tarp, Zero grabbed her in his customary suffocating grasp from behind. In his carefully chosen secluded location, he took his time to render her unconscious, prolonging his euphoria. He wanted her to know she was in big trouble. She fought back, but her 115-pound body was so small he could throw her around like a rag doll.

Rather than allowing her to come around fully conscious, as his usual routine, he injected her with his Special K to keep her unconscious. His anticipation felt like a drug high, filling him with adrenalin. How would he ever top such a sensation? What miracle of his creative intellect could bring him a more-satisfying experience in the future than his plans for that orgasmic day?

CHAPTER THIRTY-THREE

Jack and Roy returned precisely at ten o'clock. They were immediately invited into the inner sanctum.

They exchanged good mornings. "Your timing yesterday was impeccable," she said. "Nevertheless, native Hawaiians are generally known for their hospitality, but still no *lei.*"

"We'll manage without them," Jack said. "We have just a few questions. The conference Dr. Bacardi attended ended on Friday, October 14. She wasn't reported missing until the 24th when she failed to show up at her practice. The notes in the file say her Physician's Assistant relayed that she extended her time here, because she met a man she was interested in, named Zach. It mentions that an interview was done with the PA, a close friend who took the call about staying longer in Honolulu."

"Before your arrival and all hell broke loose yesterday, I reviewed the binder," the Chief said. "The case took place shortly after I took over as Chief, so I remember it better than I might otherwise. As the file details, there were interviews with the victim's father. They were estranged, and he hadn't heard from her in a long time. There were also interviews with a sister, brother, and some friends. There are few details, because no one but the PA actually heard from her."

"Of you 107 missing persons," Roy asked, "how many were resolved?"

"All but thirteen. Most turned out not to be homicides. Some turned up as vagrants who thought Hawaii would be a good place to become a beachcomber. Others were prostitutes, mostly teenagers, who took a powder while on their parents' vacations."

"So there were ninety-four resolved. How many of those were homicides?"

"You want an exact number? The best I can do is estimate around fifteen percent."

"Any others demonstrate this kind of savagery?" Jack asked.

"I don't think I've ever seen a case with this kind of savagery. It was a horrific way to die, and it was well-planned and performed with deliberate execution. I'm not supposed to show more deference to one case over the other. Being a woman, and encountering the facts of this case, well...."

"I think we have what we need, Chief Kalawai'a. We appreciate your time."

"I'm sorry. I should've invited you to call me Brandi. I'm not usually this formal."

"In that case, how did you acquire a native Hawaiian name and marry it to Brandi?"

She laughed. "Kalawai'a means fisherman, apropos for someone trying to fill her net with criminals. My dad wanted to update me a tad. He liked the song *Brandi,* so here I am."

CHAPTER THIRTY-FOUR

Sylvia woke in a prostrate position, her thighs rising at a forty-five-degree angle to her calves and knees, forming a right triangle in the sand. It was tortuously painful. In her drowsy state, she struggled to stand and relieve the strained, cramped muscles in her shins and thighs. Finally, she righted herself by grabbing her shins and pulling herself to a standing position.

Seeing her feet mired in concrete, she screamed.

"You know, Sylvia," Zach said, "I stood above the grotto and played a portable radio at ear-splitting levels, and it couldn't be heard from above. Isn't that amazing?"

She tried to turn to see him. He walked up behind her and roughly pulled her arms down, securing them with zip ties. Sauntering around to face her, he confronted her with a wicked smile.

"The system of caves absorbs sound like a sponge does water. No echo or sound escapes. Even if there were someone to hear, he wouldn't be able to share my enjoyment of your shrieking. It took me hours on Saturday to find the right place. I don't think you'll want that picnic lunch, considering what's in store for you. Sorry about the zip ties, but I can't risk my DNA being left under your fingernails."

Giving the secluded location and its natural soundproofing, he would enjoy being able to hear the unmitigated screams and entreaties of Number 60. It would be rapturous.

Zero used scissors to cut away her clothing very carefully, creasing her skin with the tips so blood trickled down over her pert, tiny breasts. Another crease directed blood into her ecstasy valley from her abdomen. When her clothing was completely removed, he began to rape her, watching her desperate features for added enjoyment.

After a short time, she went limp, as he raped her in a standing position, bending his knees to compensate for the difference in height. He was still raping her when she revived on her own.

"Dear God, Zach. What are you doing? Why?"

"Three things, actually. First, I'm raping you. Second, I'll sodomize you. With your little concrete pedestal, it should be more comfortable for me than taking you from a facing position. Of course, I won't have the gratification of seeing your facial expressions. Third, I'll take a seat on my tarp over there and eat a picnic dinner while I watch you die an excruciating death. You should be able to turn your head to the right and look up to witness my enjoyment.

"As to why, I hate *bitches,* especially ones like you who think you're superior."

"Don't do this, Zach. Please don't do this. I thought we were getting along so well and made a connection with each other."

"I have to admit, talking with you was much less inane than with most of the women I've killed. You're smart, but you need to learn who's smarter. You need to be *taught* who's smarter. My name isn't Zach. It's Zero."

"Listen, Zero. I have one of the leading pediatric practices in Philadelphia. I'm a rich woman. I could make you rich!"

"You see what I mean about trying to be superior? I don't want your fucking money! I may not have your wealth, but I'm successful and have plenty of money of my own. I can't imagine missing what's coming. It may be the pinnacle of my career. What I'm telling you is that your chatter is pointless. Scream if you want, and you will, believe me. Stop talking, though. It won't do any good."

"The high tide's coming in, isn't it? You plan to drown me? Is that it?" She tried to anticipate his plan. Her mind raced, as Zero sodomized her, fighting for consciousness over pain and terror. Zero degraded her, sodomizing her until he was satiated.

"Now, Sylvia, I promised you a surprise. You wouldn't want to spoil it, would you?" His malevolent voice pleasantly surprised even him. "I'll tell you this, though. I placed you, so water will reach only your shoulders at high tide. Don't worry about drowning. Besides, you wouldn't insult me with such mediocrity as drowning. You're Number 60, like sixty seconds in a minute and sixty minutes in an hour. You're special. You'll learn that sixty seconds can be a very long time."

He stepped forward and cut her zip ties. "It wouldn't be sporting if I didn't let you defend yourself, however ineffectual." He gave a hearty laugh. The surf was mid-thigh and rising fast. "Hint—hit the shark on the nose. Actually, there'll be dozens."

The heavy picnic basket was filled with concrete mix. She was unconscious long enough with the anesthetic for the concrete to set. Zero threw chum into the foaming water.

"Oh, God, no! You can't! It's monstrous!" She tried to sit down, hoping to drown herself.

"No, no, Sylvia. You'll spoil my fun. Sorry, Dr. Sylvia." He set down the chum and approached her. "My genius anticipated this." He picked her up with his strong arms and placed a sturdy piece of driftwood into the third hole in the concrete.

"As you can see, like a good Boy Scout, I came prepared." He tied her to the driftwood.

He was careful not to leave any DNA on the wood or allow her to scratch him with her free hands, as she tried to do. It was unlikely there would be any fingers left. What the sharks didn't get, the crabs would finish.

Zero spread more chum in a bloody circle around her, the water halfway to its full height, and picked up his tarp with latex-covered hands and gathered everything except the impressions he left in the sand, which would soon be erased.

Moving to higher ground, he sat on a rock and began eating a sandwich while he waited.

"As a doctor, you must be aware of the olfactory senses of sharks," he said, relishing his taunts. "They will smell the chum from as far away as five miles, but they'll be trying to beat the others to the prize. It shouldn't be long now."

Despite the futility, she continued fighting for her life. Water was almost up to her breasts. Soon, it would reach her shoulders.

Suddenly, an unimaginable shriek filled the night, as the first shark struck. Zero squealed with joy like a pig. A second struck, and another sound came from Sylvia that no words could describe before she lost consciousness.

Zero sighed, knowing the fun was over. He regretted that the sharks made it impossible to revive her, if she was still alive, given his normal proclivities. Still, the horror of it challenged him to excel each creative act with something even more horrific and thus more satisfying. Besides, having a single MO like all the other inferior serials would be boring. There would be no challenge to top it, which had become his intellect's pervasive preoccupation.

In the morning, he doubted more than the stubs of her legs would remain. It was, indeed, the zenith of his career.

"What say you now, Mom?" he asked. "I'll wager I'm the valedictorian of serial murderers now, don't you think?"

He walked back to his car.

CHAPTER THIRTY-FIVE

Cheri left to see what she could learn about Dr. Bacardi on the doctor's home turf.

Jack and Roy flew to Honolulu to meet with Police Chief Brandi Kalawai'a and Chief Medical Examiner Stanley Collins. Kalawai'a was Honolulu's second female police chief. Jack checked with Bureau people who knew her, and she was reputed to be a very tough cookie. They would pump her for anything on Collins when they arrived. Collins, new to his job, hadn't worked with any of Jack's contacts so far.

After Roy's misstep in calling without authorization, he was quiet for most of the flight, with a transfer in LA, although he was clearly excited about making his first sojourn into the field. Jack did his best to put him at ease, wanting him to feel comfortable. Jack felt he overreacted in the office, but Roy wasn't a very talkative fellow.

Kalawai'a let them wait for over an hour once they arrived at her office.

"Something's going down," Jack said softly.

"Lots of cops scurrying around," Roy added.

Finally, they recognized the Chief from the photos at Quantico, as she walked toward them. She blew right past them and quickly closed the door to what they assumed was her office. Almost immediately, she came out and left again.

Fifteen minutes later, she reappeared, reintroduced herself in a strictly businesslike way, and ushered them into her office.

She had the coveted corner office with windows on two walls looking out over beautifully landscaped grounds. With a name like Kalawai'a, she was obviously a native Hawaiian. She was in good shape, but her relatively flat features relegated her to competing for Miss Congeniality in a beauty contest.

"Have a seat, Gentleman," she said. "Sorry I don't have a *lei* to welcome you." She looked at Roy. "You're the young agent I spoke to on the phone?"

"Yes. This is Supervising Special Agent Jack Garvey." His introduction was a bit formal, which Jack chalked up to nerves.

"Nice to meet you, Chief Kalawai'a. Caught you on a bad day, it seems?"

"Nice to know a senior agent didn't miss that. Gives me confidence in the Bureau," she said wryly.

She shuffled through a stack of files on her desk until she found one labeled *Bacardi*. As homicide binders went, it was pretty thin. "This should give you the lowdown on Dr. Bacardi's demise."

Roy couldn't contain his curiosity any longer. "What the heck is going on around here?"

Jack gave him a frosty glare that shut him up.

She replied, "Bank robbery. When you live on an island other than Long Island, response times here are pretty quick. We caught the perps flat-footed. SWAT handled a hostage situation quickly, but there's a ton of follow-up. Let's get on with what you came here for. The file I just gave you should answer your questions."

"You were Chief a year ago when Bacardi went missing, so you must've had some involvement in the case," Jack said.

"We've had 107 missing persons in the year since I took over. When it became a homicide, I naturally explored it and made sure what could be done was getting done. Like I said, it's in the file."

"Look, can we make a bargain? Confidentially, we're working on a serial. It's possible Dr. Bacardi was one of the victims, but possibly not. Give us a room to look over the file and an appointment for tomorrow for follow-up questions, and you can go about your SWAT debriefing. Fair enough?"

She sighed, knowing there was no way out of it, since it was a possible serial. "OK."

CHAPTER THIRTY-SIX

Chief Kalawai'a arranged for the agents to meet Dr. Stanley Collins, the city's Chief Medical examiner and its highest-paid employee, right after meeting with her.

Collins wore the long white doctor's coat but no stethoscope. His patients didn't have beating hearts. He was tall, around six-one Jack surmised, with male-pattern baldness and close-cropped hair around the sides.

He made it clear he was busy in his detached, cool demeanor.

"Have you reviewed the case, and were you aware we were coming?" Jack shot back, put off by the man's lack of bedside manner.

"Didn't need to. Wasn't much to the case, forensically speaking. What do you want to know?"

"Dr. Bacardi was reported missing on October 24. According to the file we reviewed, the cement block and driftwood stake were discovered on the 21st. From what I understand, the remains were mostly bone and toenails, although they were badly degraded. How'd you make a DNA match?"

"The tissue had been consumed. There was really no way to estimate when she was murdered. The big bones of the foot's arch, the talus and navicular bones, along with the calcanean bone or what people call the heel, are the largest bones in the foot. Also, there were metatarsal bones, the toes. All of these were preserved, because the concrete filled in around them.

"When we got them to the lab, we had to break the concrete with autopsy hammers. We extracted the bone marrow, and voilà!

When we compared it to DNA from her father and other family members, we had a match. What else?" he asked impatiently.

"Could you at least fix a ballpark on the date of death?"

"I thought you guys were a little more up to speed on this stuff. No tissue means no *livor mortis*, no *rigor mortis*, and no temperature. We couldn't estimate time of death in a million years."

"I suspected so," Jack said, "but you never know. You might run into an ME who's more than average brilliant."

If Dr. Collins possessed Superman's eyes, he would've burned holes through Jack.

Within minutes, he and Roy were on their way back to the airport.

CHAPTER THIRTY-SEVEN

The following day, the team was back at Quantico for their 8:00 AM briefing. Mike Hennessey, who was present, wanted an idea of the team's progress, and said he was just there to observe.

"Cheri, please lead off," Jack said.

"I talked to the same people the Honolulu Police did," she began, "with no better result. Apparently, the only person Dr. Bacardi spoke with was the PA in her office, and the only information she had was that Bacardi met a man she wanted to get to know better and was going to stay another week. His name was Zach, and he was attending another conference the following week," she said dejectedly. "I hoped for more."

"Cheri, that wasn't in the file!" Roy said.

"What wasn't?"

"That he was attending another conference the next week!" Roy said, excited. "That's why she decided to stay on!"

"Good catch, Roy," Jack said. "It was definitely *not* in the file."

"That's a great piece of news," Mike said. "Let me ask a foundational question. Does this murder line up well with Barbara Cox's murder? Are we chasing the same perp?"

Cheri was ready to reply, but Mike was looking at Jack, who had more experience, not to mention he was unequivocal about Cox being Number 67.

"I just don't know, to tell the truth," Jack said. "Some things fit, and some don't. For instance, Cox didn't have repeated contact with our guy. Bacardi apparently did. Cox's murder was definitely hands-on, active aggression. Bacardi's was clearly passive. The perp let the sharks do his handiwork. Did repeated attacks by the sharks constitute repetitive torture? Cox went through a long ordeal. While terrifying, Bacardi's death was probably not so extensive in elapsed time. I just don't know. I think Bacardi should be followed up, though."

Jack turned to Cheri. "I want you to see if you can extrapolate a profile for each of these murders. You'll almost need MPD, because you'll have to put aside what you know about each, making them as independent as possible. Then you can try to put them together and see what kind of match we have or don't have. *Capiche*, Cheri?"

"Gotcha."

"Roy, check out the conferences the week after Dr. Bacardi's. Given that our perp travels so extensively in the east, I believe he's some kind of sales guy, regional manager, or something business related. There were probably 100 conferences that week, which included fraternal organizations, professional gatherings like the one the doctor attended, charitable and fund-raising get-togethers, and maybe political gatherings. Narrow it down to business right now and see what you find."

CHAPTER THIRTY-EIGHT

Two days later, they were together again. Mike Hennessey reserved a conference room for eight, so it was very comfortable for only four.

"I've been thinking about something that happened in our last meeting," Mike said, "and it's a good teaching perspective for our young agents. We've said before, the smallest piece of evidence or a seemingly inconsequential thought can break a case. It would be going too far to say Cheri's discovery was missed by Honolulu, or that Roy's quick recognition of its significance, have broken the case, but it does show both of you are doing the kind of job Jack and I expect of you. Keep it up. That's all I've got, Jack."

"I concur, Mike. Good job," Jack added. "OK, let's lead off with Cheri. What have you developed?"

"When you first pointed out the dichotomies presented by this murder, each point you made clearly had facts on its side. It looked like either an unsolvable conundrum or that analysis would leave us fence-sitting. In that event, the question could become whether we should invest time on it or look for more-fertile pastures.

"Let me take each of the issues Jack laid out in order, then cover some new ground. First is the issue of repeated contact that didn't appear in the Cox case. We really don't know that. In fact, there was at least one prior contact to arrange a rendezvous. There could have been more.

"Of course, in Honolulu, since Dr. Bacardi anticipated staying over a full week, it's likely that she expected to see our culprit more than once. I don't think she would've agreed to extend an additional week otherwise. As a doctor with a very successful practice, as I learned about her, she would've been more cautious about putting herself into a vulnerable position too quickly.

"The second issue was about the hands-on aspect of the Cox murder. I think that's a nonsequitur. The preparation this operation required was very hands-on. The way in which the murder was conducted required extensive thought both in the planning and execution. In reviewing the information provided by the Honolulu Police that Jack and Roy brought back, we should consider several points.

"The location had to be selected. Concrete mix had to be purchased. A piece of driftwood had to be found that would keep her erect. Once it was discovered, the perp had to set it aside while he scouted for a location. It may be hands-on in a different way than attaching jumper cables to the victim, but it was hands-on nonetheless.

"Next is the issue of passivity. Watching her, as I'm certain would've been the case with any perp who was twisted enough to create these murders, would likely involve what's called psychological projection. Usually, that's employed to avoid responsibility for negative acts against others to avoid emotional consequences, but it can also be for positive reasons, such as increasing one's exhilaration during the event. I believe that's part of the pathology in this case.

"Finally, the issue concerning the length of time the torture lasted and the amount of repetition of the torture itself. In considering this, one has to understand that the *anticipation* of this brutal plan, running repeatedly in the murderer's mind, would have provided the same or even greater gratification.

"Jack, you asked me to see if we could put the two together. I think what I outlined is persuasive that we can."

To be successful, investigation involves a lot of mental work and introspection. Each person in the room was silent, absorbing and trying to reconcile the analysis Cheri laid out.

Jack was the first to speak. "Outstanding, Cheri!" His opinion had been that the Bacardi case wouldn't link with the Cox case, but he was totally convinced by her reasoning.

He also experienced feelings he hadn't felt before. He was proud of his ability as a teacher, of the skills he acquired over the last ten years, and his students made him proud, too, but he felt the beginnings of emotional attachment. He was like a father when his toddler went off to her first day at school, except his feelings weren't paternal.

"I'll take it a step further," Mike said. "Your insight and psychological assessment are what I would expect from an experienced BAU agent. I'll be very surprised if you aren't on a path similar to Jack's. At the risk of embarrassing the man, that's a high compliment."

Roy beamed for his friend.

CHAPTER THIRTY-NINE

Still smiling, Roy said, "Jeez, Cheri, that's a hard act to follow." He looked at the others. "The conference Bacardi attended was called *Diagnosing Rare Conditions in Adolescents,* and it took place between Monday, October 10 and Friday, October 14 last year. There were a hundred trade shows, conventions, conferences, and seminars in the following week. We're focusing on October 17-21, the week after Bacardi's conference.

"My research shows there were religious conventions, such as the Knights of Columbus, a Catholic charitable organization, conferences on focusing on self-betterment like Alcoholics Anonymous and Toastmasters International, seminars such as Tony Robbins for sales and personal development, groups with a political agenda, such as NOW, as well as tradeshows.

"I was directed to look at business get-togethers, which I did. That's logical given the apparent employment nature of our perp's travel habits, but who's to say he wasn't there attending Tony Robbins? There are legitimate avenues of inquiry we aren't pursuing, and we might have to look at them in the future. One might have classified Robbins as business-related, but one of our goals, as I understand them from Jack, is to lean in the direction of limiting the scope of our exploration, at least for now.

"Thirty-five organizations were specific to industries and businesses and trade shows. Most were small. One focused specifically on technical salespeople who sold and consulted about surgery. Others included an organization of lathe manufacturers, an association of varnish manufacturers, and even one on concrete-mixing technologies.

"When I saw the concrete show, I immediately jumped. It seemed like a hell of a connection to the Bacardi case. Then I had two thoughts that redirected my efforts. I got some input from Cheri on this, too.

"First, there are two ways of looking at this. We've already concluded that the numbers our perp is using are designed to show he has a superior intellect. The temptation to reveal this intellect to the world would almost certainly surface in the crime. By that I mean he would've chosen specialized concrete that would advertise his intellectual prowess. The file from Honolulu said the concrete was scrutinized for any potential evidence, and they determined it was made from a common mix you can buy at any ACE store.

"The second thought had to do with our quarry's habits. He's been meticulous in shielding his identity. He went to great lengths to learn and apply forensics knowledge he assiduously acquired to conceal any connection with himself. It would've been out of character for him to go to a concrete-mixing trade show and then use concrete in the commission of a crime.

"Of the thirty-five business-related conferences and tradeshows, only one, held at the Hawaii Convention Center in Honolulu, was large. That was the AAUS, an automotive aftermarket trade show of specifically U.S.-based manufacturers. Large companies like Borg-Warner attended, and smaller ones that use brokers to represent them.

"It's your decision, Jack and Mike, but here's my thinking. There are two ways to approach our mission. One is that we try to pick off the thirty-four smaller organizations one-by-one and try to establish a connection to our serial.

"The second would be by trying to penetrate AAUS. The odds are in our favor, because more people attended that convention than all the other business-related programs combined. The problem with that approach, of course, is the magnitude of the job.

"Bear with me, because I'm going to get into some detail, but it'll soon be clear where I'm going. I called the Director of the AAUS, Ed Cousins. AAUS is the third-largest automotive aftermarket association. The two larger ones are SEMA and AAPEX, both held in Las Vegas in November each year at the same time. SEMA attracts 2,400 exhibitors alone, and between the two conferences, about 250,000 people attend. Both are international in nature. If our guy's a part of that conglomerate, finding him will be beyond any reasonable calculation.

"AAUS was formed to represent strictly American manufacturers and distributors, conserving tax and trade pacts, etcetera. The top reason for the creation of AAUS was to avoid being lost in the magnitude of the Las Vegas shows. The trade show in Honolulu was their second. meant to save the organization after a disastrous San Francisco premier the previous year.

"I was curious why they selected Honolulu. It was more difficult transportation-wise and more expensive for many exhibitors, purchasing agents, those who monitor industry developments, and other attendees. There were a huge number of retail and wholesale distributors of auto aftermarket products who had to consider the logistics. They faced additional business days lost and greater expense for the Hawaiian experience. Was that tradeoff successful for AAUS? Did it depress attendance at the exact time they were trying to recover from their disappointing show in Frisco?

"Cousins explained it was a gamble. It was crucial to their continued viability to be viewed with the same kind of legitimacy as the larger Vegas conventions. Honolulu, he felt, could do that. He hoped the attractiveness of the venue would overcome the obstacles.

"It looks like it worked, because Honolulu was a great success. Cousins also felt that conditions in Frisco, with its homelessness and other negatives, may have depressed attendance for their first U.S.-only trade show. While the number of vendors was steady, attendees went up by 43%, from 56,000 to 80,000.

"Atendees could purchase tickets at the door by flashing a business card. Almost everybody has one. The relevance of the card didn't seem to matter. Due to the sheer numbers involved and their more-limited resources, AAUS decided not to try to gather information on attendees. Exhibitors had to apply and provide a registration and credentials for each member of the exhibit team. On average, that was four people per exhibit. Some exhibits had fifteen or more, while others just had two to spell each other. That still means in excess of 6,000 persons to be looked at and potentially interviewed.

"Cousins provided me with a list of the roughly 1,500 exhibitors to both the San Francisco and Honolulu trade shows. I'm running it through the computer right now to look for matching exhibitors who attended both. My thought is, since our guy has been operating in the eastern U.S. for ten years, he's probably a veteran who, if he belongs to the organization, would probably have attended both.

"I'm following that up by running those names through NCIC for any criminal history. Naturally, I'm prioritizing any sex-related activity. Preliminary results suggest that's going to be a small minority of that 6,000. That'll give us only a few people to scrutinize more closely. Absent a result there, it won't limit the scope of what we have to look at."

Jack halted Ray at this point. "I just had a thought. When I was in law school at USF, I clerked for a criminal appellate attorney named Bill Oppenheimer. Bill was well-respected and had a lot of contacts in the legal profession. He was able to get me a weekend job selling legal research software at conferences. I flew out to legal conventions all across the country and worked the exhibit. I learned a little about sales and the structure of companies.

"They aren't all Goodyears out there. In a lot of cases, smaller companies, like the one I exhibited for, would be represented by brokers. They would usually have Regional Sales Managers who traveled a large geographic area and trained and supervised the brokers. The eastern U.S. could easily fit that configuration. I'd start by looking at smaller companies that might he structured that way."

"Great minds think alike," Roy quipped. "I learned that in the automotive aftermarket world, most companies have that structure and tend to be highly specialized. A company might make just a switch, for example, that triggers warning lights on the dashboard.

"If you count companies with Regional Managers that cover the eastern part of the country and limit it to the companies that distribute only in the eastern U.S., as well as the independent brokers, Ed Cousins estimated the number would be down to a thousand or three. That's better but still a significant amount of territory to cover. That could be exacerbated if our guy isn't an exhibitor.

"Here's the salient fact that made me feel attacking the AAUS initially was best. The association's third annual trade show is coming up in October. I'm not suggesting that we wait until then to explore the group. I think we ought to contemplate a calling campaign in the meantime. The upcoming trade show, however, could give us the opportunity to come face-to-face with our perp. We might even be able to identify possible persons to interview. The odds are long, but they have been ever since we started. We'd be doing something our predecessors lacked even the predicate to try. We'd be breaking new ground, however thin our postulations are, and go beyond just mailing dates.

"No matter what we do with what little we have, and with great deference for Jack's conviction about Barbara Cox, all this is still speculative. Even if he's correct, and boss, I sincerely believe you are, can we be sure that Cheri's brilliant presentation joining the two murders is correct?

"Whatever we do will be a shot in the dark. I just think that of all the options we have, this is the best."

He stopped, waiting for their reactions.

All of them were silent, processing the new information.

Mike smiled and looked to his left. "Jack?"

"I'd say both of you have outdone yourselves. Your arguments, Roy, seem strong to me. No doubt, knowing you for just a short time, you were already doing lots of statistical calculations on our chances before deciding on this recommendation?"

"Some."

"Assignments. Roy, pursue your line of reasoning with AAUS. See if you can organize a prospective calling program, but continue to check the mailing dates and any potential murders in eastern jurisdictions that might line up. Put the emphasis on the calling list.

"Cheri, you work with Roy. Call some smaller companies, to see if we get lucky. Also, act as a sounding board with Roy on any potentials. I'll keep calling local law enforcement.

"Thanks, Everyone."

CHAPTER FORTY

The team had their next meet on the following Monday. Mike was unable to attend, so it was just the three musketeers.

"You started the last meeting, Cheri," Jack said. "We'll let Roy take first crack at it today."

"If we start with the 1,000-3,000 or more of the 6,000 exhibitor personnel that are small enough to work with brokers and have either an exclusively eastern market or an eastern regional manager, there are a bunch of hurdles to get over," Roy began. "We can't call anyone but the CEO of the company these thousands work for, or we could end up talking to the perp.

"Then there's the logistics. What percentage of calls will end up with a busy signal? Will we actually reach the desired CEO without being screened out? Are they out of town? Will they just refer us to legal counsel or refuse to talk with us? We're talking about tens of thousands of calls between just the two of us."

Jack said, "I'll still be calling locals. We can call it two-and-a-half, if you like. I'll be splitting my time."

"I appreciate that," Roy said, "but that changes the equation by only 25%, a fraction of what we need. Is there no way to get additional help? We don't have much time before the next trade show in October. It would be nice to have some possibles to interview. You still think we should attend?"

"Yes, unless something less speculative presents itself. As far as the help goes, I'll see what I can do, but no promises."

"In the meantime, I'm still trying to correlate the dates of the mailings with homicides. Maybe the reason we haven't been more successful with this is that we've been looking for homicides that occurred exclusively before the mailing date. Cheri's profile suggests our man may have gone to considerable length to create confusion and make his ID more difficult. Wouldn't mailing the number first and committing the murder second do precisely that?"

"Cheri, what are your thoughts on that?" Jack asked.

"It's a good idea, Roy," she said, considering her answer. "It's definitely thinking outside the box, but it just doesn't fit the guy the way I see him. He's trying to confuse us in any number of ways. I think we all agree he's intelligent and very methodical. I'd say he's not just methodical but the very definition of OCD. The idea he'd send the number first, well, if something went awry, he'd have an inaccurate number. I don't see it. His pride in his accomplishment demands the killing be a reported fact, not a speculative one."

"That was creative, Roy," Jack said. "You might even turn out to be right, although I respect Cheri's opinion, too. Just now, though, we need to narrow the range of possibilities, not expand them. Continue thinking outside the box, but for now, work on homicides solely a week before the posted date. You could narrow that focus to only three days before, but I'll leave that up to you. A week throws a wider net. I'd stick with that for now, but, as I said, it's your call.

"If our guy is as OCD as Cheri suspects, he'll want two things. He wants to travel to another city before he mails it, to throw us off, Honolulu notwithstanding. If that weren't the case, we'd have been able to put the crimes together with the mailings, and so would the agents who worked on this before. I sense he'll also want to announce his triumph as soon as possible, but whether sooner or later is a conundrum. I concur with Cheri that mailing beforehand isn't a fit for our guy."

Jack looked at Cheri. "What did you come up with, Cheri?"

"I'm afraid a lot of it is pure conjecture. What we have from a clinical perspective is very thin. If we're right about Honolulu being

Number 60 and Adams County being Number 67, not just the brutality of the crimes but the fact that repeated infliction of pain was imposed suggests a deep, malingering hatred for women in general, possibly as an alter ego for someone. Since our serial moves around, it's a reasonable extrapolation that he didn't know either Bacardi or Cox well. Then why such brutality? Most often when we see that, it suggests an ongoing relationship with the victim.

"In this instance, I believe it fits the alter ego context the best. Since Barbara Cox was a very attractive woman, that could be a prerequisite—or not. We can't assume too much from two instances. If it's a factor, that indicates our perp may have been inflamed by repeated rejection from the trophy wife types, making him someone outwardly confident but inwardly disconsolate. Other factors might flip his switch, but we don't know what those are. Possibly he had a cleft palate or other infirmity, but that's problematic.

"In Cox's case, it appears they had a prearranged rendezvous. Certainly, there was some social contact with Bacardi. This suggests a man who is attractive to women and not likely to have encountered the kind of regular rejection that would build resentment to the level of hatred. No, I think our man hates *all* women."

"There's a hybrid you're overlooking," Jack said. "He could've been an ugly duckling—not in appearance, perhaps, but someone who experienced rejection in youth, and it carried over into adulthood. Sometimes, those wounds are the deepest."

"That was certainly the case with Jeffrey Dahmer," she said. "While his victims were men, he was driven away from women by hatred for his mother. She tied him to a tree with metal chains in the middle of a thunderstorm when he was quite young. I think we're dealing with someone with a deeply internalized and pervasive hatred of women in general. Our perp may have been driven to his hatred by a domineering, abusive mother. The women our guy murdered could have been a substitute for the perp's mom or the person who raised him, including foster care. Same motivation but manifested differently."

"That's a lot," Jack said. "I continue to be impressed with each of you. As I told Mike earlier, he's got a good eye for talent."

"Translation," Cheri said. "Jack means him!"

They laughed.

CHAPTER FORTY-ONE

Zero sat unobtrusively in a high-backed booth in a dimly lit bar in Cleveland, thinking about Number 68. He already conceptualized the exquisite torture he would inflict on the next woman to expiate his enveloping hatred. He hadn't, however, figured out how or where or when or on whom he would practice his next ritual.

It was late afternoon, and the after-work patrons hadn't yet invaded. A loud-mouthed woman bullied her husband.

"Susan look, you know I've only been on the job a short time," he replied. "We're just getting our heads above water after my not working for a while. I understand you want to give Hank a great birthday, and so do I. I just don't understand why it has to be so elaborate."

"How typical of you. You don't get much of anything, Sam! It's probably why you lost your last job. This will be Hank's sixth birthday, and he'll start first grade in a month. It may be the first birthday he remembers, and I want it to be memorable."

Susan's cell phone rang, and she picked it up. Cupping her hand over the phone, she whispered, "It's the agency." Turning back to her call, she said, "Yes, that's right. Really? He does magic tricks, too? That's great. How much more? Well, OK."

Sam kept trying to interject. Much as Zero's dad was overridden by his mom, Susan ignored him.

"I already gave you guys the address," she said. "Oh, I see. It's just to confirm? It's 18752 North Franklin Street this coming Saturday. I already gave you my credit card. Put the additional amount on that. I need to give it to you again? How efficient," she said sarcastically.

Her voice dropped too low to overhear, then it came back. "Yeah. We're having a barbecue about four o'clock for the parents of the other kids who are coming.

"Oh, I see. How much setup time do we need for the magic act? OK. Better have him come by around three, then. What's the clown's name? Pickles? How *original.* No, there won't be anyone else there. My husband's meeting the kids and other parents at an amusement park around nine that morning and won't be back before *Pickles* arrives." Her voice dripped with sarcasm over the name.

"I don't want him there before three, though. I'll be getting ready and will be working furiously. I want to do it all myself, so it'll be perfect. I guess that covers it."

Susan hung up and resumed arguing with Sam. She ignored his protestations about the additional cost. "Look, Sam, I'm tired of arguing with you. That's the way it's going to be. Maybe if you were more successful, we wouldn't have to pinch pennies and have these arguments. We're not doing any more than the Simpsons did for David."

"Exactly," Sam whined. "He's a foreman at the factory. He can afford it."

"Can't you just shut up? You're driving me nuts!"

Zero had his Number 68. Susan was the incarnation of his mother. He would enjoy Number 68 immensely. That bitch was made to order for him.

He was very auditory and never forgot anything he heard. He knew the address and timing.

CHAPTER FORTY-TWO

Zero didn't want to buy the clown suit or makeup in Cleveland. A little research found a theatrical supplies shop in Akron, about forty miles away down I-77. Akron was a medium-sized city, and no one would associate a purchase there with an event in Cleveland. With traffic, it would be a quick two-and-a-half-hour trip. He drove down on Friday.

The next day, he showed up at the house at 11:00 AM. Most people looked forward to their weekends. Zero certainly looked forward to that particular Saturday. He was in full clown regalia. When he rang the doorbell, no one responded, so he knocked heavily. His clown gloves protected him from leaving prints. He even perused the rough-hewn wood door to make sure he left no fibers from the glove.

Finally, his prey answered the door. "Hi. You're Susan? I'm Pickles the clown!" He gave her a disingenuous smile. His perverse motives undergirded the countenance he learned to display to others. "Where will I set up for the magic act?"

He wanted to make sure she was alone and also check out the surroundings.

"You're way early," she said. "Where's your stuff?"

"In my trunk. I want to see the lay of the land first. Where should I set up the stage?"

She took him to where he could see the backyard, and he quickly memorized every detail.

It was an older house, probably built in the mid-1950s. It had the vinyl siding in vogue at that time, now a weatherworn, faded façade.

The front door opened into a small entryway with a guest closet on the left. A large living room with a worn copy of an oriental rug was excellent for his purposes. Yellow cabinets were in the kitchen on the left, and a staircase with lacquered railing led upstairs.

The living room looked out onto a medium-sized backyard that would have been a great location for a magic show, if he had one. He walked back to the front door, turned toward his unwitting prey, grabbed her, and spun her into his customary chokehold. Unconsciousness came quickly.

He dropped her limp body to the faded rug, then he closed all doors and pulled all the shades, including on the doors, to make their next interaction more private. Restraining her he quickly disabled all the smoke detectors on the first and second floors.

When she came to, she was already bound with duct tape. He always bought the widely distributed Gorilla tape for its strong adhesion. Two Ping Pong balls were in her mouth, which was taped shut. Thanks to his latex gloves, there was no chance of leaving fingerprints or DNA behind. He removed the clown gloves to avoid leaving fiber evidence and continued wearing only the latex gloves. The clown gloves went into his oversized pockets.

His shoe size was camouflaged by the oversized clown shoes. His exaggerated pockets gave him plenty of room for the few items he needed.

The house reminded him of one his parents rented with a vintage '55 Chevy Bel-Aire in the driveway. His dad babied that car for years, and he and his dad loved it. Ultimately, Phoebe forced Drake to surrender it, he recalled bitterly, because they *had* to keep up with the Joneses.

Zero already saw the house had no modern security system, which fit with the family's strained finances. He anticipated that, but he always checked, one of his zero-defects habits.

He stripped her naked in the middle of the fake oriental rug, probably bought at Wal-Mart years earlier. The rug would take some damage. He explained he would rape her and berated her for not being up to his normal standards. At least she needn't fear he would kill her, as customary. He was uncomfortable with the time constraints, even though he was quite early. He had plenty of time, but unplanned interruptions from neighbors or anyone else made him prepare for tighter time constraints.

He usually avoided using the hated condoms, but he realized that was superfluous. His plan would make wearing a condom redundant. He hoped he could take care of that while she was alive, if she didn't go into shock from what he had in store.

He raped her as brutally as he could three times, the last time sodomizing her. He was sure she denied that pleasure to her husband, Sam, but he imagined she enjoyed it with him, the bitch.

It was time to move on to the real fun. He reminded her of his promise, took a small can of cigarette lighter fluid from his oversized clown pocket, and poured a small circle of it on her left nipple before lighting it. Her muffled screams were some of the most satisfying of his many escapades. He let it burn briefly, then extinguished it.

"That was excruciating, wasn't it, Susan? Care to try the other nipple?"

She shook her head vigorously.

"Would you rather I kill you?"

Again, she indicated no.

He poured more lighter fluid on her right nipple and covered more of her breast before lighting that. Eventually, he smothered the flame. He wondered how loud her screams would have been without the two Ping Pong balls and tape. The extra ball was to ensure total quiet.

A fitting analogy, he thought, *to the expression, the old ball and chain.*

Zero spurted lighter fluid onto her vagina and let it burn longer to ensure there was no trace of him inside her. He anticipated the stench of burning flesh would be foul and considered wearing nose plugs, but he decided he wanted to experience the full range of the torture and didn't bother. He might have reconsidered if he anticipated how repulsively nauseating the odor actually was.

He thought with glee that it was much more painful than the woman who scalded herself with McDonald's coffee. He continued burning her repeatedly on the thighs, abdomen, and arms, each time letting the flame burn a little longer before extinguishing it. Finally, Number 68 capitulated and began nodding to end it.

He gleefully poured an excessive amount of lighter fluid on her face, observing her terror reach an entirely new plateau. Before igniting it, he assured her that her son would, indeed, have a very special birthday.

"You're a special kind of bitch, and I'm glad to be liberating Sam."

He lit her entire head on fire, adding more fluid as needed, and left her to be found by the real Pickles, or, better yet, by Sam.

CHAPTER FORTY-THREE

The team learned that Sam Bundergast was at his sister's house across town, which was a bit of a trip. That was probably a bad thing, as it gave Sam notice and some time to organize his thoughts. Unrehearsed reactions to questions were always better.

"Why'd you tell Olenski we didn't want to talk to Bundergast, and now we're on our way there?" Roy asked.

"How'd you read Olenski?" Jack asked, playing straight man.

"Almost hostile. Territorial. Protective of his jurisdictional prerogatives."

"Here, here," Cheri added.

"So, do we want Olenski hanging around while we're looking for an opening?" Jack asked.

A short time later, they arrived. When a woman answered the door, Jack explained they wanted to talk to Sam. She tried to protest, but a man appeared behind her.

"Sis, please take Junior upstairs," he said. "I've been expecting them."

"Mr. Bundergast, my name is Jack Garvey. I'm with the FBI, as I told you." He held up his credentials. "These are my associates, Agent Cheri Hancock and Agent Rogers." He decided to avoid Roy's first name.

"There are good reasons for following up on this quickly," Jack continued, "even though we know how difficult it must be."

The man's face looked like a landscape of Hiroshima an hour after the bomb hit. Jack almost expected him to faint.

"I understand," he said numbly, opening the door wider.

The three of them went inside and sat on the couch, while Sam took a comfortable-looking chair opposite. Clearly uncomfortable, he sat on the edge of the chair, leaning forward.

"I feel like I've been run over by a truck. It was supposed to be such a wonderful day, my son's birthday. My wife and I wanted it to be memorable. He'll never forget it now...." His voice quavered.

Jack knew he wasn't about to ask the usual questions, like did Sam have any enemies or someone who would want to do such a terrible thing. "We know, of course, that the Fun Time Agency had knowledge of your plans for that day. Local police conducted interviews there, and they don't think the personnel were involved, although that's not dispositive at this time. Who else knew about your plans?"

"Besides the agency, the only people who knew were the kids and the parents of the kids who were to attend the party in the late afternoon. They were all with me at the Cedar Point amusement park before the party. Besides, I know those people. They couldn't have done such a thing!" he said with conviction.

"Not all the kids' parents were there, were they?" Cheri asked.

"Some had other commitments. I know them all, mostly from our church. It just isn't possible any of them could've done such a terrible, horrible thing." He sobbed uncontrollably.

Jack gave him time to recover but made no move to console him.

"We won't take much more of your time, Mr. Bundergast," Jack said. "Did the police tell you about the neighbor who saw another clown enter your home earlier that day?"

"Yes. I can't understand that at all," he said, bewildered.

"We believe the first clown was the person who killed your wife. We're trying to find out how he knew your plans."

"Could Fun Time have accidentally sent out two clowns in error?" Sam asked in desperation.

"The police checked into that, as I said earlier. The agency contends they didn't, and they wouldn't have made such an error. Besides, they had no other clowns who weren't occupied. It was a Saturday. They're usually booked weeks in advance, and no one called in sick." Jack's voice was muted. No matter how often he went through it, he was glad he wasn't hardened or lost his empathy. A good agent put empathy on a sidetrack and kept his focus on obtaining information.

"Did your wife tell many people about the party?"

"Just her friends at church and Junior's friends who were coming to the party, and their parents."

"Did you and your wife have any discussions about the party?" Jack asked.

"Incessantly. I was concerned about the cost. It seemed so important then but isn't at all important now." He sobbed.

Regaining his composure, Sam tried to explain. "There was a lot of tension between Susan and me over this birthday party. I was out of work for a while, and I didn't think what we were spending on the party.... Oh, my God. Susan said I didn't know what was important in life." He silently stared at the floor.

"We're all so sorry, Mr. Bundergast," Cheri said, earning a sharp look from Jack.

"Where'd you have these discussions?" Jack asked.

"Always at home. Since we were at odds, and because we're very private people, we didn't want to discuss it in public."

"The agency said they made a confirmation call and told your wife that Pickles could do magic. Do you remember that?" Jack gleaned that fact from reviewing a copy of the case file Olenski provided them under duress.

Sam's eyebrows rose, as he tried to remember. A flash of recall came to his face. "Well, yes, I do. Susan and I stopped at our local watering hole, Dan's Place. She doesn't like bars much, but after having a tug-of-war with her over this birthday thing, I needed a drink. Seriously needed one, so she relented. It was probably more of a bribe on her part than anything else. My wife is—was—a wonderful person, but she could be stubborn. When it came to Junior, she was downright intransigent."

"Who was in the bar with you?" Cheri asked.

Jack smiled. That was his next question.

"Just Dan, the owner, a real good guy. When we were talking, however, he left and went in the back to get some stock for the after-work rush. He couldn't have heard us."

When the team was outside again, Cheri confronted Jack. "What was that look about?" she asked defensively.

"First, I was conducting the interview," Jack began.

"The man was really hurting. I was just trying to be sympathetic." A little anger sounded in her voice.

"Second, you were sympathetic at exactly the wrong time. Listen up. We're investigators. Our job is to investigate, not sympathize with or make the victim's family feel better. That's not as cold as it sounds. Ultimately, the only thing that'll help Sam Bundergast is if we catch the bastard who murdered his wife. The man I was interviewing was sobbing with every other question. Your sympathy could make him break down all over again. I was trying to hold him together, so I could get information. Fortunately, we got it."

Jack's voice softened. "Focusing on the information and leaving the grieving to the family is the only way to do it."

"I'm sorry," Cheri said sincerely. "I didn't realize."

"Comfort yourself with this: if we lost every agent who made that mistake, we wouldn't have any agents, myself included." He smiled yet wondered why he was being so sympathetic toward her. He wouldn't have done it for Roy or any other female agent.

Get a grip, he told himself.

"Hey," Roy said. "Don't leave me out of this. She was only a split second ahead of me."

Jack was pleased with Roy's show of solidarity.

Closing their car doors, they looked around on the way to Dan's Place. Two seconds later, they laughed in unison.

CHAPTER FORTY-FOUR

Jack, Roy, and Cheri assembled in the office again.

"We have news," Jack began, "none of it good. The FBI looked at microscopic shavings in the striations in Barbara Cox's bones. The lab's good at identifying such things. They believe the shavings came from a spade, which is no surprise. The gray paint matches spades commonly manufactured for Craftsman tools. They were sold only by the now-defunct Sears but have been licensed to Lowe's and others before their demise.

"Chromatography was used in an attempt to pinpoint the lots that were manufactured, but there wasn't enough material to work with.

"The insects found in the mutilated body were also forwarded to the lab. They confirmed Dr. Carr's estimate of the time of the death based on adult insects and pupae. Something enticing to the insects, perhaps honey, was applied to the gaping flesh after this monster completed his handiwork, deliberately attracting the insects to further obscure evidence."

Jack paused, and Cheri saw him collect himself before delivering more bad news. It had a real impact on him.

Finally, he said, "Also, we got the Number 68 in the mail, posted from Pittsburgh."

Cheri and Roy, exchanging looks of horror, shared a sense of futile resignation.

"I also heard from the Chief in Cleveland, following up from an earlier call, to say they have a female victim who was tortured. I think we'll take the whole team this time."

Roy said, "I hate passing this up, but I'm knee-deep in the trade show thing, and I want to be where I'm most useful. I'm making real progress. Most of the specialty aftermarket manufacturers are smaller companies who work with brokers. I'm narrowing our likely possibilities to Regional Managers of small national companies or National Sales Managers of regional companies that distribute only in the east. I'm compiling a good list. We can eliminate about 20% of the exhibitors that way. I'd like to keep at it."

"You have a laptop and cell phone," Jack said firmly. "You can continue from Cleveland."

CHAPTER FORTY-FIVE

Arriving in Cleveland the following day, they picked up a full-sized van from Enterprise before driving directly to the office of the Cleveland Chief of Police, Charles Olenski, with whom they had an appointment. They had a follow-up appointment with the Cuyahoga County ME.

Olenski, gruff on the phone, was accommodating once they sat down together. "I understand you FBI types wouldn't be here if you didn't think you had something important enough to take us away from our own investigations. That usually involves telling us how we should be doing our jobs."

Jack was ready to defend their meeting, but Olenski raised his hand.

"This isn't my first rodeo, Folks," he said. "I'm not denigrating you or your agency, and I'll give you all the cooperation you need, but we had ten homicides *last night,* mostly gang-related, and yours is just one extra we're already working on with very little to go on. We have our hands full. In Cleveland, ten homicides in one day is more than unusual. The press, of course, immediately indicted the whole police force, so I'm not happy right now.

"Let's get to it." He was of medium height, clean-shaven with more than a medium-sized paunch hanging over his belt. The only way he could win a fifty-yard dash was if the competitors were Wrong-way Corrigans. His mustache revealed he slipped up when shaving, with one side shorter than the other.

"The deceased's name is Susan Bundergast, age thirty-five, with one child, Sam. Jr. She was preparing for junior's sixth birthday party. Sam, Sr. has an iron-clad alibi. He was with a dozen other kids and some of their parents at Cedar Point Amusement Park. From what our investigators learned, they were supposed to return for the party and a barbecue to entertain the adults while a clown, Pickles, was supposed to perform a magic show for the kids.

"Pickles arrived at three o'clock as scheduled. He walked in, finding the front door ajar, when no one answered. He immediately smelled something burning or burnt. Since the door was open, Pickles, whose real name is John Smoler, called for Mrs. Bundergast.

"She never spoke. Her body lay in the middle of the living room floor surrounded by a charred, or completely burned in some places, oriental rug. Her body was covered with burns, but her head was almost completely charred. We didn't recover anything of her eyes. Her husband, Sam, could only identify clothing she wore for house cleaning that had been ripped away, but it took dental records for a definitive ID.

"Smoler, with a fight-or-flight reaction, bolted. His first thought, he said, was that he might be tagged with the crime. He has a prior felony for receiving stolen property, but, after serving a two-year sentence, he's been clean ever since. Smoler quickly realized that the full-time agency that sent him had a clear record of his booking. Besides, murder is a hell of a step up from his previous record.

"He sat down on the front steps of the house, let his stomach settle, and called us with his cell. The internal body temperature told us Mrs. Bundergast was dead for a couple hours, and that fit with the timeline. Pickles can be ruled out, because he had a prior kids' party at noon."

"Could someone have filled in for Smoler at the first appointment while he was actually at the Bundergasts'?" Roy asked.

Olenski's gaze almost bored a hole through him. "I guess all you younger guys are conspiracy theorists," he said resignedly. "That would be a clever plan for a deliberate, premeditated murder. It's been done before, but it doesn't work in this instance. Smoler had no connection to the Bundergasts except through the Fun Time Agency. At least, that's all our detectives could find.

"In addition, the first appointment he had Saturday was with a family who hired Pickles before and were adamant they recognized Smoler, clown paint and all notwithstanding."

"That doesn't mean Sam Bundergast couldn't have hired someone else to wear a clown outfit and commit the murder," Roy insisted. "How else could you account for the knowledge of their plans on Saturday?"

"That's more plausible," Olenski admitted. "Even possible. We interviewed just about everyone who knew him. None of them can envision him doing such a thing. He's portrayed as very timid, and that's not usually a personality profile for someone who would have the tenacity to follow through on murder for hire."

Cheri jumped in to defend her colleague. "Sometimes timid people are bullied. Maybe he had enough."

Jack listened, giving his new agents free rein.

"He must've hated her an awful lot to have jad her killed that way. What I saw of the man at the crime scene was someone devastated by the loss of his wife. Still, it's a plausible explanation." He shrugged.

"By the time Sam Bundergast and his guests returned from Cedar Point," he continued, "we were already onsite. One of the other parents took Junior with them. We explained to Mr. Bundergast that his wife was dead. He immediately tried to bolt into the house, but we restrained him. Eventually, we needed to have him identify the body as best he could.

"Her head was badly charred and was unrecognizable even to her husband. Her torso was mostly naked, however, and he was able to make a preliminary identification based on a birthmark in an area hot affected by non-lethal burns. That, of course, wasn't an adequate ID for a murder investigation, even in their own home, so we went with dental records.

"As you might suspect, especially given the terrible degradation of the body, Bundergast was all but incoherent. No doubt you'll want to talk to him, but you might wait until tomorrow. The funeral was yesterday."

"No, I don't think so," Jack said. "Our experience is that recollections are clearer closer to the event."

"Well, you guys always know better, don't you? We'll ascertain his whereabouts and *tell you where to go,* unless you change your mind."

"I'm sure you will."

"We haven't completed our forensics evaluation yet, so it's too soon to tell. So far, nothing has jumped out at us. Even the dental records weren't a slam dunk. The teethe were in pretty bad shape, too. As I said, the lion's share of potential forensic evidence is still being processed. The Cuyahoga County ME, Dr. James Phillips, will fill you in on that. We have eight forensic pathologists, and every one has his hands full with other homicides, plus non-homicidal deaths exacerbated by ten murders.

"Jim said, since we have the *august* presence of the FBI here, however, he would take you through things personally."

"Did the husband have any idea who might have done this?" Cheri asked. "Any inkling that Mrs. Bundergast was having an affair or anyone with a motive?"

"Neighbors said the two were always sniping at each other, but they never had any knockdown, drag-out confrontations. Sam, Sr., was rather timid, and the Mrs., while always complaining, wasn't the type to have an affair. She was a fervent churchgoer and very involved in her religious community. No known enemies for either of them.

"One other thing I think is vital. We noticed two sets of what appeared to be typical oversized clown shoes. I say two sets, because they appear to be different shoes. The larger shoe impressions covered more ground than the small, worn by Smoler. This was confirmed by a neighbor, who said she saw another clown leave the Bundergast home earlier in the day. There's a strong possibility, in our opinion," he added, giving the agents a sideways glance, "that the earlier clown is our killer. She said he left in a sedan, black or dark blue."

Once they left the office and were walking back to their rental car, Cheri said, "He was a real piece of work."

Roy and Jack nodded.

"Don't think this is Number 68, though," Roy said. "This had to have been someone who was familiar with the Bundergasts' plans for the day. I think it was murder for hire, the clown suit providing perfect cover for the perp and an alibi for Sam, Sr."

"If he is as timid as people suggest," Cheri replied, "it would be hard for him to gather the resolve, unless he was really fed up with being henpecked."

"No," Jack said. "This is Number 68."

Dumbfounded, they looked at him.

"Let me explain. First, using the clown suit indicates knowledge of the Bundergasts' plans for the day, pointing the finger at Mr. Bundergast. Granted, he may not have been the brightest bulb in the chandelier, but that would've been a dumb enough move that our executioner would have begged off even if Bundergast couldn't see past his own nose. No. This is someone who wanted things to appear that way, someone very smart.

"Normally, a serial has a definite MO, as you know. The lives of the victims are almost always taken in exactly the same way. If I'm correct about our guy, he avoids such a telling methodology. Three things are, nevertheless, consistent—the mailing of the number in close proximity time-wise but from a different location. In this case, it's Pittsburgh. Then the victims are all women. The most telling of all, however, is extreme and repeated torture. Torture itself isn't that rare, but the extreme nature of this, and the way it's deliberately prolonged, is."

Roy couldn't resist. "Do you realize how long the odds are that a stranger who normally chooses his victims randomly to somehow know the Bundergasts' plans in detail?"

"That's exactly what we have to find out," Jack insisted.

CHAPTER FORTY-SIX

The county morgue was half an hour away through heavy traffic. On the way, Jack dispelled theories put forward by Cheri and Roy. One of them was that an employee of the Fun Time Agency, who would have knowledge of Pickles' schedule, was their prey.

"If I'm right about our perp," Jack said, "he's moving from major metro area to major metro area throughout the east, committing these atrocities. That precludes an employee of the Fun Time Agency as our serial. We won't interview anyone from that agency unless one of you two finds something that suggests this murder is unrelated to our serial. Until that happens, we'll leave it to the locals.

"Often new agents, by not bringing preconceived ideas to a case, can see more clearly than more experienced ones, clouded by myopia from past cases. The reason a veteran agent directs these inquiries varies with the Supervising Agent. I try very hard not to succumb to that myopia. My strength has always been my instincts about a case. I respect each of you more every day I work with you. You both will be terrific additions to the Bureau.

"I'll continue to listen to you both. Your input helps me question my conclusions, but we'll never solve this case if I abandon those instincts. We're dealing with a very clever, very twisted, insidious individual. Stay with me for the moment and see where this goes, OK?"

They nodded somewhat reluctantly. Jack knew what they were thinking. They respected his experience, but they wouldn't become good agents if they didn't believe in themselves, too, and they were right.

They arrived at the morgue and were immediately directed to the ME's office. Frosty glass on the top half of the door announced *James Phillips, MD, Cuyahoga County Medical Examiner.*

A friendly woman, adorned in unflattering whites, conveyed them directly to the doctor.

Unlike Olenski, Phillips was very affable. He looked in his mid-forties to early fifties, had thick salt-and-pepper hair, a slightly pock-marked face, and was just beginning to need Spandex pants, yet overall, he appeared better off than most men his age.

"Call me Jim. Do you want to ask specific questions, or would you prefer a general rundown?" he asked after finishing introductions.

"Let's start with a general rundown," Jack said. "If we have questions, we'll be sure to let you know."

"Cause of death was smoke inhalation. She mercifully suffocated almost immediately from the fire on her face. No external source of air except through the fire and smoke emanating from her face. There were repeated applications of an accelerate elsewhere on the body. This fiend.... I can think of no other word to describe him...."

Jack met a lot of experienced MEs and knew they usually had thick skin. They needed it to survive.

Finally, Jim said, "It's easier to demonstrate than explain. I imagine you're all vets at this sort of thing?"

"Roy and I are still novice agents," Cheri said. "I've been through this once, not very successfully."

"I haven't," Roy said, "but I have a pretty strong stomach."

Neither Cheri nor Jack said anything, but they were thinking it.

Dr. Phillips, suppressing a smile, handed each of them a barf bag. "I'm sure you'll all be OK, but a corpse smells bad. It's better to be safe."

Rolling out the body, he removed the sheet. The head was horribly burned. Cheri, remembering her first experience, was somewhat prepared, although this body was worse. Somehow, she fought off her nausea. Roy valiantly fought the urge for five seconds, then had to use the barf bag.

His bag was quickly disposed of, and he rinsed his mouth. Cheri and Jack also took a moment to fight back their nausea and adjust to what they saw.

Dr. Phillips said, "When a body burns continuously, there's a relative evenness to the charred remains, absent accelerants. Here we see an unevenness, in some cases showing the path where additional accelerant was applied. If gasoline were used, the burning would have consumed the tissue more rapidly. We also examined other, shorter-term burns at several locations on the body. These couldn't have been for any reason other than to inflict terrible pain. I could see instantly that those burns were extinguished after a relatively short period.

"A fireman can use what is called a 'fire safety cloth,' since you can't spray a fire extinguisher right into someone's face. The cloth is used to suffocate the fire. Your man probably used any available thick, nonbreathable cloth. Since the continued torturous application of accelerant was premeditated, he may even have brought one with him.

"It would be an effective way of denying a source of oxygen, smothering the fire on any part of the body other than the face. There are very few accelerants that can't be suffocated. Some will even burn underwater. Napalm is an infamous example.

"Unfortunately, we aren't dealing with napalm here." He seemed to be lost in thought, but he snapped to when he saw the confused looks on the rookies' faces. Jack, however, understood.

"Those kinds of accelerants move *very* fast," Phillips clarified. "She couldn't have suffered any longer than it continued to burn. This poor soul suffered much longer. Her killer sadistically put out the fire and started a new burn over and over. We can't tell the exact order in which the burns were applied to various parts of the body, but my guess is that each time was longer than the last based on a progression of the square centimeters of each burn. It's the only potential pattern I can see. The burns might form some kind of geometric pattern, once I've had more time to study the corpse. Like I said, a *fiend.*" He paused. "Tests have shown that the accelerant was probably lighter fluid."

"Could it have been fluid for lighting charcoal?" Roy asked.

"No. that has a different burn profile. Also, it would've been bulkier to carry. Olenski told us about the first clown. Lighter fluid for a cigarette lighter would've been easier to conceal, and the witness didn't see the first clown carrying anything. That kind of fluid also has a shorter burn life, which would explain the successful extinction and reapplication of the accelerant.

"Tissue responds different when blood flow stops, so we were able to determine that the only layers of tissue that were burned post-mortem was a large portion of the face after asphyxiation. Once the victim's face was lit, asphyxiation was mercifully rapid."

"The cranium looks disproportionately small for the body," Cheri said.

"That's because the bone literally shrinks from the degradation that takes place in extreme heat. If the head were severed and found without the body, the DNA would also be so degraded, it would've made identification very difficult. In this case, we didn't have to worry about that."

"Can you show me the birthmark her husband used for ID?" Cheri asked.

He removed the sheet from Susan Bundergast's lower body. On her right hip was a moth-like red birthmark where the skin escaped mutilation.

"If you had no other means of identification, would that have sufficed?" Roy asked.

"No. Many times, criminals burn their victims to conceal identity. Rarely is the fire so hot that even enamel and teeth are consumed. In this case, we have additional corroboration from dental records."

"No one could stand to remain still while being so severely burned," Jack observed. "How was she restrained?"

"With duct tape. We have retained some of it and already sent the larger sample to Quantico for analysis, even before we heard you were coming out here. We often take advantage of your sophisticated labs to support our humble local efforts in a homicide." He smiled paternalistically.

"Let me guess. No fingerprints?"

"Nope. The time of death was easy to determine, because discovery of the body wasn't long after death. *Rigor mortis* hadn't yet set in. Also, the body temperature after death falls at a very predictable rate. The body temperature told us that death occurred, broadly speaking, a couple hours before discovery of the body."

"We studied a bit about body temperature in a forensics context," Roy said, "but wouldn't the fact that the body was severely burned affect the temperature?"

"Not the internal temperature so much. The external sores would have begun filling with fluid, which could help cool the surface and may've had some minimal effect. Temperature-measuring devices designed for forensics penetrate deep into the body cavity and are pretty accurate. If her body had been completely consumed by fire, it would be different. Here, the burns to inflict pain were surface burns, extinguished in seconds, having minimal effect on body temperature."

Jack added his own comments. "Precise time of death is most valuable when you're dealing with a wider window of opportunity, usually with a corpse a day or more ripe. Here, we know Sam Bundergast met parents and children at an amusement park at 9:00 that morning. The real Pickles showed up at three. Dr. Phillips' estimate was pretty much in the middle. Until we find a specific suspect who can't account for his time during that narrow window, it doesn't help much," he finished.

"Don't misunderstand my last comment, doctor," he said. "You did a great job. Here's my card. Call me at the Bureau if you come up with anything else. Thanks."

If Jack seemed less than cordial with the affable ME, it was because a certain phrase kept running through his mind: *Another one on our watch!*

CHAPTER FORTY-SEVEN

Dan's Place was a typical neighborhood bar, perhaps more dimly lit than most. There was a very long wooden bar, well past its prime, with fading lacquer and plenty of nicks where beer mugs had been set down a little too energetically.

It was later in the day than when Sam coaxed Susan there, and it was a bit later today. The person behind the bar was busy with customers. The bartender eventually walked down to the three of them and asked, "What's your pleasure?"

"Just want to talk for a moment," Jack said.

"Well, I'm a friendly guy," Dan said, "but my backup bartender comes in to help with the after-work crowd, and he called in sick today. I'm afraid I have to tend the bar."

Dan froze, however, when Jack flashed his ID.

"Do you know Susan and Sam Bundergast?" Jack asked.

"Oh, God, yes." A gray shadow fell over Dan's features. "I heard about Susan. Terrible thing, just awful. Working here, I couldn't help hearing about it."

"How much to you know about it?" Roy asked with a hint of suspicion, which earned him a disdainful look from Jack, who wondered if Roy hadn't learned anything from Cheri's misstep.

"Just that she was murdered, and it was pretty messy, nothing specific."

"Relax," Jack said. "We know you had nothing to do with it. We're just looking for some information. Sam said he and Susan were here two days before she was killed. There was no one in here but the three of you, and you were in the back most of the time, right?"

"That's not quite accurate." Dan raised one eyebrow. "I don't think Sam noticed, but there was a stranger in here, too, sipping a Beam and 7 Up. He was in a dark corner booth behind Sam and Susan."

"Could the stranger have heard what they were discussing?"

"Not unusual for them, but the conversation was a bit animated. Susan got carried away sometimes. Yeah, he might've well heard them."

"What did he look like?" Cheri asked.

Jack expected that. All of them were anxious to find out.

"A tall guy, a bit over six-foot, with a medium build. He wore a hat with the brim pulled down. That was funny for such a hot day. I didn't get a look at his face because of that. I got the impression he was younger as opposed to older, but not a kid. I could tell from the way he carried himself I didn't have to card him."

"Did he pay by credit card?" Jack asked.

"Let me think. No, it was cash. I'm 100% sure. Most in the booths tend to pay by card, so I noticed. It's different at the bar."

"When he handed you the cash, what color were his hands?"

"White."

"Did you notice if he took notes while the Bundergasts talked?"

Dan squinted, trying to remember. "I don't think so. I would've noticed that. Do you think that's the guy...?"

Jack raised his hand to stop him. "We're just running down leads. People hurt each other all the time based on unfounded rumors. I don't think you're that kind of guy."

Dan looked at him and nodded.

"Anything else?" Jack asked.

"Can't think of much else. He was only here long enough to have maybe two drinks. With the bar empty before the Bundergasts came in, I usually like to engage customers. Most people like a little chitchat, but not him. He said to just get his drink. He left shortly after Sam and Susan. He had already paid."

When the three agents were outside Dan's place, Jack said, "The guy we're looking for is white, in his thirties, and is over six foot. We already knew he was smart. Now we know he has a great memory, too."

CHAPTER FORTY-EIGHT

Jack's team moved the follow-up meeting of their Cleveland trip to a conference room. Mike wanted to attend, and Jack decided it would be more comfortable for Mike if he didn't have to sit his large frame on the corner of Jack's desk. A conference room worked best for all.

The oval mahogany table sat ten. The comfortable chairs were high-backed executive chairs in deep tan fake leather. It was the kind of chair, with full lumbar support, that would be great for a nap, not that anyone at the table would snooze.

"It's essential that you all know I'm not here to scrutinize your work in the sense of being overtly critical," Mike said. "but I do need to know your progress. Jack earned my confidence a long time ago. From what I understand from him, you two are rapidly earning his. Good to hear.

"I know you're wondering about more resources. You must be thinking, 'We have, albeit theoretically, tentatively connected two homicides to the Numbers we've been receiving. Both were repeatedly raped and dreadfully tortured before being murdered.'

"You have a speculative description of the perp as White, over six-feet, with a medium build, who enjoys Beam and 7 up. Sorry, but we won't be taking volunteers to go scouting bars just yet." He stumbled a little at his attempt at humor, but no one thought less of him for trying.

"That's a thin description. Decision makers in the Bureau must make hard choices concerning the allocation of available personnel. That's always the most-critical resource and is carefully scrutinized. Jack is well-respected in the Bureau. He's made some amazing interpretations of evidence that led us to apprehending some bad folks. That buys confidence from the higher-ups, but not as much as hard evidence.

"Like all of us, he's jumped in the wrong direction, too. You won't be a good agent if you don't trust your instincts and take risks, or if you're too busy CYA-ing to take that risk. Right now, we have no suspect or evidence we can connect to anyone. It's a mixed bag. The Bureau has enough confidence in Jack and me to give this team latitude to continue, despite the resources we previously spent that led nowhere.

"They just don't feel they can give us a lot of additional personnel based on what we have, or, perhaps more accurately, what we don't have.

"I may have a question somewhere along the line today, but maybe not. Jack?"

"Thanks, Mike. We've been working on this case for almost two months. We've been doing our best. That doesn't change the fact that two women have been horribly tortured and murdered on our watch. Our task is clearly to intervene before there's another, which could be difficult.

"Cheri doesn't have a lot of experience profiling, let alone for a serial murder case. What she brings to the table, however, is a Master's degree in psychology and what appear to be great instincts. I have that experience after working with the BAU. So far, I can't disagree with any conclusion she has drawn.

"Likewise, Roy demonstrated great skill at statistical evaluation and prognosticating where to go next, like a bloodhound that picked up a scent. No offense, Roy. He has so far driven our investigation into trying to identify where our man might be found.

"Methodically going about finding the perp, while it offers the promise of eventually getting there and doing so without costly mistakes that could send us in the wrong direction, won't get us where we want to go, because it's too slow.

"We need to make some leaps of faith. We need to cut some corners, something that's rightly discouraged at the Bureau. If our guesswork and instincts are correct, we just might save a life. I've discussed Roy's ideas about focusing on AAUS with Mike, and he encouraged us to take that path if we feel it's best. Cheri and I met and reviewed an updated profile. We concur after consultation on how to move forward from here. Cheri, fill us in on that."

He couldn't help letting his thoughts digress to how much he enjoyed those meetings with Cheri and how much he looked forward to the next one. Metaphorically kicking himself in the seat of his pants, he tried to regain his bearings.

Cheri quickly glanced at Mike. She heard lots of good things from Jack about the man but so far had very little exposure to him. "Let's start with the original profile we worked up, which is thin, and then update you based on more-recent information.

"We made an immediate calculation that our serial, if he was capable of successfully murdering sixty-six women, now sixty-eight, in a ten-year time frame, is quite intelligent. If we're right about his gathering all relevant info on the Bundergasts and Pickles the clown without taking notes per the statement from the owner of Don's Place, that could be confirmation. He remembered the name of the clown, the agency that referred him, the names of Sam and Susan Bundergast and Pickles, the address, the time frame he was expected, and perhaps that he was to perform a magic act, all on a single hearing.

"His mind is agile and quick. He's as bright as we thought and possibly has perfect recall of what he hears. It would be like a photographic memory but attuned to auditory signals, not the visual channel. He might have both. That would fit with a genius-level IQ.

"He has a clear hatred for women in general. Barbara Cox was beautiful, the kind he might have found inaccessible or arrogant. That would have fueled his pathological hatred and caused him to select her. Jack and I both feel that's not where his hatred started, however. It's deeper than that. We expect it has its origins in childhood.

"Susan Bundergast wasn't the beautiful aloof woman we saw in Barbara Cox. She wasn't *un*attractive, but pictures of her portrayed what some might call a dumpy housewife. She'd put on a few pounds but was hardly obese. If our perp was the man in Dan's Place, and I believe we agree on that, then it was something he heard from her, or her body language toward Sam, that triggered him."

"It seems to me some of these conclusions about the man in the bar might be a bridge too far," Mike said. "We're assuming a patron of Dan's Place is the perp, that he has what amounts to a photographic memory, that in one day he could drop everything else he was doing and obtain a workable clown outfit to kill someone he never met. We're assuming a single conversation in a bar of short duration, overheard while having a couple drinks, moved him to murder. Certainly there were others in that agency—what did you call it? Fun Time?—who would've had the necessary information. Mrs. Bundergast might've spoken to a neighbor about it. Just because there was a guy in the bar while she was talking to Fun Time.... I respect your thoughts on this, Jack, but I just don't know."

"If we're going to get this monster," Jack retorted, "this is the kind of leap of faith we'll have to accept, especially if we want to get him before Number 69. This is precisely what I meant. It's a corner we're cutting. The corner might take almost the whole page. At the same time, Mike, you have a valid point, and we appreciate your analysis. You're my boss. If you think this is one of those infamous rabbit holes, you can redirect us," he ended.

"No, no, Jack. I wasn't suggesting that. If I had the numbers, which I don't, on how many times your instincts paid off versus how many times you went down a rabbit hole, well, Roy could give us the percentages. They'd favor following your gut by a large margin. I'll bet on you and your team, Jack. You know that," Mike said.

Jack nodded. "Working with that assumption, then, where does it take us, Cheri?"

"To catch the guy, we need some insight into his consciousness. How'd he get to be an unequivocal monster? He almost certainly had a domineering mother. His emotional development would've been severely retarded as a result. It could also account for his hatred of women, at least in part.

"Somehow, I feel that isn't enough. Dan described when the Bundergasts were there, they frequently bickered. He gave me the impression that Susan always degraded Sam, and the argument ended when he conceded to her demands. That may've been what triggered our guy.

"It leads me to believe that not only was our guy's mother a dedicated shrew, his father was probably timid and unassertive. Most likely, the perp's hatred was engendered not just by his mother but through the pain she inflicted on his father, whom he may have loved. If we get to the point of interviewing a suspect's parents, we want to look for the whole package.

"Another thing is my belief we could be looking at an only child. In many cases, only children feel familial emotions more intensely. There's no place to hide from your parents' constant scrutiny. If he grew up in such an environment, we shouldn't be surprised to find that they are in infrequent contact now, especially with his mother.

"We've been discussing the fact that this serial was able to attract a very-alluring, even beautiful woman in the case of Barbara Cox. That suggests two things: first, in addition to his better than six-foot height, he's probably a very attractive man.

"That still isn't enough. A good-looking man who's awkward or lacking confidence couldn't have lured his prey into a dangerous or compromising position. That fits with our suspected Number 60, Dr. Bacardi. In short, we should be looking for a very intelligent, handsome, outwardly secure man in his thirties or possibly forties. If we accept the mailings are for real, which we do, this started over ten years ago, and there's been little or no contact with his seminal family.

"Based on the mailing from Honolulu where, coincidentally, the second AAUS trade show was held, I think those social skills would be compatible with involvement in sales or sales management, whether in the automotive field or elsewhere."

"Very thorough, Cheri," Jack said. "Roy, you're up."

"I've been trying to find the shortcuts Jack referred to. With 80% of the vendors at AAUS utilizing brokers, that leaves 1,200 companies with a minimum of 5,000 staff at the show. How do we narrow that down?

"I'm using Cheri's profile to put together some questions that can be quickly put to these companies. We can't talk to sales or sales management or even the marketing staff. These are the same people we think could ultimately yield a suspect, but we don't want to alert our guy. We have to reach the owners and CEOs. In smaller companies like the ones we're targeting, that shouldn't be too hard. At least, that's the assumption. Jack has already informed you that using the stature of the Bureau could bring the agency's credibility into question. This demands we use discretion wisely and check our impulses.

"Nonetheless, they'll most likely be so skeptical, not to mention protective of their people, that getting a surprise call from the Bureau will only feed that skepticism. We'd probably have to give them a number to call back, where they can verify the legitimacy of the source of the call.

"Even so, some hardheads may want to talk with their lawyer or insist on written documentation. We'll need to explain, without going into specifics, that we don't want our inquiry out in the public forum. We're working on a case where time is of the essence. We'll need to be assertive, and, if we hit a roadblock, perhaps turn to local law enforcement or someone they know in law enforcement to get the information we need."

"I may be able to help with that," Mike said. "I've been around long enough. Jack, just don't tell them how long. I have a lot of contacts with local folks in many jurisdictions. Use me as a resource if you need it. To save time, you can come directly to me, as long as you tell Jack afterward. Is that OK with you, Jack?"

"Of course, Mike. We appreciate the help."

"Based on Cheri's profile," Roy resumed, "let's cut our inquiries short if the person isn't single or isn't in his thirties or forties.

Ask discretely if the man looks more like Robert Redford or Woody Allen.

"Our guy should also have a suave, appealing demeanor. His territory should be predominantly in the east. Obviously, he should have attended both AAUS trade shows as an exhibitor.

"If we get a likely, and the owner or CEO won't cooperate, Jack or Mike may be of help obtaining a subpoena *duces tecum* for the company's records. Of course, those aren't easy to get. That means we'll have to build as much info and as strong a case for the court as possible. We'll need to be very thorough in our questioning. We were taught that in training, but we'll need to take it one step further.

"That should include checking the person's whereabouts at the times of the mailings we received. If we hit the right person, it will be obvious quickly. My estimate is that a small minority of the company reps out there will fit our profile, but all we need is the right one.

"Cheri indicated in her profile that the perp would most likely be in his thirties. If he started his rampage at nineteen, he could be younger than that, but Cheri doesn't think it's likely. Similarly, he could be older, but we want to narrow our parameters. If I think of anything else we can do, I'll tell everyone."

"Neither of you disappointed," Jack encouraged.

"Actually," Mike added, "Jack has done a terrific job of indoctrinating both of you." He chuckled.

"We just think alike," Jack insisted. "Mike, I know you won't give us any more agents, at least not until we have something more concrete to go on, but how about diverting some clerical staff who have security clearances? We can't risk creating any buzz about a serial murderes even within the Bureau. Any buzz from agents who investigated this previously has probably dissipated by now, but getting additional clerical help would mean we cover the ground faster."

"I'll see what I can do," Mike said.

"To wrap up," Jack said, "we're all going to hit the phones. Roy, use your Diehard Roy Rogers to introduce some humor into the call and loosen up the business owner. Cheri, use that sexy voice of yours."

That earned him a glare from Mike.

"Roy, if some esoteric personality trait comes up, check with Cheri or me to see if it fits our profile."

"Just a second, Jack," Mike said, catching everyone's attention. "Apart from the PC and sexual harassment implications of what you just said, there's something more important here. It's one thing to cut corners, another to fly blind. However long the odds, suppose we actually hit our guy? Using a sexy voice could be deliberately provocative to him, and that could put Cheri in danger."

Cheri opened her mouth to speak, but Jack waved her off. He hadn't considered that issue. How he would address it with Mike hadn't been foremost in his mind.

A chill went through him he wasn't expecting, and that was odd. He realized his emotional detachment was in jeopardy. He took a few seconds to formulate his reply to Mike, which was completely transparent to his boss.

"You're right, Mike. I failed to consider the implications," Jack admitted. "Forget the sexy voice, Cheri. Just do your job professionally."

"You stopped me a moment ago, Jack," she said, "but I have a right to speak to this. In my career, might I not potentially go undercover at some point? Might I not need to use my physical attributes to get close to some suspected criminal, even a dangerous one? If my sex is an obstacle to that, then I really am being discriminated against. Frankly, however, you might try to put those shackles on me. If I see the opportunity to use any attribute I have to get the job done, I'll use it."

When Jack wanted to object, Mike waved him off.

"She's right, Jack. Here's the *final* word on this. Use what resources you have, Cheri, but use them judiciously. If you get *any kind* of unusual response, make the entire team aware of it and proceed with caution. Wrap it up, Jack."

"Everyone keep tabs on your calls," Jack said. "We'll each get a spreadsheet with the data that has already been provided by AAUS on the exhibitors and their staff. We'll divide the spreadsheet three ways for now until we find out if Mike can scare up any clerical staff. It's of vital importance that we know how many people become preliminarily eliminated. It's even more vital if we hit a person of interest."

He looked at the others. "Any questions?"

There were none.

CHAPTER FORTY-NINE

Jack got a call asking him to drop by Mike Hennessey's office. From Jack's office, it was around a corner and down a long, wide corridor past myriad square glass offices that all looked alike. He reached a corner office, and from there, it reminded Jack of moving a knight in chess, one to the corner, then two to the left into a much-narrower corridor. Looking straight into Mike's office, he saw Mike waiting for him.

Mike smiled broadly at Jack and made a motion that was less than a halfhearted effort to stand in greeting, then sat a whole six inches down again.

"Whassup?" Jack knew the expression annoyed Mike.

"*Whassup*? Really?" The left side of Mike's face scrunched toward his cheekbone. Mike received updates to Emily Post every six months, not because he was so conservative, but because he felt as if manners and niceties were slipping away and making society less civilized. "It's 'the best of times' when we catch creeps accessing child porn and 'the worst of times' when bodies keep piling up in our inner cities, and no one has a cure, and you want to know whassup?" Mike's metaphor would be lost on anyone who didn't know Charles Dickens.

With emphasis, Mike said, "*What is up*, is that I have the additional help you asked for. What it is *not* is another agent or even an agent-in-training. It's what you suggested at the meeting, diverting a cleared clerical staff member to help with calling and tracking. As clerical staff goes, however, I think I did very well by you.

"Her name is Anita Johnson, a third-year student in criminal justice who hopes to go on to postgrad studies in forensics. Eventually,

163

she'd like to join the Bureau. Her dad, Marcus, was one of us until he retired, similar to Cheri. I think she'll follow your instructions and will work hard. She's more excited about this assignment than the transcription I took her from. She'll be at tomorrow morning's meeting. I won't attend that one. I don't want to take anything away from your team's focus. You'll have a lot to cover.

"I've taken the liberty to have your calling lists divided by four. Cheri, Roy, and Anita will each get 30% of the calls. You get 10%. That's how I want it. None of these people, while committed and hard-working, have your eye for spotting something that may appear insignificant to a less-practiced eye. I need you to use a significant part of your time following their efforts, trying to spot something one of them missed."

Jack hesitated, looking down at the tile floor. Mike's office was somewhat more spacious than his own, which was expected for a member of senior staff. Finally, he looked up. "I hoped to simply cover more ground faster." His lips puckered, as he considered Mike's point. "As usual, you're right. Still, it wouldn't have been possible without your scaring up this Anita person. I appreciate the assistance. We'll be a first-class telesales team for the next week or two. It'll take some salesmanship to convince these business owners to cooperate. I think Cheri and Roy will be good at this. I'll keep you informed.

"Oh, yeah. Could you have Ms. Johnson come in a bit early, say twenty minutes before the meeting tomorrow? It'll give us a little time to get acquainted."

Jack walked back to his office with a little more spring in his step. "We're going to do this," he said softly, although he had never doubted it.

CHAPTER FIFTY

Anita Johnson showed up at exactly 7:40 AM the following morning. She wasn't what Jack expected. She looked like an Amazon. She was twenty-one and six-feet tall, with biceps from bodybuilding that make Jack envious.

Anita's jaw line was square, like the Marlboro man, and she gave the impression she had *Don't Tread on Me* tattooed on her forehead. Any factor of intimidation was shattered, however, when she gave him a disarmingly wide Julia Roberts smile.

Jack, always cordial, made a particular effort to put Anita at ease and feel welcome. The additional help was sorely needed, and he wanted to integrate her into the team rapidly.

"My dad was a big guy himself," she began with a broad smile. "I mention that, because I always get a brief instant's reaction when I meet people. I run marathons, too."

They laughed. Jack knew instantly when he liked someone.

Anita told him about her dedication to join the Bureau and how her dad retired from the FBI, which he already knew.

"Well, when you get there," Jack joked, "and we're chasing a perp together, don't make me look too bad."

He was surprised when she gave a child-like giggle.

"I won't give you the rundown on today's meeting, as I want you to hear the same information as the others on the team at the same time. As far as the case itself goes, I know Managing Special Agent Hennessey has given you something of a rundown on the case."

"He's Uncle Mike. Not my real uncle, but my dad and he are close friends even now. They have an annual fishing trip."

"Ach! Mike's always trying to get me to go fishing with him. I haven't fished since I was a boy. I think there's a reason for that. I suppose you fish?"

"Yup."

"Well, right now, we're swapping the fish-that-got-away story for a we-caught-this-monster story. Did Mike fill you in?"

"I think so, but it's hard to say without the context of having been involved up to now. Mike said I'd be making a volume of calls to exhibitors from the AAUS trade show, trying to find a match to the profile you and Cheri developed."

Jack was impressed. "You seem to have a good grasp of the task we have for you, but understanding certain aspects of this guy we're looking for would be helpful. Did Mike discuss our profile with you?"

"Your guy picks on attractive women, rapes them, then tortures them on a level rarely seen even in the Bureau. He's most likely in his thirties or forties, single, yet has unusual coping mechanisms for someone with mental problems. This includes the ability to be ingratiating to people and doing it quickly, based on the Cox case.

"He's bright and seems to have done some forensics reading based on his facility of methodically avoiding leaving evidence. The only things he leaves behind are the victim's bodies, which he wants found. Like other serials, he does this for personal gratification and to foster recognition of his intelligence, but unlike many serials, not out of a desire to be caught.

"I'm probably missing some stuff, but that's what I have right now," she finished.

"That isn't OK."

He waited for her stunned reaction.

"You aren't even in the Bureau yet, and you're already gunning for my job!"

He couldn't remember when he was so impressed. He wondered if she would return to transcription duties as early as Mike anticipated.

CHAPTER FIFTY-ONE

The eight-o'clock meeting was held in one of the conference rooms. Jack gave perfunctory introductions and added, "Ms. Johnson—I think we'll be less formal and call her Anita—will be a valuable addition for at least the next week or two while we get through these calls. Like Cheri, her dad is an alumnus of the Bureau club. I guess that leaves Roy and me out."

They smiled.

"There are a few things I want to cover with you this morning," he continued. "Foremost is that the persons we're calling will be dubious about the authenticity of the call. No one expects a call from the FBI, which will make them nervous and tentative. Each of you has a printout of the calls we want you to make. At the top of each page is a Bureau number the person can call to verify the origin of the call is with the Bureau. That person won't be able to transfer any calls to you, because you should already be making the next call. You'll get any messages virtually in real time. Return them promptly.

"We've been joking about doing telesales. That's *no joke*. We're all going to put on our sales hats. Many of these companies will be focused on protecting their employees. They won't think of any of them as potential criminals. The people in this room are already certain one of them is.

"First, even if we had the time to go after a subpoena *duces tecum*—which asks for records instead of getting a person to testify, Anita—there's no evidence to ask for one from a court. Bluffing the

168

people we're talking to should be a last resort. If we need to get back to them in the future, we'll lose credibility, which means no cooperation.

"We need to be persuasive, and we must do it without using the words 'serial murder,' most notably the 'serial' part. We don't even want to use 'murder.' That word makes people crawl into their shells and creates defensiveness. We're simply looking for a witness who may be able to help us with a crime.

"They'll want to know what crime, but we need to resist. If they press you, say we're looking for a witness to an identity theft ring. We don't want to talk to a sales manager, because he could be our guy. Stay with the owner or CEO. If you can't get the person's cooperation, and you can swear the owner to secrecy—not that it will help, mind you—use 'murder' to underscore the gravity of the situation. Try to avoid it if you can. Definitely avoid the word 'serial.'

"Some will cooperate immediately when they hear FBI or have confirmed that fact. They'll do it out of a sense of duty. Others may push you to the wall. It'll create some ripples here at the Bureau, and Mike will do what he can to run interference, but if you have no other recourse, tell the person refusing to cooperate in a homicide investigation could make him or her an accessory after the fact. That's a dangerous practice. Without specific intent to aid a known perpetrator, what we'd be saying isn't absolutely true. It's one of those corners we need to cut to catch this monster. Cheri and Roy have seen why no other word fits.

"We need to find him before he kills again. Mike and I like doing things by the book. The only book I'm interested in right now, however, is the Bible. The one being read over the graves of these women and my own, that I read to get through this."

He paused to collect his thoughts. "I'm adding something to our profile. To impose this kind of torture on anyone, and, from my perspective, a woman, our target is a sociopath, lacking anything remotely resembling empathy. Don't make the mistake the person is or isn't religious. For some individuals, John Brown during the Civil War, and, more recently, Jim Jones, come to mind. Both were apparently religious and just as certainly sociopaths who would kill anyone opposed to their aims.

"I happen to be Catholic. Like all Christians, Jews, non-jihadist Muslims, and subscribers to all legitimate religions, we're guided by faith to do good, not evil. Religion, however, can be perverted to commit awful atrocities. It can even play a factor in creating rather than preventing this kind of perversion, cruelty, and *evil*, the word which fits best for me, that we see in this case. Our man could be truly religious, although to a rational person, that might sound contradictory. He could be outwardly religious to distance himself from suspicion, or he could be an atheist, agnostic, or just disinterested, so don't use that as a measuring stick.

"We believe our serial is a loner, which also argues against organized religion except as a ruse. We already know the guy is very intelligent, someone who likes to organize rather than rationalize. I think he'll have tried to be definitive about a higher power, whatever his actual beliefs. Don't use this as a line in the sand, but I believe he'll be an atheist, expressed or no. A clever atheist might use the cover of religion to create a misleading façade of reverent belief. The bottom line is, ignore that aspect.

"If you think you've got a prospective candidate in other ways, and he pronounces himself to be an atheist, which this guy probably won't, that's one more check on your list, but that's all it is. These days, there are only half the churchgoers there used to be.

"Mostly, we've prepared a script, like any good telesales operation. I did telesales while I worked my way through college. Verbatim scripts were highly favored. This situation, however, doesn't lend itself to verbatim. There are too many opportunities to digress to even use what is called a branching script, that, as the name implies, allows you to branch off. This will be your first opportunity to conduct interviews.

"Everyone has instincts. It's important to listen to yours. It's the instinct that you don't follow that could be key. You have to freewheel intellectually to be successful in what we're doing." Jack picked up three collated copies, having already taken one out of the pile for himself. Mike had his copy.

"Pass these around. They're the questions you should ask to guide your interviews. Don't assume the status of the person you talk to. Don't ask if he or she is the president of the company. Screeners will say 'sure' to screen out callers, getting brownie points for saving the boss the trouble."

All three received their copies.

"Don't take this as an inflexible outline. Jump around as needed. The cover story is we're looking for a witness to a white-collar crime. You could engender skepticism if the interviewee thinks you know too much about a witness. Your job is to eliminate companies that don't potentially employ our perp. If you get a live one, you may need to follow through on all the questions. That might compromise our cover story. If necessary, so be it, but try not to."

Jack prepared to read the list aloud. "Just listen right now, and ask questions afterward."

- Ask the person for his or her title. If he isn't who you want, get transferred.
- When you have the right person, identify yourself as an agent of the FBI.
- Offer the phone number for verification right away if you encounter skepticism.
- Make a note to follow up if you don't hear back within twenty-four hours.
- Do not use our profile to describe the person.
- Explain we're looking for a witness to the crime, not a perp.
- This person must have attended the AAUS trade show in Honolulu.
- The person is male. (Take the following questions one at a time.)
- Does this person have a territory? Eliminate western or national territories.

- Is the person married?
- Is the person religious? (Again, discount this aspect, but we want the information.)
- Does he travel extensively?
- Where does he travel? (Look for major cities throughout the east.)
- What is his personality type? (Engaging?)
- What is his personal appearance like? (Attractive?)
- How long has he been with the company? (Ten years plus or could have changed jobs.)
- Does he socialize within the company? (Probably not.)
- Any unusual habits or traits?
- Does he have family living, and/or is he close to them? (Probably not.)
- Add questions as the flow of the interview necessitates.

"I want to emphasize that last one. It gets back to using your gut feeling. These are questions not to ask, as well as ask. Save time by not continuing the questions if you can see you're on the wrong track. That seems obvious, and I don't mean to talk down to you, but time is our most-precious commodity.

"Some of these questions may seem strange to our interviewee. For instance, why would socializing within the company be a factor in identifying the witness? Explain that it may not be clear to someone at first glance, but to make it understandable would require divulging confidential information. That, hopefully, will enhance the person's sense of importance and facilitate the rest of the interview as well as discourage more questions."

He looked at them. "Questions?"

"You added to our profile this morning the atheist thing," Cheri said. "If we think we have something else that should be added to the profile, how do you want us to handle it?"

"Bring it to me right away. If it fits, if we think it has merit, we'll pass it along to your cohorts. That reminds me. First, you have to really crank the phone. Cover a lot of territory quickly. That doesn't mean you shouldn't bounce ideas off each other. Synergy is an important arrow in your quiver. Just don't get carried away to the exclusion of calling. I will be calling, too, but on a more-limited basis. I want to work closely with each of you. I have an open-door policy. Yes, I know that's a cliché, but in this case, utilize your access. Other questions?"

"Sometimes people react to authority," Anita said. "Pulling a Supervising or Managing Special Agent out of a hat might sound intimidating to some. You or Mike might get traction where we can't. Can we utilize you in that way?"

"Well, I just told you that you have good access, and you do. That should be a judgment call, especially where Mike is concerned. He has other cases, though this is number one for him. If I'm not around, go to Mike. Remember, you're perceived as agents of the FBI, which should be enough clout; but yes, you can if your gut says it's the only way to get to first base."

"Will we meet every other weekday as usual?" Roy asked.

"Instead of every other day for our six-day work week, for now it'll just be Wednesdays and Fridays, so we can use our Monday time for calling.

"We can't send you into the field, Anita, as your preliminary training here has to wait for later. Friday after our meeting, Roy, Cheri, and I will fly to different destinations to interview our most-fruitful prospects in person. This means interviewing potential suspects. I can't emphasize enough the peril that involves and the absolute necessity of being cautious and protective of your safety.

"This particularly applies to Cheri. It's not because I'm sexist, but because she fits the profile of one of the victims."

"What about keeping you up-to-date on our progress?" Roy asked.

"I need a twice-daily email from each of you. It should have five numbers: the number of calls made, companies eliminated for now, companies not reached, companies remaining to be called, and the number of those who won't cooperate. I want the names of the companies in that last category and the contact information for their top dude. They'll have the pleasure of making my acquaintance." He had the attitude of a Great Dane ready to steal his master's porterhouse.

"There should be a detailed addendum giving me information on any suspect individuals. Specify why you think each one warrants an in-person interview. I'll prioritize and arrange for transportation to one or more sites for each of us for our Saturdays. We'll use Saturdays to keep a low profile for the person to be interviewed away from his job. If someone insists on a weekday interview, inform me.

"If you're hot to trot on somebody, I'll consider a midweek flight. I'll probably conduct those interviews myself. Cheri, if someone you think could be a fit balks at talking with you because of your sex, that's a red flag. Avoid snap decisions. I'll trust your judgment."

After there were no more questions, Jack escorted the group to their new conjoined offices, with directions to get settled, move any necessary items from their old digs, and start making calls.

He counted on their long-shot process to produce something before Number 69.

CHAPTER FIFTY-TWO

The following day began with an email from Jack to Mike, Cheri, Roy, and Anita.

Chief Olenski tells me their forensics staff from the Cleveland Fire Department determined that the perp stayed until Mrs. Bundergast was dead, as would be expected from the degree of damage inflicted on the skull. He smothered the fire with a throw rug. The analysis suggests it may've been done multiple times to prevent the fire from spreading. It was then tossed aside and left in the living room. There was a small amount of slow-moving accelerant. Police forensics say the discarded throw rug had no fingerprints or extraneous fibers.

A short time later, Cheri sent an email to the group.

He extinguished the fire, because he didn't want the abomination he created to go unnoticed. That's why the Cox woman was found with loose dirt tossed on her body, deliberately ravaged after death to eliminate evidence, and left only a few feet off a trodden path. He always wants the corpses found. This confirms Jack's hypothesis that this guy wants an awareness of what he has accomplished to demonstrate his superior intellect. By isolating himself from all potential forensics evidence for our 68 suspected ritual murders, the perp is showing he doesn't want to be caught.

The murders of Cox and Bundergast fit Jack's theory. I think our guy believes he can be the most-prolific killer and still evade detection. That would ultimately elevate him beyond any other known serial within our borders, if unchecked. He's close to surpassing Ridgway. He'll set his sights on Little, the number-one in the U.S.

Since he's exhilarated by each murder, I doubt he'll ever stop. That means his ongoing handiwork won't stop even if he surpasses the 218 known and 250 suspected murders of "Dr. Death," Dr. Harold Shipman, in England. I doubt his lust for death knows any limits.

CHAPTER FIFTY-THREE

Friday morning's meeting arrived. The team had been calling for two full days without much to show for it. Mike Hennessey attended, and Jack led off.

"Mike and I want to thank you for your hard work for the last couple of days," Jack said. "Having the phone glued to your ear all day can be exhausting. In a lot of ways, it's typical of the job. We turn over rocks to see what's under them. That's what investigation is all about. Each of you averaged a couple hundred calls a day, which is a great effort.

"There's a gorilla in the room that needs to be addressed. Roy recommended, and properly so, that there were more exhibitors at the AAUS than the other thirty-four conferences or trade shows combined, so as a matter of percentages, we should concentrate on AAUS. I believe you're also thinking if our guy isn't in that group, we have an almost-equal number to look at in the other thirty-four.

"If you're tackling the entirety of the job on those terms, it will seem overwhelming, particularly if you don't turn up something that prompts the decision-makers to provide us more assistance. We're all dedicated, determined professionals, but I can tell you from experience that if you're thinking in those terms, it can exacerbate your feelings of exhaustion. That can make you let something slip by, removing some of the sharpness to your effort.

"Don't do that to yourself. When I've done that in the past, it cost me my efforts and my consistency, which led to errors. Don't think about what's to come. Give what's in front of you your full effort, and we'll find a way to move forward without putting you in the hospital from exhaustion. The odds are still in our favor. Stay focused.

"Moving on to AAUS, there are a few things that need clarification. First, the main problem we're having is that actually reaching an owner or CEO has been more difficult than anticipated. J. Edgar Hoover calling from the grave may be the only thing that would move one of these bozos. We're learning that if he or she is in a meeting, it won't be interrupted. Often the person we need is traveling,. In other instances, we're directed to legal counsel. That most often occurs with medium-sized companies, rather than smaller ones.

"As we said at the onset, the really large manufacturers, the Goodyears or Borg Warners, have been purged from your lists. Their territories are very small, and their national and regional sales managers are often confined to headquarters, relying on district managers with small, local territories to handle day-to-day sales operations. They travel, but not as extensively as our guy.

"This leads to an issue I'm confident you've already inferred on your own. Besides the often-typical structure of a national sales manager who supervises eastern and western regional managers, who, in turn, supervise the divided network, many companies have regions of only four or five states.

"That could fit our perp, augmented by an occasional trip to Nashville, where we only got one number for instance. We're looking for a very definite structure. Add a reference to companies you've identified as having either structure in your daily email, and I'll follow up on those with you individually.

"Next, we generally look at someone to see if he has an alibi. That's next to impossible here. One of the corners we're cutting involves the assumption that the murder represented by the most-recent mailing was committed prior to the mailing, not after. Cheri and I still believe that's the case. Do you still concur, Cheri?"

"Yes, I do," she replied. "Our guy has, in the way I view him, obsessive compulsive disorder, OCD. Not having committed the act for which he made the mailing would be like a picture hung unevenly. He'd be beside himself until it was straightened."

"Cheri and I have also concluded that the mailings are done from locations and at times that are meant to mislead us," Jack continued, "making it almost impossible to know when and where the murder occurred. That's why alibi isn't among our scripted questions. There are circumstances where we could use alibi to eliminate someone, however. For instance, someone sent to Europe for a month prior to a mailing to scout product pricing in that market, or a person in the hospital for an operation that required long-term recuperation, could be eliminated. Be on the lookout, and remember, eliminating potentials is a step forward."

"We've all learned that two weeks from tomorrow, AAUS is having its third annual trade show," Roy said. "Wouldn't going to that and seeing some people up close and personal be a good idea?"

"Great minds think alike." Mike grinned. "Jack and I have been discussing that. I'm going to let him give you the lowdown."

"The reason we didn't jump into that is threefold," Jack said. "First, we wanted to concentrate our efforts on the calling. Perhaps that was my bad. I've said more than once that the last two murders, no matter what we faced in terms of odds, happened on our watch. I always feel that way, and I want you to think in those terms as part of growing as an agent. Waiting three weeks would be traumatizing if we received another Number before the trade show. In preparation for the trade show, our guy might be occupied and out of commission, which could buy us some time. Sixty-eight murders in the roughly ten years we've been receiving the Numbers is a little more than one every two months. Much beyond that, and his itch needs to be scratched.

"We'll still fly out tomorrow to interview the persons of interest at the top of our list. I believe we each have one person who agreed to cooperate and will meet us. Anita has one that fits our criteria, but we can't put her into the field. We'll try to look at him when we get to AAUS, which we decided to do. Roy, Cheri, and I will report back on these interviews at next Wednesday's meeting. In the meantime, we'll continue calling on Monday.

"Mike, as a Managing Agent, has other investigations he's overseeing and won't attend the trade show. To guide us in further calls, I want each of you to give us a rundown on the person you feel fits our profile. Cheri, you've been working most closely with me on profiling, so why don't you begin?"

"One moment," Mike said. "I doubt this needs saying, but if you don't know Jack as well as I do, he may unintentionally make it sound as though I'm only tangentially involved in our investigation. Thant's incorrect. Given the sheer potential number of victims, this case is my top priority.

"Jack and I are conferencing on this daily. If any of you needs help, and Jack isn't available, I'm up to speed. Just as he has an open door, so do I. Go ahead, Cheri."

"There's a regional manager covering the eastern U.S. for CBP, Inc. His name is Fred Maduro. He doesn't fit the profile perfectly, but he's close. For instance, he isn't an only child. He's set apart from his siblings, however, because he's the only one who's adopted. When I set up the appointment with him, he volunteered that his mother had a medically necessary hysterectomy after her fourth child. His parents later decided they wanted another child, so they adopted him.

"If he was treated differently from the others, it could have engendered the kind of antisocial behavior of someone who fits the profile. The second way he differs is that he has been married and has children of his own, CBP's owner told us. He's known the man for many years. According to the owner, Mr. Maduro's divorce was hotly contested. Being separated from his children could have nurtured a hatred for women."

"I have a question," Roy said. "My understanding is that probably our guy wouldn't have children. He isolates himself from other people while using interpersonal capabilities that reflect his intelligence to accomplish his goal, such as being successfully in sales or in attracting women. How does that fit with the guy you're describing?"

"I considered that," Cheri said. "I said his divorce was hotly contested. I believe he was happy to shed the responsibility of the kids, but was OCD dedicated to being territorial, with the children as part of his landscape. I'll find out whether that's an accurate portrayal when I interview him. That's just a capsule. Jack suggested to me that we should avoid getting too far into the weeds before the interview. If he's our guy, he could easily pick up on clues we don't want him to have." She nodded to Jack to indicate she was done.

"What about him *does* fit the profile?" Mike asked her.

"Several things. First, the business owner said he was pretty standoffish with his fellow employees to the point of not being well-liked. He's Eastern Regional Manager and travels to all the cities from which we've had mailings and has attended the AAUS in the last two years. He accidentally got credit card receipts from strip clubs mixed in with his expense reports, though. I don't think his boss likes him much more than his ex."

"Good job, Cheri," Jack said. "Roy, you're next."

"Similar picture here. A fellow works for a small manufacturer of gaskets. He's not a perfect fit. He's single, and, according to his boss, affable. He's an only child. He's been on the job for five years as Eastern Regional Manager, too. Before that, he handled a territory for Union Carbide in batteries and was relocated several times to start new territories when there was a change in personnel.

"I don't know that his name is important here. What may be important, however, is that he's gay." Roy looked at the others to gauge their reactions. "I'm aware, of course, that our serial had sex with the victims. We base that on the damage done to the vaginal cavity to remove semen.

"There are two possible scenarios here," Roy said. "First, while he's out of the closet, his homosexuality might reflect an animosity toward women with an underlying bisexual proclivity...."

"Leave it to our statistician to use a word like proclivity," Jack said.

"...a proclivity," Roy continued, "that may've been suppressed by a domineering mother, which fits our profile.

"The second scenario is even more intriguing and also fits behavior we can attribute to our perp. What if the removal of much of the pelvic cavity in the Cox case and the destruction of the vaginal cavity in the Bundergast case were attempts to destroy the principle symbol of the female gender? His gayness could have commenced during puberty after a hostility toward women surfaced. Is that too far-fetched?"

The others thought about that for a moment.

"No," Jack said, "I don't think so. What do you think, Mike?"

"That's thinking outside the box, pun intended. Seriously, though, Roy's thoughts could very well have merit," Mike said.

"I agree. Good work, Roy. You're multifaceted as well as a multi-tasker."

"I almost forgot," Roy added. "He's based in Cleveland."

Eyebrows rose.

"As afterthoughts go, Roy, that's a humdinger," Mike commented.

"Guess that leaves you and me, Anita," Jack said. "Show us what you've got."

"My guy is almost certainly not the serial we're looking for," she began. "That would be too easy. He's a perfect fit for the profile. His name is Lawrence Todd, a well-liked member of his sales team but someone who doesn't socialize with his coworkers. He's been with the company for ten years, handling the entire east coast up to the Mississippi. Mr. Todd was recommended to the owner of AFI, which stands for Able Fasteners, Incorporated, by one of the brokers who represents them. The broker called on Todd at Todd's retail job for a couple years, when he was just a teenager.

"He's currently thirty-one, single, and an only child. The CEO knew Todd's father well, and I guess that sealed the deal despite his youth. He was only twenty-one when he joined AFI. He's been a very productive employee with the retailer, is tops in sales, earns employee of the month, that sort of thing. I never spoke to the guy, but I think we should try to see him at AAUS."

Jack nodded. "Thanks. I have a pretty good fit, too. Mine is thirty-eight, twelve years with the company, came to them from a competitor within the industry. The boss said this man traveled too much to find a wife. Also, he's an only child. His boss, whose father started the company said he went out of his way for the brokers who represented the company. He's very amicable within the company but wouldn't cross the street to make a friend. He said he suspected the man might have a drinking problem. The people they knew in common usually knew him from a bar. He might fit well into Dan's Place, another potential fit."

Mike finished the meeting with a pep talk and encouragement for their progress. He said he looked forward to Wednesday's meeting to hear about the weekend interview.

"Roy and Cheri," he added, "stop by Jack's office after the meeting to collect your airline tickets."

CHAPTER FIFTY-FOUR

After Jack debriefed Roy and Cheri about their Saturday interviews, he made sure Mike was informed. Wednesday's meeting with just Jack and his team served two purposes. One was to review orally Cheri and Roy's reports, with Jack's added to the mix. The second purpose was to complete their preliminary planning for the upcoming AAUS trade show.

"So, Roy, let's have it. Did you nail our guy?" Jack teased.

"Oh, yeah," he replied sarcastically. "I didn't name him or his company at our last meeting, which I understand you want on the record for the tape of this meeting. His name is Chris Turner, and he works for General Gaskets and Seals.

"We know from his boss he's openly gay, and I could pick that up, though subtly, when I set up the appointment. I have to tell you I can't visualize him as our man. He's about as inoffensive as Serge from *Beverly Hills Cop*, and like Serge, he's very anxious to please. Unlike Serge, his gayness is very understated.

"His mom and dad aren't rooted in any religion. You could call them modern-day secularists. They're more like agnostics than atheists, to hear Turner tell it. They had doubts, but it ends there for him and his parents. They didn't lay any guilt trips on him that would've driven him into the closet or made him fear homophobes. They knew he was different at an early age, and they accepted it. He says there were no guilt trips at all.

"Far from hating women, he has many female friends. He simply prefers men when it comes to his romantic proclivities. Yeah, I used that word again. It's my vocabulary word for the month. He's well-adjusted and incapable of the kind of horror we've seen inflicted.

"His boss and I discussed Turner and his work. He's a very inoffensive person but so ingratiating on a personal level that even people who might otherwise feel a bit uncomfortable about his lifestyle are completely disarmed. I can see where, in time, given his desire to please his customers, he would build sincere, long-lasting relationships.

"He's a lanky, just-under-six-foot guy with close-cropped brown hair, and looks very average. He's not swishy. That's another place the Serge analogy goes wrong. He's got Serge's desire to please but with a very subdued sexuality. He most definitely wouldn't be alluring to Barbara Cox. I don't wear hats, but if I did, I'd eat mine if he turns out to be our guy, even if he's from Cleveland."

"Comprehensive interview, Roy, You have a proclivity for this kind of work. I'll note that in your file," he added with a half-smile. "Cheri?"

"I said I'd find out in the interview if some of my predictions about him were true, whether some of my ruminations about him constituted an accurate portrayal. I don't think the picture I foresaw was in any way on target. True, he had a hotly contested divorce. There was nothing territorial about wanting the children, though. He loves his kids, and his ex has relented. He has joint custody and a workable relationship with his ex.

"He's had a number of intimate relationships with women, some of them while he was still with his former wife. He's engaged again. Mr. Maduro could play the lead in *The Man Who Loved Women*. He likes them, is attracted to them, loves them, and purports to put them on a pedestal. He's not our guy."

"Jack said, "My guy was Bernard Levi, Jewish by nationality and religion. Sundown Friday to sundown Saturday, he claims he never goes out, rides in a car, or uses the phone. His company, Auto Abstracts, always schedules his flights to get him home before dark on Fridays to observe the Sabath.

"Auto Abstracts farms out the manufacture of some novelty accessories and then has the brokers sell them. Last year's best-selling item was a leather steering wheel wrap in genuine cowhide that could be imprinted with a company's logo. They made nice gifts for the imprinting company's clients."

"You think you could ask Mike to add some of those to the budget with FBI logos?" Cheri joked. "Sounds cute to me."

Jack would normally have felt that was an annoying off-topic digression, but for some reason he was just beginning to become aware of, he couldn't do that with Cheri.

"I'll continue after that outburst," he said, his body language signaling his comment was tongue-in-cheek, despite feeling weary from the grind. "His boss was right about a drinking problem. When it's the Sabbath, he drinks at home. The rest of the time, he drinks at the closest watering hole, whether at home or while traveling. He purports to be starting AA, Twelve Steps, and the whole thing. He knows his boss is aware of his drinking, and he's worried about his job.

"He never drinks on the job, though. He feels if he crosses that line, he's a goner. I suspect he slipped a bit on his AA commitment before our interview. He refused to meet me before sundown and then not at his place. He said it was messy. I'd guess it's a hovel. The bottom line, though, is he's incapable, in his usual inebriated state, of the detailed planning and anticipation that characterizes our serial. His free time is consumed with his drinking. I confirmed that by visiting his favorite watering hole near his house. Any thoughts or input?"

They shook their heads.

"We knew going in that none of these guys were made to order," Jack continued. "We made our selections based on the most probable of those we talked to, with their cooperative employer's input and the person's cooperation, so I'm not surprised or discouraged, and neither should you be. Finding the right guy in this situation won't be easy. We'll just keep plowing ahead until we get there. There's a reason the Bureau hasn't found him up to now, but we will.

"Let's plan for next week's trade show. In calculating your numbers from the daily email, a significant number of companies are still withholding cooperation. That'll be my first priority next week. I've made a list to get with the head honchos of those companies at the show. When you flash a badge, it has more impact than a demanding text or email. I can also leverage the public setting. I can't actually create a disturbance, which would go sour quickly, but the threat should be enough.

"Cheri and Roy, leave the heavy lifting to me. You both need to keep a low profile at the show. Bring your observations and hurdles to me. You'll be undercover. I'll explain that in a bit."

He was saving the details to build excitement in his rookies. It wasn't a big deal to an old pro, but he saw anticipation in their body language. Both of them sat up more erect, and he caught a flash in their eyes.

"Wish you could be with us, Anita, but I want you to know you've done a remarkably good job. You follow through and get those degrees, and you'll be welcome on any team I'm supervising. A note will be made to your record.

"The next thing on my agenda is to interview this Lawrence Todd you came up with, Anita. Add to that anyone we uncover in our calling this week. I'll do those interviews, too. Don't think I'm cutting you two out of the loop." He eyed Roy and Cheri. When he locked gazes with Cheri, he thought he saw something new there, and whatever she communicated made him a bit uncomfortable.

"Your jobs will be to make the rounds of the vendors, scrutinize what you see in detail, and retain what you can or take notes in a restroom. Don't be obvious. Pass those observations along to me. With all the small- to medium-sized vendors there, you'll be busy.

"We're flying out Sunday morning to get situated in our hotel early in the afternoon, which will give us a chance to familiarize ourselves with the surroundings. I don't want anyone working this Saturday. Kick back and enjoy the day, so you're fresh for the trip. I arranged with Ed Cousins, the Executive Director, for your trade show credentials to be at AAUS will-call.

"You two should make as many contacts as possible. I'll be the only one flashing credentials. These trade-show organizations tend to be incestuous. Most exhibitors know each other. Each of you will be a sympathetic neophyte who wants to learn from the master. Mike was able to angle some NAPA clothing for both of you. That's why I mentioned the undercover bit. As far as anyone else knows, you're just another attendee. As is often the case with members of the same company, you'll have adjoining rooms, and I'll be on a separate floor.

"While your rooms are together, though, you'll be in a different location from the other NAPA staff. Your cover story is you had late registrations. You may be tempted to hang with other people from NAPA. Don't. There's too much chance you'll blow your cover.

"Draw out the exhibitors. Cheri, flirt a bit, remembering that any one of the guys could be our man and the risk inherent in doing that. Be very wary. Being a guy, Roy can tell you that's an effective methodology. As Mike reminded us, though, it can be dangerous." He was careful to use Roy as an example instead of himself, and he thought he saw a bit of disappointment in Cheri's eyes.

"Since you and Roy will both be in NAPA garb, it won't seem strange if you're together off the trade show floor. Don't fly solo, Cheri. The guy we're looking for is too cautious to act out at the trade show—we think. I don't think Roy's a likely target," he added humorously. "Still, keep an eye out for her, Roy.

"Keep your contacts to the exhibit floor. You might be tempted to learn more about a subject by having a cocktail with him after the show closes. Don't. You're both ambitious, but don't be stupid. You might get a reaction you don't expect. Roy, you might think all this is directed at Cheri. I was joking a moment ago, but if our guy feels threatened, you could be at risk, too. You're both perceptive but still inexperienced. If anything rings a bell, I want to know immediately. *Immediately.*" His tone left no room for misunderstanding.

"Your status with NAPA will be as Manager Trainees. You were just hired. Top management at NAPA listed you as 'floaters,' meaning you can be assigned to any store where you're needed. Avoid involving anyone at the store level as a precautionary measure. You'll each get a packet on NAPA given to new employees from me Sunday morning. You can read them on the plane and in your hotel room. That should be enough to fake it.

"You're attempting to acquaint yourself with the industry in general and the vendors NAPA stores work with. You're vulnerable, because you don't have field experience. You just joined the company, so you don't know the lingo yet. It's a good idea to look at NAPA's website and familiarize yourself with the company to the level of a trainee at least. Your hotel rooms will have wi-fi, so do it then, so it'll be fresher. You need to know a little of what a NAPA store looks like, so you might want a quick visit on your Saturday off if you've never seen one. That won't take much time. I want you to rest. Go to the zoo or do something relaxing."

"Considering we're looking for an animal," Cheri said, "that might be considered work."

CHAPTER FIFTY-FIVE

Zero Defects indeed, he thought.

The realization he made a mistake echoed loudly even before the envelope, released from his latex-gloved hands, hit the bottom of the mail bin in Honolulu. He just performed a mailing that coincided in a location with a Number, although not plausibly with AAUS.

He comforted himself with the thought that it wasn't enough to make a connection with him personally. That would require a second error. He certainly wouldn't mail anything from Naples, Florida, where the present year's event was being held. Zero couldn't conceive of adding a Number during the show, but he always prepared for the unexpected.

It was the first day of the show. Regardless of his former resolve, he was itching to continue his delicious carnage. He could metaphorically taste it. The two weeks before the show, he had to oversee prospective mailings to his brokers and their customers, inviting them to visit him at the trade show, then place follow-up calls to the same people.

Premium pens were included with the mailings. They weren't the run-of-the-mill pens given out by other vendors. These were a definite upgrade. His customers always looked forward to those pens. That year would be augmented differently, though. Zero finally got the old man to pop for something a little extra that was his own idea. The old man was stuck with what he traditionally did, and why not? He was successful. Zero told him that giving a decent but not top-of-the-line bottle of red or white wine with a visit to their exhibit could put them in the big time.

Zero was on a break and was in line for a Philly cheese steak when he saw her. He hated women, although he loved their bodies. He was a leg man, and this semi-tall woman had legs as long as the Nile River. The rest of her was fabulous, too, and she walked like she knew it.

When women knew men wanted them, they always flaunted it. He knew they enjoyed the taunting, deriving the same kind of pleasure a mean person savored when she put a dog's food dish one foot farther away than the leash could reach.

After Zero saw her, his itch became a raging rash that he had to scratch, but he mustn't. That would be his second error. Even after she left his sight, the image of that magnificent body, along with her arrogant self-awareness of it, kept invading his thoughts. What a perfect Number 69.

He saw her prancing around in a tight black skirt, two-thirds thigh length, with her blue blouse and six-sided blue and yellow NAPA logo embroidered just above her C-cup left breast. Zero never wanted a woman more. The orgasmic imposition of his will on that one would be a new zenith of pleasure. He always compulsively wanted more stimulation than the last. He wondered if he would ever reach an apex that couldn't be topped. If he did, he'd still keep trying.

He recalled when, after drooling lighter fluid on Susan's face, she realized that was how he would grant her request for death. Sitting in his hotel room after the first night, after all the cocktail parties and back-slapping, he thought about the NAPA girl and ejaculated in his pants. That made him furious. She caused it! Messing himself like that was emasculating! There must be retribution.

CHAPTER FIFTY-SIX

The brand-new Naples Convention Center was adjacent to the always-upscale Ritz-Carlton Hotel. The new convention center provided 600,000-square-feet exhibit space, half the size of the largest floor space at Chicago's famous McCormick Place, the largest trade show facility in the U.S. Booths at the Naples facility varied in size from the standard 15 x 15 to much larger ones to accommodate the Borg Warners and other large companies in attendance.

The Ritz-Carlton had a 60,000-foot-square area used in the evening for hospitality, providing libations and attractive female staff that were definitely on company time and not pros. Pros couldn't work at the Ritz, but the company still attracted flirtatious clientele. Smaller organizations had suites at the convention center for hospitality purposes that were cheaper, with fewer commercial trapping than renting booths at the Ritz. Many attendees went back and forth between the private suites and the flashy ones within the Ritz at night.

The Ritz-Carlton Hotel in Naples was an ideal venue for the AAUS trade show in other ways. Like all Ritz Carltons, the hotel was luxurious, a requirement for a setting needed to follow up the previous year's Honolulu venue. The Ritz sat right on one of the white-sand beaches interspersed on Florida's Gulf Coast, and participants could take a quick dip in the Gulf after a short walk from the hotel.

Both the exhibitors and attendees went back and forth between the convention center exhibits, the hospitality suites, their rooms, and the beach until late in the evening. Booths needed to be spruced up for the following day's activities, and orders and leads required attention, too. The trade show ran from Monday morning through Friday noon. Friday mornings, exhibitors broke down their booths, somehow compacting them into containers that looked woefully inadequate before heading home on their flights.

Monday night, the exhausted agents went to bed early. Tuesday night, Jack wanted them to have dinner together to summarize their progress. After showering in their hotel rooms Tuesday, they met at a discreet table Jack reserved at a restaurant away from the hotel.

Cheri and Roy still wore their NAPA clothing to avoid attracting attention when leaving the hotel. They took an Über together, while Jack took a taxi and met them. Soon, they were at a table in the Red Lobster not far from the hotel.

"I spent most of my time so far chasing down honchos who weren't being very cooperative," Jack said. "My cover story was that hundreds of thousands of dollars had been stolen through identity theft at the first two AAUS events. It worked better than expected.

"To extricate the company's employees from involvement, I used our tactic that we're only looking for an unidentified witness who we knew was an exhibitor the last two years. I explained the Bureau received a report that a desk clerk noticed someone with multiple IDs and too many credit cards at Honolulu's main even hotel. Unfortunately, the clerk failed to take it seriously and didn't report it in a timely fashion. The thief had an official badge, but the desk clerk couldn't remember the name. I suggested it would have been an alias, anyway.

"Another exhibitor commented on his array of cards and intimated he knew the guy. Our suspect, as the story goes, was a handsome man, and the clerk expressed her enthusiasm. The fictional female at the front desk was too busy dreaming about her new heartthrob, who resembled George Clooney. Flirting briefly and ignoring her suspicions, especially after he mentioned he would 'see her later,' she remembered little more.

"It was all a fabrication, of course, and I honestly can't believe how many of these so-called sharp honchos swallowed it. I can't see myself doing that.

"Our real prey probably looks nothing like George Clooney," Jack said, laughing, "but it conveyed the image of a GQ sophisticate, which might be helpful. The cover story worked to get a degree of cooperation. Face-to-face after a credential is flashed in someone's face, well, it made the difference we hoped. Those I talked with didn't identify any new potentials. Most of the reps turned out to be married, and many brought their wives with them. The wives sunbathed or shopped during the day and met their husbands later in the evening.

"Cheri, given this guy's hatred for women, is it possible he would marry? Your prior analysis said no. Perhaps he had a bad relationship tied together by children or other factors, someone who feels trapped in the relationship? Would that compel his otherwise inexplicable actions? You invested the time to interview such a guy on Saturday, so you must've considered the possibility." Jack, clearly frustrated, wondered aloud.

He had a lot of respect for Roy, but he gravitated toward Cheri. He told himself it was because of their shared background in psychology, but he was becoming increasingly aware of it and tried to even things with a question for her, then one for Roy. Jack could tell something was happening, but he couldn't, or more likely wouldn't, put a name to it.

"Given the depth of vitriol our man feels toward women in general, I think it's unlikely he'd keep the lid on things. It would require superhuman effort. He's been methodical as hell, committing atrocities for ten years, as near as we can tell, and he takes the time to plan meticulously. That's why we receive the numbers every couple of months. We've generated the best possibilities for interviews but not likely suspects.

"If it weren't for the perp's meticulous planning I think he would murder every day. Continuous confrontations with a spouse or significant other would build his fury geometrically. Even if he could keep a lid on it with a spouse, I'd expect an increase in the frequency of the murders as part of an uncontrolled reaction. He'd lose his methodical discipline, as his contact with his significant other and the frustration with the necessary compromises that exist in a relationship went forward. We haven't seen that yet."

"That's quite a mouthful, Cheri. Good thing you haven't given it much thought," he teased. "The restaurant closes in a couple hours."

"I'll say," Roy added humorously.

He received blank stares from his dinner companions. Hoping to recover his credibility, he launched a diatribe of his own. "Besides, if we expanded our profile to include married men, the task of identifying our culprit would become almost insurmountable. It would expand the number of possibles by five or six times. We'd have to wait for this very careful, very intelligent doer to make a mistake, which so far, he's assiduously avoided. It makes me shiver even to think how many more victims...."

Like an auctioneer, Jack said, "Sooold American!" It came out awkwardly, perhaps because he felt off balance.

"Just calculating the sheer numbers," Roy finished sheepishly.

"We get it," Jack said, annoyed at the prospect. "We need to continue our focus on single men. That brings me to Anita's 'perfect fit' fellow. His name is Lawrence Todd. I interviewed him today. I can't see him as our guy. Sociopaths sometimes fool polygraphs. Fortunately, I'm not a machine. When confronted with law enforcement the first time, there's almost always a tell if the subject is the actual perp. I'm a poker player when the job infrequently allows me to make some *dinero,* and I'm fairly good.

"One reason is that I can pick up tells. I'm even better when I encounter a perp. It could be that he's overly solicitous. It could be a trace of nervousness, like tapping a foot when there's no music playing or diverting his eyes. Coming up with a reason he needs to go soon during the interview is one of the many things they do, none of which Todd demonstrated.

"He doesn't like being called Larry, but that's not unusual. I know men named Ronald that don't like being called Ron, ane someone named Thomas who doesn't like Tom.

"He's single but claims to have relationships with women. He says his travel, which his boss told me was about eighty percent of the time, makes it difficult to maintain a bond under such circumstances. I imagine he's right. I tried tactfully to probe for specifics, but he asked why his sex life was of interest if all we wanted was a witness to identity theft."

"You can't fault a guy for trying not to involve someone with whom he's having an affair," Roy said.

"Are you sure that's what he's doing?" Cheri asked.

"Yes, I believe so. There was no discomfort on his part, no telltale disdain he might feel for a person trying to nail him. If Todd was our man, it would be very hard to completely conceal any concern about our real motives in questioning him."

"What about the rest of our profile?" Cheri asked.

"His parents raised him as a Christian. He's a regular church member but doesn't make it every week. When he travels a lot, he sometimes sleeps in on Sunday. He seemed to feel guilty about that. Few people make it to church every week these days. He says he has a personal relationship with God and told me the Ten Commandments are God's law, defining what is sin and certain things we're supposed to do, like honoring your mother and father, the failure to do that being a sin. An affirmative act, such as coveting your neighbor's wife, is also sinful. Our serial would never have picked that example. It's too close to home," he said.

"Todd distinguished the Commandments, which are primarily definitions of sin, from an outline of how we're to live our lives in positive terms. Those, he said, are found in the Beatitudes. When I asked him for an example, he said he loved the Beatitudes and proceeded proudly to recite them in their entirety. I had a good religious upbringing but not enough to recall them all. Todd's favorite was the first one, 'Blessed are the poor in spirit, for theirs is the kingdom of heaven.' He's a bit of a holy roller."

"Could be a smoke screen," Cheri persisted skeptically.

"Could be. I think it would be very difficult for this monster to completely ignore direct challenges without one of my tells, such as becoming defensive. I tried bating him and said I was single, too, and I found many women to be disingenuous. He suggested I keep looking, saying there were some wonderful, sincere females out there.

"He's about six-two, which fits our description of the man in Dan's Place. He reminds me of an old-time actor named Tyrone Power. Todd would certainly be attractive to most women. That part fits. I just can't see him as the man we're looking for. Maybe he snowed me. Maybe I missed a step, but I think we need to continue searching. We have a lot of ground to cover and only more days to do it. We won't get much attention from people Friday morning when they're breaking down the booths and trying to catch planes."

Jack turned to his two agents. Cheri inferred she used her genetic attributes to entice exhibitors into conversation, hoping one would betray tendencies consistent with their profile. She probed for any hostility underlying a man's outward personality. All she got was an endless number of proposals for dinner, or, inanely, coffee from the less-assertive types.

Roy tried to assess what percentage of those encountered were single and weren't handsome enough to attract Barbara Cox.

"Didn't know you were so attuned to evaluating attractive men, Roy," Jack said.

He and Cheri enjoyed a chuckle at Roy's expense.

Ignoring their perverse sense of humor, Roy continued his statistical analysis. "A high percentage were present in Honolulu. My original estimate that fully twenty percent might be a fit for our perp was exaggerated, though. I'd say it's more like ten percent or less, based on my census of the last two days. Of course, with anecdotal evidence of that kind, I have no idea what the margin of error is. When you're looking for a needle in a haystack, repetitive searching may dull our observations. The more we look for a potential fit, the more likely we are to fall into a malaise and overlook the needle."

"I think he's right about that," Cheri encouraged. She glanced at Jack, wondering about his opinion.

"Sounds unanimous," Jack said with a dash of levity.

Their food arrived. The team took a respite from the long day to enjoy it.

CHAPTER FIFTY-SEVEN

What bullshit! Zero thought. *That FBI asshole wouldn't be here investigating identity theft.*

He was confident his interview with Agent Garvey threw him off the scent. He would never suspect Lawrence Todd again. For the first time he could remember, he could thank Phoebe for all that religious stuff she forced him to learn. How could a Supervising Special Agent, as the card identified the man, who was knee-deep in the carnage Zero left behind, persist in such rot. Clearly, that Garvey fellow still clung to his beliefs.

His first instinct was to back away from his near compulsion to exact revenge on the FBI by adding the NAPA woman he desired to his Numbers. The fact that the FBI was there demonstrated that mailing a Number from Honolulu was a mistake that required him to back off.

The NAPA woman humiliated him by controlling his impulses. She sullied him with his own semen. She *controlled* him!

Years earlier, he promised himself two things. First, no woman would ever exert the kind of control over him that his mother used to suffocate him and his father. He would be a man, not a milksop like his father, whom Phoebe easily manipulated.

Still, he should back off. Then he had an inspiration. The death of the NAPA woman right after his interview would point suspicion at almost anyone at the trade show but himself. Who, after an interview with the FBI would immediately go out to commit another atrocity? Instead, they would become intensely focused on the person they had so far missed. They'd run off in a thousand different directions.

He came prepared, too. When he bought the clown outfit in Akron, a never-to-be-discovered weighted package at the bottom of a deep Ohio lake, he bought a second disguise. Feeling the itch, he brought it with him.

A lesser man would have felt the urge to flee even after what appeared to be a successful encounter with Supervising Special Agent Garvey, Zero thought derisively. Fleeing demonstrated what law enforcement would call consciousness of guilt.

He would stay put, but not in the way they expected.

CHAPTER FIFTY-EIGHT

The three continued their efforts Wednesday and Thursday, frustratingly without result. Wednesday, Cheri had the odd sensation she was being followed but didn't see anyone or anything to confirm it. When she was a kid playing Hide and Seek, she was always good at sensing when someone was near and returned to a place that had already been checked.

Dismissing her feeling as paranoia, she wondered about having someone watch her back and thought of Jack.

After dinner, they said their good nights. Cheri and Jack said they were beat and were going to sleep. Roy headed to a lounge at the Ritz to relax.

A bit later, Jack flicked on the news and tried to wind down from the day when someone banged on his door. Drawing his weapon, he rushed to answer.

A hysterical Cheri fell against him, holding him urgently. He moved her to a couch, sat her down, and tried to comfort her to no avail. His rookie Special Agent, whom he judged would be calm under fire, was hyperventilating. He feared she might lose consciousness. It was always different when an agent was the victim.

Unable to think of anything else to calm her, he slapped her face hard, leaving a rose-colored mark. He realized that might complicate forensics if something serious happened, but he had little choice.

Luckily, Cheri's breathing slowed, and her sobs became shallower.

"Calm down, Cheri," Jack said. "You're safe now."

He instantly knew she'd been attacked by the serial. Time was critical. "I want you to do your best to compose yourself. I believe I can guess what happened. Where'd the attack take place?"

"In m...my room," she stammered.

"I won't leave you. Can you give me sixty seconds to make a phone call?"

"Yes." She forced herself to become calm.

Jack knew that Cheri and Roy had adjoining rooms without a connecting door. Cheri was in 1025, Roy in 1027. He didn't know which bar Roy was in, but the evidence had to be preserved. Cheri also needed him, and that was suddenly more important than he would have thought.

He called the front desk.

"Hello," a woman said, "may I put you on a brief hold?"

"This is Special Agent Garvey of the FBI. Don't you *dare* put me on hold. I have an emergency, and I need to speak with the most-senior manger you have *right now!*"

"It's a she."

"Put her on the phone *now!*"

It took much longer than he would have liked, but finally, a woman's voice said, "This is the Night Manager. How can I help you?"

"Listen to me very carefully. I will only say this once. You might want to take notes. This is not a prank. I can provide you with credentials later. My name is Jack Garvey, and I'm a Supervising Special Agent with the FBI. I'm here with another agent named Roy Rogers, and that's not a joke, either. He's in one of your bars. Page him...."

"I'm sorry, Sir, but hotel policy is not to use the paging system unless it's an emergency."

"I already told you this is an emergency. What's your name?"

"Night Manager Emily Thompson."

"I will provide you with credentials, as I said. There's been a serious attack in your hotel. I need to reach Agent Rogers immediately. Please page him and have him call room 325. Unless you want to be looking for a day job tomorrow, do it right now!" He hung up.

A minute later, Roy called and asked, "Jack? What's going on?"

"Cheri's been attacked, I think by our guy. Do the following. Go to her room." He turned aside. "Cheri, did you leave your room open?"

"I wasn't thinking about preserving the crime scene," she said uncomfortably.

"She left it open, Roy. You need to get up there right away to preserve evidence and to prevent anyone from entering. Call the night manager. Her name is Emily Thompson. Have her call the locals. Emphasize this is an ongoing FBI investigation and have them put up crime-scene tape. Don't let them enter.

"Then call the closest Bureau field office and have them get personnel down here prepared to collect evidence. Also have them obtain security footage from the cameras on the tenth floor. Tell the night manager we'll want to check the tapes from all the floors later."

Jack hung up, returned to the couch, and put an arm around Cheri. Melting against him, she put her head on his shoulder. She felt so good and natural there, as if she belonged there in a crisis.

Jack and Cheri knew there was some undefined tension between them, but that wasn't the time to explore it. Jack waited a few seconds until she seemed more composed.

"Cheri, you know we need to talk," he said.

"Yes, I know."

"Tell me what happened chronologically and as clearly as you can."

"I opened the door to my room," she said calmly, like the buttoned-up agent she appeared to be. "He must've been inside already. I sensed him without seeing him. He immediately grasped my neck in the crook of his arm and placed pressure on the back of my head, like we were taught at the academy with an unruly perp we wanted to render unconscious.

"I knew I had only seconds to react. My shoes are blunt and have medium heels, but they could hurt his shin. He was too fast. He must've drawn his leg back to avoid the blow, because I didn't make contact.

"I felt he lost his balance, though. The room has a heavy, round, beveled glass coffee table with three legs. The glass is supported by cushions just above each leg. We fell forward onto the table, landing between two of the legs, making the glass flip at an angle. Thank God it was too heavy to shatter, or I might've been in a bad way."

"Dear God," Jack said.

"It made a hell of a clatter. I was stunned, maybe from hitting my head on the glass. By the time I recovered, he was gone. I tentatively peered into the hall, wishing my gun wasn't in my luggage, and then I ran after him, but he disappeared. He was too fast. It's a long hall, and there was no one in either direction. A fire exit led to the stairs, and that must be where he went.

"All I could think of was getting to Roy next door, because he was the nearest, but I knew he was in one of the bars. Then I just needed to get to you." She began weeping again.

"You didn't see anything of him?"

She shook her head.

"Any sense of his height?"

"From the position he held my head, he was definitely taller than me."

CHAPTER FIFTY-NINE

Zero, furious with himself, couldn't believe his plan for the NAPA woman's demise had been aborted. He had to concentrate on avoiding detection. His preparation would still insulate him from identification.

The disguise he used was that of a Hasidic Jew. His clothes, as were traditional, were entirely black. The wig displayed the hanging curls that characterized the sect, complete with a full beard and yarmulke.

Zero knew if he left his room in the disguise, the extensive security cameras would lead the authorities right back to him, so he left the hotel in his regular business clothes. His disguise was in his deep but lightweight aluminum briefcase. He calmly went to his rental car and drove to an abandoned gas station he scouted earlier. It was out of business for some time, had no cameras, and provided cover from the unchecked growth of foliage at the back.

He left the rental car there and quickly transformed into a Hasidic Jew. He hailed a taxi and returned to the hotel, entering via the main entrance in full view of the many cameras.

Then he went to the NAPA lady's room, taking the elevator to the tenth floor, which he already scouted when he followed her to learn her room number. It was *his* NAPA woman, because when he undertook a mission, he owned his victims through controlling their fate.

Zero used a passkey he stole from an inattentive maid's cleaning cart to gain entry. Then he waited.

After the debacle, Zero disappeared into the fire exit on the tenth-floor stairs and reemerged on the ninth floor. The stairs had security cameras and afforded no better camouflage. He rode the elevator down to the lobby and walked out of the hotel to catch another taxi, taking it in the opposite direction to a cab stand he saw as a backup. After switching cabs, he returned to the abandoned gas station.

Once there, he quickly shed his disguise and disposed of his entire briefcase, including costume. It was clean of prints when he dropped it into a huge Dumpster that would soon be emptied into the city dump. He would buy an identical briefcase when he returned home after the last day of the show. His fellow workers would be too occupied to notice he didn't have a briefcase, and all his business papers were saved to a flash drive.

There was nothing to connect him to the events of earlier that evening. They would have a video of a Hasidic Jew walking down the hall to the NAPA bitch's room, but that would lead nowhere. He completely removed the business clothes he wore prior to his Hasidic costume until he was totally naked, then he carefully placed those clothes into a plastic bag and sealed it, segregating it from the others. He dressed again and went to the subbasement of the hotel to dump the bag of clothing into the incinerator.

Taking great care to shield his face from the few locations in the subbasement that had cameras, he left no forensic evidence.

He deliberately had a late dinner at one of the Ritz restaurants. The wait staff who wanted to go home would clearly remember him. He made a rare appearance at a bar his coworkers talked about and stayed with him for two Beams with 7-Up. The head honcho, Will Armstrong, and the Western Regional Manager, were both there. Despite their surprise at seeing him, they welcomed him warmly.

The following day, he would go home and put it all behind him. He would find a new 69.

CHAPTER SIXTY

"I'm OK now, Jack," Cheri said. "If I'm not mistaken, and I'm still part of the team, we have work to do." Her mood brightened considerably.

"Of course you're part of the team," Jack said. "It's probably not necessary now, but I promised the Night Manager I would give her my credentials. It'll take only a minute."

They rode the elevator down to the lobby, where Jack asked for Emily Thompson. She appeared instantly and introduced the hotel manager, who she called in to meet Jack.

Jack reached for his credentials, but they waved him off.

"Local police and your fellow agent gave us what we need," Manager Bernie Reynolds assured him. "Is this the young lady who was attacked?"

"Yes," Cheri said. "I'm OK now."

"We at the Ritz Carlton Hotel are very sorry this happened."

"It wasn't your fault," she said.

"Mr. Reynolds," Jack proceeded, "we need to see all your surveillance videos. We'll start with the tenth floor and work down from there."

"Your Agent Rogers already informed us. I understand agents are flying in here from your Tampa office. The local cops are giving Mr. Rogers a hard time. He might need you.

"We have a major trade show going on, and we've done everything we can to cooperate. The lower the profile you can keep on this, the better. We would really appreciate it."

"Comprende," Jack said in his limited Spanish why he wasn't sure. "I'll do what I can."

Jack and Cheri didn't need any further invitation. When they arrived at room 1025, Roy looked like a home plate umpire going head to head with a very animated team manager.

"Excuse me," Jack said.

"Who are you?" an authoritative police figure demanded.

"I'm Supervising Special Agent Jack Garvey of the FBI."

"I'm Lieutenant Pollack, of the Naples Police Department. Anytime anything comes up at the Ritz, I'm called in. I understand this involves an assault on a young woman. Is this she?"

Cheri nodded, showing her exasperation.

"I don't know why you guys are here or how you got called in so fast, but assault is a local crime with local jurisdiction. You need to let us into her room. I suggest you do so right now."

"I hate to disappoint you, Lieutenant, but this young woman is Special Agent Cheryl Hancock." He used their formal titles to establish his authority. "An assault on an FBI agent is a federal crime, which gives us jurisdiction. Why we're here is none of your damn business. We'll cooperate with you to the extent of giving you the vitals when we're ready. May I suggest that you and your men remain here? We may need assistance.

"In the meantime, Agents Rogers, Hancock, and I will be in Ms. Hancock's room. I'd appreciate it if you and your officers would make sure no one else enters the crime scene until our Bureau technicians arrive."

CHAPTER SIXTY-ONE

Back at Quantico that Saturday, Mike Hennessey called a rare weekend meeting of the group. Anita immediately embraced Cheri with the empathy only two women would share. They exchanged knowing half-smiles.

"You OK, Cheri?" Mike asked.

"Yeah, I am. It kind of brings the whole thing home to you. It's the why of what we do."

"If we could definitely connect what happened to our case, you'd have to be removed, you know."

Cheri was instantly dejected. "If he's our guy, I'm the only one who had actual contact with him."

"Don't worry. We haven't made the connection yet. I have only preliminary findings from our forensics techs. It'll be awhile before we have a complete report and can connect all the dots. Jack already emailed a rundown of what occurred.

"Jack, what did you do to that Naples lieutenant? He and his chief are hopping mad."

"They wanted to tromp all over our scene before the technicians got there. I had to pull rank, and then I didn't give them a clue what we were working on."

"I've seen you do that, Jack. Ever hear of using tact?" Mike gave him a sidelong glance. Jack's formality was an obvious effort to put some distance between himself and Cheri, but it was transparent as hell to Mike. "We learned the only prints found on the glass table belong to Agent Hancock. She probably tried to catch the table to break her fall."

"There weren't even any residual prints. "The maid just Windexed the table. We found fibers and think they belong to the Hasidic wig the perp wore. Our lab guys are trying to track them down. You'll know as soon as Jack and I do.

"We have a reasonably short amount of time captured by the hotel's tapes. We can see the attacker entering the hotel around seven o'clock through the main doors, wearing his Hasidic outfit. From what Jack told me, you three returned from dinner around eight, and Cheri went straight to her room, where she was attacked immediately. The bastard was waiting for her."

"A bit embarrassing for the hotel," Jack said. "Mike said one of the maids was missing a passkey. The perp must've lifted it."

"The security tapes suggest he was six-one or six-two," Mike continued, "which aligns pretty well with the description from Dan's Place in Cleveland. We even had an estimate that he wears size eleven or twelve shoes. The techs were able to get that using known measurements in the corridor as a backdrop with the pattern in the carpet."

"There isn't much more yet," Jack said, sounding slightly disappointed. "We're slowly gaining a pattern, a volume of information that will eventually connect. Once it demonstrates we aren't chasing our tails following up on someone's very long-term prank and can show hard evidence that we have a big-time serial on our hands, we'll get a force of agents together and nail this son of a bitch."

CHAPTER SIXTY-TWO

Jack, concerned about Cheri, felt she was more traumatized by the incident in Naples than she let on. They'd been working six-day weeks since they received Number 67. Roy and Cheri fully accepted that any woman who died from that point forward did so on their watch.

Jack had been attacked on the job more than once. He wasn't as sexist as some people joked, even though they knew him well enough to know it wasn't true. He was simply old-fashioned. He didn't think it was chauvinistic to open a door or pull out a chair for a woman. Instead of diminishing them, he felt it elevated them. That was how he was raised.

When someone was exposed to danger, especially more than once, he or she tended to insulate himself from the experience. Time created a protective buffer between the person and the next incident. All agents knew they might put their lives on the line someday. No one, unless he idealized the job and lied to himself about the eventuality of danger, was immune from the first confrontation. Absent the scab that would grow over the peril, the first time had a huge impact.

No one but Cheri could feel that. It was one thing to be on a stakeout when danger was anticipated. Being attacked unaware in her own hotel room by a suspected serial murderer, rapist, and torturer was something else.

Jack deceived himself that he could talk with Cheri and somehow ease her pain. He imagined her having been sleepless since the event. Worse, she might be experiencing the trauma repeatedly, manifested by nightmares. He believed his words and empathy could help her through the experience until she insulated or prepared herself for the next time.

He knew if he called her, she might rebuff him and put professional distance between them. She could also misinterpret his intentions, so he didn't call. He showed up at her apartment and knocked on her door rather reluctantly.

When she didn't answer, he knocked harder. Maybe she was out. Was she taking too long, or was that just his nerves?

"Just a minute," Cheri called.

His heart caught in his throat. The proverbial fight-or-flight response made him want to run, but he felt a different kind of urgency. Suddenly, he was transported to a place he hadn't been since high school. Jack, a confident man, wasn't accustomed to the sudden rush of emotion.

The door swung open to reveal Cheri in a plush pink bathrobe. "Jack?" She sounded genuinely surprised.

He wanted to flee again.

Cheri, wondering what he was doing at her apartment, was elated to see him and somewhat apprehensive, too. Jack was a complex man who always put his job and career first. That could include checking on her well-being, trying to determine her state of mind or fitness to continue, or it could be he wanted to let her down easier than taking her off the case while at the office. That thought gave her the jitters. It never entered her mind his visit might be personal.

Cheri had feelings for Jack, although she couldn't clearly define them. She was confident of her abilities in the Bureau, and, when she was involved in Bureau business, she felt fine. In a personal setting, like the dinner they had in Brighton, she felt ill at ease, even nervous.

"Hi," he said timidly. "Bad time?" He hoped and feared rejection simultaneously.

Instead of giving him the predictable, "Why are you here?" she simply invited him in.

"I think I caught you at a bad time," he tried again.

"I've just been lounging around this morning. I usually go to church every Sunday, but I wasn't motivated. Please, come in. Have a seat anywhere. I'll go change."

"Oh, well, your bathrobe is very chaste. I really don't want to interrupt your relaxation."

"OK."

He sat in a chair opposite the loveseat, while Cheri sat in the corner of it across from him. Moving from the dorms at Quantico usually meant the new Special Agents were on a tight budget. The loveseat and chair were new, but they weren't Broyhill. Neither were the furnishings at Jack's condo. Still, Cheri used her resources to make an inviting, comfy place.

Jack practiced being observant, which was useful in his profession. Her small, one-bedroom apartment, with a cramped living space that merged into a small kitchenette was neat and had very few accoutrements. A print of Monet's "La Japanaise" adorned one wall adding rilliant color to what could have been a drab apartment. Camille Monet posed in a kimono. Recalling the Renoir in Jack's office, Cheri offered, "I see we both enjoy impressionism.

"Usually when something traumatizing happens in your life," Cheri said, "turning to God can be very comforting. Monet's simplicity I find soothing in a different way. It's normally how I cope. Somehow, this Sunday, I didn't want to face people. I needed time to adjust."

"You needn't feel bad. That's a normal, healthy reaction. Calm introspection and time alone are exactly what you need." Wanting to escape, he knew he shouldn't be there.

"If something developed with the case, I'm sure you would've called."

"You're asking why I'm here. I wanted to know how you're doing. I can't get your expression when I first saw you after the attack out of my head. The experience must've been terrible. We didn't have time to focus on you with everything else going on. I'm concerned about all members of my team," he finished weakly.

"That's very nice." She almost said it was sweet but stopped herself. "Can I get you a cup of coffee? I just made some, and heaven knows I could use it."

"I'd love a cup. You aren't sleeping too well? That's understandable."

Cheri walked into her efficiency kitchen. "Not altogether. I haven't woken up in the night shrieking or anything, just...." She glanced down for a second, then prepared the coffee without finishing.

"I'm afraid I haven't had much time since getting out of the dorm at Quantico," she continued. "Twenty weeks there was quite enough. It's your fault the apartment is in this condition, you know," she teased. "This case has kept all of us hopping. My place is still sparsely decorated."

"The Monet adds a nice ambiance," Jack offered.

"Ever since my parents let me go to Paris during summer break between high school and college. It was an organized, chaperoned trip set up by the National Honor Society. Being chaperoned was the only way Dad would let me go. Coming from the Bureau, you can imagine he leaned in the direction of being protective.

"I was awed and amazed by the Louvre. The Renaissance painters were incredible geniuses. Rembrandt was startling in his intensity, yet he could capture a facial expression that put me in the painting. The Mona Lisa was wonderful, I suppose, but it didn't speak to me.

"It was when I got to the Impressionist Museum that I lost my heart. I think Monet is my favorite, but it might be Renoir. Did you know they were best friends and even had houses built next to each other in Giverny, France? The pond in Monet's garden was where he painted his famous water lilies. It takes 120 gardeners to keep up the place now. I keep changing my mind.

"Van Gogh's bedroom and self-portraits I love, too. *Starry Night* is like a trip to another dimension. The ceiling of the Paris Opera House by Chagall takes my breath away. Then there's always Gaugin!" She blushed as if embarrassed. "I can really get on a soapbox about Impressionist painters."

Jack sensed that letting her talk would be therapeutic, filling what otherwise would have been taut silence, giving their encounter an air of normalcy.

Cheri ran off and returned with a tray with two cups of coffee and two Danishes. "I know from the office you take your coffee black, no sugar. Me, too."

"Thanks." He somehow felt traumatized just being there. It was an unusual sensation for him. It almost felt like cowardice. He knew his visit would be frowned upon by the Bureau, but he also knew that wasn't what he felt.

"If you're worried about me, don't be, Jack. I know I was a mess Thursday night."

"I think you came through pretty well for a rookie." He allowed himself to chuckle. "Actually, if I'd known about your literacy in Impressionism, I would've come much sooner. I'm a fan, too."

"I was a little disappointed in myself," Cheri confessed. I signed on knowing something like that could happen. I felt like a soldier in his first combat when the shelling started. I didn't run, but I froze in the foxhole. I may've been stunned, but I still feel like I should have done better."

"If you had, well, let's just say it wouldn't have been using good judgment. You weren't armed, because passing through the security metal detectors at the Convention center would have blown your cover. At the moment, he probably was, too."

"Yes. I try to console myself with that thought. I could use some consoling right now." Her voice shook slightly.

Jack, moving to the love seat to comfort her, put an arm around her, intending nothing more, but she rose up to kiss him.

"Cheri, we can't!" he implored.

"I don't give a damn." She began to undress him.

Jack never wanted a woman so much. She was everything missing in his life. He needed her. Suddenly, he didn't give a damn, either.

His hand slipped inside her bathrobe to fondle her breast. The nipple was already hard, and, when he touched it, she stiffened. Kissing him, she embraced his mouth fully and urgently.

Each was astonished when they found themselves completely naked, taking in the sight of the other's body. Jack wanted to unleash her passion, to do it as no one ever had. He instinctively went to her long, pale thighs, tracing his tongue slowly up them to where they converged. A flood of passion enveloped her. Both hoped her apartment walls were soundproof.

Jack rose up, looking into her eyes, and gently entered her. Their cadence grew in rapidity and intensity until they found each other on the small loveseat lying awkwardly, looking at each other as if they crossed into a new horizon into an unfamiliar but welcome landscape.

CHAPTER SIXTY-THREE

Jack, concerned about Cheri, felt she was more traumatized by the incident in Naples than she let on. They'd been working six-day weeks since they received Number 67. Roy and Cheri fully accepted that any woman who died from that point forward did so on their watch.

Jack had been attacked on the job more than once. He wasn't as sexist as some people joked, even though they knew him well enough to know it wasn't true. He was simply old-fashioned. He didn't think it was chauvinistic to open a door or pull out a chair for a woman. Instead of diminishing them, he felt it elevated them. That was how he was raised.

When someone was exposed to danger, especially more than once, he or she tended to insulate himself from the experience. Time created a protective buffer between the person and the next incident. All agents knew they might put their lives on the line someday. No one, unless he idealized the job and lied to himself about the eventuality of danger, was immune from the first confrontation. Absent the scab that would grow over the peril, the first time had a huge impact.

No one but Cheri could feel that. It was one thing to be on a stakeout when danger was anticipated. Being attacked unaware in her own hotel room by a suspected serial murderer, rapist, and torturer was something else.

Jack deceived himself that he could talk with Cheri and somehow ease her pain. He imagined her having been sleepless since the event. Worse, she might be experiencing the trauma repeatedly, manifested by nightmares. He believed his words and empathy could help

217

her through the experience until she insulated or prepared herself for the next time.

He knew if he called her, she might rebuff him and put professional distance between them. She could also misinterpret his intentions, so he didn't call. He showed up at her apartment and knocked on her door rather reluctantly.

When she didn't answer, he knocked harder. Maybe she was out. Was she taking too long, or was that just his nerves?

"Just a minute," Cheri called.

His heart caught in his throat. The proverbial fight-or-flight response made him want to run, but he felt a different kind of urgency. Suddenly, he was transported to a place he hadn't been since high school. Jack, a confident man, wasn't accustomed to the sudden rush of emotion.

The door swung open to reveal Cheri in a plush pink bathrobe. "Jack?" She sounded genuinely surprised.

He wanted to flee again.

Cheri, wondering what he was doing at her apartment, was elated to see him and somewhat apprehensive, too. Jack was a complex man who always put his job and career first. That could include checking on her well-being, trying to determine her state of mind or fitness to continue, or it could be he wanted to let her down easier than taking her off the case while at the office. That thought gave her the jitters. It never entered her mind his visit might be personal.

Cheri had feelings for Jack, although she couldn't clearly define them. She was confident of her abilities in the Bureau, and, when she was involved in Bureau business, she felt fine. In a personal setting, like the dinner they had in Brighton, she felt ill at ease, even nervous.

"Hi," he said timidly. "Bad time?" He hoped and feared rejection simultaneously.

Instead of giving him the predictable, "Why are you here?" she simply invited him in.

"I think I caught you at a bad time," he tried again.

"I've just been lounging around this morning. I usually go to church every Sunday, but I wasn't motivated. Please, come in. Have a seat anywhere. I'll go change."

"Oh, well, your bathrobe is very chaste. I really don't want to interrupt your relaxation."

"OK."

He sat in a chair opposite the loveseat, while Cheri sat in the corner of it across from him. Moving from the dorms at Quantico usually meant the new Special Agents were on a tight budget. The loveseat and chair were new, but they weren't Broyhill. Neither were the furnishings at Jack's condo. Still, Cheri used her resources to make an inviting, comfy place.

Jack practiced being observant, which was useful in his profession. Her small, one-bedroom apartment, with a cramped living space that merged into a small kitchenette was neat and had very few accoutrements. A print of Monet's "La Japanaise" adorned one wall adding rilliant color to what could have been a drab apartment. Camille Monet posed in a kimono. Recalling the Renoir in Jack's office, Cheri offered, "I see we both enjoy impressionism.

"Usually when something traumatizing happens in your life," Cheri said, "turning to God can be very comforting. Monet's simplicity I find soothing in a different way. It's normally how I cope. Somehow, this Sunday, I didn't want to face people. I needed time to adjust."

"You needn't feel bad. That's a normal, healthy reaction. Calm introspection and time alone are exactly what you need." Wanting to escape, he knew he shouldn't be there.

"If something developed with the case, I'm sure you would've called."

"You're asking why I'm here. I wanted to know how you're doing. I can't get your expression when I first saw you after the attack out of my head. The experience must've been terrible. We didn't have time to focus on you with everything else going on. I'm concerned about all members of my team," he finished weakly.

"That's very nice." She almost said it was sweet but stopped herself. "Can I get you a cup of coffee? I just made some, and heaven knows I could use it."

"I'd love a cup. You aren't sleeping too well? That's understandable."

Cheri walked into her efficiency kitchen. "Not altogether. I haven't woken up in the night shrieking or anything, just...." She glanced down for a second, then prepared the coffee without finishing.

"I'm afraid I haven't had much time since getting out of the dorm at Quantico," she continued. "Twenty weeks there was quite enough. It's your fault the apartment is in this condition, you know," she teased. "This case has kept all of us hopping. My place is still sparsely decorated."

"The Monet adds a nice ambiance," Jack offered.

"Ever since my parents let me go to Paris during summer break between high school and college. It was an organized, chaperoned trip set up by the National Honor Society. Being chaperoned was the only way Dad would let me go. Coming from the Bureau, you can imagine he leaned in the direction of being protective.

"I was awed and amazed by the Louvre. The Renaissance painters were incredible geniuses. Rembrandt was startling in his intensity, yet he could capture a facial expression that put me in the painting. The Mona Lisa was wonderful, I suppose, but it didn't speak to me.

"It was when I got to the Impressionist Museum that I lost my heart. I think Monet is my favorite, but it might be Renoir. Did you know they were best friends and even had houses built next to each other in Giverny, France? The pond in Monet's garden was where he painted his famous water lilies. It takes 120 gardeners to keep up the place now. I keep changing my mind.

"Van Gogh's bedroom and self-portraits I love, too. *Starry Night* is like a trip to another dimension. The ceiling of the Paris Opera House by Chagall takes my breath away. Then there's always Gaugin!" She blushed as if embarrassed. "I can really get on a soapbox about Impressionist painters."

Jack sensed that letting her talk would be therapeutic, filling what otherwise would have been taut silence, giving their encounter an air of normalcy.

Cheri ran off and returned with a tray with two cups of coffee and two Danishes. "I know from the office you take your coffee black, no sugar. Me, too."

"Thanks." He somehow felt traumatized just being there. It was an unusual sensation for him. It almost felt like cowardice. He knew his visit would be frowned upon by the Bureau, but he also knew that wasn't what he felt.

"If you're worried about me, don't be, Jack. I know I was a mess Thursday night."

"I think you came through pretty well for a rookie." He allowed himself to chuckle. "Actually, if I'd known about your literacy in Impressionism, I would've come much sooner. I'm a fan, too."

"I was a little disappointed in myself," Cheri confessed. I signed on knowing something like that could happen. I felt like a soldier in his first combat when the shelling started. I didn't run, but I froze in the foxhole. I may've been stunned, but I still feel like I should have done better."

"If you had, well, let's just say it wouldn't have been using good judgment. You weren't armed, because passing through the security metal detectors at the Convention center would have blown your cover. At the moment, he probably was, too."

"Yes. I try to console myself with that thought. I could use some consoling right now." Her voice shook slightly.

Jack, moving to the love seat to comfort her, put an arm around her, intending nothing more, but she rose up to kiss him.

"Cheri, we can't!" he implored.

"I don't give a damn." She began to undress him.

Jack never wanted a woman so much. She was everything missing in his life. He needed her. Suddenly, he didn't give a damn, either.

His hand slipped inside her bathrobe to fondle her breast. The nipple was already hard, and, when he touched it, she stiffened. Kissing him, she embraced his mouth fully and urgently.

Each was astonished when they found themselves completely naked, taking in the sight of the other's body. Jack wanted to unleash her passion, to do it as no one ever had. He instinctively went to her long, pale thighs, tracing his tongue slowly up them to where they converged. A flood of passion enveloped her. Both hoped her apartment walls were soundproof.

Jack rose up, looking into her eyes, and gently entered her. Their cadence grew in rapidity and intensity until they found each other on the small loveseat lying awkwardly, looking at each other as if they crossed into a new horizon into an unfamiliar but welcome landscape.

CHAPTER SIXTY-FOUR

Jack asked to conference with Mike Tuesday morning in Mike's office.

"Whassup?" Mike asked mockingly.

"I want to go to Chicago to interview the President of AFI that our person of interest works for. Todd's the guy. I can feel it in my bones.

"I've already given the team assignments to keep them productively occupied. They'll try to find the origin of those costumes. If they do, it would add another ribbon to the bow we're tying."

"Can't you wait until we have something to tie to him directly beyond the coincidence of interviewing Todd and the attack? After all, Jack, he wasn't the only person the team looked at. Your first impression of Todd was exculpatory. Suppose Roy or Cheri misread one of the people they met? Suppose it was Cheri? Suppose this admittedly smart perp read her better than she read him? There'd be a more-tangible connection."

"My instincts are on fire, and I'm rarely wrong."

"I know, Jack. What do you hope to accomplish?"

"I want to convince Wilbur Armstrong, *the Third*, to cooperate. He reluctantly agreed to let us interview Todd. I think he was just being cooperative. I need to inform him more fully about the case. That's the only way I can think of to gain his cooperation."

"Let me see if I get this straight," Mike said acerbically. "This guy, Armstrong, *the Third*, has a very productive employee who is central to the success of his business. Initially, before you twisted his arm—I know how you work, Jack—he resisted giving you information. He finally relented, because he believes in Todd, and you are, after all, just looking for a witness to a white-collar crime. He sounds like a guy who respects the agency and doesn't want to be uncooperative.

"Now you want to tell him that Todd is a serial murder person of interest. What comes after that, Jack?"

"I want him to open his expense reports to tell us where Todd has been and when. We can correlate that with mailings, or, more importantly, murders with excessive repeated torture and rape. That sums it up." He gave a broad, self-serving smile.

"Jack, you've done a great job for me. You've made me look good. If you hadn't, I'm pretty sure I'd be throwing you out of my office right now!"

"Does that mean I'm going? May I buy tickets for tomorrow?"

"You'll have to call Armstrong first."

"I've already called to confirm he'll be there. I won't set an appointment. If I try, I'll strike out before I'm at the plate."

"Now I *am* throwing you out!" He paused. "I'll have the tickets on your desk within the hour."

CHAPTER SIXTY-FIVE

Jack gazed around the modest but successful-looking offices of Able Fasteners, Incorporated, more commonly referred to as AFI, hoping Todd wasn't there. He didn't see him.

The receptionist was typical for that position, reasonably attractive, young, a bit perky, but very businesslike. "May I help you, sir?"

"I need to see Mr. Armstrong."

"Do you have an appointment, Mr...?"

"Garvey. Jack Garvey." It sounded to him like someone saying, "Bond. James Bond." "I'm afraid I don't have an appointment."

"I'm sorry, we just came back from a big trade show. Mr. Armstrong is going down for the third time."

"Look, *seriously,* please keep this under your hat. Like I said, I need to see him." He discreetly flashed his credentials.

Expecting anything but that, she seemed slightly shaken. "I'll see what I can do."

Two minutes later, Jack was shuttled into Armstrong's office. The two men shook hands perfunctorily.

"Have a seat, Agent Garvey."

Jack perused the office. Pictures of the Armstrong family were prominently displayed, along with a hole-in-one trophy.

"You have a beautiful family," Jack said. "Quite the golfer, too, I see."

"I'd be very surprised if you came here to discuss either of those things," Armstrong said with a hint of hostility. "I wasn't expecting to see you again—ever. What do you want?"

"I want to see all of Mr. Todd's itineraries and expense reports as far back as you have them."

"What the hell?" Armstrong was stunned speechless for a moment. "You must have a subpoena or a search warrant or some such," he said angrily. "I assure you Lawrence Todd makes very good living here and isn't involved with any kind of identity theft!"

"I'm sure he isn't, Mr. Armstrong. I lied to you about that."

"What else did you lie about? Can I see your credentials again?"

Jack handed them over.

"Supervising Special Agent Jack Garvey, eh?"

"Yes. You may call FBI headquarters in Quantico and speak to Managing Special Agent Mike Hennessey, my boss. I have his number here if you'd like."

Armstrong, calling in his personal secretary, handed her the number Jack gave, along with Hennessey's name and title.

The two men waited uncomfortably while the call was placed. Armstrong tried to size up his visitor.

The secretary was back within a moment. "I spoke to Mr. Hennessey. He was expecting the call. It was definitely the FBI on the other end of the line."

"You spoke to Agent Garvey when he came in, didn't you??" Armstrong asked.

"Yes, I did."

"Did you mention to anyone else that someone from the FBI was here?"

"As you know, Mr. Armstrong, I've been here awhile, and my mother was here before that. We've always looked out for you and the company, so no," she answered as if hurt.

"Thank you, Alecia. Let's keep it that way. This truly is routine, but you know how the office buzz makes things into something when they're nothing. I'm very grateful."

Alecia left.

"So you aren't looking for an identity theft ring after all," Armstrong said. "What kind of criminal are you looking for?"

"A serial murderer."

"You think Lawrence Todd witnessed a murder?"

"No. Mr. Todd is a person of interest *for* serial murder."

Armstrong leaned back and laughed heartily.

Jack waited.

Armstrong said, "That's the most-ridiculous thing I ever heard. He's church-going, everyone likes him, and I've never had a complaint about him. The FBI just lost several notches in my estimation. How absurd."

"You told me he's church-going. How do you know that?"

"Easy. He goes to my church, First Lutheran."

"Is he there every Sunday?"

"No. Is that a crime? Many parishioners don't."

"I'm guessing he goes less than half the time, maybe a lot less."

"And how would you know that? Really, Agent Garvey, I'm a very busy man. You were at the trade show. You know how much activity there was. I don't have time for this nonsense."

"I'm betting you go to your church just about every Sunday. I'm a Christian myself. My job takes me away when I least expect it, but I make it whenever I can, almost every Sunday."

"Good for you," he said sarcastically. "People who don't go to church every Sunday, like you, are serial murders? You must have a lot of work. I think you should go."

"Mr. Armstrong, I just want you to listen. Then, if you want to throw me out of your office, I'll go peaceably. The Bureau never shares confidential information. We don't have that latitude. I'm going to stick my neck out and do it anyway, which makes me vulnerable. I need you to keep everything I tell you confidential. Will you do that?"

Armstrong, clearly under pressure to return to work, was already perturbed with Jack. "I'll keep any confidences you relate, but I'm still not sure I'm inclined to let you relate them."

"I'm going to pull out the big guns, Mr. Armstrong, and I hate doing that, because it's a low blow, and I think you're a decent man. I told you this is a serial-murder case. Multiple women have been grievously tortured and murdered, more than you would imagine. If one woman died because you wouldn't listen to me, how would that square with your Christianity?"

Armstrong looked like he'd been punched in the gut. After a few seconds, he said, "OK, Agent. I'll listen."

"Let me start with two points. First, you've heard about the Bureau's system of profiling. Since you're an intelligent, and, I assume, well-read man, you know it's been very successful at identifying some of the worst perpetrators to have affected our country. As Christians, we feel the power of the devil. He's very strong.

"Second, in many, if not most of these cases, the people who knew these butchers the best had no clue about their nefarious activities. Most famously, Ted Bundy's fiancée initially swore he wasn't capable of such heinous acts. So did his law professors, political figures, clergy, and almost everyone who knew him. There are thirty-three known women, which some have estimated should be almost one hundred, who are dead, some as young as twelve. John Wayne Gacy put on shows in clown suits for children with diseases. He had photos of himself shaking hands with First Lady Rosalynn Carter.

"We're all capable of being fooled by these people." Jack almost said "monsters," but he didn't want to drive Armstrong away.

"Let me go over our profile with you. First, our culprit is male. There have been a few female serials, but none of them ever focused exclusively on women. We also believe he's a handsome devil. Sorry, that was an unintended reference. The reason we know this is that he has successfully seduced some beautiful women. I think you'd agree Mr. Todd is a handsome man by any woman's calculation.

"This man is very intelligent. He has a grasp of forensic evidence that rivals some of our own experts. It allowed him to evade justice, and more startlingly, commit dozens—yes, dozens—of murders. In most cases, he left behind no detectable forensic evidence. If you've ever watched *Forensics Files* on TV, you have some concept of how impossibly difficult that is to do. I believe you'd agree that Mr. Todd is intelligent."

"Wait a minute. Are you saying you're taking a shot in the dark? That after several murders, you have no forensic evidence that would connect Lawrence?"

"Actually, we have a video tape of a man who is Todd's height attacking a female agent. I don't know if you heard anything about a commotion that took place at the Ritz on Thursday night."

"At little. I was with Lawrence that night."

"What time?"

"Oh, I don't know. He'd just had dinner and joined a few of us at the bar, somewhere between ten and eleven, I'd say."

"The attack took place a bit after eight. Does Todd often socialize with his coworkers?"

"No. Not usually."

Jack refrained from a comment on that. "I can't go into the details of the torture that was imposed on these women repeatedly, but it would turn your stomach."

"I just can't see Lawrence doing such a thing. I've known him for years, even as a child, long before he came to work here."

"Our profile suggests that the man who did these things has excellent interpersonal skills and would be very successful in his job, especially in sales."

"Can we back up a minute? You said you had a video of the man who attacked your agent, no? Case closed. You should know if it's him."

"The person who attacked our agent was disguised," Jack was forced to admit.

"Come now, Agent Garvey. You had me going for a minute. What kind of disguise is going to obscure someone's face to the extent that you can't make an identification?" Armstrong was upset.

"If it was Todd, he wore the costume of a Hasidic Jew, complete with temple curls, yarmulke, and full beard. The murderer we're looking for sent us evidence from Honolulu last year attending a trade show. That's why we were at the AAUS. If you'll let us have the itineraries and expense reports we need, it will likely eliminate Todd as a suspect, and you'll never hear from us again."

Pausing, he looked into the man's eyes. "The alternative is a lot of sleepless nights for you. If I'm right, he'll kill again as soon as he can outlast our resources. We can't surveil him forever."

Armstrong was silent for a while. "You'd normally have a subpoena or warrant or something, but you can't, because you don't have the evidence. No court would give you one."

Jack's heart sank.

"From my point of view, I want to minimize the consternation within my office. First, I want you to make a big noise about a wild goose chase on your way out. Second, you bring just one other agent with you on Saturday. Because of the trade show, I had several people coming in on Saturday. I'll tell everyone they worked hard enough at the show to get the weekend off. They won't object. That might hurt us as a company, but I have enough sleepless nights already. I don't need any more. I'm looking forward to proving you wrong."

CHAPTER SIXTY-SIX

Mike Hennessey missed the previous team meeting due to other commitments, but he was there for Wednesday's scheduled meeting.

"I'll turn the floor over to Jack in just a moment. I don't know if you noticed, but Jack was absent here yesterday. I'll let him brief you about what he was doing.

"Some information came in from our lab that I haven't had time to share with Jack. It isn't what we hoped for, and there are no discretionary decisions to be made about it, so I'll review it with you now. Basically, it comes down to this. The main component in identifying a fiber, unless you have enough from the same lot for a match, which we don't, is the dye and type of fiber. In this case, the fiber was polyester, and it doesn't get much more common than that.

"The lab ran a combined liquid chromatography and mass spectrometry test on the dye. The black dye from the wig was very common. It's almost impossible, without an exemplar, to identify a specific manufacturer. There's no way our perp could've known that. He just got lucky. Looks like another dead end."

Mick shrugged, and nodded at Jack.

"Thanks for the rundown, Mike," Jack said. "I was in Chicago yesterday at Lawrence Todd's company, AFI, speaking with the owner, Wilbur Armstrong the third."

Roy snorted softly.

"I can't see where someone with the moniker of Roy Rogers has any room for comment," Jack quipped. "It was a hard sell, but I got a very skeptical Armstrong to let us look at Todd's itineraries and expense reports. Between the two, we should be able to place his whereabouts at the time of any murders involving torture. If it was in a localized area, we could probably connect enough of them to Todd to be considered circumstantial evidence, at least a cog in the wheel of probable cause.

"There are so many murders that involved some degree of torture, and the landscape is so large, that we'd have an uphill battle to obtain that circumstantial evidence, but I still think we can do it. Roy, you'll have help from all of us on this, but I want you to keep it organized. The rest of this week will continue our search for the costume store. We'll see if we can get lucky. Even if we do, it won't be positive of anything, just suggestive.

"There's one exception to that. We have reproduced a photo from Todd's driver's license obtained from the Illinois DMV. If a person in that costume store could ID Todd for us, that would be a big break.

"Next week, I'll put all of us on calling major metro law enforcement. We'll cover all aspects, particularly MEs who remember cases where torture was imposed on a repeated basis. The key is *repeated.* Our perp inflicts punishment, revives his target, and does it again, apparently until he loses interest. That was the case with both Cox and Bundergast, although with Bundergast, time was more restrictive.

"Of course, we'll keep talking to chiefs, sheriffs, cold-case investigators, or anyone else who can potentially provide a connection. The usual reference to an MO is to identify a particular way of committing the offense, like strangulation or slashing a throat with a buck knife. Sometimes there'll be a specific type of victim, like Ridgway's prostitutes. Todd scrupulously avoided adherence to any recognizable MO.

"If that weren't the case, we would've connected the crimes to the existence of a serial murderer a long time ago. We are concluding our guy committed the murders in Wisconsin and Ohio and probably

Hawaii near Honolulu. The MO we have is only that he commits torture on a repeated basis.

"Our focus will be on three factors. First, what murders took place within a reasonable radius of where Todd was or from which a mailing was made. Reasonable radius is hard to define. For Cox, it was only 200 miles. In other cases, it could be a crime in Nashville and a mailing from New York or wherever his business took him.

"Second, was there evidence of genuinely *cruel* torture inflicted on repetitive basis before the culprit dispatched his victim?" He paused to look at the team. "Finally, what was the lapsed time between the potentially connected murder and when the mailing was made? With Cox, it was five days, while with Bundergast, it was four."

Anita tentatively raised her hand.

"We don't raise hands around here, Anita," Jack said. "If you have something to say, say it."

"What if your conviction about Todd is wrong?"

"Then I've invested a lot of resources and sent us off in the wrong direction while we continue to receive more Numbers in the mail. I'll have screwed this up big time.

"Mr. Armstrong placed limitations on our review of his records. One, we must look on a Saturday when none of his other employees will be there, essentially because he furloughed them for the weekend. He'll let us in and will stay to observe our activity.

"Two, we're limited to the itineraries and expense reports for Todd, which is fine. Third, we're limited to me and only one other agent to review the docs.

"Armstrong is a good man, following his conscience. That doesn't mean he wants a lot of activity in his office that might attract attention to AFI.

"Cheri will be the other agent. If Armstrong gets cold feet, it'll be harder for him to confront a twenty-six-year-old woman who was just attacked. Sorry, Cheri, but we may need to use that. I don't like it, knowing how painful it might be for you. Armstrong is skittish as hell, and I believe he holds the key to proving Todd's involvement. If we can do it, we can save lives.

"The major factor in swaying him to give up the records was how well Todd fit our profile. Cheri and I worked most closely on that, and that's why I want her to accompany me."

The meeting broke up, but Mike stayed behind. "Something going on between you and Cheri, Jack?"

"What? Because I'm taking her to Chicago?"

"Not exactly. You aren't in the habit of explaining your decision. You assign whom you assign."

Jack, prepared for that, didn't express surprise or trepidation. "Roy went on the last trip, because I felt his grasp of statistics would be helpful. The reason I gave in the meeting accomplished two things. First, it laid a perfectly legitimate basis for taking her along, and second, it prevented Roy from feeling disenfranchised about being left behind."

Jack didn't want to lie to Mike, so he rationalized that he was telling the truth, just not the whole truth.

It wasn't just Jack's career in jeopardy. Cheri's career was, too. He wasn't about to damage her career.

As well as he and Mike knew each other, though, Jack's answer got both of them off the hook—for now.

CHAPTER SIXTY-SEVEN

Roy, seeing Jack's office door ajar, burst in, blurting, "Bingo! All in One Costume in Akron, Ohio, forty miles south of Cleveland."

He had Jack's full attention. "Tell me."

"I called there before and spoke to the manager. He wasn't aware of anyone buying both a clown's outfit and a Hasidic Jew costume, but I guess the call from the FBI prompted him to ask his employees. One was on vacation. Her name is Tamara Roth, and when she got back, she heard about the inquiry. She remembers thinking it was an odd combination of costumes to rent together.

"Another thing was unusual. Generally, the store rents costumes, not sells them. That's the case for most outlets I checked with my calls. Some costumes are quite pricey. This guy insisted on buying them and paying cash. They have a purchase price listed for each costume, but it's not an option many people take. Tamara also recalls the guy was good-looking. She said she even flirted with him a bit.

"Then here's the bad news. She couldn't recognize him from the license photo we faxed. She said she doesn't have a good memory for names or faces, just bodies. It's like a bar girl who likes football for the tight ends."

Jack realized Roy was trying to be clever, but he would be better off sticking with stats.

"I sent her a blown-up copy of the license photo that was retouched to add clarity, but she still didn't remember him well enough to say he was the guy," Roy said.

There was a moment of silence, and Roy looked deflated. "I guess it didn't get us the ID we're looking for, did it?"

"You're missing the big picture. It connects the Bundergast murder and the attack on Cheri. It might not allow us to arrest Todd, but it confirms we're on the right path. This is major, Roy. Excellent job!"

An expansive smile crossed Roy's face.

"I usually pass developments along to Mike, but I'm a bit occupied right now," Jack said. "How about you run down to his office and fill him in on what you dug up?"

Roy's expression lit up like a neon sign. After being left behind on Saturday's excursion, the news would cement his place on the team.

That was what Jack intended. He wanted Roy review his methodology in uncovering the connection and expand on the feedback from Ms. Roth at Friday's upcoming meeting.

Jack and Cheri had tickets for a late-afternoon flight to Chicago on Friday, where they had two hotel rooms near each other. The early arrival was calculated to head off any buyer's remorse on Armstrong's part. It would be more difficult to send them back if they were already in town. Jack was counting on the kind of man Armstrong was. He didn't think he would get cold feet, but it was best to hedge his bets.

He wouldn't mind spending the evening with Cheri, either. The way he looked at the situation, they both deserved some R&R.

CHAPTER SIXTY-EIGHT

Armstrong was there on time, not very pleased, but at least he was there.

Once they were inside the office, Armstrong unlocked two filing cabinets. He removed Todd's itineraries, in a separate hanging file that contained twelve monthly itineraries for five years.

"We have to keep ten years of expense reports in case of an IRS audit," Armstrong explained. "It's required by law. We have only five years of itineraries, though, because there's no legal requirement. Five years is sufficient for any kind of historic record of where we go on a seasonal basis. For instance, we go to cold climates more often in the winter, because there are more auto breakdowns. Anyone in Chicago can tell you about the potholes."

He showed them the second cabinet with the expense reports.

"Can we make copies?" Jack asked. "We'll pay for them."

Armstrong balked. "I'm being quite hospitable letting you look these over. I'm not sure I want copies of proprietary information leaving here."

Jack anticipated making copies that would allow them to study the documents in detail, so he was a bit let down by the man's attitude, calling him "Wilbur" in his mind. He made a mental note not to let that slip out.

Now that Jack had to adjust his plan, and given that Wilbur insisted on being present throughout, he was forced to give Cheri direction without any cover. Idly, Jack wondered what would happen if Wilbur had to take a leak.

"Cheri, I want you to work on the itineraries while I look at the expense reports. Mr. Armstrong, one of the things we discussed on Tuesday was the profile we developed. Cheri spearheaded that effort. She'll be happy to answer any questions. You could help her with questions about the itineraries."

"Sure."

Jack knew Cheri would quickly have the man eating out of her hand. Wilbur might be a churchgoing man and devout Christian, but no man would be completely immune to her charm. Jack knew Cheri didn't like it, but she also knew sometimes it came with the territory, within limits.

"We're looking for dates and locations," Jack said. "Since there's a large amount of material, we'll need to note this information as we go, being careful not to make errors. You'll have to move rapidly if Mr. Armstrong is going to salvage any of his Saturday to spend with his family," he said sympathetically, "and if we're going to make our flight.

"I'll do the same with requests for expense reimbursement. I doubt it'll be relevant, Mr. Armstrong, but I may have questions about any unusually large reimbursements. Also, I'd like to note the credit card numbers used for those transactions."

"You won't find any," Wilbur said. "Lawrence has a penchant for privacy. By the time he came to work for us, identity theft was in full swing. If there's such a thing as identity-theft paranoia, Lawrence has it. He refused a corporate credit card and said he had enough savings to float any expenses he needed. He paid cash and gave us a printed or handwritten receipt for everything. We were skeptical at first and verified some of his expenses when he started working here, but every detail checked out."

Jack and Cheri exchanged a sidelong glance.

"Hotels and rental cars require a credit card," Jack said. "How did Todd work around that?"

"We were skeptical about that, too, at first. He had a great recommendation from his previous employer, but it was odd how he wanted to handle those transactions. He wouldn't have access to a credit card, but he wanted the company to pay for his hotels and rental cars. He said he didn't have bad credit. He just hadn't established any.

"We weren't going to hire him, but he proposed he would give us a $5,000 bond until he earned our confidence, even though he didn't have access to a card. That impressed us. Lawrence clearly wanted the job. We also viewed it as one hell of a sales job on his part.

"On his second Christmas with the company, we returned his $5,000 by adding it to his rather large Christmas bonus. He increased our business year over year by 15%!"

Other than the quick glance the two agents gave each other initially, neither of them gave any sort of tell when Armstrong revealed more information. Cheri acted like a pro. She and Jack were amazed at the man's naïveté.

When Armstrong finished Jack said matter-of-factly" "Well, let's have at it."

CHAPTER SIXTY-NINE

Jack, working at a furious pace, went backward through the ledgers, looking for the most-current information in case he didn't get to check all the documents. That improved his chances of finding dates and locations that might coincide with Ohio and Wisconsin. He had a lot more material to cover than Cheri. Although he focused on dates and locations, he also looked for anything unusual that might prove inculpatory. He hoped she would finish and then help him with the expenses.

He was right about Cheri's charm. She quickly had Armstrong laughing and almost enjoying the experience.

AFI was an old building on State and Madison in downtown Chicago. Originally made of slate gray granite, it collected so much soot and pollution over the years it appeared black. Rather than do a full renovation to restore the building's original color and beauty, gold paint was added to the large window frames to make the building resemble the black-and-gold nearby Union Carbide building on the same side of the Chicago River.

The 1930s interior was also dated. AFI even had a holdover waist-high barrier when someone entered the office, and a swinging door where Jack met Alecia on Tuesday. It looked like a set borrowed from a '30s or '40s *noir* movie.

All three worked so diligently they never heard the key flipping the lock on the office door. When they heard the door creak, they looked up quickly and found themselves staring into the face of Lawrence Todd.

Armstrong blushed, while Jack and Cheri simply stared. Todd gazed at Jack for two seconds with no reaction. Jack knew the man was a cool character.

When Todd saw Cheri, however, he gave a tell that Jack caught. He glared at her, just to see if it provoked a reaction. Despite never having seen him before, she froze for a second. From Jack and Armstrong's reactions, she knew it was Todd, and his focused stare sent a shiver down her spine.

Todd sent Armstrong a withering look. "What's going on here, Will?" He glanced at Jack.

"Hello, Mr. Todd," Jack said. "Nice to see you again."

"OK. I'll ask you the same thing, Agent Garvey." He gave Jack a jaw-clenching stare.

Although Jack and Cheri quickly covered the material they were examining, the open file cabinets were obvious.

"Just routine Mr. Todd," Jack replied. "You don't suppose you were the only one we interviewed in connection with this case, do you? All our interviews were satisfactory, so we're taking the next logical step to see if we can learn anything to help identify our witness. We're investigating a few specific companies. AFI is just one of them. It's strictly routine.

"Mr. Armstrong has been cooperative, a good citizen. You have nothing to worry about. Mr. Todd. Your interview with me was quite satisfactory. However, I have to ask you to leave, so we can finish with our work." Jack looked at Armstrong, no longer thinking of him as Wilbur.

"Lawrence, you're a valuable member of the AFI team," Armstrong said. "Agent Garvey is satisfied where you're concerned. They were just about to leave."

"Seems to me I heard him say they needed to finish up," Todd said.

"Agent Garvey was asking you to leave, but instead, I'm suggesting he and his associate leave, OK, Agent Garvey? Why don't you go ahead into your office, Lawrence, while we put things away? I'll join you there in a minute and take you out for a cocktail or two. If you have any questions, I'll fill you in to the extent I'm familiar. This is much ado about nothing."

Todd, avoiding giving away any more tells, walked down a corridor on the way to his office.

After Todd was out of earshot, Armstrong said, "I should've known he'd come in on a weekend after a trade show, no matter what the others did! Damn it! My cooperation is at an end. Don't call me or make any more requests. You've probably cost me my best regional manager on what I'm certain is foundationless snooping."

Jack doubted Armstrong really believed that. Something must have snapped when he was talking with them.

Armstrong, collecting the files, angrily thrust them into the cabinets before escorting the two agents out the door.

CHAPTER SEVENTY

That fucking bitch! Zero thought. *An FBI agent, and she came onto me and made a goddamn fool out of me!*

Anytime he wanted a woman, she always came onto him. That was how he viewed his encounters, even when his first lascivious thoughts about her happened when he saw her from behind.

Zero had to think things through. His top priority was to avoid detection of any evidence that would tie him to his recreational activities. *I can wait those FBI bastards out. If I don't give them anything else to go on, they'll eventually have to move on.*

That brought up the second contingency. He would need an income while he waited for the FBI to exhaust its efforts. He wouldn't let any goddamn bitch drive him away from an income he invested ten years of his life building. He had a comfortable nest egg, but he was consumed by the agent who aroused his prurient side and made him mess himself. She was the one who wanted to take it all away.

His thoughts returned to his meeting with Armstrong. They went out for a couple of cocktails. Lawrence could hold his liquor, but he carefully limited his intake that day. Will, who betrayed him, as he saw it, was giving him all kinds of assurances. His boss repeated the lies the agents told him.

Armstrong's hope must have been that the naïveté with which he bought into Garvey's story might lose plausibility over time. Reviewing records of all the employees to find a witness for a white-collar crime? Did they think he'd swallow that lie twice? It was infuriating that they thought so little of his intelligence.

Briefly, he considered adding Armstrong to his list, but there were several reasons that would be unworkable. First, it would increase the FBI's focus on him. Next, his job was at stake. No one else in the Armstrong family was prepared to step in to run the company. It occurred to him they might ask him to fill Will's shoes, but he didn't know the financial end of the business.

Finally, he rationalized his acts as ridding mankind of beautiful, manipulative teasers who inflicted pain on men. Their desire for those bitches raged within them but when they were turned away, did nothing. Only Zero had the fortitude to undertake what needed to be done: restore balance to the inimical designs of these Delilahs.

He knew the women wanted it, too, at least the sex. He wouldn't deny them that. Each would be given her desired debauchery. Like a black widow spider or praying mantis, a woman's goal was only to consume men as if they were merely fodder. Zero consumed them instead in ways that would instruct the world.

Zero read the Koran. Extremist Islamists, the few among their religion who got it right, treated women as chattel to be killed as the men's fancy demanded. As Muhammed professed, women had only half the value of a man. History recorded that Muhammed raped many women, including very young ones whom he sometimes took as wives. It was better to rape women under the cloak of Sharia Law, requiring four or five male witnesses as corroboration to prosecute, as was done in the most-radical states. A woman could be stoned to death for infidelity in those states on the word of a single male witness, often her husband.

Number 48 was killed similarly. Zero selected his chosen victim, secured her with ropes staked to the ground, and draped her in a mantle of white sheet. He hit her in her torso with rocks, breaking her arms and legs to prolong the agony. When she finally asked him to end her ordeal, he did it in stages, giving her a glancing blow on the head that would render her unconscious and create a blood stain on the white sheet mimicking what he saw in an internet video of an actual stoning. Zero's was far more merciless, because he withheld potentially lethal blows.

He used smelling salts, through a slit in the sheet, to bring her back, then hit her with another glancing blow that added another crimson brand to his masterpiece. Because of the broken arms and legs, she was a lump of humanity he could form into whatever shape, excruciating for the victim, before he delivered the next blow. The final glancing blows to her head prolonged her torment. When he could no longer revive her, he pounded her repeatedly, giving full vent to his fury, until her skull was reduced to splintered pieces of bone floating in a gelatinous goo.

Normally, he avoided forensically telltale blood splatter. He was inspired to do Number 48 after seeing that internet video. Carried out by Muslim extremists pursuant to Sharia Law, each impact stained the cloth red. Zero expected the woman to die quickly, but somehow, she clung to life. How much more punishment could be inflicted if the blows were intentionally non-lethal for as long as possible. He had to find out. Having no interest in Islam, he was intrigued by the torture.

To protect himself from blood spatter, he wore transparent vinyl rainwear. The jacket's hoodie he wore backward so even his face was protected. He wiped blood away from the vinyl to clear his vision. The pants covered him to his ankles, and his feet were in booties. It was a simple matter to dispose of the gear, melting the vinyl into unrecognizable sludge and sinking it in a lake, his favorite evidence graveyard. Trained bloodhounds can't smell underwater.

Lawrence Todd would never be a member of any religion beyond a façade he created to cloak his nefarious activities. His father favored exposure to religion but wanted him to acquire his own beliefs. As usual, his father had a vaporous spine while his wife dragged him to her Christian church each Sunday. All he could see was indoctrination and hypocrisy in her religion, the same one Jack and Cheri and millions of fools practiced, revered, and found solace in.

He didn't reject Christianity specifically. He would never consider or convert to any religion. Islam had an allure, because radical Islamists treated women as chattel. Such a world would admire his achievements and elevate him to a position of prominence. No matter how correct the few, controlling the diabolical females in their midst was righteous. They were far outnumbered by those who viewed their religion as an instrument of gentility and peace. How had the hypocrites, the ones who didn't want to impose the legal step of genital mutilation on women, prevailed?

Armstrong had friends who were fervent members of Islam. Will even accepted an invitation to attend services during Ramadan. The fervent sometimes prayed until three o'clock in the morning, or all night on days of great importance. During Ramadan, believers could hear the reading, delivered poetically, of the entire Koran.

Armstrong, a committed Christian in his own beliefs, went to honor the good friend who invited him and was exposed to a religion about which he knew little. For days afterward, Will went on about how beautiful the ceremonies were and how welcome he was. Even the gentlest of Islamists, the majority who would never support the radicals or their acts, still separated men and women during prayer in obedience to the Koran.

Catholics still wouldn't ordain women priests. How could those religions distinguish between men and women with theology that endorsed that women were inherently unequal and yet not embrace retribution upon them for their evil nature? Wasn't religion supposed to be about punishing evildoers?

There would be no religion for Zero but the one he made to effect vengeance on women. There could be no other, because there was no God, only the devil inhabiting women exclusively.

Zero's mind wandered. His thoughts and acts were always structured and organized. He jerked himself away from his ruminations to the job at hand and mentally created an outline for his plans to move forward.

1. He would give no indication to Armstrong that he hadn't bought into his apologetic, almost desperate, reassurances. He would even gleefully accept the additional bonus he was offered to assuage his concerns over Will's cooperation with the FBI.

2. He would keep a profile so low, it wouldn't even be in the strike zone until the FBI abandoned what would prove a fruitless line of investigation.

3. He would ultimately kill the NAPA woman, as he thought of her, patiently waiting to torture her as he never tortured any woman before.

4. His patience might be limitless, but her destiny was the same whether sooner or later. The passage of time and a lack of forensic evidence to connect him would distance him from the FBI's unsustainable scrutiny.

It would be an easy transition. He grinned to himself. He would wire the money offshore, saved from his frugal ways and a small inheritance from his father. It was one of the few assertive acts his father took. That would enable him to transition into a serial murderer protective plan of his own device.

Zero's rituals would begin again in a new location with an altered image and new name. He could hardly wait to begin, free of the watchful eyes of Agent Garvey and the Bureau. Agent Hancock, when the time was right, would go first. Oh, how exquisite would be her demise.

CHAPTER SEVENTY-ONE

Jack and Cheri enjoyed their time together Friday night. Cheri was a mature twenty-six, and Jack was a sexually detached thirty-five. He wasn't inexperienced at lovemaking. Having feelings for the women he'd been with, he even felt some Christian guilt about sex outside marriage, making him a throwback.

There was no guilt with Cheri. She was very open to her own feelings and his. There was no awkwardness or hesitation between them. Given the depth of their feelings, it was revelatory they developed so quickly.

Their lovemaking was spontaneous, gentle, and explosive. Jack touched her all over. It was as if anywhere one touched, the other had an erogenous zone. It was impossible to touch without an immediate response. Their emotions went quickly from a resistible simmer to a boiling inferno. Jack never imagined it could be like that.

Still, their careers were important to them. They already backed away from their commitment to keep things professional until the case was over. They couldn't keep their hands off each other, especially in the anonymity of Chicago.

Married agents within the Bureau weren't supposed to work on cases together. Mike was already suspicious. The reasons Jack gave to bring Cheri to Chicago with him were logical, and Mike accepted the story, if a bit skeptically. Jack thought about confessing everything and taking Cheri off the case. They could survive that, but Cheri was as dedicated as he was to shackling Todd, maybe more after the attack. That made it personal, and she would be wounded if she had to quit the case.

With the situation going to pieces on the case, though, their raging fires had to be extinguished at least for a while after Chicago.

CHAPTER SEVENTY-TWO

Jack wangled a meeting with Mike early on Monday afternoon. Mondays were Mike's busy days, with plenty to catch up on, but he could read Jack easily and knew immediately something was up.

"OK, Jack," Mike said. "Tell me what happened in Chicago."

Jack outlined the entire meeting, explaining how he thought they won over Armstrong only to have the situation backfire when the business was threatened, and the owner's worst fears were realized.

"The worst thing is that while we have some information, it's limited and can only be checked against the last four or five years. The itineraries were simpler, and Cheri was also occupied with winning over Armstrong and answering his questions. I don't know if the way it ended was for Todd's benefit or if Armstrong really closed us out. Armstrong is running scared, almost panicked.

"However, we're beginning to connect some dots. We know our killer purchased the clown outfit for the Bundergast murder and the Hasidic Jew costume at the All in One Costume Store in Akron, forty-four miles south of Cleveland, an easy round trip. The store found the receipt, dated one day before the Cleveland attack.

"Roy will make a good agent. He checked the security footage at All in One and surrounding stores in the strip mall. Since there were no significant crimes in recent years, almost all of the tapes were reused. There are circumstances where we can recover a once-overwritten tape or CD but not multiple times. Few of the businesses upgraded to the more modern, HD-capable equipment that leaves a recoverable imprint.

"The strip mall is in a nice area with little concern for robberies, meaning no footage of our culprit.

"We also know from both the itineraries and the expense reports that Todd was in Cleveland doing product training with one of AFI's brokers for two days before the Bundergast murder. He must've finished for the day when he went to Dan's Place.

"We can also make a connection with the Cox murder, although it's tangential and requires a bit of theorizing. He met with the brokers who handle Milwaukee and Madison, Wisconsin. He was in Milwaukee on Monday and Madison on Tuesday. He noted he took a vacation day Wednesday. Armstrong told us Todd earned a lot of vacation pay over the years. He never takes off for a week or two at a time, just an occasional day or two.

"I don't have to tell him that it certainly fits our puzzle. My guess is that he met Cox on Wednesday in the Dells, went to Peoria, Illinois, on Thursday, as shown by his expenses and itinerary, and he kept his rendezvous with Cox on Friday, which he listed as a travel day, which is common whether flying or driving.

"Usually, Todd flies from metro area to metro area. When he has multiple brokers in a compact area close to Chicago or not near a city airport, he drives. Cox's body was found on Saturday of that week." Discouragement filled Jack's voice.

"You lay out a nice timeline, Jack, but we still don't have a single scrap of direct evidence to make a case against Todd."

"He's going to lie low and start killing again once he feels safe," Jack said. "More women will die. It's time to get us some help, for God's sake!"

Mike sat silently, obviously swayed by Jack's inspired pitch but still contemplating if he could sell his bosses on approving more manpower.

Jack said, "Mike, Todd recognized Cheri. You should've seen the look on his face when he saw her. She's at risk!"

Mike was clearly perturbed by that. "You should see the way *you* look at her, Jack. I'm a better detective than you give me credit for."

Jack realized he had gone where he didn't want to go.

"I'm disappointed you didn't confide in me, Jack," Mike said calmly. "You know I'll have to take her off the case."

"Then I'm off it too, Mike."

Mike was startled. "Jack, you've needed someone like Cheri for a long time. You think I don't know that? There are good reasons for avoiding these conflicts in an investigation. I feel like I'm teaching a course in Ethics 101 at the academy! When you get too close to a situation, you make mistakes, and a mistake could jeopardize Cheri. She's been part of my life for many years. I won't let anything happen to her.

"You're on the trail of this maniac. A new agent to head the investigation will take time to get up to speed. He or she will lose the thread. You'll be risking the lives of future victims, and you know that, damn it!"

Jack gave Mike a moment to regain his composure. He'd never seen the man so upset. He was usually the most-controlled, measured man Jack knew.

After a few moments to calm down, Jack said, "I care about future victims. You know that. Right now, though, Cheri's life is my pre-eminent concern. I can't lose her now that I've found her."

"My point exactly. How can you head an investigation putting one individual above your job? You just spelled it out!"

"I know this guy, Mike. He travels extensively, and we need help to surveil him. We have his planned itinerary for the rest of the year. We know what airlines he'll be on and what dates, where he's going, and when he'll arrive. With enough manpower, the kind that a serial murderer of this many women warrants, we can be on him every second.

"But he's a very intelligent, slippery perp. He'll get past us sooner or later, if only for a short time. It will be long enough to get to her. If I'm off chasing him down, and that happens, you know he'll kill Cheri. The only way I can protect her is to have her with me, Mike."

"I have the reputation of being a stickler for procedure," Mike reminded him. "There's a good reason for it. I've learned over the years that when you violate protocol, bad things happen. I have the ultimate responsibility for Cheri."

"I respect you more than anyone I know, Mike. I'll be with Cheri every minute until this is over, on or off the case. I have a *lot* of vacation time coming. I'll respect whatever decision you make, but you'll have to decide. If you keep me on, I'll get this guy with the help of my team, including Cheri."

"I'm really surprised at you, Jack, and a bit disappointed. I think this budding relationship with Cheri, who's precious to me, too, is a good thing. What surprises me is that you'd put the entire investigation in peril. By the time a new supervisor is in place, we'll almost certainly lose additional victims and the thread on Todd. I would never have thought you'd do that."

"I can understand how you feel, Mike. Very few people in my life have been as loyal to me, and no one taught me more about honesty and integrity. What you just said hurts, but it's justifiable. Let me recall a conversation we had some time ago.

"We talked about the death penalty. After Governor Pataki pushed it through for new York, death-eligible murders went down from 3,600 to 2,700, in round numbers, the first year it was in force. That was a 25% reduction, and it continued going down for some time. We agreed we'd be prepared to take guilty lives to save 900 innocent ones.

"Cheri's and my relationship isn't a 'budding' one. I haven't waited all these years to find her just to lose her to a horrible death at the hands of a maniacal killer. I'm willing to part with another woman's life, if necessary, to save Cheri's. I'll remain at her side until this monster is in shackles or dead. The only thing I won't do is send her directly into a known dangerous situation. When I know where Todd is, Cheri will be somewhere else. Until then, I'm her personal bodyguard, even if that means the end of my career at the Bureau. The Bureau has been my life, but now Cheri is.

"If you decide to keep me on, we must surveil this guy, and we need more manpower to do it. I've outlined what we have, and we're getting more by the minute. You have two decisions to make. Will you keep me on the case, with Cheri, and will you go to the mat to get us that help? It's time."

CHAPTER SEVENTY-THREE

The Friday meeting arrived following Jack's ultimatum. No matter what the decision was, he wouldn't waver from the position he took with Mike.

Walking into the room, he saw two more people at the table, and he knew them both. Tim Stein was a forensics specialist. Leland Burns was a Special Agent whose strong suit was logistics. Jack greeted each of them.

"It seems the powers that be are seeing it our way, Jack," Mike began.

Jack knew he really meant *your way*.

"Last night I gave each of them a quick review of what we're dealing with. Tim will act as liaison to run down and inform you about any forensics evidence you collect in the field. The way our serial operates, that could be a boring job.

"It'll be different for Leland. Our guy probably won't strike for a while, considering last Saturday's visit. We can't get anything in place until Monday. We can't have agents leaving home base and flying around the country with Todd, but we'll have Bureau locals travel with him to the airport and others waiting for him when he lands.

"Leland, why don't you give Jack and the rest of our team the lowdown on your role?"

"OK," Leland said. "Tim and I have worked with Mike and Jack several times. The rest of you are new to us, as we are to you. Roy, Cheri, and Anita, it was nice meeting all of you this morning. It's nice to see someone beating Jack to the punch, or at least to the meeting." He chuckled.

"I'll tell you about Tim what he won't say. He'll doggedly pursue the smallest piece of forensic evidence you send him. He'll drive the lab guys nuts until he has something for you. If they come back with nothing, he'll make them do it again."

Tim squirmed uncomfortably.

"It's my job to track the whereabouts of Mr. Lawrence Todd while he's sleeping, waking, or already awake. I'll schedule an agent to follow him from his residence in the morning to the airport. I'll schedule someone to be there when he exits the gate at the other end. An agent will see him to bed at night and bring him his orange juice in the morning. If this asshole killed as many women as you believe, we'll do everything to help you bring him in. Tim, you got anything to add?"

"Yeah, I do. From what I understand, this dude is trying to be as good at forensics as we are. That truly pisses me off. Mike told me he's given us nothing to go on for nearly a decade. I would've said that's impossible, because *it is*. Bring me next to nothing, and let's nail this fucker."

He paused. "Sorry, Ladies. Most of us older guys don't speak that way. Long-time Bureau folks, like Mike and Leland and I, get pretty pissed off when there's this high a body count. I'm passionate about getting this fool, but I won't apologize for it."

"I know I speak for everyone here when I say we're glad to have your expertise added to our team." Mike looked at the agents. Tim always reminded him of Woody Allen, short and looking like he'd lose a wet T-shirt wrestling match in the lightweight category. Leland looked like a Dwayne Johnson clone.

The team was a liberal's dream of diversity—White, Black, male, female, younger, and older. It was a true mix constituted for the people's skills, not for diversity. The only common denominator was their commitment to the Bureau.

"Jack, I gotta get back," Mike said. "If you need anything else, you probably won't get it, but try, anyway." He left the room.

Jack nodded at the others. "First, feel free to jump in. The Bureau believes in brainstorming. There are no bad or stupid ideas. We've heard that before, because it's important. It's the thing nobody wants to bring up, because it seems unimportant or foolish sometimes, that can blow up in our faces or fail to bring down our perp. We have a broad range of specialties here from the least experienced to agents with years of experience. Give that experience respect but not deference. Everyone in this group contributed well. The addition of Leland and Tim is a boon."

He turned to look at Leland. "What kind of limitations have we been given on surveillance in terms of manpower, budget, and in general?"

"I'm going to request the best surveillance guy in each location. We don't have the latitude of putting more than one person on our guy at a time. If we're talking about a large hotel, they have their own dicks, and those people usually cooperate with us. That's important if this Todd guy tries to slip out through a different entrance.

"We can keep an agent on him for twenty-four hours in eight-hour shifts. If Todd is as smart as you say, he can still give us the slip, but we'll be ready for him when he returns. We'll be able to use the hotel's video to give us the exact time he departs and returns down to the millisecond. In a different environment, it's tougher, so I'm asking for the best available. What's your goal, Jack?"

"Ideally to catch him in the act. That's a perilous undertaking, though. If he knows we're tailing him, he'll retract into his shell. If he doesn't, it's a balancing act between getting there on time or arriving too late or not at all. That's not an option. I want our people to err on the side of forcing him to curtail his activities instead of increasing the risk. That approach risks pushing him underground, though.

"If he decides to try to evade us, we're getting into dicey territory. If he can slip past a surveillance agent no matter when we arrive, it's probably too late. You know how I feel about letting that happen on our watch. None of us ever wants to receive another number. Leland, what do you think about using female agents for surveillance?"

"It depends on who you're watching. Mike gave me the profile you and Cheri developed, and it sounds like he'll be more alert to women than men. I'm hardly a chauvinist, but I think we stand a better chance of staying under his radar with just males. One of our agents already caught his eye," he added sympathetically, looking at Cheri.

"I agree," Cheri said. "We need to note, however, that I wasn't trailing him. I could tell by the way he looked at me Saturday that he had no prior idea I was an agent. Nevertheless, he's in the habit of scouting women. I think he studies every woman he encounters as a potential opportunity, then he stalks her, so I think Leland is right. Men are better in this case, because they won't get the same attention."

Leland said, "There's an important limitation we didn't mention. Mike's been instructed that we'll surveil Todd in two-week increments. Every two weeks, we need to get a reassessed nod from upstairs. There are a lot of unsolved homicides out there. The Bureau is aware of that, but we can't spend what we did on the Iraq War. Two weeks, four, or eight—I don't think anyone really knows right now."

"We have to concentrate on what we have, not on what we might not get," Jack said. "I want to get to assignments. Roy," he paused and looked at the two newcomers. "Would you believe this joker's name is actually Roy Rogers?"

Roy looked more frustrated than sheepish, but the comment drew chuckles all around.

"So I've heard." Tim grinned.

"Isn't this getting a little old," Roy implored.

"Roy, you've proven you're good at turning over rocks and finding what's under them. Finding the source of those costumes south of Cleveland was crucial. So has Anita. She found Lawrence Todd. I want Anita to assist you, Roy. We need to make matches with more torture-homicides than just the ones in Wisconsin and Ohio, with a likely Number 60 in Hawaii. We still need to connect that last one.

"You two will take on my role contacting local law enforcement. If we can find matches to our notes from AFI's itineraries or expense records, it'll be important in two ways. First, it could be foundational in trying to get more internal help, and second, it might leverage more assistance from Armstrong. Tim, Leland, you know who Armstrong is?"

They two men nodded.

"When we can demonstrate the synergy between where Todd was and the occurrence of female torture-murders, it'll gives us more leverage to have continued surveillance approved. One of the problems you'll have is discerning which torture-murders fit Todd and which don't. That'll be Cheri's job. When you find a potential, I want Cheri to dig into it and see what kind of fit it is. Cheri, your profiling and instincts are excellent, but don't let that stop you from using me as a sounding board."

He paused. "You've got the easy jobs. All I've got to do is follow up on what y'all are doin' and feed it to Mike without getting my ass chewed out."

CHAPTER SEVENTY-FOUR

Lawrence Todd's itinerary for the week had him on a flight to Louisville for a day's meeting to train a broker about some innovative new products AFI was promoting, then another flight to spend a similar day in Nashville, followed by two days in Memphis to train yet another broker, with Friday as a travel day.

He didn't notice the agent who was twenty people behind him, as he passed through security at Chicago's Midway Airport on Monday morning. However, he remained vigilant.

When he exited his aircraft in Louisville, he noticed a man lounging behind a newspaper at his gate. When he looked behind him, the man folded his newspaper under his arm and was at the top of the escalator leading to the rental car that AFI reserved for Todd. Passengers don't read newspapers after exiting a flight and when heading out of a terminal.

He wasn't surprised or even annoyed. He was enjoying himself. The game was afoot. He was enthralled with the idea of toying with the FBI. He wasn't sure how long it would take them to give up, but they couldn't tail him forever without evidence that might connect him to the Numbers.

CHAPTER SEVENTY-FIVE

Roy and Anita had two sets of data to work with—itineraries that reflected planned travel, and expense accounts that pinpointed where Todd had actually been. Cheri completed her notes on the five years of itineraries, but Jack was able to sort through only about four years of expense reports, because they contained lots of extraneous info. His notes were specific about location and date but nothing else. If they wanted to know which broker or customer Todd saw on a particular day, it was necessary to check the itinerary.

They quickly observed occasional discrepancies. Planned itineraries were modified, most likely due to business demands. A routine visit to one broker would be supplanted by a higher priority trip to a different location. If the itinerary changed, they wouldn't know the details. Business was never static.

An added complication was that some receipts, such as a lunch at "Terry's diner," were sometimes lacking an address. Some hotel receipts were missing, whether by unintended omission or simple loss. Roy and Anita felt they were deliberately removed from the files.

Occasions where the itinerary was altered, and information was missing, were considered of singular importance. Was there a Number added? The two of them agreed it was possible, if not likely. Without a fix on location, and Jack had since ascertained a continuing lack of cooperation from Armstrong, what could they do? How could they look for a torture-murder without an inkling where it occurred?

Because the itineraries could be altered, and because many receipts, hotel receipts in particular, more consistently included a location, which Jack noted, they decided to work from his expense report notes as their primary avenue of investigation.

They would use the itineraries for two purposes. First, they would cross-reference questionable or nonspecific receipts. Second, they would search for murders that occurred on dates where the planned itinerary deviated while staying within a reasonable orbit of the original itinerary. Todd could have been diverted from Montgomery, Alabama, to New York City, which explained why Armstrong's cooperation was so important.

Mike allowed Cheri to consult with local law enforcement more openly about a serial-murder investigation while Roy and Anita kept digging. Working backward would mean they'd encounter the Wisconsin and Ohio murders first, since no new Numbers were received. Instead, they decided to work forward from the earliest of Jack's notes, going back four years.

As anticipated, there were many unsolved murders that involved some form of torture. As Roy and Anita found homicides in proximity to Todd's location, Cheri was consulted. She would get more details from the police or sheriff's department or state bureau of investigation. As she did, many possibilities were methodically eliminated.

Some more resembled an act perpetrated in the heat of the moment, called "heat of passion" in legal parlance, such as finding one's spouse in bed with someone else, or an out-of-hand confrontation with a neighbor. Killings like that were usually called manslaughter, not murder. They most commonly reflected a perp who knew the victim. A female stabbed repeatedly, maybe twenty or thirty times, when loss of blood was abated, because the heart no longer pumped after the fourth blow, didn't work. Stab wounds the victim couldn't feel wouldn't satisfy Todd's lust for imposing pain on the hated sex. Such acts also didn't fulfill his ego-driven demonstration of creativity and repetitive torture. While Todd clearly had a high level of internalized rage toward women, his profile suggested he was cool carrying out the murders.

In other cases, forensic evidence, minimal or substantial, wasn't connected to anyone. Based on the suspected Numbers 60, 67, and 68,

Todd was meticulous in avoiding the availability of forensic evidence capable of analysis. Cheri also excluded unsolved murders from additional follow-up where DNA, fingerprints, or sloppy execution provided obvious forensic evidence, even if it wasn't clear.

In still other instances, there were suspected serial murder cases that followed specific MOs, like consistent strangulation, as in Albert DeSalvo, the Boston Strangler. Bodies were sometimes deliberately posed a certain way or had symbols carved on the corpses, like the Zodiac Killer.

Even after segregating those from the remaining cases, they had many examples of murder-torture only a few or even one of which could have been committed by Todd and were absent any clear way of distinguishing them from non-applicable homicide. Cheri looked at those and ranked them by the most-horrific tortures. Those that fell into that category, after applying the other parameters, successfully isolated a single murder in locations where they knew Todd was within striking distance. There were twenty-five of those, including the three suspected Numbers, that Roy and Anita pinpointed and Cheri considered consistent in the four years they studied.

CHAPTER SEVENTY-SIX

Jack's team wasn't afforded the opportunity to obtain fresh forensic evidence from the new possible cases. Learning twenty-two unsolved torture-murders were verifiably within Todd's reach at a time corroborated by receipts and/or itineraries prompted Jack to assign Tim Stein a major role in the investigation.

Stein was sent to meet with MEs and anyone else who might have studied the forensics in the cases. His job was to review and determine if anything had been overlooked. His objective was to confirm consistencies with the profile—after a thorough briefing by Jack and Cheri—and to eliminate murders that didn't belong on their list based on inconsistencies. Tim had a lot of traveling to do.

Leland, meanwhile, regularly reported on Todd's surveillance. Jack was informed each time he boarded or debarked a plane. Todd was followed to his hotel room, where the team had access to security cameras that showed if he left his room. The agents had to secure the cooperation of the hotel managers and keep a low profile to avoid alerting Todd. Agents trailed him to his business appointments and followed him onto the next plane in his itinerary.

As the investigation progressed, Tim's feedback confirmed most of the suspected murders he was sent to check were consistent with Todd's behavior. All demonstrated repeated, horrific torture. Because each murder was executed in a different way, Tim was wary about including one that might be misleading.

Suddenly, the situation began moving more rapidly. Once the team uncovered more logistics evidence, Mike authorized additional agents for surveillance. Todd was officially classified as a suspect. Access in time and location to twenty-five murders by one person defied any realistic probability there was a different perp. Roy assured them of that after figuring the odds, which were very long, indeed.

Necessary coordination and assignment of additional agents precluded the implementation of the expanded surveillance into the second week of Cozy, as they decided to name it. Cozy would be as airtight as the Bureau could make it. Once they had Cozy in place, Jack would breathe more easily. He wasn't entirely uncomfortable with their present efforts after they kept a close watch on Todd all week.

The following week, Todd would be in Philly on Monday, then to Fatlanta, as Jack called Atlanta, because he didn't like the Falcons, followed by his usual travel day. The second week would have his entire agenda in place the way he envisioned. Todd, as cool as he was, would eventually break under the pressure—they hoped.

Agents would be placed surreptitiously at all entrances to Todd's hotels. His rental cars would be monitored until he moved to the next city. When agents had the opportunity, magnetized tracking devices were hidden on those car bodies. Infrared night-vision binoculars and thermal-sensitive equipment were used at night.

With all the personnel and technology implemented, it would be as difficult for Todd to escape their dragnet as it would be for the proverbial camel to pass through the eye of a needle. As a Christian, Jack liked such references. If there was any justice, Todd wouldn't pass through the eye of the needle, nor would he pass Go. Instead, he would go straight to hell. Jack knew he should pray for the man's redemption and soul, but Jack couldn't do that. He still had vivid images of Todd's handiwork on Cox and Bundergast careening around in his head and a vision of Dr. Bacardi that was more than chilling.

Everyone was relieved when Leland reported Todd boarded his Chicago-bound flight Friday morning. Todd would continue to be watched during the weekend until he boarded his flight to Philly on Monday morning. After that, surveillance would continue until he broke, or, under pressure, made a mistake in attempting Number 69.

Jack invited Cheri to relax their self-imposed moratorium and shed their tensions with a nice dinner at his place. He chose an aperitif of Cointreau to kick off the night.

Jack felt knots in his shoulders the size of shooter marbles. Cheri had marvelous, strong hands no one could have anticipated from her doll-sized waist and hour-glass figure. Her deceptively delicate frame masked a moderately muscled upper torso suggesting surprising strength. Todd had learned that.

Jack, feeling her massaging out the kinks, slumped into his favorite chair, while she stood behind him, working her magic.

Jack liked to cook. Cheri was amazed at his facility to whip up a gourmet meal. A wine connoisseur, he chose the perfect vintage for their meal. Both fell into sublime relaxation in a Shangri-La of their own making. When Cheri initiated what she anticipated would be their love-making, Jack resisted.

"I want you as much as you want me, Cheri. We've already broken rules, but that's not what's bothering me. I deceived a friend with half-truths. I promised Mike we'd hold back until this case is over. I feel guilty even being here. I made this whole arrangement more difficult for both of us. I know we want to finish this case together, so we have to wait."

"You're right on both counts. I need to finish this case, and *you shouldn't have put us in this position!*" she said angrily.

Before he could object, she slipped on her flats and left.

CHAPTER SEVENTY-SEVEN

Cheri eagerly awaited Jack's arrival, wanting to say he was right and to clear the air between them. She wanted to keep faith with Mike, too, given Jack's promise.

He returned her call from his office, where he was tying up loose ends. She was only five minutes from Quantico, and he would be leaving any second.

She started two glacier-thick Porterhouse steaks on low broil and promised Jack they would only eat and enjoy each other's company. She would obey the rules.

Each liked steak medium-rare, and she wanted it to be just the way he liked it. Nothing was as disappointing as the perfect steak done imperfectly. She would have to greet him and immediately retreat to the kitchen when he arrived.

There was his knock! She wiped her hands on her apron and ran to the door, throwing it wide.

"Hello, Ms. Hancock," Todd said. "We meet again!"

Her first instinct was to go for her weapon, which was in a nightstand drawer beside her bed. She checked that impulse, knowing she'd never make it. It would mean turning her back on him, and that could be fatal. She had experienced his embrace from behind.

She retreated three steps into the living room and took a defensive posture, arms raised and fists clenched.

"Really, Ms. Hancock," Todd said in a cool, even voice. "There's no need. First, I have no weapon." He held out his hands, palms up. "Second, how foolish would it be to come here after evading your tail this morning and attack you? Your friends at the Bureau, as I think you call it, could easily track me using the many cameras at the Nashville Airport to see the Washington flight I caught to get here."

"If you aren't planning to attack me, why are you here?" She wanted it to sound like a demand, but it came out like a plea.

"Because I'm an innocent man. You and your comrades are persecuting me without reason. I haven't done anything!"

"Maybe you're innocent. I was never convinced you're the guy we're looking for. You're not the only one we're considering, but you shouldn't be here right now. It won't help your cause. I'll certainly pass on that you convincingly maintained your innocence. It might even help you that you came to me about this, *if* you leave right now."

"OK, I'll go. Please try to help me. I'm an innocent man."

Turning with the precision of a military right-face, he walked down the hall.

CHAPTER SEVENTY-EIGHT

Zero, very satisfied with himself, spotted the agent who watched him board the flight to Chicago and waited until the passenger boarding bridge was ready to detach from the plane and the agent tailing him was confident he was onboard.

Just as the flight attendant started to close the door, he screamed, "I can't do it! I can't! Let me off! I'm claustrophobic!"

He ran for the almost-closed door. The flight attendant stepped aside, not wanting to confront a large man who appeared panicked. Zero shoved the door open and was gone.

Once alerted by the shaken attendant, the copilot called airport security, who immediately closed in and grabbed Todd. The flight attendant confirmed he had only one carry-on. As far as she knew, it hadn't been opened, and nothing was left behind. The overhead compartment Zero used was searched to make certain no clandestine package had been left.

Two TSA officers took Todd to a nondescript office. He offered no resistance and gave an Academy Award performance right down to the convulsive shaking of a phobic.

A senior officer shortly joined them. The other officers swept Todd with a wand, pronouncing him clean.

"My name is Dan Bailey," the man said. "I'm the Assistant Chief of Security at the airport." At six-four, Bailey had a physique that would have been intimidating even to someone of Todd's six-two frame. "You could be in deep shit, you know. What's going on here?"

"Hello, Officer," Todd said deferentially. "My name is Lawrence Todd." He offered his ID.

Baily took a moment to look through the wallet before returning it.

"I'm claustrophobic," Todd explained. "When they started to close the door, I panicked."

"You caused a hell of a ruckus, Mr. Todd," Bailey said sternly.

"I know. I'm sorry."

"Why were you getting on a plane if you're claustrophobic?"

Todd feigned heavy breathing to calm himself. "I'm still trying to compose myself, Officer Bailey. First, you'll notice my ticket was purchased on a corporate credit card. I was flying home to Chicago to relax for the weekend in preparation for a big meeting Monday. Usually, I drive home. I'm a sales rep."

He offered Bailey his card. "The boss pressured me to take this flight. He's having a barbecue tomorrow for a big client. On Monday, I spearhead a presentation to the client, and the barbecue was supposed to be an icebreaker. I couldn't make it driving, and the boss already rented a car, so my car wouldn't be stranded here. After years of flying, only recently I developed this claustrophobia. Your records should show I've flown with your airline many times. I thought I could work through it."

"You certainly failed on that count. Didn't your boss know you were claustrophobic?"

"Well, yes and no." He looked at the quizzical faces around him. "It's a bit of a long story."

"That's OK," Bailey said skeptically. "We've got the time."

"I've flown without any problem until recently. A few months ago, I was driving south on Sheridan Road, near the end of Lake Shore Drive in Chicago. I had all green lights ahead of me for the next couple of intersections, so I was doing the speed limit. At the second intersection, a guy in a U-Haul truck with its left turn signal on was coming north. He could have turned long before I got there, but he didn't."

"Go on."

"I'm driving my vintage Porsche 914. That's a midengine Porsche...."

"I'm familiar with it. Vintage. I'm a fan. Go ahead."

"Then you know it has a solid roll bar the width of the car. Just as I got to the intersection where the U-Haul was, the driver gunned it and killed his engine. I had nowhere to go. If I hadn't ducked, I would've been decapitated. It took out the whole windshield and roof, right up to the roll bar."

"I'm going to interrupt. Bill, I want you to call this company. It's AFI on the business card. Confirm that Mr. Todd works there."

"Officer Bailey, that's fine, but may I ask a favor?" Todd implored.

"What?"

"My boss isn't the most-sympathetic guy. He thinks I have to confront my fears. You'll soon understand why I'm claustrophobic. He doesn't. You've already seen my ID and business card. You know who I am, and anyone who answers the phone can confirm I work there...." His voice trailed off.

"I get the idea. Bill, just confirm he works there. Don't give details." He eyed Todd. "Go on."

"Well, I was wedged under the bottom of the truck and couldn't move. I was almost swallowing my stick shift. I saw gasoline trickling into the car from a puncture in the truck's tank! I really panicked when I saw from the corner of my eye the idiot who was driving the truck lighting a cigarette.

"I screamed at him, but he didn't acknowledge me. I learned later he spoke only Japanese. I've got nothing against the Japanese, but I wasn't very fond of him. It took the fire department forty-five minutes to get there, take away his smokes, and extricate me from the car."

"And this made you claustrophobic?" Bailey asked, nodding assent.

Bill stuck his head through the door. "The person who answered says he's worked there for ten years."

"We're gonna turn you loose, Mr. Todd. Just do me a favor. Don't try to fly out of my airport again until you have a handle on this claustrophobia thing."

"Don't think you need to worry about that."

Everything went as planned. He made sure he wasn't tailed after leaving the airport security office. If Bailey wanted to alert all the other airlines, it would take time. Zero's performance was pretty convincing, so Bailey might not bother, but he might.

He had to move quickly. Planning ahead, he knew his alternatives. He went to the appropriate airline counter and traded his ticket to Chicago for one to Washington. He was already savoring the reaction and fear his visit would instill in Agent Hancock.

He never really wanted to convince her of his innocence. He wanted her to know he could get to her anytime, anywhere. Zero wanted her to live with that fear. He would kill her and was already designing a fitting end for that cunt. It would be at a place and time of his choosing. It would be exquisite, a crowning achievement befitting his creativity and superior intellect.

CHAPTER SEVENTY-NINE

Mike burst into Jack's office, expecting he'd already left for the day, but he hadn't. Mike grabbed his phone, which had just rung. "Leland? Yeah, Jack's here with me. I'm putting you on speaker phone."

"Jack," Leland said, "our agent in Nashville saw Todd get onto the plane and waited until departure time before leaving. The agent in Chicago just called. The plane's departure was delayed, but we don't know why. When the plane arrived in Chicago, Todd wasn't on it."

"Do you think he has Number 69 on tap?" Mike asked. "It's probably in Nashville. We're notifying the authorities there."

"Fuck that!" Jack shrieked. "He's after Cheri!" He raced out the door and down the hall. "Warn her!" he shouted to Mike.

Five minutes later, Jack kicked in the door to Cheri's apartment without waiting for an answer to his knock. Cheri ran to him. Only then did she begin shaking. A few minutes later, Mike and a SWAT team ran through the unhinged door.

Cheri immediately composed herself. She couldn't show weakness in front of her peers, not again.

When it was obvious Todd wasn't there, and all the consternation settled down, Mike released the other agents after ordering round-the-clock protection for Cheri. Leland was there by then, and only Jack, Mike, and Leland remained to debrief her.

Cheri, taking a deep breath, recounted her eerie encounter with Lawrence Todd. When she finished, Mike and Leland looked at each other, but Jack was fixated on Cheri. He wanted to help her through the situation but decided he couldn't bring himself to participate in the upcoming interrogation.

"Did he make any threatening gestures?" Mike asked, hoping for any excuse to arrest the guy. That would've been harmful to their investigation, but it didn't seem like anyone cared.

"Other than just being here? No. He didn't even trespass or cross the threshold. He showed me empty hands and didn't threaten me."

"You said he showed you his hands," Mike said. "Could he have been carrying a concealed weapon?"

"He just came through the metal detectors at the airport," she replied. "I doubt he was carrying anything. In Washington, it's next to impossible to get a handgun between his flight and here before you were notified he wasn't in Chicago. It's equally unlikely his business contacts would supply him with one, but he can buy a knife anywhere, if he was intent on harming me. As I see it, this was all about messaging."

"We don't know how long he was here," Leland said thoughtfully. "We'll track down the flight from Nashville. Despite your analysis, he could have picked up a weapon between flights."

"Then why not use it?" she asked. "I believe his understated threat was all the more cogent and terrifying. Imposing terror on a woman is his central theme. It's imperative. We included that in his profile."

"Maybe you didn't make a mistake he was counting on," Mike said. "You said you were careful not to turn your back on him."

"I don't think so. He's been very careful until now. That doesn't fit with coming here to commit murder when he could be easily traced from Nashville. He even pointed it out himself. It's more of his gamesmanship."

Leland's cell rang. The others paused to let him finish the call.

"That was our man in Nashville," he reported. "Todd faked claustrophobia to get off the flight.. Dealing with a feigned claustrophobic delayed that flight. Diverting a scheduled flight is a federal crime."

"Don't do anything about that," Mike commanded. "That would

derail our investigation, and that might be what he's trying to accomplish."

"It might also keep Cheri safe for a while." Jack asked, "Anyone think of that?"

"You might ask me if that's the kind of shelter I want," Cheri said.

"I'll broadcast a memo as soon as I'm back in the office," Leland said. "No one shadowing Todd in the future leaves the gate until he can see the jet's contrail as it leaves. I'll have the gate ramp checked, too.

"There's more, though. The Assistant Security Chief in Nashville, Dan Bailey, interrogated Todd. Bailey bought Todd's cock-and-bull story about how he was trapped in an auto accident. Apparently, it was either richly rehearsed or an actual experience he or someone he knew had.

"We'll have a local agent interview him first thing tomorrow. He's already left for the day. There's no need to go to his home. It won't insulate Cheri. What we know now, we gathered over the phone.

"I know Burt Huntley in Nashville fairly well. He's a good man and was able to learn Todd swapped his ticket to Chicago for one to Reagan National. That's how he got here so fast." Leland sighed, as if the entire incident were his fault instead of being one of the agents on his watch who slipped up.

They sat in silence until Jack said, "Cheri's had an unnerving time. I demolished her door. You said you have two men to watch her twenty-four seven until we can devise a better plan. I'll notify the building that the door needs to be fixed right away. In the meantime, plant a guy here. Alert him that our guy might return. I don't think so, but it can't hurt.

"I'll drive Cheri to a hotel. Have your other agent follow us. I'll see her into her room and get a suite for myself. When I'm sure she's OK, I'll leave. It isn't very often someone encounters a serial killer for the second time. I'll call the second agent's cell and plant him in Cheri's sitting room. For all we know, Todd is watching us now. We'll make sure we aren't shadowed."

"You're doing a lot of planting tonight, Jack," Cheri said, attempting to be humorous for the men but mostly for herself. "Maybe you should consider opening a landscaping company," she said, putting on a brave face.

CHAPTER EIGHTY

It looked like Todd would carry through as if nothing happened. Leland soon informed the team that agents recouped Todd's surveillance. Todd was on his way back to Chicago from Washington that afternoon, and his arrival was confirmed.

At no point over the weekend did he lose his tail or attempt to. On Monday, out of O'Hare Airport, an agent informed Leland that the suspect was on his way to Philadelphia, as planned. "He's on the jet this time," Leland told the team. "Our agent all but boarded with him and waited to see the plane's contrail."

Monday, the Bureau convinced a judge there was too much coincidence for one man to be in such close proximity to twenty-five murders, all involving the repeated torture of women and all occurring within a small window of time that coincided with Todd's itineraries and expenses. The court issued a search warrant for his home and a subpoena *duces tecum* for the records from AFI.

Tuesday, Jack was waiting when AFI opened. He was let into the office by the office manager and sat to wait for Armstrong. He arrived five minutes later. When he saw Jack, he flushed red.

Before the man could speak, Jack stood very close to him and unobtrusively slapped his chest with a folded document. The word *Subpoena* was clearly visible at the top.

"You might want to keep a lid on this," Jack said very softly. "Your office?"

Armstrong's jaw clenched, and he went through the swinging door toward his centralized office with Jack following. Once inside,

Armstrong sat down with a thud, making a whoosh of air when he hit the cushioned seat.

"You guys are unbelievable," Armstrong began. "First, you come here with unsubstantiated allegations against one of the best employees I ever had, and now you're back. You can't find the real murderer, so you've fixated on Lawrence? This is an abuse of your authority. I'm calling my attorney!"

"I wouldn't do that if I were you. I think I can satisfy you that Lawrence Todd is a monstrous serial murderer."

Armstrong's hand lay on the phone receiver while the two men stared at each other. Armstrong flinched first and let his had slide away. "I don't think you have a chance in hell, but I'll let you try. If there's something to it, I'd like to keep a low profile for obvious reasons."

"We've already discussed that Lawrence Todd fits our profile like a glove."

"Yes, yes."

"You remember Cheri, the young agent who was with me last time?"

"Yes, of course."

Jack's eyes squinted slyly, as he prepared to drop a hand grenade into the conversation. "On Friday night, he was at Cheri's apartment, scaring the hell out of her."

Armstrong looked like he'd been hit in the stomach by Muhammad Ali. "What happened?"

"Not much. He didn't assault or threaten her. He said he knew we were following him, and he wanted to prove his innocence."

"Well, there you go." He didn't sound convinced, though, because it wasn't the kind of thing he ever thought Lawrence would do.

"Do you believe in coincidence, Mr. Armstrong?"

"Sometimes. We've all had those *déjà vu* experiences. You're sure you've been someplace or done something or seen someone before. Maybe you have, and maybe you haven't. I've heard TV shrinks say it's based on a similar occurrence we don 't remember specifically.

"Then you encounter someone you haven't seen for years, and you just happen to run into each other at a train station or something. Coincidence happens."

Jack was ready to let him have it. "How much would you believe in coincidence if it happened twenty-five times? That's how many women were murdered in a location where Todd was."

Armstrong almost reeled from his chair. Jack moved to the edge of the chair and prepared to catch him, thinking the man might faint. He waited until color returned to Armstrong's face. A few minutes earlier, his face was red with anger. It turned white.

Jack could sympathize. He may have inherited the business from his father, but it was obvious he poured a lot of his own sweat into it. Such a story could potentially ruin a small business, although Jack didn't think that was foremost in Armstrong's mind.

"Tell me everything you can," Armstrong said weakly. "Don't hold anything back. I want to know."

"Mr. Armstrong, you're a good man. I take no pleasure in this."

He nodded sadly.

"This subpoena is to obtain all of Todd's itineraries, expense reports, and any data you have from his original hiring. That includes anything you might have in your files about his parents.

"The main things we need are the itineraries and expense reports. We've collected twenty-five murders that we think are connected to Todd based on the notes Agent Hancock and I took when we were here. Now we want the originals. Of course I know you must make copies for taxes and other records. That's fine. We need the originals for evidentiary purposes."

"Why aren't you arresting him right now?" he asked.

"You've been around him for years. Is he intelligent?"

"I think he might be the most-intelligent man I've ever known. He had a good track record with one of our customers before starting here, but that alone won't usually land a Regional Manager's spot managing brokers, most especially when the candidate is twenty-one at the time. His father was a college professor and a very smart man. He was a friend of mine until he passed. Lawrence is even smarter, maybe by a lot."

"We haven't arrested him yet, because he's been very smart and appears to be very well-read about forensics. One person being within the orbit of twenty-five monstrous murders defies any kind of logic that it could be anyone else. That's enough for this subpoena and the warrant we obtained to search his residence. In a court of law, though, that's just circumstantial evidence with no direct or forensic evidence to back it. In these days DNA can be gathered with superglue even where a culprit touched someone's skin or a garment, spraying luminol to detect blood stains and so forth, some indicium of forensic evidence is expected."

Armstrong, a proud man, slowly gathered himself together. "You want to go back further. You think there are more?" he managed to ask.

"We think there are forty-three more, giving a total of sixty-eight." Jack hated doing that to the man.

Armstrong reeled again, and Jack gave him time. Eventually, he leaned forward and pressed a button on his desk. "Alecia, I don't want any calls or interruptions. Not for any reason."

"Are you all right, Mr. Armstrong?"

"Yes, just no interruptions," he said.

It was as if Armstrong had become one of Todd's torture victims. The news was tearing him apart.

"Agent Hancock has a Master's in Psychology and helped me work up the profile. Since you know Todd's family, she'll be calling you for more information. We can hold off on that for a day," he added sympathetically.

"You didn't just say serial murderer," Armstrong said slowly. "You said he is a monstrous serial murderer. What did you mean?"

"I can't go into detail about the crimes, sir." He wasn't allowed to share the information, but he also wanted to spare Armstrong further anguish.

"You're going to say the rules preclude my knowing, that telling me would jeopardize the investigation. I watch a lot of movies. I'm co-operating because I want to, but I promise you not a word of anything you tell me will leave this office. Mr. Garvey, I need to know!"

Jack sat there for a minute in silence. Finally, he asked, "What exactly do you want to know?"

"What did you mean by monstrous?"

"If I tell you anything, I put myself in a precarious position with the FBI. I have a career to protect, just as you have a company. I'm not a rule-breaker. I feel a great deal of sympathy for someone I feel is a good man."

"Thank you, Agent Garvey. I won't break your confidence. What did you mean by monstrous?"

"Do you remember Todd taking a vacation last summer? He was in Madison, and he was headed to Peoria, with a day to kill. Sorry. That was a poor word choice."

"I gave him the day off and told him I wouldn't charge it as a vacation day. What about it?"

"We think he met a woman that day and went back on Friday, his travel day, to meet her. I can't tell you her name. that's non-negotiable, though you could probably track her down using the internet. Still, I won't make your job any easier, and I can still disclaim having told you.

"Todd used jumper cables hooked up to a gas-powered electric generator to shock her, burn her, revive her, and shock her again repeatedly. Finally, he threw her in a tub of water to finish the job. Enough?" Jack prayed he wouldn't ask for more.

As if through a fog, Armstrong said softly, "If there's more, I guess I want to hear the rest."

"His pattern is to rape his victims vaginally multiple times and then sodomize them before starting his torture. He was afraid of leaving semen in his victim here, so he used a spade to dig out her entire pelvic cavity."

Armstrong looked ready to vomit. Finally, he stammered, "Wh...what do you want from me?"

"I mentioned in the lobby keeping a lid on this. The Bureau doesn't want to hurt you or your company if we can prevent it. Do you have someone here, one person who's been with you for a while, you can trust?"

"Yes, my office manager, Alecia. You met her last time you were here. Her mother, Betty, worked here before her."

"We have to maintain what is called a 'chain of custody.' That means it can't be out of my sight once we begin to gather it. Here's what I suggest. She has already seen my credentials, so there's no hiding that. Your cover story will be that I'm collecting data for a joint FBI-Treasury Department investigation involving a money-laundering scheme. She'll quickly ascertain that all the documents will pertain to Todd. Just tell her I'm doing a routine audit to see if we can find any connection to him, but it's mainly to eliminate him as a suspect."

He glanced at Armstrong. "Alecia showed a desire to protect you the last time we were here. I have the impression she'll do so again?"

"Yes, I believe so. Betty was my dad's personal secretary and mine. She retired, and Alecia stepped in. I trust her."

"She oversees the office, so she can keep people too occupied to snoop into what we're doing. An audit is disconcerting, but it's nothing to what you, unfortunately, will have to face down the road, because this will eventually become public.

"Alecia and I can't share the photocopying duties. I must stay with the originals because of the chain of custody, so she'll have to do it all. I'll want the three things we discussed, the originals of all five years of itineraries, all ten years of expense records, and his personnel file. When I leave, you'll be out of this for the time being, except for a phone interview with Agent Hancock to see what we can glean about how Lawrence Todd became who he is.

"There are two other things. I'll need you to sign a prepared affidavit I brought, swearing under penalty of perjury, that the documents taken pursuant to the subpoena are the originals. That and my own affidavit will be sufficient for the chain of custody."

"And the other thing?"

"What are your plans for Lawrence Todd?"

"What do you think? He's history."

"I wouldn't do that, Mr. Armstrong. We've beefed up our personnel, and we're surveilling him around the clock. We want him to continue to do his job while we gather additional evidence."

"I have to consider my staff, especially the women, since that seems to be his penchant."

"He's never chosen anyone here. You're too close to home. He knows right now what we have constitutes very long odds that anyone else could have done this, but there's little or no forensics to back it up. We need time, sir."

Armstrong deliberated for a long time. "I wasn't very cooperative at first. That weighs heavily on me. I'll give you that time."

"When this is all over, I'll see if we can draft a statement that your cooperation was instrumental in apprehending Todd. Maybe that will mitigate the fallout where your company is concerned."

Armstrong stared at him blankly. Seeing how hard the man fought to maintain his composure, Jack admired him for it.

CHAPTER EIGHTY-ONE

Wednesday, Jack was back at Quantico with Mike and the rest of the team for their regular meeting. With the sense that their efforts were finally winnowing down Todd's avenues for escape, everyone was excited and looking forward to their next steps.

Their inward enthusiasm was stifled somewhat by the news of what happened to Cheri. She rebounded well, as Jack expected. Cheri was a strong person.

"We won't make a big deal about what happened to Cheri," Mike said, beginning the meeting. "We'll just say she demonstrated the kind of mettle good agents should be made of. However, there's a reason I brought it up."

He paused. "We all need to be cautious and aware from now on. Todd appears to be going about his regular business activity. I'll let Jack brief you on that. It's his baby, but you're my agents and staff. Stay alert and watch your backs.

"We don't even know how he got Cheri's address. He's a charmer. He probably wangled it from someone who should've known better. We're checking our tapes, and, if we find that person, there'll be serious disciplinary action. Personal information about our agents is *verboten.* If he can show up at her apartment, he can also show up where you live. He's like a wounded animal, and we're his tormentors. So far as we know, he's never harmed anyone except women, but he might make an exception for one of us. Don't take chances, and don't let your guard down. Jack?"

"Leland, bring us current with Todd," Jack said.

"We determined Todd switched his Chicago ticket for one to Reagan National, and that's how he got to Cheri so quickly. He's sticking to his planned itinerary so far this week. He flew out of Chicago, landed in Philly for a quick meeting Monday, and stayed over at the Hyatt Monday night. We tracked him to his Atlanta flight from Philly and confirmed his arrival at the Atlanta airport yesterday. Todd will be making his regular rounds with the broker's salespeople according to the owner of AFI, who is cooperating. Todd will also call on a couple of key auto aftermarket customers, like the Firestone regional office.

"Friday is Todd's typical travel day, and we know the time of his planned departure from Atlanta on Friday morning. We have agents on him every minute around the clock."

"Are we informing local law enforcement?" Roy asked.

"Only to the extent that we're on their turf and doing surveillance activity of some importance," Jack said. "Local law enforcement are great people, irrespective of the times we have jurisdictional clashes. Their rumor mills occasionally leak information we don't want leaked, especially when a possible serial murderer is involved.

"Agent Stein is trying to hunt down any forensic or other evidence that may have been overlooked by local police in the cases we've identified as probable Todd homicides. Give us some good news, Tim," Jack finished.

"Jack, I should've known you'd set me up," he said, joining the banter. "This piece-of-shit Todd is well-read regarding forensics. In the *two whole days* I've had to explore errors and omissions," he added with sarcasm, "I've found jack shit. I am, however, extraordinarily stubborn, which accounts for having almost no friends. Give me a little more than two days."

"We have to push your buttons, Tim. It inspires you." Jack chuckled. "Jack shit, hmmm?"

As the meeting went on, Cheri sensed the others trying to portray an atmosphere of everyday routine. Their concern for her made them a bit uncomfortable. It would have been worse to mention it, though, in an attempt to put them at ease. That would only make the situation worse. They just needed time. She prepared for being Jack's next person to be called.

"Cheri, I understand you've spoken with Armstrong," Jack said. "Fill us in."

"I heard from you after your early morning meeting with him, and I called right away, not wanting him to get cold feet. I understand the whole dynamic now. Armstrong took this hard.

"He was more than anxious to get the interview over. I think he needed to put it all behind him, at least for now, and buy himself a few hours' respite. I mention all this, because in probing what he knows about Todd's family life and development, we must understand we're seeing it through the lens of Wilbur Armstrong, the Third, and his emotional turmoil.

"He's a very religious man, but he also has unusual compassion and a desire to see only the best in people. That's why he initially gave us resistance. He looked at Todd and saw only what he wanted to see, the good. Todd is probably a genius, a great actor, and a manipulator who puts a very good first foot forward with others. That first impression had years of reinforcement. Now that Armstrong's bubble has burst, he's likely to feel greatly disillusioned, so that may color his testimony.

"His observations, however, are valid. Lawrence's father was an academician. Like many, at least of the older generation, he was retiring by nature, even timid. Lawrence's mother had no such trepidations. She was controlling in the extreme. Lawrence sensed his father's gentleness and sincere love for his son.

"Armstrong believes Lawrence hates both his parents, his father for his weakness and his mother for her domineering ways. He's disappointed in his old, deceased friend and the potential destruction it wrought on him.

"I think differently. I believe Todd found his father empathetic. Every time his mother bullied his father, he saw every manipulation of his father as a wound they shared. It was also another account to be settled. Lawrence learned from an early age he was impotent to help his father, mostly because his father intervened on his mother's part, incongruously enough.

"If Todd had been ambivalent in his feelings about his parents, he wouldn't have developed the terrible rage that manifests in these killings.

"As Lawrence went through puberty, he became interested in sex. Unlike a young man who develops normally, he wanted girls, but he envisioned them as adversaries initially, then later on, as repugnant, making a relationship impossible. According to Armstrong, Lawrence Todd had a very good relationship with women in a business context.

"The interview with Armstrong added aspects to our profile. To interact in a productive rather than a destructive way, Todd had to segregate some women as unapproachable as targets. His business relationships were in one category, while potential victims were in another, so AFI's people aren't at risk, although Armstrong is naturally reluctant to accept that.

"This also means that Todd is capable of compartmentalization. Our first profile suggested he wouldn't walk away from the job or the life he created for himself, because he would regard it as a loss in a win/lose proposition. Now we have to be prepared for him to walk away, possibly suddenly. My analysis still suggests, however, that he'd have to be driven to the wall to do that. The question is, will searching his home push him that far?"

"Are we trying to put a lid on things as far as Todd's being notified of the search of his home?" Anita asked.

"Good question, Anita," Jack said. "Todd owns a nice, single-family home in an upscale neighborhood. He wasn't home, so we were forced to breach the door, hopefully discretely in terms of not doing much damage, and enter to initiate a search pursuant to the warrant. It would be helpful to talk with Todd's neighbors about his habits, comings and goings, and visitors.

"However, we *are* trying to keep a lid on it. With the number of agents involved and the computer and other items we marched out of the home, we attracted some attention. The few neighbors who approached us out of curiosity told us they had almost no contact with Todd. What little information we have suggests he keeps to himself and makes no effort to know any of his neighbors. The most anyone admitted to were a couple of hellos shouted across their lawns, always initiated by the neighbor. Neither of them had his phone number or contact info for him.

"If possible," Jack continued, "we'd like Todd to return from Atlanta unaware the search took place until he gets home. I'm trusting the people in this room to keep a confidence. The law requires that if we have knowledge of the whereabouts of the person subject to a warrant, and have reasonable access, we're required to inform him even if he isn't at the premises where the search is executed."

Jack lowered his voice to emphasize the seriousness of his words. "There are a lot of agents in operation right now. It seems the right hand didn't know what the left was doing? We each thought someone else made the call. That's our problem.

"Mike will tell you that we're both sticklers for procedure. We're trying to save lives. We're truly up against evil, as I've never seen if before. This is up close and personal. We normally don't look at crimes that way, but if Todd isn't evil, I don't know who is.

"Cheri, do you have anything to add?"

"Todd's hatred for women was formed before puberty and grew with every interaction between his parents and girls and women from adolescence on. It's been festering for a long time, so he's dangerous and volatile."

"Roy, you and Anita just got the documents from AFI before this meeting," Jack said. "You have five additional years of expense reports to check. Those will give you new locations and time frames. It's possible that some of the twenty-two murders you've already identified as potentials, in addition to the three we know about, don't belong to Todd. Whether we're looking for forty-one, forty-three, or forty-five more to get to the Number 68 is unimportant. What *is* important is to get to the suspect ones we haven't identified. If we get to a higher number, then we'll look for those who don't fit, like the time frame is wrong or the torture pattern doesn't fit.

"We need to find the most-likely sixty-eight that we can. We need to put our rather stretched resources where they can do the most good. Continue to check with Cheri or me about the psychological issues. What do you say, Roy?"

"Just this," Roy began. "Anita and I feel pretty good about the ones we identified. In every case, Todd, from a timeline perspective, could have done the deed. Every single one involved not just horrific torture but repeated torture and revival. I'd be surprised if any of them belonged to another perp.

"I tend to look at things from a statistical perspective. How likely is it that this would occur and be accomplished by another perp? How likely is it the opportunity would present itself to a person in Todd's position in AFI? I'll look at a group of homicides and whittle away at them from a statistical starting point.

"Anita sees things differently. Do the homicides we're looking at follow a pattern that can be put together like pieces of a puzzle? We augment each other well. We'll have our choices for the top sixty-eight by the end of next week, if our dialing fingers don't give out first."

"Great reports, Everybody," Jack said. "We have a lot of work ahead. Let's keep in touch. Synergistic decisions and inputs always work better than a combination of individually formed ones."

CHAPTER EIGHTY-TWO

One hour after their Friday meeting, Jack was looking at the homicides Roy and Anita proposed to add to their list of probables when the phone rang. It was Leland, and Jack knew it meant trouble.

"Whassup, Leland?"

"We lost Todd again," he said sheepishly.

"Shit! Fill me in."

"Our agent was tailing him when he came out of his hotel with a typical carry-on. He got into a cab, and the agent followed. Todd exited the cab at the airport and headed for the terminal. Our guy kept him in sight the whole time, but, when they got to security, he got a good look, and it wasn't Todd.

"Agent Duncan knew that information was time-critical, so he approached the man, who was of similar height and physique, dressed in a dark suit. He told Duncan he had a cocktail with Todd the previous night, which was reported by the agent who watched him, but it looked like an unplanned encounter.

"Todd learned that Blaine Wilson was headed to the airport the next morning and asked Wilson if he could grab a cab and pull it up for Todd. They'd share a ride to the airport, and Todd would pay the tab. Wilson thought it a little strange that Todd wanted him to get the taxi, but if he was willing to pay for the trip, why not? Wilson left the cab, and Duncan followed." Leland was so furious, he spoke through clenched teeth.

"It wasn't Duncan's fault or yours," Jack said, letting him down easy. "There's no end to Todd's resourcefulness. Cheri was right about

290

his taking off. It just came sooner than anticipated. We need to act fast on several fronts. I assume you've already told the Atlanta agent about the situation?"

"Yeah. I called him before calling you."

"I'll talk to Cheri and see if her crystal ball has any idea where Todd might be headed. Leland, I think we need to bring in the locals and get a picture of Todd distributed? Can you take care of that?"

"Sure, Jack."

"I'll ask Roy if he sees any pattern that might help us figure out what he's doing or where he's going. I'll consult with Mike to see what he thinks of using the media to broadcast a photo of Todd as a person of interest, although I don't think that'll go anywhere."

"Sounds good, Jack. I'll get right on the local thing."

"Let them know Todd's suspected in a homicide and is very dangerous. Keep a low profile on the serial thing. We don't want to panic the public if this leaks."

"Gotcha."

CHAPTER EIGHTY-THREE

Lawrence Todd was gone. Remaining was just Zero, intent on inflicting punishment on his adversaries at the FBI, especially Cheri Hancock. His smartphone warned him that his home security system was breached, and he knew the FBI finally obtained a warrant to search his home.

He wasn't concerned about anything in the house incriminating him. Unlike his predecessors in serial murder, he wasn't stupid enough to take souvenirs. All clothing he wore during any of his ritual was disposed of before he entered the house. He could relive the rituals in his mind, using his supreme brain. Only weaker specimens needed the crutch of a physical connection to their victims. Zero remembered every single ecstatic dispatch of his women. He thought of himself as a polygamist, married to each by a ritual experience they shared.

The search warrant changed everything. It meant his case had changed from being a short-term interest into their keeping tabs on his every move. There was no going back now, no relinquishing their attention on him. The FBI was fully committed.

Almost concurrent with the notification, he went to the bank on Thursday and withdrew half of the $100,000 from one of his accounts. That money was enough for him to move forward on his devastatingly depraved plan. It would've attracted too much attention to take out all the cash and close the account. He tossed his cell phone and bought an anonymous prepaid phone.

He already had multiple passports and driver's licenses, each with a different photo. In some he was a redhead, some had his natural brown hair, and some showed him with a beard, while in others he was clean-shaven.

His long-term planning anticipated the recent developments. Zero had several surprises planned for his friends at the Bureau, and then he would disappear and begin a whole new serial murder career. When added to his prodigious accomplishments to date, he would become the most-prolific serial murderer in American history, surpassing victim counts of the Green River Killer, with seventy-one victims, and Samuel Little at ninety-three.

His rightful place was to be Number 1, and he would surpass both of them.

CHAPTER EIGHTY-FOUR

Jack immediately called Mike and told him about Todd's latest escapade. Mike told him to come to the office immediately.

When Jack walked in, Mike said, "I spoke to Leland while you were on your way over. He feels terrible."

"This isn't his fault or Duncan's. If Leland filled you in, you know that. I'm pretty sure under this scenario, I would've been fooled, too. You have to be close enough to keep the guy in sight, but not so close that you'll tip him off. Both men wore dark business suits and were the same height with one carry-on. Todd's clever and cool."

"How do you suppose he coordinated the dark suit thing? Was Todd just playing the odds? His fellow passenger would have thought it even odder if asked about the clothes he planned to wear that morning."

"He probably complimented the guy on his suit and got him to talk about his wardrobe. Most men don't feel comfortable talking about those things. If Blaine Wilson were ego-driven, though, who knows?"

"What do we do now?"

"Leland already transmitted our best picture of Todd to the locals in Atlanta. They know he's a person of interest in a homicide, but that's all. Since you're smarter than I am, Mike, I thought we should kick around what to do from here."

"When you were a Special Agent, I told you not to bring me a problem unless you could offer a solution. I haven't forgotten that. 'You're smarter than I am, Mike.' What crap!"

"You might prefer that to what I'm about to say. We don't know if he targeted anyone in Atlanta. We need to do what we can, however insufficient to potentially save a life. I want to broadcast his picture on the major TV stations in Atlanta as a person of interest in a murder."

"Jesus. A person of interest? It's one thing to go to local law enforcement and quite another to broadcast it to a million people in the Atlanta metropolis. That could bring out his mercenary side. He could pop up, attorney in tow, and ask us what direct evidence we have of his culpability for murder, then sue the Bureau. I'm as passionate about protecting his potential victims as you are. Remember, other than the very long odds of the coincidence of his being near two dozen homicides, which all have different MOs, we don't have a thing on this guy! Do you really want us to fall on our swords?"

That brought Jack to his fallback position. "All right. How about just saying he's wanted for questioning in a homicide case? When you specifically say 'homicide,' it scares the public a lot less than murder, although it's essentially the same thing."

"You always scare me when you say 'essentially,'" Mike complained.

He mulled it over for a few seconds. "All right. Do it before the brass can refuse. I'll cover for you and say I gave you broad discretion given the imminent danger Todd poses. 'Wanted for questioning,' right? I'll claim insanity if necessary. Isn't there another call you need to make?"

"It's physically impossible for Todd to have gotten up here by now. I rang Cheri on my cell on the way over."

"You really like this girl, eh?"

"And then some."

"How'd she react?"

"Like a trooper. We could tell the media he has been known to wear disguises, although we can't prove he was our clown or Hasidic Jew. Besides, it he's wearing one, it isn't like it would do any good."

"It might also diminish the importance of the photo. Let's leave out the disguise. I'll turn this over to our media people and get it moving right away."

There was one other call Jack had to make—to Armstrong. He didn't want him to hear about the situation on the news.

CHAPTER EIGHTY-FIVE

When Jack spoke to Armstrong, he heard a predominant mood of resignation. Jack tried to encourage him, repeating the prospect that a press release, praising Armstrong's cooperation in taking a dangerous serial murderer off the streets, might mitigate the damage to AFI once the case was over.

Jack's encouragement couldn't assuage Armstrong's self-flagellation for giving Lawrence Todd a significant job that provided a platform for what the man did. Todd would have murdered no matter who employed him. Armstrong didn't want to hear it.

It was incongruous that good people, the ones who lived by their honesty, integrity, and commitment to do right by others, were also the ones who lived with the anguish caused by those who didn't. Perhaps that was why so many turned to faith as the answer. Jack recalled times when faith sustained him and remembered saying a short prayer when he viewed Susan Bundergast's mutilated body.

The sociopath who created such carnage was incapable of fully comprehending the evil he did. It was impossible without an understanding of morality and empathy. Todd rejected morality and couldn't conceptualize empathy.

After his call to Armstrong, Jack sent agents and other trained resources to handle the inevitable inbound calls. Broadcasts always generate large numbers of leads, most of which are kooks and dead ends. Judgments had to be made over which were crank calls, which descriptions didn't fit Todd, and which might potentially be a serious lead. If it was viable, did the caller get a name the person was using or have any current knowledge of his whereabouts? Those calls had to be routed to the more-experienced staff. Potentially hundreds of calls would come in immediately, overwhelming Bureau resources. Jack saw to it that the lines were activated quickly, with as many staff to answer as possible. Fortunately, the FBI had contingency plans for such situations and was good at a rapid roll-out.

Jack received a quick call from Leland to say, "We're on!" As a logistics man, Leland was very good.

Shortly thereafter, Todd's face was splashed on TV screens throughout the Atlanta area. Within minutes of the first broadcast, hundreds of tips about the possible whereabouts of Lawrence Todd came in like an avalanche—slow at first then rising to crushing volume.

Every lead was followed, some of which showed promise. Those were quickly effused. Each time the stations broadcast a re-minder, they received fewer calls that might be hopeful. As the calls di-minished, so did everyone's hope that Todd would be apprehended.

Jack and Mike worked shoulder-to-shoulder for over thirty hours. Finally, Jack turned numbly to Mike and asked, "What now?"

"Did we have any luck tracking down the taxi driver who pulled away with Todd at the airport?" Mike was grasping at straws.

"Yeah, just a minute ago. We got our first forensic evidence re-lated to our guy. The taxi took Todd to a used-car lot, where he used his real ID and paid cash for one of the best cars on the lot, a five-year-old black Camaro for $9,999. Any time a dealer gets ten grand or more in cash for a car, it must be reported to the Feds because of potential money-laundering."

"This guy knows too damned much!" Mike snapped.

"Todd told the dealer he needed something fast and dependable and drove it off the lot, which was our first break."

"How so?" He could use some good news.

"The used-car dealer didn't have much inventory coming in. The front tires were on asphalt, but the rear tires rested on loose dirt. They never parked another car there after Todd took off, and there's been no rain. We have clear molds of the rear tire impressions for the Camaro. Tim had local agents pour the molds and send them to him right away."

"If we find those at a crime scene, we might have something." Mike felt it was wishful thinking.

The two men fell into a brief silence. One of the things the Bureau emphasized *ad infinitum* was that an agent's first responsibility was to follow orders. The second was to think.

"If he was being so open about his identity, he'd probably already changed the plates on the car and his own face, so he won't be easily recognized from the photo we've been circulating."

"Feels like he's always one step ahead of us," Jack said with more anger than frustration.

Each was silent for several minutes, biting their lips in thought.

"What else do you have us doing on this?" Mike asked.

"We're canvassing motels and hotels throughout the Atlanta area. Motels seem a more-likely place to lie low and not attract attention. A big hotel has too many eyes. There are a lot more motels than hotels. The good news is, he's probably not moving around but staying put somewhere. If we find that place, we'll have him."

"We still can't arrest him, just bring him in for questioning. He'll probably lawyer-up right away and take another hike."

The frustration in the room was growing.

"At least if we find him, we can try tracking him again and keep him in sight as long as we can." Seeing Leland approaching, he said, "Speak of the devil."

"Hey, Fellas," Leland said.

"Hey, Leland," they replied in unison.

"We were just having a conversation you should be part of," Mike said. "There are two possibilities. First, Todd is still in Atlanta, because he's got a target. Jack just brought up the second by asking if he might have flown the coop."

"That's why I came by. We've been checking the enforcement cameras at all tolls coming out of the Atlanta area. There are a lot of black Camaros. None so far have the dealer plates on the car Todd bought, so there's no ID. The cameras are positioned to get the plates. With a huge volume of cars, even if we find a match, which is doubtful, Todd will probably be long gone by the time we get the info."

"Mike and I were just thinking about that," Jack said. "This cookie quickly swapped the plates. If you don't know, Tim got some back-wheel molds of the car Todd bought."

"Yeah, he texted me."

"So where does that leave us?" Mike stared at the two agents, as he leaned back in his chair, hands clasped behind his head in exasperation. "It feels like Todd has us running in circles."

"We've asked the locals to report anyone missing plates," Leland said. "I expect he went to an auto wrecker, ostensibly for a part, looked around, and lifted a couple plates from a wreck that won't be missed. He might have found a car on blocks and stolen them. I'm willing to bet they didn't come off a car in active use."

"Now we wait for Todd to make the next move," Jack said.

CHAPTER EIGHTY-SIX

Zero watched with elation when he saw his face plastered all over the TV. He planned to remain anonymous forever, but the attention he intended to avoid was more satisfying that he could have imagined.

He looked in the mirror, not recognizing himself. In the week since he gave the FBI the slip, he grew a close-cropped beard, had the sides of his head shaved with a number-one setting, and shortened his normally longer, curlier hair, dying hair and beard to a bleached-blond surfer look. He looked more like twenty-one than thirty-one.

Suddenly he got more attention from women than ever before. *A demonstration of women's shallowness,* he thought gleefully.

When his current plans were culminated, his younger look would make him geometrically more successful in his second career. He'd have to change his appearance afterward, just to be safe, but he would keep it on the younger side.

"A purple mohawk?" he mused.

Would that attract too much attention? Probably not from the kind of women he wanted to punish, one of the beautiful people. One who had money, youth, and a sense of entitlement. Oh, the arrogance! It would be one who knew she could have anyone she wanted, and when she wanted Zero, she'd pay dearly for that miscalculation.

It was more than three months since Cleveland, and his itch had to be scratched soon.

Much planning went into his next adventure. His preparations were almost complete. The hour of his triumph would arrive in a few more days. He always used the word "exquisite" to describe the experience. Forcing unwanted sex on a woman who would withhold it from a man after she made him desire her was always exquisite. Domination of her body through the creative imposition of his choosing was exquisite. The revival of his object when she imagined death had finally released her, only to know it was starting all over, would be exquisite, too. When death finally came, that was exquisitely exhilarating. It was what he lived for.

Effectuating his plans for Cheri Hancock would be the most-exquisite sensation of all his adventures. Zero took great care to impose pain on his chosen ones. He subjected them to pain that required his genius even to conceive. The pain he planned for Agent Cheri Hancock would be breathtaking in its conception and imposition, almost as breathtaking as her desire to take her last breath, only to know it wouldn't come for a long time. She would beg for it. She would pray for it to Phoebe's godless God to no avail. Ultimately, as the creative pinnacle of his achievements, she would thank him for allowing her the opportunity to end her life. Although it would be painful, she would accept it gratefully.

It would, indeed, be exquisite.

CHAPTER EIGHTY-SEVEN

The entire team assembled in one of the larger conference rooms for an emergency meeting. The extra seats would accommodate top members of the Bureau. As was often the case, they were confident in having delegated such a potentially historic case to Mike Hennessey. Jack, too, was growing in their esteem and confidence based on his past cases.

"I'll let Jack lead off today," Mike began simply.

"We've received Number 69 and Number 70," Jack announced. "Having two together has never happened before. They were mailed together, and Cheri and I agree we're dealing with a double homicide."

"Not two women killed in quick succession at different locations," Cheri added. "We believe Todd's sending us a message. He killed them together. Todd's pathology is rigid. If he sends two Numbers together, it means he killed the two women together."

"The mailing came from Atlanta," Jack said. "There are three possibilities. One is that Todd identified his targets in Atlanta, killed them, and is laying low. Another is that he is doing something entirely new, to make us chase our tails more than we already are, so he sent them to us in advance. Cheri and I agree that such a strategy doesn't fit Todd.

"The other chance is that he's being entirely consistent. As in every case, he mailed the numbers from a location other than where the murders took place. Since they were mailed in Atlanta, the murders were committed someplace we don't know about...maybe.

"I feel that's the situation. Roy and Anita have already looked into multiple murders involving two persons, or even just two missing persons. They're using the ripple method. For Anita's benefit, that means we begin with Atlanta as the epicenter and work our way outward, like dropping a pebble in water. In the southeastern U.S. in the past week, there have been three double murders or disappearances. The first involved a male and a female. We ruled that one out. Even without any details on the other two, I believe I know where Todd is. I'll let Cheri get into the psychobabble of Todd's pathology."

"Psychobabble, indeed," she replied. "Jack, for a guy with a degree in psychology and a lot to say, well.... Lawrence Todd is a crisscross of latent pathologies that came to the surface in early-to-late adolescence and early manhood. His hatred for women is the most dominant.

"We briefed you before on the reasons for that. Next is a kind of lust to dominate the women and control them as his mother controlled him during his development. Speaking of Phoebe Todd, she has been completely uncooperative. But there's sexual lust, too. He can resist but can't deny his sexual appetites. The third is to use what he can control to inflict severe punishment on the women as surrogates for punishing his mother.

"Lastly, he has OCD, Obsessive Compulsive Disorder."

She understood that all of them knew the term, but it was important, though speculative, to have it on the record. All meetings on the case were to be recorded going forward.

"We think this particular facet of his makeup tells us two things. First, it's almost impossible for him to vary his actions from the structure he created. If he mailed the Numbers from Atlanta, he didn't kill them there. Additionally, there hasn't been a double murder yet discovered in Atlanta, at least according to the authorities. Jack has a theory about the second prong of this, so I think he should elaborate."

"Can we hold on for a second?" Leland asked. "If I remember your excellent treatise, Number 60 is believed to have been committed in Honolulu, and the number was mailed from there. How does that fit with your OCD concept?"

Jack sat back confidently to let her handle the question. She glanced at him for the go-ahead.

"If you score two runs and your opponent one, who wins?" she asked. "Todd no doubt wanted to avoid mailing from the site of one of his most-vicious murders, but he had two OCD components in conflict. He found Dr. Bacardi an irresistible target. As one of the foremost pediatricians in Philadelphia, and one on the leading edge, she may have been the only woman to challenge Todd intellectually. According to Armstrong, Todd's mother, was extremely controlling and constantly upbraided him for his average academic performance in spite of his rocket-scientist intelligence. Here was a female in his face, and I doubt he could abide it. She was too irresistible.

"Secondly, there was his self-imposed consistency of rubbing our noses in the timeliness of the mailings. Armstrong told us that Todd was stuck going to Hawaii a week early and staying afterward to handle business he normally didn't have to, based on the illness of the Western Regional Manager. Since that, too, was an OCD parameter he couldn't ignore, the final score was 2-1."

Jack said, "That helps me transition to another, though unrelated, compulsion which tells me where I believe Todd is. He's attempting to demonstrate to himself, us, and his mother, principally, the he *is* mentally superior to his father, the university professor she so methodically castigated. For all his mother's constant harassments, he could surpass his father's accomplishments in a way she would find abhorrent.

"We have to go back to why these Numbers are sent. Most serial murders have an inborn psychological desire to be caught. Sometimes it's a desire to stop the carnage, while some want finally to receive the recognition they feel they deserve for their accomplishments.

"I don't think either of these apply to Todd. He has consistently refrained from giving us any forensic evidence that could be connected to him. Rather than coveting the recognition, he tried to escape detection. Far from wanting to be stopped, he has a strong compulsion perpetually to inflict pain on women. He can't continue to feed his impulses from a jail cell.

"His compulsion is to add to his Numbers until he exceeds any other American serial. After that, he might look beyond our borders for continued motivation. His lust for torture and death is without limit. I believe there's a concentric circle of acts within the overall goal of exceeding what any other serial may have done. Even though he killed a woman, and not a man, the use of the clown suit may have modified a murder by John Wayne Gacy, who entertained children in a clown suit while committing heinous murders of men, because he was homosexual.

"I believe Todd is duplicating another and wants to exceed an accomplishment of Ted Bundy. Bundy broke into a sorority at Florida State University in Tallahassee, which isn't far from Atlanta. He killed two sorority sisters in the Chi Omega house. Todd would never be that bold. It's not because he lacks nerve, but because it doesn't fit his overall goal of killing while demonstrating a superior intellect and having the isolation to inflict repeated torture on his victims. That wouldn't be possible within the confines of a sorority house.

"Two young women from Chi Omega in Tallahassee are missing. I believe they're Numbers 69 and 70, dead by Todd's hands. I've already notified the Tallahassee police. Our team needs to get down there before Todd kills again. I doubt he'll leave Tallahassee until he exceeds Bundy's two Chi Omega murders and can tie or exceed Gary Ridgway's seventy-one."

CHAPTER EIGHTY-EIGHT

As was their habit of late, Jack and Cheri met at some discreet hole-in-the-wall, absent bad food, restaurant for dinner. It seemed less dangerous, as Jack tried to keep his word to Mike, and Cheri tried to help. She would've preferred tearing off his clothes, as she had more than once in the past.

After they perused the menu and ordered, Cheri asked, "Why weren't the tickets to Tallahassee handed out at the meeting?"

"We didn't want to embarrass anyone. Anita has worked hard and done some good things since joining the team, even if unofficially. Mike has the tickets."

"Do you have my tickets? You didn't direct me to his office." Her expression turned hard.

"You aren't going, Cheri. We already know you're target Number 1 on Todd's list. Mike and I feel it would be an unwarranted risk for you and a distraction for the team."

Cheri slammed the table so hard with her open hand, she flipped over an empty salad plate and sent it crashing to the floor, shattering and drawing everyone's attention.

"You and *Mike?* Bullshit!"

"Mike was concerned about your going."

"And you did everything you could to dissuade him? Double bullshit," she said angrily.

"No, I didn't. Mike had some trepidations, which I agree with. I don't want you going, truthfully. It's too risky, and it would shift the emphasis to protecting you."

She was furious. "We had an agreement! We wouldn't let our personal relationship interfere with this case. Do you have any idea how hard it was for me to stay away from you so you could keep your commitment to your boss? And you did it without consulting me?"

"There's more to it than that, and you know it. Bureau policy won't permit it. We already sent your assault down a different track, so you wouldn't be a material witness, not to mention normal Bureau policy. After this, we'll take steps to avoid working on the same cases, as you agreed." He was angry, too, but he was on the defensive.

"I was an integral part of this team you said! Step-by-step from the get-go!" she shouted.

"Cheri, calm down. Mike knew without my telling him we had something going on. I had to fight like hell to keep you on the case after Naples. He had to fudge a bit to convince the Executive Special Agent to keep the assault and murder cases under separate investigations. You can't say we both haven't gone to bat for you!

"Cheri, please listen. When I said those things, they were true, but you hadn't been attacked by Todd once and confronted by him another time. It's a different landscape now!"

He was suddenly alone at the table. Cheri ran toward the door, while he scrambled to pay the check. By the time he paid for the meal they never ate and rushed outside, she already found a cab and was gone.

CHAPTER EIGHTY-NINE

Mike notified everyone their commercial airline tickets were canceled. To get there sooner, they would take a military plane. A group formed on the tarmac, and Jack was surprised to see Cheri ready to board. He went to Mike for an explanation.

"What the hell's going on?" he asked. "We talked this through."

"We've always had an open-door policy, Jack. She went over your head."

"And you acquiesced? I don't believe it. She's Todd's prime target. He failed with her in Naples, then he tracked her to her apartment. He'll pursue her relentlessly until we capture him or put him down. This isn't good judgment on your part!" he almost shouted.

"You must have Dissociative Identity Disorder. Don't you remember arguing that you needed to be by her side to protect her?" Mike, also angry, was tired of being caught between them.

"We didn't know at that point we'd be going to a location Todd chose and where he was lying in wait. If I have DID, then you must've completely lost it."

All of them had to board the aircraft. Onboard, Jack and Mike continued their conversation, while Cheri sat as far from them as possible.

In a low, deliberate voice, forcing his tone to remain calm, Mike said, "Watch it, Jack. We're friends, but I'm still your superior. You'd best change your tone of voice from what I heard on the tarmac. I've taken steps to protect Cheri."

"Like what?"

"You know Neil Duncan from the Atlanta office?"

"I've had contact with him a time or two. He seemed like a good man."

"He was able to see that the guy he followed in Atlanta wasn't the guy going through security. He noticed it at a bit more distance than most. Tallahassee is less than a five-hour drive from Atlanta, and I added him to the task force. He might be able to see Todd in disguise when someone else wouldn't.

"We have a communications truck on the scene near the Chi Omega sorority house. All our agents will be wearing body cams, and several monitors in the truck will display what each sees. Cheri and Duncan will be the two best agents to spot Todd, and she'll be safe in a communications van, locked from the inside, with other agents all around. I assigned her to the safer day shift, too. That's the one I supervise."

"You're forgetting our agreement. I said I'd be at her side as long as she and Todd were at a distance. We both agreed we wouldn't send her into a dangerous situation given her history with Todd. Why'd you change your mind?" Although he spoke softer than before, he was still incensed.

"You forget that I have a longer standing relationship with her. It's different in every way, but she's important to me. I love her in a different way than you do. I suspect she'll be one of our best agents someday. She threatened to resign over this. Normally, at this stage of development with an agent, I would've agreed, but not with her. We both owe her a better shot than that. That's why these relationships juxtapose priorities and are discouraged at the Bureau."

"A little late to pull that one out of your hat," Jack said, simmering.

They both fell silent.

CHAPTER NINETY

When they finally landed in Tallahassee, Mike was informed he had a message waiting and was to meet Duncan at the office of the base commandant.

Mike and Jack went through the perfunctory greetings with Duncan.

"We have all your personnel on their way to their hotel, three or four together, in unmarked cars. Ms. Hancock will room with a female agent from our Atlanta office. Mike already explained the heightened security issues around her.

"I hate to hit you with this right off the bat, but the Tallahassee police found the bodies of two Chi Omega students in a nature park a little less than ten miles from the Florida State Campus. Both were bound with Gorilla tape, their hands behind them, with two Ping Pong balls in each of their mouths. They never had a chance." He shook his head.

After Duncan gave them the coordinates of the location, Mike called Tim Stein but couldn't raise him on his cell, so he left word at the hotel. When they heard back from Tim, Mike directed Stein to the murder scene, a heavily wooded area off an asphalt road in the park, and told him to take charge of the crime scene whether the locals liked it or not.

"Shall I tell you the method used?" Jack asked. "They were strangled with nylon stockings."

"Just like Bundy, eh?" Mike asked. "This time, a garrote was used in each instance. The bodies were found early this morning soon

311

after we boarded our flight. It took a bit of time to get someone from Chi Omega to go to the morgue to make positive IDs. I've got a car waiting to take us to the Leon County ME's office, where an autopsy is being done." Mike saw he took some of the wind out of Jack's sails.

Getting into the waiting car, they were off. Less than half an hour later, they were introduced to Reagan Dudley, Chief Assistant ME.

"I hope I'll do," she said. "The big boss is off fishing. I expect he'll be headed back now. He's at the Michigan's Upper Peninsula, so I don't know when to expect him. He told me to carry on."

Dr. Dudley was absolutely stunning, easily six-feet tall, very slender with a tiny waist. Her black hair and elongated face gave her a look most people would remember, and she seemed out of place in a morgue.

"We understand a garrote was used for strangulation," Jack said.

"The garrotes were left at the scene. There were no finger-prints. They were made of women's hose, and attached to sturdy pieces of hardwood to twist the hose."

That sounded odd. Todd never left evidence at the scene.

"Were the women strangled just once, or were there repeated attempts?" Jack asked.

"Strange you should ask." She seemed a bit incredulous. "From the look of the ligature marks on their necks, each was strangled repeatedly. Bruise marks show up differently postmortem. They aren't as pronounced, because of more limited blood flow. We think each was strangled to the point of unconsciousness and revived several times. It makes the most sense, from an elapsed-time perspective, that the perpe-trator was alternating from one to the other.

"Both women were freshmen. One was eighteen, the other sev-enteen." She shook her head.

"Were they raped?" Mike asked.

"I've done only a preliminary examination. It appears there was a significant amount of vaginal tearing, more than would be normal for consensual intercourse. So far, however, there's no obvious semen. The chances are the rapist used a condom."

"That doesn't fit our guy, does it?" Mike asked tentatively, knowing it wasn't what Jack wanted to hear.

"I know this isn't your territory," Jack asked the ME, "but what do you know about the crime scene? Anything?"

"Only that this guy had brass balls. It appears he alternately raped and strangled each. It took some time. He did it in deep, thick foliage just a few feet from a dirt path on one side and an asphalt road on the other."

"If the women had been strangled with just the hose but without the wood as a tool to tighten it repeatedly, would the murderer have been able to accomplish the same thing? I don't mean in terms of death, but the repeated strangulations alternating between the women?"

"What a question!" Dr. Dudley said. "They train you well at the Bureau. I hadn't thought of that. Based on the ligature marks on their necks, each went through three or four rounds of...what I would call withheld strangulation. The murderer would've exhausted himself and cost himself time, too. The wood pieces made his job easier and faster."

In amazement, she asked, "May I ask what prompted that question?"

Mike knew where Jack was going with that line of thought, but he should tell the doctor.

Jack looked at Mike almost triumphantly and said, "One policeman to another? Someone around here will make the connection anyway, maybe an old-timer, like the doc who's off fishing."

Jack glanced back the ME. "I'll say just three things—two coeds, Chi Omega, and strangulations."

"Bundy!" she said very soberly. "It's a copycat."

"The difference here is that Bundy was into necrophilia. He often strangled the women with the stocking before committing the sex act. Because he strangled the two women once apiece, he didn't need the wood for the garotte.

"Others will put that together. I want you to characterize this as a one-timer, just another double homicide. Once the new media picks up on Chi Omega, it'll be all over the place. Maybe we can keep the lid on it for a short while.

"It would help us a great deal, Doctor, to catch the man who did this," he pleaded. He once told Cheri she might have to turn up the heat. Maybe it was his turn.

"What about the other Chi Omega coeds who are at risk?" she asked.

"We already have people stationed unobtrusively all around the sorority house," Mike said. "It's about as secure as Fort Knox. We have a much better chance of catching this guy before he kills again with your cooperation than without it."

She nodded slowly, thinking hard, looking each agent in the eye. "I'm glad you mentioned the necrophilia. I couldn't be sure, but I thought there was less bleeding than one would expect with the degree of vaginal tearing I observed. My best guess is he raped them and strangled them slowly, on an alternating basis, then he raped them again once they were dead. I think it was just once.

"The vaginal tearing would be consistent with multiple entries by the perp. Since each of the victims displayed free-flowing blood from the vaginal tearing at times, and dissipated flow on another, I believe some part of the rape was probably *postmortem*. If you're right about the Bundy copycat, he would have wanted to duplicate Bundy's necrophilia, as I understand was done to many of his earlier victims, including the earlier Chi Omega women."

"You're well-informed about Bundy," Jack said. "As forensic pathologists go, I have to compliment you. Bundy's murders of the Chi Omega women, however, didn't involve necrophilia, but several of his other murders did. It wasn't unusual for him to decapitate a victim and take the head home, apply makeup to it, and then engage in masturbation using the heads for stimulus. The four Chi Omega women were bludgeoned, but Bundy only killed two and left hurriedly after just half an hour. That allowed insufficient time for necrophilia. Here, I don't think our guy had either the time or the inclination for decapitation."

"We're pursuing a specific suspect for these crimes," Mike explained. "Our guy normally engages in sodomy. Was there any evidence of that here?"

"No."

"The absence of sodomy could be meant to confuse us, but I don't think so," Jack said thoughtfully. "Instead, I believe it was intended to leave a further indicium that was consistent with Bundy's repertoire here, a confirmation he wanted to be sure we understood. I'm certain our man won't be satisfied until he has topped Bundy's Chi Omega body count. I predict another one soon."

Meeting with the ME first gave the team new avenues of inquiry with the locals investigating the murder scene. Normally, Jack reversed the process, but because he felt his team presumptively knew the perp's identity and while the autopsy was in progress, Jack went along with Duncan's suggestion to start with Dr. Dudley. Since the crime scene was still being scrutinized by the locals, he felt it was best to wait.

Jack figured they might be too far along for Tim realistically to take charge on the local level. Coming to the case late could arouse animosity from the locals. His instructions to Stein notwithstanding, Jack felt it was best to leave them alone. He was confident Stein would use good judgment.

After the inquiries with Dr. Dudley, she directed them to the police headquarters, adjacent to the morgue. Thanking her, they moved on.

At headquarters, they learned the supposed kidnapper was seen by students who knew the victims. It was from too great a distance for a usable identification, but they saw their sorority sisters give a lift to a blonde man with a crutch and cast on his right leg. The witnesses said the two women drove a white sedan. A white Toyota Camry was found at the scene, and their forensics team was going over it very carefully.

"We have to let Tim know ASAP about the Camry, in case the auto description wasn't mentioned at the crime scene," Mike suggested.

"Knowing Tim, he would probably sniff that out," Jack replied, "but you're right. It's better to be sure. By the time Tim gets to the car, it might mean being filled in by the locals. If they're as good as Reagan Dudley, that might be good enough."

He and Mike were in full investigative mode, their earlier confrontation set aside for the moment.

On the way back to the hotel, Jack called Tim and told him to take charge of the Camry.

"I was surprised at two things that I think were meant to mislead us," Jack mused. "Todd has never left any evidence at a crime scene before, but those garrotes were left deliberately. Also, he has never, that we know of, used a condom before. Our assumption was that he was ineffectual bordering on impotent if he tried to use one. That may've been wrong."

"Or this isn't your guy," Duncan said.

"Oh, yes, it is." Jack was adamant.

"Tell us why," Mike said.

"I can give four reasons. First, the thing that brought us down here was two Numbers in a single envelope, practically a road map to his intentions. Initially, he wanted to equal Bundy's two at Chi Omega in this specific instance. He selected it, because it was within short range of Atlanta.

"Second the nylon garrotes were left to confirm that. That's how Bundy killed the two Chi Omega girls forty-plus years ago, with nylon hose, although he bludgeoned three others unconscious without killing them—two at Chi Omega and another at a nearby home.

"Third, the method of abduction. Bundy raped the two women in their sorority dorm room. Our guy didn't abduct them. In prior murders, Bundy wore an arm cast supported by a sling. Todd simply substituted a leg cast and crutch. The arm and sling might have rung too many bells, making them an unnecessary risk. Using a fake cast was his MO for Bundy's murders. He enlisted the victims' empathy and then murdered them.

"Fourth, the repeated near strangulation, revival, and repetition until he either killed them accidentally or grew bored with the process. That's Todd's moniker. It's him, all right.

"There's another reason he may be picking up Bundy's legacy. While Little's ninety-three and Ridgway's seventy-one murders are considered the top two serial killers, Bundy confessed to thirty-three murders, but some in law enforcement speculated he may have killed as many as one hundred. Todd's trying to cover all the bases."

CHAPTER NINETY-ONE

After interviewing with Jack Garvey at the AAUS tradeshow, Zero knew he faced an agile adversary. He felt certain he fooled Garvey, and the interview took the path his superior intellect wanted. A few days later, he found Garvey going over his records at AFI with that bitch at his side, the gorgeous one who knew it.

He was on the brink of exacting his rapturous revenge on Agent Cheryl Hancock. Like everything he attempted, it was planned in excruciating detail, with every contingency covered. His anticipation was so intense, containing it was almost impossible. He would exact a price from Supervising Agent Garvey and embarrass him by carrying out his plan right under their noses.

He reminisced about Numbers 69 and 70. Since Bundy killed two sorority sisters from Chi Omega in 1978, his oft-used technique of feigning injury with a fake arm cast and a sling became infamous. It would be even more so at Chi Omega, although there was no certainty the youngsters would know it. A simple switch from the arm to the leg, and *voilà!* He improved his odds.

When the two young coeds stopped at a red light, where he tactically positioned himself at a bus stop, he feigned losing his balance and falling. He appeared to lunge at a nearby bench. When the girls drove up, he clumsily dropped his crutch. The coeds pulled over and helped him get situated on the bench.

"Are you OK?" asked the first.

"Oh, sure, sure." He winked. "I'm not used to this crutch. Still haven't figured out how I'll get on the bus with it."

"Where are you going?" the second asked.

"Oh, I don't want to put you out. Where are you headed?"

"We're going to the mall. We just moved into our sorority house and need a few things," the recipient of his wink said brightly, thinking he was cute.

"That's amazing. I was going to take the bus to the mall. It probably wouldn't be a problem if it weren't for the crutch and this darn bag. I think that's what put me off balance."

They tossed his bag into the middle of the back seat and helped him in beside it, handing him the crutch. Zero insisted he didn't want to separate the two roommates and would ride in the back of the late model, rich-kid, Camry Sport.

A few blocks away, he pulled out his Ruger 9mm, a weapon easy to conceal but powerful, and told them to take the next left—or else. He directed them to a wildlife preserve he scouted earlier. There was no foot traffic at that time of day. He made them turn off into an oft-used natural clearing alongside the road.

They got out, and Zero duct taped their hands behind them. He walked them into the heavy bushes that would conceal them in the pre-selected clearing, reached into a bag, and withdrew a large burlap tarp big enough for both of them to lie on. He staked them on the tarp side-by-side, their arms still underneath them, with stakes under their armpits and their ankles spread apart to facilitate the impending rapes. After inserting two Ping Pong balls into their mouths, he taped them shut.

In his perverse way, he put one Ping Pong in a victim's mouth if he wanted to hear their low, muffled screams, but he used two, making it impossible for anything to be heard.

He promised he'd only rape them, not kill them, if they didn't resist. Once they were unable to resist, he told them they were going to die. He fed on their fear, like a hungry lion feeding on a newly killed carcass.

Zero was ready to begin a new life filled with new conquests, new ecstasy, and more death. He had no time to cleanse their bodies of semen as usual. He hated condoms, but he needed to prevent anything that might connect him to the victims. With no forensic evidence, a conviction would be difficult to obtain.

He raped one, then put on a new condom and raped the other, being careful to place the two used condoms in a sealed bag he would discard later. His latex-covered hands put a garrote made of small but sturdy blocks of wood and a stretch of nylon hose around each coed's neck. He thought back to how he strangled Number 1, how satisfying it was slowly to tighten his latex-covered hands and render her unconscious, then immediately withdraw and let her regain consciousness, only to do it again.

The first coed looked at him, eyes bulging, as he incrementally tightened the garrote as he raped her, until all went gray, and then black. It wasn't permanent black, though.

He moved to the other girl and every so slowly raped her and drained away her consciousness, then stopped the instant she lost complete awareness. He thought he would inflict that twice on each girl, but he prematurely finished off one. Finishing the second, he worried about his potential exposure.

Following one of Bundy's practices, he raped each of the dead bodies once again, sealing the used condoms in a plastic bag he took with him.

He walked 100 feet to a pond wearing oversized shoes and waded into the shoulder-deep center, dropping his weighted bag in what he surmised was the deepest water. He waded out of the pond in a different place where dry shoes of his own size waited, then he put them on and walked back to the Camaro, sitting on asphalt a short distance from the entrance to the preserve.

At the car, he had dry clothes waiting. One mile from where he left the lifeless Chi Omegas, he disposed of the wet clothing, then he changed into dry clothes and drove away. Fibers from his own clothing, kept separate at all times from the deceased coeds', could not incriminate him once disposed of.

CHAPTER NINETY-TWO

Two days after the team began their Chi Omega surveillance, there was still no sign of Todd. Jack, whose track record warranted being listened to, assured everyone Todd would emerge. Meanwhile gathering evidence on the Chi Omega murders was top priority.

Tim Stein tried to pull rank on the locals by impressing upon them that the murders were part of an ongoing FBI investigation. The Tallahassee police and the Leon County Sheriff's office had two murders that normally would fall under their individual jurisdictions. A major part of the wildlife preserve was outside the city of Tallahassee, but the Camry was parked on the right side of the paved road, which was the dividing line between the city and the county.

Tim Stein's reputation in forensics had people looking to him for guidance. Incredibly, the ME still hadn't returned and was apparently still fishing. Impressions of the Camry tire tracks were added to those collected in Atlanta. Since the Camry belonged to Sonja Carlson, one of the murdered Chi Omegas, it led to an in-depth forensic examination. Eyewitness testimony put the perp in the Camry.

There was no blood on the interior, so they assumed no attack took place in the vehicle. Many fibers were found in the car that could have come from multiple sources, most of which were probably not related to the crimes. It would take significant time to sort that all out. Fibers from Zero's wet clothing before they were wet were probably among them. Possibly even a small sample of skin or oil from one fiber would include DNA. DNA identification had become increasingly sophisticated over the years, and blood or a large sample was no longer needed.

Too many people walked back and forth on the earth between the Camry and where the naked, staked bodies of the two young women were found. In the effort to gather evidence, some had probably been destroyed.

Tim found size-fourteen shoeprints leading away from the staked bodies, but he also noticed the way the impressions were formed revealed the person who wore them had an actual shoe size smaller than fourteen. The person was deliberately trying to deceive whoever found the tracks. He already knew that Todd wore size 11½ from shoes recovered from the search warrant.

Tim followed the oversized shoeprints to the edge of a pond. He ordered scuba divers to look for evidence in the murky water. Tim carefully circumscribed the perimeter of the pond, searching for a place where someone may have left the water in size-fourteen shoes. Instead, he found shoes in Todd's size exiting the pond about a third of the way around.

Impressions of both shoe sizes were taken. The team's job was to find who'd been wearing them. Stein and the rest of the Bureau's team thought Todd wore them both. Once Stein put that theory forward, the other forensics personnel fell in behind. He and everyone on the team continued to be impressed, although not with any admiration, of Todd's preparation and planning.

After a couple days of the locals examining the crime scene and concluding there was nothing more to discover, Stein walked up and down the area, gradually expanding the perimeter, looking for an error on the part of his quarry.

About one mile from where the Chi Omega sisters met their horrible ends, he found something he recognized. It was part of a tire track off the road, indicating the other part of the left rear tire had been on the asphalt. A cut in the tread matched the impression taken from the used car lot in Atlanta. He was elated. Finally, they had evidence directly tied to Todd.

Stein was almost carried on the shoulders of the rest of the team when he reported the news at their daily powwow that evening.

"The tracks were a mile away from the scene," he said. "Lots of people hike in that preserve. Will the distance be an issue?"

"It's the total picture," Jack said. "Before we left Quantico, you and Cheri," he saw her avert her eyes at the mention of her name, "found what you prioritized as sixty-eight murders fitting the total picture. A few could be off, but his presence around all of them is very strong circumstantial evidence. He leaves his job and apparently flees, or disappears, and now we can add tire tracks belonging to his car.

"In a court of law," Jack said, showing his experience from law school, "the jury can be instructed that flight shows a 'consciousness of guilt.' Then there are the tire tracks. We're close to a winnable case." Smiling, he looked at her, but she looked away as if something behind her demanded her attention.

CHAPTER NINETY-THREE

Zero carefully surveilled those who were surveilling him. He rented an apartment near Chi Omega, paying the first month's rent and security deposit in cash and using a fake ID with a photo to match his altered appearance. He was as resourceful as the agents hypothesized. Across the street from Chi Omega was a parking lot, and on both sides of Chi Omega and the lot were dormitories and administrative FSU buildings.

He went to several no-kill shelters, using one of his available IDs and adopted one dog at each. He would pose as a dog walker. With his close-cropped hair on the side, longer hair on top worn like a punk rocker, and new blond color, he looked nothing like his former self except for his height. Dog walking, the perfect cover, would allow him to saunter, looking around casually and spot the agents who in no way looked like they fit on the FSU campus.

Figuring the Camaro he bought was known to his adversaries, he bought a Rent-a-Wreck truck with camper shell, stowed the Camaro in his assigned underground parking spot with its changed plates, and camped out in the shell of his truck while watching the comings and goings of the agents who were watching him.

From the way Jack and Cheri looked at each other when he surprised them at AFI, and from comments Armstrong made at the cocktail hour, Zero assumed the two agents had something going. It was very rewarding to him that, with Cheri's demise, Jack Garvey would pay a dear price, too.

Zero knew to protect Cheri from him, the Bureau took extraordinary steps. A van with a decal promoting *Superior Plumbing* on the side was undoubtedly where their mobile communications center was located. Cheri was assigned to the day shift, imagining that was safer. At the end of the shift, an agent got into the driver's seat and drove away, only to be replaced by a similar van promoting *Comcast Cable*, carrying the FBI's night crew.

Zero easily followed Superior Plumbing to the Hyatt Regency Hotel, which Mike and Jack's joint team used as central command. There was no chance to intercept Cheri there. She had a female agent for a roommate and other agents' rooms clustered around her. One of the reasons the FBI chose the Hyatt was the large, open foyer encompassing much of the eating space provided by multiple restaurants at the hotel.

Mike instructed them to go to dinner within the Marriott and in groups. Eventually, however, Zero found a way to surmount all those obstacles. One thing worked to his advantage. Cheri worked a twelve-hour day shift, while Jack had the night shift. In '79 when Bundy killed his victims, he did it at night and in the sorority house.

Based on that, Jack assumed Todd's next attempt would be at night. Jack wanted to check in with the day crew and give any new instructions to agents coming on duty. That left a short period of time before the night crew arrived when both Cheri and Jack were together.

Zero knew the placement of every agent on the day and night crews and that they changed shifts at dusk. He prepared to tie Gary Ridgway's postulated seventy-one kills with his third kill on the FSU campus within view of Chi Omega, topping Bundy. Making that tie with the exquisite experience that would be the end of Cheri Hancock would be his crowning achievement.

CHAPTER NINETY-FOUR

Jack placed an agent near each of the of the Chi Omega sorority house's three entrances. The building had typical front and rear entrances and an emergency exit at the end of a long corridor with rooms on each side. Each room was shared by two sorority sisters. The emergency exit was on the first floor at the end of the corridor.

An agent watching the emergency exit pretended to be an HVAC repairman in the day, with another agent stationed on the roof of a non-Greek dorm adjacent to Chi Omega at night. Each had what appeared to be a toolbox but actually contained a collapsed rifle that included scopes for day and night vision. The agents could assemble their rifles in seconds. Although they couldn't cover all locations from their positions, they could see most and were able to communicate instantly with anyone on the team. The rear door was watched by an agent who appeared to be a student repairing a motorcycle.

The front door was visible from the communications van. Each agent outside the van had a Kevlar vest and body cam completely hidden from view. Monitors inside the van had views of all the body cams. Whoever was in the van could see everything the agents saw in real time.

In addition to Agent Duncan and Hancock in the communications van, another agent, who intentionally appeared to be napping, was in the parking lot across the street from Chi Omega. He was to respond to any potential sighting of Todd or any exigent circumstance. Jack, a football guy, considered that man his safety.

It was still half an hour before the shift change when Jack opened the door and slid in next to the parking lot agent, who Todd spotted days before. Zero was amused that he and the agent used nearly the same vantage point to watch the sorority house.

Twelve-hour shifts were necessary to provide twenty-four-hour surveillance with the personnel. Some agents were called back to Atlanta after the first forty-eight hours. Zero realized the timing for his plan was nearly perfect. Garvey was sure that any attempt would be later at night, conforming to what Bundy did.

After twelve hours, the agents' attention would be wavering, but they were well-trained at Quantico. Still, fatigue was fatigue.

After touching base with the parking-lot guy, Jack left the vehicle and took a circuitous route to speak to the motorcycle repairman. Jack headed for his normal nighttime assignment in the bushes halfway between the motorcycle guy and the communications van. His position was obscured by the van.

As he approached his hiding spot, a campus police officer came toward him.

"Good evening, Sir," he said, staring down at his clipboard. "You don't appear to be a student here. I was just looking over a list of new faculty this year. Could I ask your name?"

It took a moment for Jack to recognize the voice, and that was too long. Before he could react, he was knocked out by Zero's Ruger striking him in the temple.

The image on the monitor tracking Jack's body cam showed a blue uniform from the shoulders down, then the picture careened toward the ground and went black when it hit the grass.

"Jack Garvey's down!" Duncan broadcast to the other agents. "Agent down! One hundred yards southeast of Chi Omega! Agent down!"

Neil Duncan, looking to his right, saw the rear doors of the communications van wide open, and Cheri was gone.

"Agent Hancock has left the van!" he broadcast. "Hancock's on her way to assist! Intercept Hancock!"

Neil's first instinct was to pursue, but, if he did, the team would suddenly be without communication or coordination. Instead, he went to the rear of the van to close and lock the doors.

Like two vehicles heading toward each other, the campus police officer and Cheri closed the distance in half the time. By the time she recognized the officer as Todd, his Ruger drawn as if responding to an emergency, he had her.

"Well, well, *moi cheri*, we meet again." His poor French was accompanied by a grin of malignant evil.

Zero spun her around, holstered his gun, and placed a knife to the right side of her throat, where the carotid artery throbbed.

"Our carriage awaits!" he declared. "I've always detested handguns. So unromantic, so quick, so not fun!"

Cheri fought like a cornered animal, ignoring his threats. Zero, stronger, easily dragged her to his car, a trickle of blood running down her throat.

Zero and his prey were just around the corner from Chi Omega. Dusk had turned to an overcast night with limited visibility.

"Freeze, Todd," a familiar voice said.

Zero didn't need a clear evening to recognize that voice. "I thought you'd be out a lot longer, Agent Garvey. You'd better have your other agents back off, or I'll slit her throat from ear to ear while you watch."

"Duncan, tell everyone to back off. Do it now!"

"OK, Jack." After a brief pause, Duncan said. "They're pulled back, Jack, but not far. Our roof guy has an infrared scope on his rifle, but there's a tree in the way."

Todd's back was to the Rent-a-Wreck truck with Cheri directly in front of him. Jack was the only agent in position to shoot.

"You're a tough dude, Jack," Zero said in admiration.

"You don't have to hurt her, Mr. Todd."

"Oh, but I do. First, I don't want to live in a cage for the rest of my life. Of course, they have the death penalty in Florida, not to mention several other states where I enjoyed my hobby."

"Neither of those things need to happen to you, Mr. Todd."

"I'm no longer Lawrence Todd. I am Zero."

"You know Agent Hancock and I work in the BAU, the behavioral unit. Several analysts maintain you're clearly insane. I'll testify for you myself." He slowly moved to get an acceptable shot.

"Stop moving! If I don't take her with me, I'll fall short of both Little and Ridgway. That would make me a third-rate serial murderer. My mother told my dad he was a third-rate professor. There's nothing third-rate about Zero!"

Jack was a good shot even by Bureau standards. He had only once fired his sidearm as an agent, and that time there was no hostage, particularly one for whom he had feelings.

Zero's head was almost directly behind Cheri's. All Jack could see was his right eye socket. Two inches to the right, and he would kill Cheri.

"Things seem to be building to a climax, Supervising Special Agent Garvey," Zero said in contempt. "Let me introduce myself. Lawrence Todd died with Drake Todd, but Zero was born. When they write about me, remind them that I am Zero. Unfortunately, I won't have the exacerbated pleasure I anticipated, the slow build to a triumphant climax, just a quick, lethal slice." He smiled.

Jack fired, sending his bullet through Zero's right eye. To his horror, Zero anticipated him and sliced Cheri's neck wide open. Blood shot out in a ghastly, life-spilling spurt from her carotid artery.

"Agent down! Agent down! Get me an ambulance now!" Jack screamed.

"I had one standing by," Duncan said. "It's pulling up now."

CHAPTER NINETY-FIVE

Jack ran to an unconscious Cheri, her life's blood gushing like an open fire hydrant. He knew he should put pressure on an open wound, so he ripped off his shirt and pressed it against the wound. It was soaked in seconds with no stoppage of flow.

"Stay with me, Cheri! Stay with me!" He knew she couldn't hear him. He was supposed to be knowledgeable about his craft, but he never felt so helpless.

From the recesses of his mind came a case involving a similar wound. With one hand behind her head, he forced it forward in an attempt to stem the blood flow.

An ambulance with *FSU Hospital* emblazed on the side arrived, and paramedics rushed out.

"We'll take it from here," the EMT said.

"I'm going with you," Jack said.

"I'm sorry, you can't...."

"I'm the goddamn FBI, and I'm goddamn going with you!" He jumped into the back of the ambulance after Cheri's gurney was loaded, and they were off.

The EMTs pulled out rolls of gauze and towels to apply pressure, once again to no affect, as the artery gushed blood.

Jack tried to pull her head forward again.

"FBI or no, you have to let us do our job!" the man said.

Jack drew his gun. "I don't have time to argue. Put cushions behind her head and close the neck as much as possible. If you don't, there'll be two dead bodies when we reach the morgue."

They arrived at the hospital within two minutes, where doctors were waiting. Jack jumped down, the EMTs still too terrified to alter his instructions. A doctor who appeared to be in charge grabbed the front of the gurney and took Cheri away, her head still bent forward.

Jack walked to an empty chair in ER and collapsed. As much as he wanted to be with Cheri, he knew he wouldn't be allowed in the operating room and would just be in the way. Completely overcome and drained, he didn't know what to do except sit there and feel dizzy and fight the urge to pass out.

Duncan soon arrived, and then the other members of the team trickled in. Mike, who'd been at the Hyatt, was the first to arrive from the hotel. Agents always felt kinship with each other, especially the more serious the condition. Most knew Jack and Cheri had feelings for each other, though neither said a word. Some things just showed.

Everyone was suddenly fixated on a fully sheeted gurney being wheeled into ER. Jack ran up and pulled off the sheet, freezing when he saw the face. He didn't know how to react. He spat in Zero's face, and the staff immediately took the gurney down the hall.

Duncan and most of the others settled Jack back in his chair, all placing a hand briefly on his shoulder without speaking.

After a moment Mike asked, "How bad is it, Jack?"

"Bad. I'm praying like I never prayed before. It'll take a miracle, Mike." He lowered his face into his hands.

Mike never thought he'd see such a reaction from Jack Garvey, and not because he ever felt the man was unfeeling. Mike felt as all of them did when a comrade fell.

Jack's body shook uncontrollably. Mike feared for his "niece."

When Mike asked about Cheri's condition at the ER desk, all the staff could say was she was in surgery. He would be notified as soon as there was news.

Returning to the seat beside Jack, he sat quietly. Jack composed himself somewhat by then. When he lifted his head, He saw

Duncan, Rogers, and others from their detail sitting nearby. All were silent. One prayed with a rosary.

Seeing their somber faces, he knew they were his friends—Mike Hennessey, Tim Stein, Leland Burns, Neil Duncan, and the oft-abused Roy Rogers. There should have been comfort with that thought, but there wouldn't be any for him until he knew Cheri would make it. Jack recognized the agent praying with her rosary was Cheri's roommate in Florida. Jack believed in miracles, and he never wanted one so fervently.

Mike looked almost as forlorn as Jack, and he knew why.

"I know we clashed over whether Cheri should come or not," Jack said softly. "You made the right call. We both know there was no holding her back. She would have booked her own flight and showed up to challenge you to a duel. She couldn't step back from this any more than the rest of us. She had to be here, because he attacked her. It was wrong of me to try."

Mike looked him in the eye and didn't believe it. Maybe he would someday.

They waited, hoped, and prayed. No one knew, the longer the surgery took, if it was a hopeful sign or one of desperation.

Five hours passed. The hospital staff, having a vague idea of the situation, encouraged the agents to visit the hospital cafeteria. They promised to notify them the instant there was anything to report.

Some asked about a hospital chapel, but ultimately no one moved.

Finally, two automatic doors opened, and a doctor stepped through, his scrubs splattered with blood. Exhausted, he somehow managed a weak, whimsical, half-smile.

"I'm Dr. Lincoln, a cardio-pulmonary microsurgeon. That means I can sew things together under a microscope that look too small to be worked on. Your young lady will be fine." He broke into a wide grin.

Jack's gasp sounded like air escaping from a tire. He couldn't speak, and his eyes welled with tears, although he fought them back.

"Someone pulled a gun on our EMTs, I understand?"

Jack finally found his voice. "That was me."

"We have some sheepish EMTs in the back. You saved her life. No doubt about it. You have medical training?"

"Not at all."

"Then how...?"

"There was a serial murder case in San Diego, man named David Allen Lucas. His favorite method of dispatching his victims was to slit their throats down to the anterior surface of the cervical vertebrae. One of them lived to testify against him. He tossed her into a ditch, and her head fell forward, closing the carotid artery on itself. That stayed with me, I guess."

"Ms. Hancock is in ICU and will be for a while. After that, she'll need extensive recuperation and rehab. It'll be some time before she can talk. After micro-surgery, we're keeping her head immobile and sedating her to keep her in a coma. You can see her in a few days, but she won't be able to speak for a while.

"I feel like I did a fine job. She'll probably end up with a very fine scar, similar to what she would have after a scalpel cut. Whatever was used on her was nearly as sharp, which is good.

"She'll need a lot of emotional support. From what I can see looking around, she'll have it."

He lightly chucked Jack's shoulder and left.

CHAPTER NINETY-SIX

It was two days in ICU before the doctors allowed Cheri to return to a conscious state, then another day before she was moved to a private room, and still another day before she was allowed visitors.

Her head was encased in a contraption with shiny metal bars that functioned like a cage, restraining her neck movement. Dr. Emmanuel Cash, another cardiovascular surgeon, explained what seemed obvious—micro-surgery was delicate, and those contraptions were for Cheri's protection.

The four days Jack spent waiting to see her were the longest in his life. The rest of the team returned to Atlanta or Quantico. Cheri was under orders not to speak.

Jack refused to go anywhere unless she could go with him. Her room was filled with flowers from well-wishers at the Bureau. She was an only child. Her mother died from cancer just after she graduated high school. Her father, Tom Hancock, was there, but the doctors allowed only one visitor at a time. The temptation to look from one person to the other wasn't anything the doctors were willing to permit.

Jack knew of Tom from Mike. Tom was Mike's Managing Special Agent when Mike was a Supervising Agent, and they became good friends. Tom was the quintessential Bureau man, a real by-the-book guy, tough as nails, but compassionate when called for. Jack was glad to meet him and put a face to the legend. Tom knew of Jack from Cheri's letters. She felt email was too impersonal for someone she loved.

Tom greeted Jack warmly when he arrived at FSU Hospital the day after Zero's attack. Being a Bureau man, he had no recriminations against Jack. Mike already tried to take responsibility for Cheri's being exposed to danger, but Tom didn't buy that, either.

"Nice to meet you, Jack." He grasped Jack's hand firmly. "My little girl thinks a lot of you."

"I think a lot of her, sir." Jack wasn't quite able to manage a smile under the circumstances.

Tom smiled first. "More than a lot, if my little girl isn't exaggerating. Don't mind my calling her that. Here she is, a very competent Bureau agent, but she'll always be my little girl." A shadow briefly crossed his face.

Tom was allowed to see her first. When he came out, Jack asked, "Please, Tom. How's she doing?"

Tom looked down at the floor for a moment, then he looked up with his lips pursed in a way that reminded Jack of Tom Selleck. "Cheri's tough, much like her mom. She'll come through this just fine. It'll take time to work through some things and absorb what happened and reconcile herself with it. The physical recuperation will be the least of it. Trauma like this changes you. Still, it won't be long before our Cheri is back."

Jack was pleased to hear Tom call her *our* Cheri. He hoped she would still be his for a long time. Jack wondered how much psychological damage was done. Her injury was severe. He'd seen amputees hit by IEDs who suffered PTSD and wondered if Cheri would have to face that. An image of Congresswoman Ilhan Omar trivializing PTSD came to his mind, but he let it go. Cheri was strong, and he and Tom and the rest of the Bureau would be there for her.

Roy wanted badly to be there. He and Cheri started at the Bureau together and quickly formed a close friendship. Mike knew Jack was waiting at the hospital, while Tom was on his way. Mike felt it best if Roy went back to Quantico and ordered him to return.

"I understand you saved my little girl's life," Tom said. "Mike told me how you applied what you learned from the Lucas case. I'm forever grateful."

Jack squirmed but was saved from replying when Dr. Lincoln emerged from Cheri's room.

"Our patient is doing just fine," he announced. "Mr. Garvey, I already advised her dad that we need to keep these visits short. Cheri's still heavily medicated and isn't permitted to even attempt to speak. She has a small notebook and pen, which has to suffice for now. Limit that, too. She holds it up to write, but the temptation is to look down at it. The less of that, the better.

"She became a bit emotional when she saw her dad. Don't think it'll be any different with you. Do your best to calm her, and keep it short. Keep a lid on your own emotions, too. That's a must.

"Moving her eyes should be kept to a minimum, because it increases the likelihood she'll unintentionally move her neck. Stand at the foot of her bed. The head of the bed has been raised, so she can see you more easily without movement.

"You can go in now."

Jack stood there for a moment, trying to collect himself. He and Tom exchanged a quick glance, and he walked the short distance down the hall to her room.

Jack put on his Novocain face and didn't react when he saw the headgear or the many wires and IVs going all over. Her eyes welled up immediately, and tears ran down her face.

"Now, now. None of that." Jack grabbed tissues and dried her cheeks through the cage. "I didn't know someone could have all these attachments and still be so beautiful."

Cheri wrote on her pad and turned it around to show him. *Don't make me laugh. It hurts.* She turned it back and wrote again, then showed him words that simply read, *I love you.*

Jack had an inspiration and gently took the pad and pen from her. He wrote, *I love you, too, very much.* He handed it back, and she acknowledged with her eyes.

She wrote again. *I'm sorry I was so stubborn. You were only trying to protect me. Doctor tells me you saved my life.*

He took the pad and wrote, *We'll have none of that. I like your dad. We're both here for you. I'm hoping he'll let me take care of you forever.*

Her expression brightened considerably when she saw that. If she could have, she would have jumped out of the bed.

Instead, she wrote, *This is the 21st century. What are you going to do, ask him for my hand?*

He wrote back, *I already have.*

CHAPTER NINETY-SEVEN

As Cheri's recuperation progressed, she was soon able to speak. It would take time before she sounded like her normal self, but fortunately, her larynx wasn't damaged. The doctors said it was probably residual hesitation on her part in using her throat. She worked at it and quickly overcame it.

By the time he was ready to leave the hospital, she wore Jack's engagement ring.

Dr. Lincoln suggested they return to Quantico by car. The changes in air pressure on a plane weren't dangerous, but the eustachian tubes went from her ears to her throat, and they might cause her discomfort she would be best to avoid, even if only psychologically. Knowing the kind of mettle Cheri was made of, Jack knew that problem wouldn't exist for long.

It was understandable that she felt self-conscious about her scar. It was a thin line six inches long across the right side of her neck where the carotid artery was almost completely severed. The scar was so thin, because Todd's buck knife was honed as sharp as a scalpel. A duller knife would've done a lot more damage.

A nurse wheeled Cheri down to where Jack brought his rental car for their trip back to Virginia. At first, conversation was inane chatter. Jack, placing a call to Mike, asked him to explore a statement that would minimize the fallout on Will Armstrong's AFI. He and Cheri felt sympathetic for the man. If Todd could avoid attracting the attention of the FBI for ten years, what chance did Armstrong have?

After the monotony of fence posts and telephone poles whisking past, Cheri broke the silence.

"I've been wondering about something. I can't figure out why didn't Todd just kill you? That would've created a diversion, and he probably would've kidnapped me successfully. It would also have meant my death would have been unspeakable. Why didn't he at least hit you hard enough to knock you out longer?"

Jack turned to her and smiled. "You've been thinking a lot about this, I see. Me, too. I think I've got some answers. Todd never took to religion on a conscious level. His mother pushed it so hard, he developed an animus toward anything religious. On a subconscious level, though, some concept of right and wrong stuck, in however perverted a form."

"That makes no sense to me. His acts were so existentially evil, unchecked by any feeling a normal person could contemplate."

"You went further with your psychology education than I did, but you're too close to the situation. Todd's sense of right and wrong, as it existed in his warped mind, ended at the edge of a person's sex. I believe he loved his father very much. He didn't want to kill me, just incapacitate me.

"There's something else. I was probably the first man he ever attacked. For a split second, an image of him hitting his father may've come to his mind. That would make him hesitate just long enough, to hold back enough, that I came to quickly.

"Todd saw himself as something of an avenging angel, ridding the world of women who taunted men only to reject them. That was another form of the kind of control Phoebe exerted on him and his father. It happened to him, I believe, many times, each time engendering a deeper hatred of women. When he found a target, he disciplined himself to be a completely different person than he was otherwise. The same thing with his customers, especially the female ones, because his sustenance depended on it.

"When he approached a woman as himself, the veneer washed off. Women could see something indefinable, something that made them uncomfortable and caused them to withdraw.

"Ultimately, Todd thought of himself as someone who could rid the world of the most-attractive, and thus most-sinister, women. Attacking a male was something different. In a man, he saw an image of his father. We have no evidence to suggest he ever attacked a man before. At the cabin in the Dells, he went to great lengths to avoid contact with Beau Williams.

"I think when he hit me, he hesitated. When he saw I was unconscious, he accomplished what he set out to do. It may have even sickened him a little. There was a buffer between how he perceived an act against a woman and inflicting pain on a man, a person who shared his gender and his father's."

"I see where you're coming from, but how did he know what I would do? He obviously cased the scene, because he knew where I was. I was the only female agent there, but we've been trained to stay put when we're in a communications center. Todd was smart enough to know our protocols."

"While we're on the subject, this is probably the last order I'll give you within the Bureau. Next time, follow protocol," he said sternly, then smiled.

"Everyone who knew Todd viewed him as a genius. His mental acuity extended to reading people and situations. When he entered AFI's offices that Saturday and saw us together, we immediately glanced at each other. You were startled, even a bit afraid, after your encounter with him in Naples. My body language, the tensing of my muscles and readiness to pounce, were evident, too. He knew there was a relationship between us, much as Mike knew for some time, maybe before we did.

"Protocol or no, when I went down, he knew you'd run to me. He knew where every agent was and the route you had to take, and he waited in his campus police costume. Except for that hesitation when he hit me, he would've been successful in abducting you. I don't think either of us should think beyond that, because he did hesitate. Seriously, don't," he begged.

A funereal silence filled the car. Cheri wished she could rest her head on Jack's shoulder, but the bucket seats and her reluctance to bend her neck prevented it.

"Burma Shave," she said. "You remember those ads on fence posts when you were young? I almost missed seeing them. The one's we're driving past are badly faded. They haven't been repainted in ages. I just saw one that was all but withered away. It got so you *just had* to read them. OCD in my own right," she joked.

"I think Todd's OCD is what got him caught," she added, waiting for Jack's response.

Jack knew what she meant but pretended otherwise. "How so?"

"He always held the Numbers, so he could send them in soon after the killing, but not too much later. It would've ruined the game if he sent the next Number too long afterward. I think he figured the one time in Honolulu would be viewed as either an aberration, or we'd try to connect it to a Hawaii murder. In Honolulu, I think he felt the method of killing where he didn't inflict the punishment made it different enough to evade a connection. My bet is he realized his mistake soon after. That probably tortured *him* for a change," she said in an attempt at humor.

"He got a very little of his own back."

The thought gave each of them a thread of satisfaction. Jack wondered if that was un-Christian and said an unspoken, brief prayer for the tortured man's soul. He hated the man, which he knew was a natural reaction.

Suddenly, he thought of what Todd suffered to become such a monstrous human being. Jack didn't pray for Todd, but he prayed for the grace that would allow him, someday, to pray for forgiveness in his own soul.

There was still a very pregnant question in the air. After more telephone poles went by, it inevitably came up.

"We know about our future together no matter what," Jack said. "Have you decided what you want to do about the Bureau?"

She didn't answer right away. Finally, she said, "I planned my life around the Bureau since my mom died. My parents were my heroes. My dad loves the Bureau, and he's still a giant in my eyes. It was all I wanted to do, and I didn't think that would ever change."

She was silent again, and Jack didn't press her.

"Anyone who contemplates a career at the Bureau knows she's risking her life. If I had been killed back there, well, that was a sacrifice I was prepared to make. This experience wasn't anywhere in the realm of what I ever contemplated. It had a traumatizing impact."

Once again, she paused. "The way it happened left an indelible mark on my psyche. I don't want to return unless I can do the job at the level of excellence I always believed I would, without hesitation, and without my decisions being colored by this experience. That's going to take some time. Mike gave me ninety days of recuperative paid leave, starting today.

"Then there's you and me. It would be a conflict for us to work on the same cases. We'd be working different cases, traveling at different times. As long as Mike's around, he promised to keep us both based at Quantico, working on different cases. We probably would see each other on weekends, but maybe not always."

"When we started this," Jack said, "I told you my definition of commitment: The thing is already done; only the doing remains. I've already lived my life with you, knowing that's the only way for us both to be happy. Only the wonderful years of our love remain.

"I can't imagine leaving the Bureau any more than I can imagine being without you," he confessed. "I haven't been through what you have. My gut tells me you'll be back. If not, or if so, we'll work it out," he said with conviction.

John Duby received his Juris Doctor degree from Empire College School of Law in Santa Rosa, California, in 1996 at the age of forty-eight. He became National Sales Manager for FORECITE Legal Publications, which provided defense-oriented criminal jury instructions. Periodically, he handled the publication's hotline, offering assistance to criminal defense attorneys and organizations.

Mr. Duby conducted training in person for public-defender organizations throughout the state of California for his expertise in criminal jury instructions. This was augmented by telephone training in the application of FORECITE's instructions for public defender organizations in Alaska, Arizona, the death penalty unit of the Cook County Public Defender organization, and assistance in FORECITE's instructions for a trial conducted by the University of Tennessee in Knoxville. The publisher of FORECITE is a criminal defense appellate attorney specializing in murder and death penalty appeals.

Mr. Duby's work for the attorney-publisher provided him with an entrée to doing *habeas corpus* investigation for some high-profile cases, including a prominent serial murder case, *People v. David Allen Lucas*, among others. In this capacity, Mr. Duby conducted interviews with jurors and the family of the appellant as well as the appellant himself conducted in San Quentin Prison.

While handling the hotline for FORECITE, Mr. Duby suggested a defense theory in the felony assault case of actor Alec Baldwin used in his trial, which ended in acquittal. He trained the judge and a member of the defense team in FORECITE's jury instruction software for the O. J. Simpson case.

He is now retired and enjoys writing fiction. *The Zero Conundrum is* his first novel.

Lightning Source UK Ltd.
Milton Keynes UK
UKHW010628160921
390678UK00001B/56